FRED RANKIN was born in Belfast and educated at the Royal Belfast Academical Institution. He qualified as a Pharmaceutical Chemist in 1949 and, after some years in the family business, he became Northern Ireland manager for an international chemical company, retiring in 1992.

He is a parishoner (and Honorary Treasurer) of Drumbo in the Diocese of Down and published a history of the parish in 1981. A member and one-time chairman of the Lisburn Historical Society, he has contributed to its journal; he is also chairman of the Lecale Historical Society and has contributed to the *Lecale Miscellany*.

Fred Rankin has been secretary to the Diocesan Library Committee for many years and was actively involved in the publication of the *Succession Lists of the Clergy of Connor and of Down and Dromore*; for the latter he wrote short histories of each parish in the diocese. Both of these books were published by the Ulster Historical Foundation. He is a member of the Diocesan Council and is a representative of the Council on the Board of Down Cathedral, in whose work he is deeply involved. He represents the diocese on the Representative Church Body and is currently the chairman of its sub-committee on Library and Archives.

GW00686140

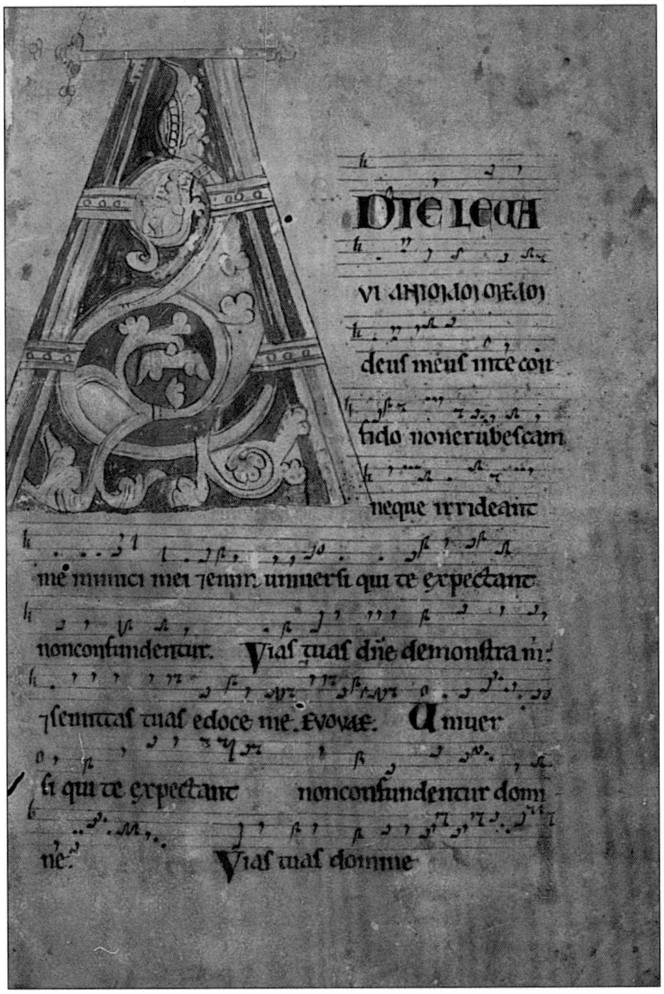

The Down Gradual Folio 1.
The opening of the Chant for Advent Sunday
THE BODLEIAN LIBRARY, OXFORD
RAWLINSON C.892

DOWN CATHEDRAL

The Church of Saint Patrick of Down

J. FREDERICK RANKIN

ULSTER HISTORICAL
FOUNDATION

First published 1997
by the Ulster Historical Foundation
12 College Square East, Belfast, BT1 6DD
in association with The Board of Down Cathedral

All rights reserved. No part of this publication may be reproduced, stored in a retrieval system or transmitted in any form or by any means, mechanical or otherwise without permission of the publisher

© J Frederick Rankin, 1997

ISBN 0-901905-85-2 (paperback)
ISBN 0-901905-86-0 (hardback)

Typeset by the Ulster Historical Foundation
Printed by Nicholson & Bass Ltd.
Cover and Design by Dunbar Design

Cover illustration: Down Cathedral by James Glen Wilson, (1827-1863) *Ulster Museum*

CONTENTS

DEDICATION
FOR
KATHLEEN

FOREWORD

The Most Rev. Dr R H A Eames
Archbishop of Armagh, Primate of All Ireland

It is a great privilege and pleasure to pen this Foreword.

Anyone who has served or lived in the Diocese of Down will readily understand something of the affection in which the Cathedral is held by the entire Diocese. I well recall the late Sir John Betjeman speaking to me years ago of his interest and regard for Down Cathedral. While he held his own characteristic views on aspects of the building it was obvious to me that he had the highest regard for its significance as a Cathedral within the Anglican Communion. Quite apart from its historic links with the *St Patrick of Lecale*, its importance to the diocese of Down as a focal point for diocesan and community occasions, a place of pilgrimage and a scene of ecumenical endeavour, it is a *living* cathedral with regular worship of Almighty God attended by some of the most loyal of members in the Church of Ireland.

As a former bishop of the diocese I know something of the faithful work which has been involved by several generations to ensure the upkeep and maintenance of this ancient place of God. I recall the restoration work of the 1980s, the launching of the appeal which was so well supported by the community at large, the renovation of the magnificent organ with which I will always associate the late Lord Henry Dunleath, the numerous visitors from all over the world and of course my memories as a young curate in the diocese of the annual St Patrick's Day pilgrimages linking Saul and Downpatrick in the episcopate of the late Bishop F J Mitchell.

I gladly share the gratitude of the many I hope will read this book to Mr Fred Rankin who has found the time and the energy to produce such a worthwhile history of the Cathedral. When I first suggested to him that he might consider undertaking such a task I had every confidence that he would write a book of accuracy and integrity. Not only has he completed the task involving many hours of his spare time but he has brought to the work his genuine love of history, ability to discern the real significance of historical land-marks and obvious love for his Church but he has given us a most readable account of Down Cathedral. At this time there is a renewed interest throughout the Church Catholic in the role and significance of Cathedrals. The Cathedral of the Holy Trinity at Downpatrick can take its place without apology as a living and vibrant part of Anglican cathedral heritage. This book will be an invaluable contribution to our appreciation of all it has, does and under God, will continue to epitomise.

✠ROBERT ARMAGH
JULY 1997

ABBREVIATIONS

A.F.M.	Annals of the Four Masters
A.U.	Annals of Ulster
B.L.	British Library
C.D.I.	Calendar of Documents [relating to] Ireland
C.J.R.	Calendar of Justiciary Rolls
C.P.L.	Calendar of Papal Letters
C.P.R.	Calendar of Patent Rolls
C.S.P.I.	Calendar of State Papers, Ireland
H.M.S.O.	Her Majesty's Stationery Office
O.S.A.	Order of Saint Augustine
O.S.B.	Order of Saint Benedict
P.R.O.	Public Record Office [London]
P.R.O.N.I.	Public Record Office of Northern Ireland
Q.U.B.	Queen's University, Belfast
R.D.K.I.	Report of the Deputy Keeper [of the Records], Ireland
T.C.D.	Trinity College, Dublin

INTRODUCTION AND ACKNOWLEDGMENTS

THE RESTORATION OF DOWN Cathedral in the late 1980s marked a watershed in its history. It coincided with a period of change in the outreach of the Cathedral, and indeed the Church of Ireland, towards its role in the community, a role which, in earlier years, may retrospectively be seen to have been somewhat defensive and inward looking. Many factors played their part in this metamorphosis, not least the changes in society which were taking place with almost alarming rapidity. The considerable sum of money which had to be raised in order to undertake the restoration of the Cathedral at that time was indeed responsible for a re-awakening on the part of the Board and Chapter to the realisation that, in Down Cathedral, they were trustees of a valuable diocesan and community asset. No longer was the Cathedral, aloft on the Hill of Down, with the grave of Saint Patrick nearby, a place which could be visited on Sundays and Saint Patrick's Day; it was a resource, albeit with a long history, to be used by the community. It was, to use that horrible jargon, to be marketed. The late twentieth century tide of tourism was just beginning and the Diocese of Down found itself with a major tourist attraction on its hands. Marrying its primary function as a House of God and centre of Christian worship with that as a focal point for tourists in the Barony of Lecale, was no different from the problems faced by the medieval monks, to whom the hordes of pilgrims visiting the Patrician site, were a source of alms and wealth.

As a facet of the outreach of the Cathedral, the then Bishop of Down and Dromore, the Rt Rev. Dr R. H. A. Eames, invited me to consider the possibility of writing a history of the Cathedral. There had been previous histories written in connection with earlier appeals for money, but they were all out of print and of doubtful accuracy, as each had more or less copied the previous one, repeating errors without recourse to original sources. Before accepting the commission, I took some time to examine the possible sources which I might use; the more I searched, the more I realised that there was a story needing to be told. There was a vast amount of information available in sources which had not been tapped by previous historians of the Cathedral; all this information needed to be brought together into one book.

This book is the result of more than ten years work, for the most part spare time as I was still in full time employment. To say that I have enjoyed the work would be an understatement; it has brought me into contact with many people to whom I have turned for advice and help and those people have remained firm friends. It has taken me to other record repositories in Ireland and in Britain and also to the monastery of le Bec in Normandy, from where one can trace the origins of the Benedictine House founded in Down in 1183.

Whilst I lay claim to being the author and therefore am responsible for any mistakes which may be found, I must acknowledge a huge debt to a few individuals along the way. In the early days, Mr William Kerr, sometime senior classics inspector with the Ministry of Education and an ecclesiastical history scholar of considerable repute, read the manuscript, chapter by chapter, and gave me much sound advice as well as providing translations for latin texts as necessary; in the later period, Mr Gordon Wheeler, Humanities Librarian in Queen's University and on retirement, resident in Downpatrick, read through the manuscript and made many positive suggestions. His bibliographical knowledge has been invaluable. Happily the early part of the work coincided with the archaeological excavation being carried out on the Hill of Down under the leadership of Mr Nick Brannon from the Archaeological Service of the Department of the Environment; the opportunity of the Cathedral being stripped to the bare walls was too good for Nick to miss. Nick used the opportunity to considerable profit and I am grateful to him for his interpretation of his findings. My thanks also to Dr Brian Turner, of Down County Museum, for his continuing interest and contribution and also to Ms Lesley Simpson, Keeper of the Collections in the museum for her assistance in locating many illustrations and artefacts. Dr Ann Hamlin, Director of the Built Heritage in the Environment and Heritage Service, and an acknowledged authority on the Early Christian Church, was kind enough to read the first four chapters and comment on them; her knowledge of the sources sent me in directions which I had overlooked. Richard Warner, Cormac Bourke and Trevor Parkhill, all of the Ulster Museum, gave much help in their respective spheres, the two former in the Department of Antiquities and the latter in the Department of Local History. My daughter Dr Susan Rankin, Director of Music at Emmanuel College, Cambridge took me through the Bodleian gradual discussed in Chapter 5.

Dorinda, Lady Dunleath allowed me to peruse a very considerable file of correpondence relating, not only to the organ as one might expect, but also to the detail of the 1980s restoration, which had been gathered by her late husband Henry, Lord Dunleath. Most of my research on the history of the organ was fortunately complete before his untimely death and no-one was more delighted than he when the true history of the organ became clear, doing away with the undocumented myths which had accumulated over the years. Dr Kay Muhr, of the Northern Ireland Place-Name Project in Queen's University, gave much help in identifying the place names discussed in Appendices 1 and 2. The groundwork for Appendix 5, the Heraldic Achievements, was carried out by the late Lt Col. J. R. H. Greeves, who became an authority on the language of heraldry; before his death he gave permission for this work to be published.

I was allowed to examine in depth the archives still retained by the Cathedral; these are all post 1790 but are nevertheless invaluable in painting a picture of that restoration and later events; I record my thanks particularly to Dean Hamilton Leckey and the Chapter for this facility. The archival resource has been supplemented by contemporary newspaper files, in particular the Downpatrick Recorder, later the Down Recorder; these were consulted at the SE Education and Library Board's headquarters at Ballynahinch, where the index for the first fifty years 1837-1887, compiled by the late Jack McCoy, proved invaluable. Down County Museum is fortunate to have in its possession a complete run of the Downshire Protestant, which provided a rare insight into local politics in the 1850s and 1860s. The museum also allowed me to read through Aynsworth Pilson's diary, without which no history of Downpatrick could be contemplated.

Needless to say, a host of other people have answered my questions and given me much encouragement over the years; if I single out two, may I be forgiven for not mentioning others, whose help was sought and granted. Firstly, Monsignor Dr J. J. Maguire of Saint Patrick's Roman Catholic Church who, as well as being a good friend of the Cathedral, has answered my many questions. Secondly, Mr Anthony Wilson, whose book entitled *Saint Patrick's Town* was being written at the same time; we exchanged much information along the way. To all of these people, my grateful thanks. Photographs and illustrations have been individually acknowledged. My wife Kathleen, as well as being of great help with word processing skills, has made many suggestions with regard to the final shape of the work. At all times she has taken a great interest in it and my debt to her is enormous.

Finally, I must pay a sincere tribute to those who have provided a large part of the funding for this book: the Esme Mitchell Trust and the Ulster Local History Trust; the Chapter, Board and Friends of Down Cathedral have also provided substantial support from a legacy bequeathed by Mrs Kathleen Mitchell, widow of Bishop F. J. Mitchell, who did so much to create the Cathedral structure as we know it now. Without the financial sponsorship which they have provided, this book might not have been published.

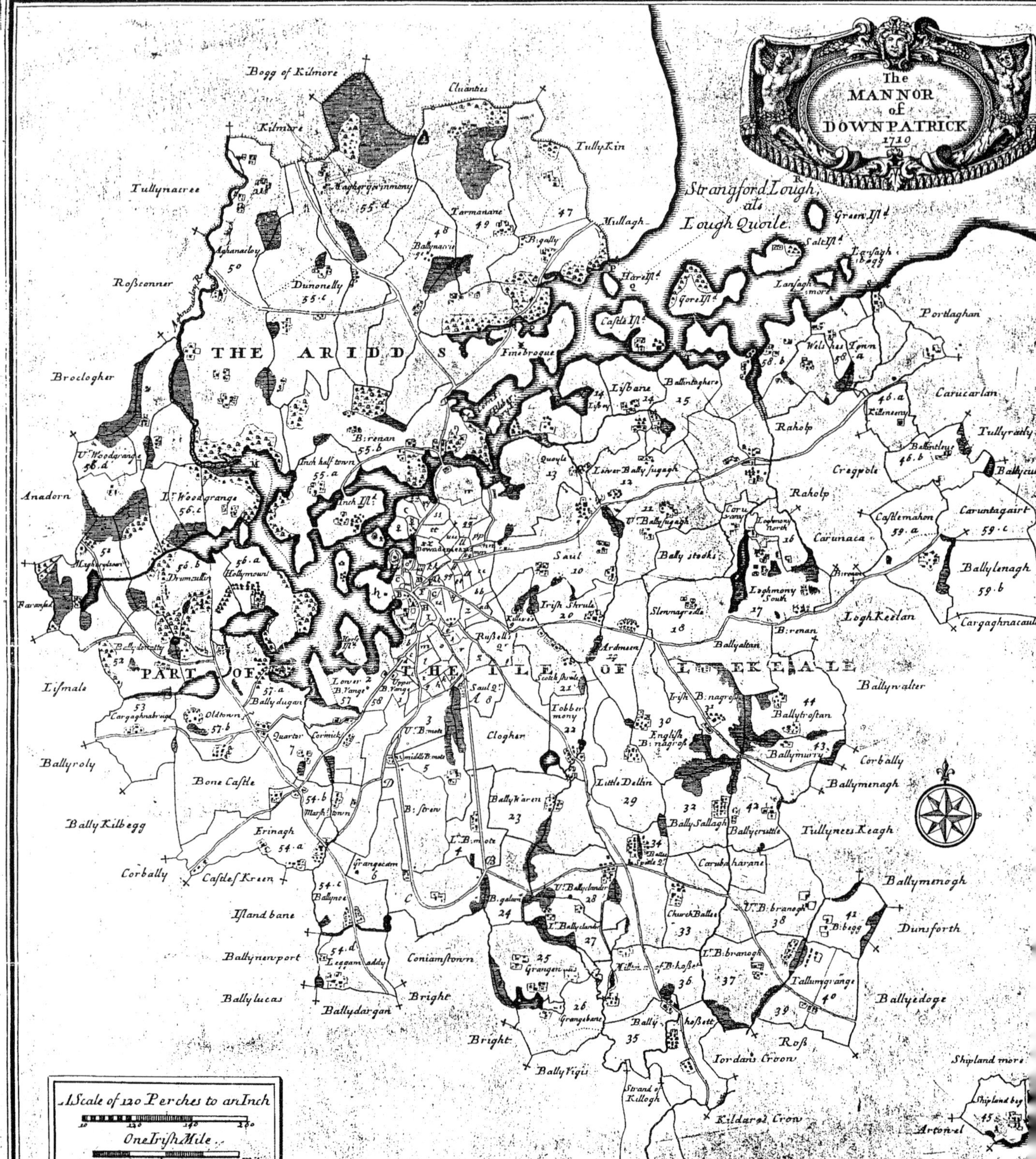
The MANNOR of DOWNPATRICK 1710
Strangford Lough als Lough Quoile
THE ARIDDS
PART OF THE ILE OF LEKEALE
A Scale of 120 Perches to an Inch
One Irish Mile
Bogg of Kilmore
Kilmore
Cluanties
Tully Kin
Tullynacree
Tarmanane
Mullagh
Aghanailoy
Roßconner
Dunonelly
Broclogher
Finebroque
Lisbane
Ballintoghers
Portlaghan
Caricarlan
Tullyratty
Rakolp
Cregpole
Castlemahon
Caruntagairt
Carunaca
Ballylenagh
Anadorn
Saul
Irish Shrule
Slevnagredle
Logh Keelan
Cargaghnacault
Ballyalton
Ballywalter
Lismale
Ballydugan
Oldtown
Quarter
Cormick
Clogher
Ballytrostan
Corbally
Ballymenagh
Ballyroly
Bone Castle
Little Dellin
Bally Sallagh
Tullynees Keagh
Bally Kilbegg
Erinagh
Ballycruttle
Corbally
Castles Kreen
Grangecam
Ballymenogh
Island bane
Ballynoe
Church Ballee
Dunsforth
Ballynewport
Coniamstown
Tallumgrange
Ballylucas
Bright
Ballydargan
Ballyedoge
Bright
Grangebane
Roß
Iordans Croon
Shipland more
Bally Vigis
Strand of Killogh
Kildarel Crow
Shipland beg
Artonel

ONE

FROM PREHISTORY TO PATRICK

DOWNPATRICK, TO GIVE THE TOWN the name by which it is known in modern times, stands on the River Quoile as it flows towards Strangford Lough. The surrounding area is low lying, having originally been a tidal estuary, and it is only within the last two centuries that much of it has been drained and turned into agricultural land. Old maps of the town, of which the best known is perhaps the Southwell Estate map of 1729, show Cathedral Hill surrounded by water on three sides, its only link to the rest of the town being the neck of land now followed by English Street. The Barony of Lecale, on whose northern edge stands the town of Downpatrick, was known by the ancient name *Magh-inis*, anglicised to 'island plain'; this aptly describes how the area was cut off from the rest of Ulster; indeed, a description of Lecale as late as 1680 tells of only two land passes leading into it, those at Blackstaff and at Annadorn.[1] The area possessed neither wood nor turf and was supplied with coals from England by boats sailing into Strangford.

To stand on Cathedral Hill and survey the surrounding countryside is to understand the importance of the place and why it achieved a position of eminence from the earliest times; surrounded by so much water and marshland, it was ideally suited, not only as a trading centre, but also as an easily defended situation. The name by which it was known, *Dún,* tells us that a fortified place existed here but scholars are uncertain as to whether this name referred to the ecclesiastical site on Cathedral Hill or to the Mound of Down, a short distance to the north. Archaeological excavations which took place on the hill during the 1950s and 1980s suggest that the Hill has been occupied almost continuously from the Neolithic, through the Late Bronze Age to the Early Christian Period.

Nevertheless, the history of the hill would be incomplete without reference to the discovery of what has become known as the Downpatrick Gold Hoard. In May 1954, whilst digging a grave some 100 yards south-west of the Cathedral Tower, Mr A. J. Pollock, the Cathedral Verger, discovered a number of gold hoard. They were found at a depth of almost three feet in undisturbed clay, carefully covered with stones in such a manner as to suggest that security was the reason for their abandonment. Mr Pollock called in professional advice; the objects were identified as ten bracelets, a fragment of another and a fragment of

Opposite:
The Manor of Down 1710

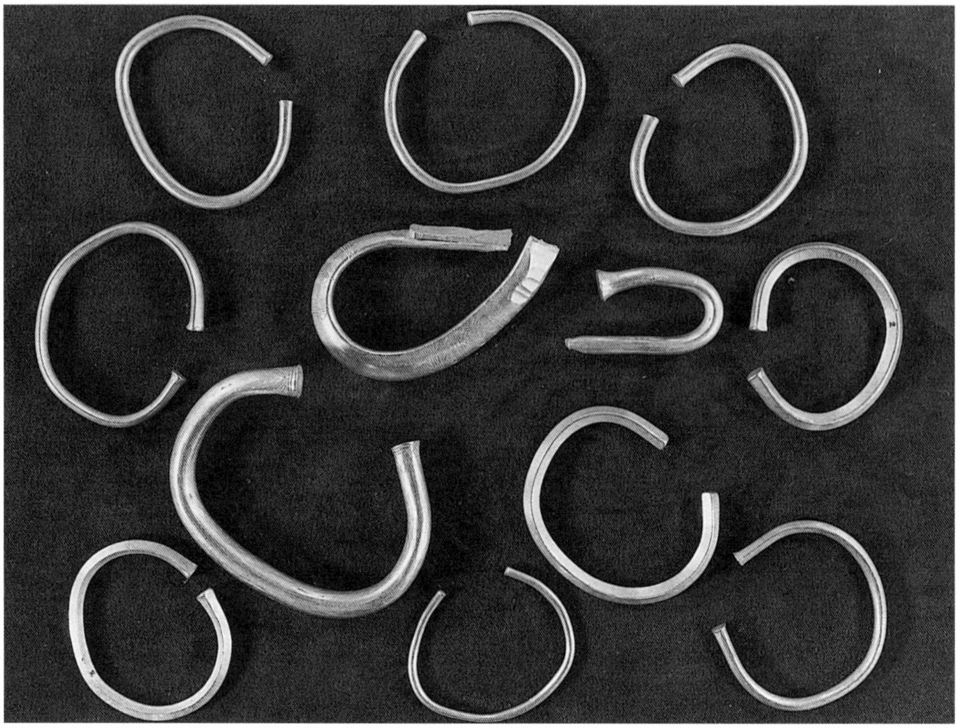

The Downpatrick Gold Hoard
ULSTER MUSEUM

a gold collar. They were declared Treasure Trove and are now in the possession of the Crown, but can be seen on display in the Ulster and Down County Museums.[2] The deposition of the hoard has been dated to between 1300 BC and 1000 BC, during the transition from the Middle to the Late Bronze Ages; the bracelets are highly decorated with chevrons, crosslines and zigzags.[3]

Archaeological excavations took place on Cathedral Hill during the 1950s which uncovered a massive ditch around the hilltop, assumed to have been dug for defensive purposes during the late Bronze Age.[4] However, when further

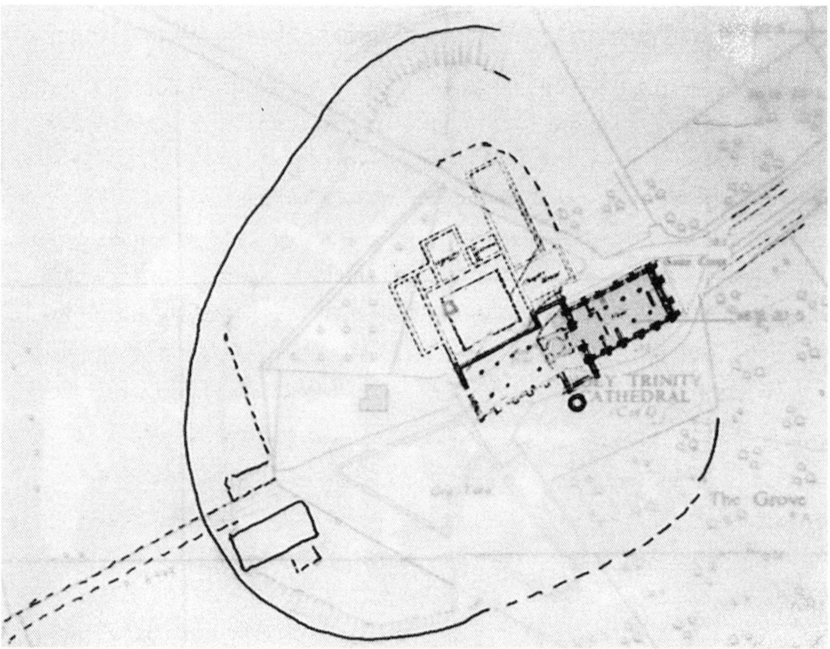

The line of the early Christian ditch around the hill top, which is, with the western entrance from the sea, associated with medieval buildings
CHANNEL 4 TELEVISION

excavations were undertaken during the 1980s by archaeologists from the Department of the Environment, Northern Ireland, that theory was questioned. The ditch is now known to have been dug no earlier than the Early Christian Period and was probably no more than a defensive boundary to the early monastery with its many outbuildings on the top of the hill. Over a period of centuries, the ditch gradually filled in but appears to have been re-dug during the medieval period. Further excavation will be necessary before any conclusion can be reached on the dating of this complex of ditches. A curious feature of the recent excavation was the discovery of Early Christian structures and indeed burials outside the line of this ditch; the implications of this are, as yet, unexplained. Why was it necessary to construct a defensive ditch when the hill itself was almost totally surrounded by water?[5] Much of the present landscape may, in fact, reflect the medieval landscape when the monastery was active over a large area. In September 1997, the Time Team from Channel 4 Television excavated on the northern slopes of the hill after geophysical examination. Further evidence of the early christian ditch was found, thus proving, by extension that the ditch encircled the hill top.

The written record, as preserved in the Annals, supports this sequence of ecclesiastical events; the secular history is less easy to piece together. It was not until the late eleventh century that the great heroic tales were committed to writing – the descendants of an oral tradition preserved by the *seanchaí* through the centuries. The Ulster Cycle, of which the principal and best known is the *Táin Bó Cúalnge,* the Cattle Raid of Cooley, revolves around the exploits of the warriors of Ulster in their battles with the *Connachta* from Connaught. *Conchobar mac Nessa,* King of the *Ulaid,* together with *Cú Chulainn* and *Celtchair* were famed for their fearlessness in battle. *Celtchair* is described as:

> . . . a wrathful, terrible, fearsome man. He was big-nosed, big-eared and with prominent eyes. Rough grizzled hair he had. A striped cloak he wore and in that cloak over his breast an iron stake which reaches from shoulder to shoulder. A rough, plaited shirt next to his skin. Along the side of his back a sword of refined iron, tempered seven times in the heat. A brown mound, to wit, his shield, he carried. A great, grey spear with thirty rivets through its socket, in his hand. He is half a battle (in himself), he is a leader of strife, he is a chief in valour. That was *Celtchair Mór mac Uthechair* from *Lethglais* in the north.[6]

Modern scholars believe that, whilst the sagas are the result of an oral tradition lasting some hundreds of years, they have little foundation in historical fact and that the characters depicted therein are wholly mythological. Nevertheless it would be tempting to give *Celtchair* from *Lethglais* a place in history as the founding father of Downpatrick!

Three distinct peoples comprised the *Ulaid*: the *Dál Riata* who lived in north

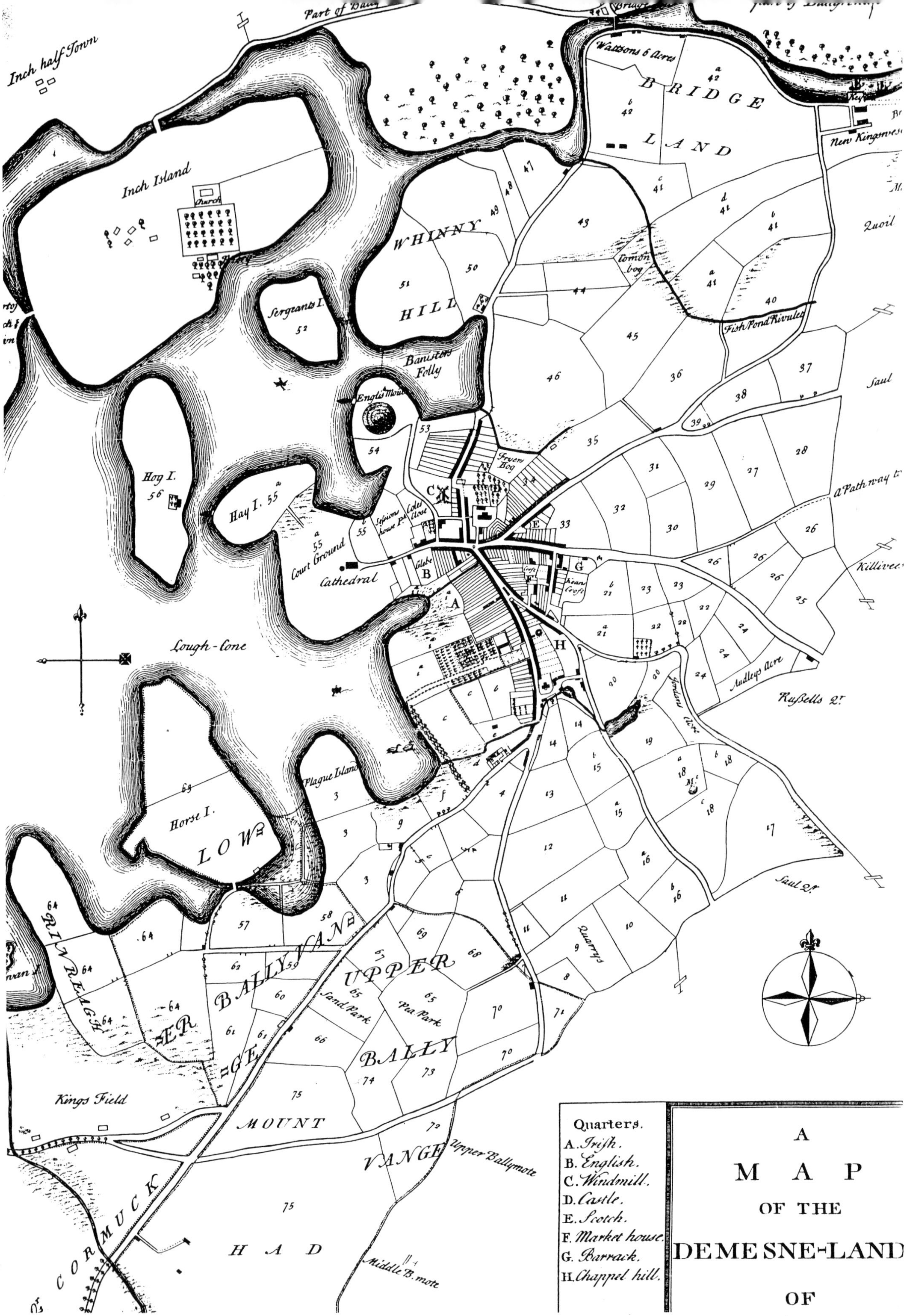

A MAP OF THE DEMESNE-LAND OF
Quarters.
A. Irish.
B. English.
C. Windmill.
D. Castle.
E. Scotch.
F. Market house.
G. Barrack.
H. Chappel hill.
Inch half Town
Inch Island
Church
Wattsons 6 Acres
BRIDGE LAND
New Kingsmes
WHINNY HILL
Comon bog
Fish Pond Rivulet
Quoil
Saul
Sergeants I.
Banisters Folly
English Mount
Hog I.
Hay I.
Court Ground
Cathedral
Glebe
Fryers Bog
Sesions house
Coles Closet
Kean Croft
A Path way to
Killivee
Lough-Cone
Audleys Acre
Russells Q.
Plague Island
Horse I.
LOW
Saul Q.
Quarry
RIVREAGH
BALLYVAN
UPPER BALLY
Sand Park
Pea Park
Kings Field
MOUNT
VANGE
Upper Ballymote
HAD
Middle B. mote
CORMUCK

Antrim, the *Dál nAraide* of south Antrim and north Down and the *Dál Fiatach* of the Ards and south east Down. *Dún* was, in fact, the seat or chief residence of this last people, the *Dál Fiatach*. In pre-historic times, *Emain Macha*, or Navan Fort, near Armagh, was the centre of the territory occupied by the *Ulaid*, the territory extending across the country north of a line drawn from the estuary of the Boyne to Sligo. In their struggle for supremacy, the *Uí Néill*, from the south and west, drove the *Ulaid* eastwards beyond the River Bann, roughly the modern county of Down.[7] The Four Masters date the fall of *Emain* at 331 AD which, if we accept its accuracy, would give an approximate date for the arrival of the *Dál Fiatach* at *Dún,* as we approach the historical period.

Although there is a fairly constant record of raiding each other's territory by the various peoples on both sides of the Celtic Sea, the distribution of finds of pottery, coins and other artefacts of the Roman period indicates that there was also a considerable volume of peaceful trading. It must be remembered that the Roman advance through Western Europe and Britain stopped short at Ireland, but this did not stop small-scale raiding in each direction. We know that raids by the Irish on mainland Britain were well established from the late third until the early fifth century.[8] It was on one of these raids that Patrick was kidnapped and brought back to a life of slavery in Ireland.

Much scholarly ink has been expended in recent decades on the subject of Patrick, the Apostle of Ireland, in addition to numerous books and articles of a more popular nature. The Roman church in Ireland celebrated the 1500th anniversary of the obit of Patrick in 1961 and this event gave rise to an entirely fresh initiative from the academic world to the subject. Books have continued to appear with unabated regularity, demonstrating the ever increasing interest in the subject. The most recent, by a group of Cambridge scholars, has re-examined every aspect of the matter, using manuscript and secondary sources, and arrived at a largely different set of conclusions from the received version of recent years. Their book was published in 1993, to celebrate their well-argued obit date of 493.[9]

In spite of the abundance of such work, Patrick remains a shadowy figure. Who, then, was this man called Patrick? In attempting to separate the real historical Patrick from the Patrick of the legend, modern scholars are agreed on one point; the only genuine facts on which we can rely are those contained in the writings which Patrick himself has left, the *Confession* and the so-called *Letter to Coroticus*. The origin of the legend can be found in the biographies by *Muirchú* and *Tírechán*, both of which date from the latter half of the seventh century (and are so radically different that they cannot both be true), the *Book of the Angel* of the same period and the *Tripartite Life* which dates from the ninth or tenth century. The *Muirchú* and *Tírechán* lives together with the *Book of the Angel* can all be found in the *Book of Armagh.*[10] As Patrick lived in the

Opposite:
Demesne of Down 1729

Down Cathedral as seen from Inch Abbey across the Quoile
W. A. GREEN COLLECTION
ULSTER FOLK AND TRANSPORT MUSEUM

fifth century, we must accept that none of the information contained in these lives is first hand; it is also coloured by typical hagiographical lore. Indeed, these writings and the statements which they make were the product of the politico-ecclesiastical requirements of their period and of the necessity to proclaim Armagh as the ecclesiastical capital of Ireland, a position which it has retained to the present day.

Patrick was a Briton, brought up in an educated post-Roman society. His father, Calpernius, was a deacon and the family would very probably have been bilingual, using the vernacular British tongue but fully conversant with Latin. Patrick tells us that he was captured at the age of sixteen and taken to Ireland where he tended sheep, but he does not tell us where those flocks were. During this time of captivity, he spent much time in prayer:

> . . . in one day I would say as many as a hundred prayers and nearly as many at night.[11]

After six years, he heard a voice telling him to return to his country and that a ship was ready, but was two hundred miles distant. When he eventually reached the ship, it was only with difficulty that he persuaded the sailors to take him on board. After three days at sea, they made landfall and thereafter they travelled through uninhabited country, during which time their food ran out. The pagan captain said to Patrick:

> What now, Christian? You say that your God is great and almighty, why then can you not pray for us, because we are in danger of starvation?[12]

Patrick replied:

> Turn in faith with all your heart to the Lord my God, because nothing is impossible to him, that he may to-day send food across your way until you are full because he has abundant resources everywhere.[13]

Patrick then tells us that a herd of pigs appeared in front of them and they killed many of them and stayed there for two nights to refresh themselves. After that they gave thanks to God and from that day onwards they had ample food.

Some years later Patrick was back with his parents, who earnestly asked him never to leave them again. Some years pass in the story before Patrick dreamed of a man named Victoricus, who had with him an uncountable number of letters, one of which was headed 'The Cry of the Irish'. While Patrick was reading this letter, he heard the voices of those who were by the wood of *Foclut* near the western sea crying with one voice 'Holy Boy, we are asking you to come and walk among us again'.[14] Patrick heeded the call and set sail for Ireland.

Thus far we have used Patrick's own words, as written in the *Confession* and the divergences from the biographies of later centuries will already be apparent. Nowhere does Patrick mention tending flocks of sheep on Slemish; in his dream he recalls the Wood of *Foclut* – the only place name in the entire Confession – as the place of his early captivity. *Foclut* has been identified as being near Killala in county Mayo – near the western sea. *Tírechán*, one of the early biographers,[15] includes *Foclut* on the circuit of western Ireland which he attributes to Patrick whereas *Sliab Mis* [Slemish] was introduced into the canon by *Muirchú*.[16] Patrick, it will be remembered, tells us that he travelled 200 miles before reaching the coast to embark for a foreign country; a location in Mayo

The Saint Patrick Window
in Down Cathedral
PHOTOGRAPH BY T.KENNETH ANDERSON

fits in well with an embarkation point on the Wicklow or Wexford coast. It must be pointed out, however, that if we accept Foclut as being in Mayo, it tells us nothing about Patrick tending sheep there; it also flies in the face of all the accumulated legend about Slemish, which is also about 200 miles from an embarkation point on the south-east coast. The boat in which Patrick sailed was at sea for three days before reaching land and thereafter the party walked for twenty eight days. Did the party land in Britain or Gaul? Patrick does not tell us. *Muirchú* writes that he travelled through Gaul reaching the city of Auxerre (then the intellectual capital of northern Gaul) where he met Bishop Germanus, the Papal Legate, remaining there for forty, or perhaps thirty years.[17] *Tírechán,* on the other hand, notes that he stayed for thirty years on *Aralanensis*, identified as *Lérins*, an island in the Tyrrhenian Sea off the southern coast of Gaul on which a monastery had been founded.[18]

We shall return to the *Confession* to discover what we can about Patrick's missionary years in Ireland. He gives us neither dates nor places, but he does reveal the tremendous difficulties under which he laboured in his work and the struggles and persecutions which he suffered:

> . . . no thanks to me, but it was God who prevailed in me and withstood them all, to enable me to come and preach the Gospel to Irish tribes and endure insults from unbelievers, to bear the reproach of my pilgrimage and many persecutions, even as far as being thrown into irons, and to sacrifice my free status for the good of others and, if I were worthy, I am ready to give my life unhesitatingly and willingly for His name and I want to sacrifice it there even if it involves death, if God were to kindly grant this to me.[19]

The *Confession*, Patrick tells us, was written in old age and in it are set down his innermost thoughts on his ministry among the Irish. His writing displays a deep sincerity and humility, the result of a lifetime spent in the service of the church. The youthful experience of being kidnapped had left behind a determination and will to overcome adversity and without doubt he found an inner peace in his deep faith and trust in God.

For the accounts of Patrick's missionary journeys in Ireland, we have to rely on the biographies left to us by *Muirchú* and *Tírechán,* both of which were written towards the end of the seventh century. Patrick's name, indeed, occurs only once in any writings attributable to an earlier date: a letter from *Cummian*, Abbot of Durrow (632/3), to *Segene,* Abbot of Iona, on the subject of the Easter controversy, in which Patrick is referred to as 'our father'.[20] No references are to be found in the writings of Columcille or Columbanus, nor in the life of Brigid by Cogitosus. The Venerable Bede, that early chronicler of the British church, does not mention him. The absence of any reference to Patrick in the sixth and early seventh centuries would suggest that, whilst he may have left a legacy of communities converted to Christianity across Ireland, when viewed against the politico-ecclesiastical background of western Europe in those centuries, this was perhaps not an unusual or isolated development. Rather was it the necessity within the political framework of seventh-century Ireland to assert the supremacy of the northern *Uí Néill* over all Ireland and the cult of Patrick was created in order to help achieve that goal. The second half of the first millennium saw the rise in political supremacy of the northern *Uí Néill*, whose subject tribes controlled Armagh west of the Bann, consolidating their hold on the high kingship of Ireland. The spread of Christianity went hand-in-hand with that rise; if Patrick had never existed, it would have been necessary to invent him in order to achieve that supremacy for Armagh. Indeed, suggests Kenney,[21] later supported by Binchy,[22] it may be that the struggle for supremacy in the northern half of the country, which eventually became the Province of Armagh, is allied to the fact that Christianity in that part had conformed with Rome on the vexatious Easter question and that the clergy of Armagh were advocates of a closer union with mainland European Christianity.

Nevertheless, a very strong oral tradition survived, a tradition based on the northern half of the country where Patrick had spent his years of missionary labours. It is this oral tradition which *Muirchú* and *Tírechán* committed to writing, based on their intimate knowledge of the topography of the country together with a desire to associate as many churches and foundations as possible with the saint. Neither account can now be accepted as founded on any degree of fact; both were set down with specific political aims in view.

There is little doubt that Patrick did not convert all of Ireland any more than that he was not the first or only Christian missionary here. But he left behind a rudimentary structure of ecclesiastical administration whose logical development was carried forward in succeeding centuries; it was not a church of ascetic monasticism, rather a church which was at once pastoral and missionary in its outlook.

An outline of the narrative as told by *Muirchú* will act as a pointer towards the reason for focussing the story in the north-east of Ireland and the rise of Down as the cult centre. *Muirchú,* a scribe, wrote his account at the behest of Bishop *Áedh* of *Slébte* [Sletty]. The narrative commences with Patrick's arrival on the coast of Wicklow and his subsequent voyage northwards where he eventually landed at the mouth of the River Slaney, which flows into Strangford Lough, close to its entrance to the Irish Sea. Patrick and his followers met the local chieftain – *Dichu* – whom he converted to Christianity and who, in turn, gave him a barn, *Sabhall,* [Saul], as his first church; Saul has, therefore, the tradition of being the site of the first church founded by Patrick in Ireland. From Saul, Patrick travelled to Slemish to meet his former master, *Miliucc*, whose flocks he had tended, but, forewarned of his approach and not wanting to be converted, *Miliucc* set fire to himself in an act of suicide, a deed which caused Patrick to fall into silent meditation for almost three hours. The party returned to Saul from where they set sail again in their boat, landing at the estuary of the Boyne, from where they followed the northern bank of the river as far as Slane. It being Easter, Patrick lit a Paschal fire on the hill of Slane which could be seen by *Laoghaire*, the King of Ireland, encamped on the hill of Tara some ten miles distant. *Laoghaire* was presiding over an assembly of his people for a pagan festival; it was the custom that anyone who lit his fire before he did, should forfeit his life. The King demanded:

> Who is the man who has dared to do such a wicked thing in my Kingdom? He shall die![23]

The chariots were ordered from Tara to Slane in order to sieze the newcomers. *Muirchú* relates some of the extraordinary deeds performed by Patrick on *Laoghaire's* followers after which *Laoghaire* was converted to the new faith.

We next find Patrick in Armagh, where he met the local chieftain, *Dáire*, from whom he requested a plot of land on which to build a church. He specifically requested a piece of high ground which was initially refused, but was finally granted, together with the conversion of *Dáire* to Christianity.

Back in Saul and sensing his approaching death, Patrick let it be known that he wished to die in Armagh and began to make his way there. He was interrupted, however, by the angel Victor telling him to return to Saul. In his last moments, he was given the viaticum, or last rites, by Bishop *Tassach* of Raholp. *Muirchú* describes his burial with a tremendous sense of drama:

> Let two untamed oxen be chosen and let them go wherever they will with the cart that carries your body, and wherever they stand still, there a church in honour of your body shall be erected. And, as the angel had said, untamed oxen were chosen and they steadily drew the cart containing the holy body placed on their necks. . . . . . And, guided by the will of God, they went out to *Dún Lethglaisse*, where Patrick lies buried.[24]

Muirchú's work gives many clues which help place Patrick's mission into its geographical context, whilst *Tírechán* places the mission in a different context. *Muirchú* displays an intimate knowledge of the topography of the north-east of Ireland and of the tradition of the *Ulaid*, the people occupying that territory, but a scant knowledge of other parts of the country, whereas *Tírechán* bases the mission largely in the west and north of the country. It is clear that in the seventh century there were strong traditions of a missionary saint – Patrick – in Lecale, especially in the *Dún* area, traditions so strong that Armagh was never able to claim Patrick's burial.[25] Some scholars go so far as to suggest that Patrick spent his entire ministry in Ireland within the Lecale area.[26]

Given the political background of fifth century Ireland and the fact that most of our information on Patrick is from later sources, it is too much to expect the modern reader to give credence to all aspects of the Patrick legend. However, peering through those mists, we can discern certain facts which bear the stamp of a well authenticated tradition and which we can therefore accept as basis for fact. That he was born in Britain from a Romano-British background, was kidnapped by Irish raiders, escaped some six years later and left Ireland, is in no doubt. On his eventual return to Ireland, we can accept that his missionary activities took him to many places within the northern half of the country and that, according to *Muirchú,* he founded his principal church at Armagh. The proximity of *Emain Macha* seems to have been the chief reason for his choice of Armagh, as well as being a reasonably central position from which to journey both east and west. Unfortunately, if we accept this theory, it throws into doubt the sacking of *Emain Macha* in 331, which date in the Annals seems to be more correct. In the light of recent research, scholars question if, in fact, Patrick ever set foot in Armagh or if it was the political requirements of a later century which gave that city its ecclesiastical primacy. The problem has been discussed in a recent paper in which the apostolic foundation of the See of Armagh has been called into question owing to the time lapse between Patrick's life and the late seventh century when it was first documented historically as a prominent ecclesiastical centre.[27] Should this have been the case, the argument for a ministry in Lecale is given much weight.

The last word has certainly not been written about Saint Patrick; scholars will continue the debate for as long as we have a Christian church in Ireland. Whilst the notes supplementary to *Tírechán's* account state variously that 'nobody knows where his bones lie' and that 'his grave is in Saulpatrick, in the church near the sea', *Muirchú* leaves us in no doubt that he lies in *Dún Lethglaise.* To the present day, most biographers accept the tradition that he lies at Down, a tradition which stems from the very strong link which *Muirchú* had with the territory of the *Ulaid* and the fact that Down has been established as the cult centre, certainly since the time when *Muirchú* was writing. The truth is that we will never know the correct location.

The Cathedral of the Holy Trinity, which today rises on the Hill of Down, is the living symbol of Patrick, with whose name the founding of Christianity in Ireland will be for ever linked.

TWO

THE EARLY CHURCH

WITH THE ADVENT OF WRITTEN records in the post-Patrician period, in particular the various series of Annals, it becomes clear that the name Downpatrick was not known; it did not, in fact, come into use until the early seventeenth century. It was then that the name 'Patrick' was added to 'Down', the latter word, derived from the Irish *'Dún'*, meaning a fort, being used either on its own or in either of two alternative forms. In the earliest documents, those prior to the eleventh century, we find variants of *Dún Lethglaise* but from the Norman period onwards, the form *Dún dá Lethglas* comes into general use, along with the shortened form, *Dún,* which eventually became the norm.[1]

This chapter will focus on the centuries between the death of Patrick and the arrival of the Anglo-Normans, some seven hundred years later. This is generally known as the Early Christian period when the embryonic Christian church gathered momentum within the Celtic-speaking world, still very much part of and interlinked with the tribal structure of society. Patrick's legacy was an outward-looking and missionary church, the bishops (and their successors) being part of the local tribe or even smaller population unit, having no jurisdiction beyond the lands of that tribe. Thus, when the Annals of Ulster record the death in 584 of *Fearghus,* Bishop of *Druim lethglaise*, who founded *Cell Biain,* we have no reason to suppose that he was other than an ordained member of the *Dál Fiatach,* the branch of the *Ulaid* which occupied much of the modern County Down. The Annals of Ulster had earlier recorded the storming of *Dún lethglaissi* in 495 and again in 497. This is the earliest use of the place-name, but apart from the implication that a fort existed, we cannot assume that any ecclesiastical activity was taking place. Archaeological excavations during the years 1985-7 established the existence of a large ditch which may have been dug during this period and also the existence of a number of burials which were also thought to date from the same period.[2]

By the sixth and early seventh centuries, the Irish church had been strongly influenced by the pursuit of monastic asceticism; the movement had spread into Ireland from both Britain and continental sources in the wake of the missionary activities of earlier centuries. Today the names of the founders of many of these

Opposite:
The High Cross
R. J. WELCH COLLECTION
ULSTER MUSEUM

early monasteries are remembered in the dedications of our churches; the three great foundations in county Down were Bangor, founded by Comgall in 555 or 558; Movilla, founded by Finnian in 540 and Nendrum, thought to have been founded by *Mochaoi* during Patrick's lifetime. It has been suggested that the monastery at *Dún Lethglaise* was founded not earlier than the eighth century under the royal patronage of the *Dál Fiatach*[3] but there is no evidence that it was a great centre of learning like Bangor which supported a monastic school attended by, we are told, thousands of students. Bangor was also the springboard from where Columbanus and Gall and no doubt many others, left these shores to spread the gospel across Europe. A reference to a scribe at Bangor, whose pupil worked on an island called *Crannach* at *Dún* can be found in a note to the Wurzburg Codex – a copy of Saint Matthew's gospel with a commentary:

> *Mosinu maccumin,* scribe and abbot of Bangor, first of the Irish, learned a computus by heart from a certain learned Greek. Then *Mocuoroc maccumin semon,* whom the Romans called the teacher of the whole world and who was a pupil of the aforesaid scribe committed to writing this knowledge on the island which is called *Crannach Duinlethglaisse.*[4]

The name and location of this place cannot be identified precisely; a number of nearby drumlins, at that time islands in the estuary, could be suggested.

The earliest annalistic record of *Dún lethglaise* is in 753 when the death of *Scannlán* is noted; he may have been the abbot. The abbot was the head of the monastery, very often in hereditary succession to the founder and not necessarily in clerical orders. There are many instances, particularly in later centuries, where the offices of bishop and abbot were held by one and the same individual. If, however, the abbot was not in orders, the monastery would have retained a bishop, normally resident with the monastic brothers but whose role was to ordain and carry out other sacramental functions. The abbot was responsible for maintaining the temporalities of the monastery and wielded considerable power and authority. A monastic establishment could acquire substantial wealth from the lands bequeathed to it by dynastic families or granted by local rulers; very often these lands were not in the immediate vicinity and it is known that *Dún Lethglaise* possessed large tracts of land across Lecale and indeed further afield.

Monasteries were, of course, an important feature in the pattern of early Irish society; they varied greatly in size and may have housed anything from a handful of monks to a large community of both lay and ordained brothers. Lay brothers were those who were responsible for manual labour and farming the monastic lands, the produce of which became the property of the monastery. Unfortunately the present Cathedral at Downpatrick may have obliterated any possibility of excavating the nucleus of the monastic enclosure, which would seem to have occupied a wide area around the brow of the hill.

Life in the monastery naturally centred round the church, almost certainly built of wood in this part of the country, with thatch or shingles for roofing. Other buildings, also wooden-built, within the monastic enclosure would have been the refectory with its nearby kitchen, possibly a granary and other associated storehouses, the abbot's house and the cells in which the individual monk, or possibly two or three, lived. Luckily we do have pictorial evidence of the one great vestige of the monastic community at *Dún Lethglaise* – the round tower. Eighteenth-century illustrations of the abbey ruins suggest that it stood a short distance to the south of the Cathedral tower, probably about the spot where the memorial stone to Saint Patrick lies,[5] but a recently discovered scale plan shows it to have stood 42 feet and 6 inches to the west of the west wall of the nave.[6] An early nineteenth-century English traveller recorded that it was 66 feet in height, with walls 3 feet thick and 8 feet in diameter. When demolished, the mortar with which it was built was so firm, that the structure remained entire. The same traveller tells us that when the foundation was cleared away, another foundation was discovered under it, running directly across the site of the tower, which appeared to be a continuation of the church wall.[7] In September 1997 the area on which the round tower was shown on the plan was excavated by the Channel 4 Television Time Team. Unfortunately no trace of the tower was found, indicating that, when demolished, even the foundations were robbed. Round towers are considered to have been built over a period between the tenth and twelfth centuries, probably as a response to the attacks by Vikings and other warring families. Serving a variety of purposes, they were primarily bell towers, serving also as stone refuges for both the members of the community and their books and treasures. Without exception, round towers are associated with ecclesiastical sites and whilst there are many examples in the rest of Ireland, it is a matter of great regret that those responsible for the restoration of the Cathedral in 1790 saw fit to pull down the *Dún Lethglaise* tower and quarry its stones in that restoration.

This piece of pink granite, built into the wall at the north-west corner of the cathedral, has a diamond pattern and a roll moulding along the edge. It can be dated to the twelfth century, is of Romanesque style and may originally have been a part of a high cross, now on its side.
PHOTOGRAPH BY A. W. K. COLMER

In an early Irish monastery the graveyard was a very important feature. The possession of the grave of a powerful saint was an influential factor in the growth of the monastery and acted as a focus for pilgrimage. The saint's body was believed to hallow the ground so that other people were eager to be buried alongside him, bringing burial fees and wealth to the monastery.[8] Here we have in *Dún Lethglaise* an early tradition of the burial place of Patrick, which seems to have become firmly established by the eighth and ninth centuries: Saint Patrick, the most powerful saint in all Ireland. Little wonder, therefore, that the place became the focus of de Courcy's attack at a later date and that he adopted the place as his headquarters. In more recent centuries the graveyard has become the resting place of rich and poor, lay and clergy alike, in the ground hallowed by the founding saint of Christianity in Ireland.

Figure of Abbot or Bishop, possibly twelfth century

A number of other reminders of the Early Christian period are still in the possession of Down Cathedral. First, there is the high cross which can be found outside the East window; it anciently stood at the crossroads at the foot of English Street, where it was known as the Town Cross. In the past, probably the early eighteenth century when the town as we now know it was taking shape, it either fell down or was pulled down to make way for houses and the various fragments into which it was broken were lost in different places in the town.[9] F.J. Bigger, an enthusiastic antiquarian, collected the pieces together and had them re-erected in the present position in 1897. The granite cross, probably dating from the tenth century, is badly weathered and it is therefore difficult to interpret the iconography of the panels on each of the faces. Such an interpretation has, however, recently been attempted by Dr Peter Harbison; the head of the cross on the east face, he suggests, is the crucified Christ with outstretched arms, his robe reaching to his knees. Beneath his arms are the early martyrs, Stephaton and Longinus, angels are above the arms and at each end are the thieves. The lower panels on the east face have been tentatively suggested as scenes from the early life of the Virgin taken from the apocryphal Book of James, known as the Protevangelium, similar to panels on the north cross at Duleek in County Louth. The head of the cross on the west face represents the Last Judgment, whilst two of the panels represent Adam and Eve with an apple tree and Cain and Abel; the other two are too worn to hazard an interpretation. The south face has continuous interlace whilst the north face has no decoration.[10] Throughout Ireland there are many superior specimens and we can only guess at the origin of the *Dún* cross by analogy. Its position at the foot of English Street would have marked the entrance to the monastery (it will be remembered that this was the only land access) and whilst its primary significance was religious, crosses were also the focal point for trading and dealing. There can also be seen in the entrance porch three fragments which probably belonged to two other crosses. Nearby is an early grave slab and detail with an incised cross; these slabs, with a wide variety of cross designs, are relatively common throughout Ireland but little is known of their date beyond the approximate Early Christian period. It may even antedate the free-standing high crosses by several centuries.

Carved figure of Bishop, possibly twelfth century

Down Cathedral possesses two small figures carved in stone, at present mounted on the wall above the door to the Chapter Room. These are thought to date from the twelfth century, later than the high crosses; each carving represents a bishop and it is said that the smaller one was formerly inset above the west door. The larger carving depicts a cleric clad in rich vestments, holding a book (symbolically the gospel) in his left hand and a crozier in his right. No mitre or other form of headdress is visible but from the roughness of the stone at this point, it would seem that the upper portion of the face is missing. The figure is set against a stylised form of wheeled cross and the feet are resting on a footstool.

The smaller fragment has been variously interpreted; Harbison suggests that the cleric is holding a saltire-cross decorated book[11] but it has been suggested elsewhere[12] that the figure (missing below the waist) is wearing a *rationale* or breastplate; the *rationale* was a little-known ornament worn by Celtic bishops and was hung from the neck outside any other vestments. It was known in a variety of shapes and designs, often heavily jewelled but the most common form was rectangular as here. The *rationale* re-appeared in the Anglo-Norman period but had dropped out of use by the fourteenth century; it was relatively rare in the western church, being found more frequently in the art of the Orthodox church, having been developed from the *ephod* of Judaism.[13] Exodus, Chapter 28, wherein are described the priestly garments of Aaron, puts the ornament into its biblical perspective.[14]

Coffin lid, early Christian, in porch of Down Cathedral

Monasteries were not exempt from the vicissitudes of tribal warfare; attacks on ecclesiastical property were at one time thought to have belonged to the period of the Viking invasion (the first recorded Viking attack in Ireland was in 795) but an analysis has shown that, where the identity of the aggressor can be established, approximately the same number of attacks are recorded where the neighbouring tribe is the aggressor as those in which the attackers are 'foreigners' or 'heathen', the names by which the Vikings are known in the Annals.[15] Records of both plundering and burning can be found in the Annals and it can be assumed that some of the burnings were accidental; however, whilst plundering implies a deliberate act, it may not always have involved total destruction. Often it involved the theft of the precious treasures of the monastery; archaeological evidence of such activity has turned up from time to time in Scandinavia.

Fragment of stone cross, early Christian, in porch of Down Cathedral

The Vikings, probably based in Waterford, had a fleet in Strangford Lough on at least two occasions, both of which have been recorded in the Annals:The first took place in 825:

> *Dún Lethglaise* was plundered by the heathen. *Mag Bile* [Moville] with its oratories was burned by the heathen. The *Ulaid* inflicted a rout on the heathen in *Mag Inis* [Lecale], in which very many fell.[16]

Again in 942:

> *Dún Lethglaise* was plundered by the foreigners, God and Patrick avenged it on them, causing them to go overseas and taking their island from them so that their king stole away and was killed by the Irish on land.[17]

In 989 the place was plundered and burned by foreigners and again in 1016 it was burned. The earlier wooden buildings had by now probably given way to more substantial structures built of stone, partly as a response to attacks but also due to advancing technology. The reputed grave of King Magnus Barfod of Norway, supposedly ambushed by the Irish in 1103, is to this day one of the tourist attractions of Downpatrick. We read of further burnings in 1040 and 1069 but on these occasions the aggressor is not identified. Lightning struck in 1111 and there was further plundering, along with Saul, Newry, Antrim and Ballyclug in 1164, during a hosting by the *Cinél Conaill* and *Cinél Eogain* (both tribes from west of Lough Neagh) into *Ulaid* territory. There is an entry of some interest in the Annals of Ulster in the year 1007 when *Matudán,* son of *Domnall*, King of *Ulaid* was killed by the *Torc* in Brigid's church in the middle of *Dún dá Lethglas.* We can only conjecture the location of Brigid's church, but here we have the only pre-Norman reference to a specific church with a dedication in *Dún.*

It is appropriate to list here the names of those clerics and/or laymen associated with the early church at Down, which have come down to us through the Annals. This list has been compiled from the Annals of Ulster, unless otherwise stated; the date given usually represents the obit:

584	Fergus, bishop
753	Scannlán
780	Maicnia, son of Cellach, abbot
790	Dúngal, son of Lóegaire, abbot
800	Loingsech, son of Fiachna, abbot
823	Suibhne, son of Fearghus, abbot, anchorite and bishop (AFM – not in AU)
882	Scannlán, superior, killed by the Ulaid
941	Aenacán, priest
953	Máel Martain, son of Maenach, priest
956	Gaíthéne, the learned
962	Finghin, distinguished bishop (AFM – not in AU)
972	Cathasach, son of Fergusán, coarb
988	Máelmoghna Uá Cairill, erenagh (AFM – not in AU)
992	Macléighinn, son of Dúnghalán, erenagh (AFM - not in AU)
	Dúnchadh, lector (AFM – not in AU)
1010	Scannlán uá Dúngalán, superior, abducted and blinded
1015	Cernach, son of Cathusach, superior
1026	Máelpádraig uá Ailecáin, lector (AFM – not in AU)
1043	Flaithbheartach, bishop (AFM – not in AU)
1057	Echmarcach, son of Cernach, superior, went on pilgrimage
1067	Scolaige, son of Innrechtach, superior (AFM – unnamed in AU)
1068	Domnall uá Cathasaigh, superior
1083	Muirchertach uá Cairill, superior, eminent in law and history
1086	Máel Coeimghein, chief bishop of the Ulaid

(Down not mentioned)
1099 Diarmait uá Máelaithgein, superior
1102 Cú Maigi uá Cairill, superior
1117 Máel Muire uá Dúnáin, an eminent bishop of the Irish and the head of the clerics of Ireland and a lord of the alms of the world, in the seventy seventh year of his age, on the ninth of the Kalends of January [24 December] completed the excellent course of his great religion (AFM states Bishop of Dún)
1148 Máel m'Aedhog uá Morgair, bishop (AFM only) (Malachy 1)
1175* Máel Ísu (namely, son of the 'Stooped Cleric') bishop of Ulidia (Down) master of wisdom and piety rested full of days in Christ

AFM = Annals of the Four Masters

Among these names are several who were members of the ruling *Dál Fiatach* dynasty, descendants of the Kings of the *Ulaid* at *Emain Macha;* it is important to emphasize that the ruling *Dál Fiatach* supplied the ecclesiastical, as well as the secular leadership, and that this was likely to have been the chief reason for the choice of *Dún Lethglaise* as their ecclesiastical centre. The monastery at *Dún Lethglaise* continued to play an integral part in the prestige of that dynasty, even though they had, by the ninth century, moved the centre of their operations northward to *Dún Echdach* [Duneight – near Lisburn][18]. Fiachna, whose son Loingsech died as abbot in 800, was King of the *Dál Fiatach.* The title passed to Loingsech's brother Cairill, from whom were descended Máelmoghna (+988), Muirchertach (+1083) and Cú Maigi (+1102), each of whom held the office of *erenagh* or superior at *Dún.*

If the eleventh and twelfth centuries were periods of continual internecine warfare throughout Ireland, they were also centuries during which the Irish church underwent fundamental change; indeed the twelfth-century reformation, whilst overshadowed in the history books by that of the sixteenth, was just as far-reaching in its effect. From the many annalistic references to visits to Rome and other places in Europe by clergy, it is evident that the church in Ireland was opening its doors to the influence of a wider sphere of Christianity than that in which it had been nurtured. A journey to Rome and back, it would seem, took approximately twelve months and the opportunity was nearly always taken to visit monasteries or other ecclesiastical centres on the route in Britain or Gaul. Although the Vikings established bridgeheads to create dioceses based on Dublin, Waterford and Limerick, they were careful to appoint native Irishmen as bishops. Thus it was Gilbert, Bishop of Limerick and Papal Legate, who gathered the clergy of Ireland together for the Synod of *Ráth breasail* in 1111. This synod was responsible for the division of Ireland into dioceses on the Roman model, giving for the first time to each of the bishops who were appointed a territorial area over which episcopal jurisdiction was exercised. Almost at one stroke, the administrative structure of the Irish church – if it could have been referred to as such – was overturned; Ireland was divided into two Provinces, each of which was further divided into twelve dioceses. Each diocese, including Connor and *Dún dá Lethglas*, had an episcopal see, but, in delineating the boundaries of each diocese, we find that Connor encompassed not only the area still recognised as Connor, but also the areas now occupied by the dioceses of Down and Dromore as well as a small portion of Derry east of the Bann [19]. If we were to superimpose the diocesan map of the north east of Ireland onto the tribal/political map of the time, we would find that the dioceses of Connor, Down and Dromore virtually recognised in ecclesiastical administration the lands of the *Ulaid*.

Needless to say, the statutes of *Ráth breasail* could only be put into operation on the next vacancy and coincidentally the reigning bishops of Connor and Down, *Flann uá Scula* and *Máelmuire,* both died in 1117. No record survives of an appointment to the sees, if indeed there was one, until 1124 when *Máel m'Aedhog uá Morgair*, better known as Malachy, was elected to Connor and Down. Malachy's connection with *Dún dá Lethglas*, it is fair to say, was somewhat tenuous, but his career in the wider sphere shows him to have been a prelate of considerable influence in the reform movement, a man of outstanding ability allied to a deep devotion to his faith in Christ. He is the earliest cleric from the pre-Norman church for whom we are fortunate to have some biographical information, our indebtedness for which is due to Saint Bernard of Clairvaux, one of his closest friends; the two men clearly held each other in the highest esteem.[20] Born in 1094 in Armagh, Malachy spent his childhood and formative years under Imar, as ascetic monk of the monastery of Saint Peter and Saint Paul in that city. On his maternal side, it is said that he was related to the Abbot of Bangor. He adopted the latin form of his name, Malachias, and, after ordination at the age of 25, he spent some time acting as Vicar for Cellach, the then Archbishop of Armagh, who spent long periods on visitation in other parts of the country. He is credited with the introduction of the Roman method of chanting services at the office hours and after two years of practical experience in the ministry, he left for the monastery at Lismore, whose bishop, Malchus, had been a Benedictine monk at Winchester before his consecration as Bishop of Waterford and Lismore and subsequent translation as Archbishop of Cashel. The period spent at Lismore at the feet of Malchus taught Malachy much about the wider church in both Britain and western Europe and was to be the foundation of his thought in later life.

On the death of the Abbot of Bangor (at Lismore) in 1123, Malachy was sent north to refound the Abbey of Saint Comgall in Bangor; he was simultaneously consecrated Bishop of Connor, the lands of which still included the diocese of *Dún dá Lethglas*. Prolonged raiding and plundering of the *Ulaid* by the *Cinél Eogain*, however, forced Malachy to return to Lismore in 1127 where he remained until his recall to assume the Primatial See of Armagh on the death of

Cellach in 1132. His heart was, nevertheless, in Bangor and after spending only five years at Armagh, he resigned the archbishopric in order to return to Bangor, separating the two dioceses and appointing another as Bishop of Connor. As Bishop of *Dún dá Lethglas*, it is quite clear that he administered the diocese from Bangor and not from *Dún dá Lethglas*, but, as part of his advocacy of reform and the drawing of the Irish church closer to Rome, he introduced a community of Augustinian canons at *Dún dá Lethglas*, dedicated to Saint John the Evangelist. This priory appears to have been a separate foundation from the community on the Hill of Down – still the original community – and was known as the Monastery of the Irish; it is said to have been at Toberglory, close to the road leading to Saul.[21]

Malachy was now regarded as being in the forefront of the reform movement and he determined to make the journey to Rome in order to receive the Pope's blessing and authority for this movement and, at the same time, he hoped to receive from the Pope the pallium, a form of scarf personally given by the Pope to an archbishop. His journey took him through Scotland and England, then through France where he spent some time at Clairvaux with Bernard, on whom he made a profound impression. On reaching Rome, he was received by the Pope, Innocent II, with whom he had, we are told, many conversations on the state of the church in Ireland. It will be remembered that the office of Papal Legate in Ireland was held by Gilbert, Bishop of Limerick; owing to age and infirmity, Gilbert was no longer able to carry out the duties of his office and in his stead, the Pope offered the post to Malachy. However, that for which Malachy had hoped for on his visit was not granted; the pallium for each of the metropolitan sees of Armagh and Cashel. Instead he was asked by Pope Innocent to hold a general council of all the clergy in Ireland and, provided they agreed by a vote of the entire assembly to apply formally for the pallia, they would be granted.

In spite of this disappointment, Malachy, on his return to Ireland, appears to have thrown himself into the duties of Papal Legate with enthusiasm and travelled all over the country in their performance. Almost a decade later, a general synod of all the clergy in Ireland was convened at Inispatrick, an island off the east coast, near present day Skerries, in order to make a formal request at Rome for the pallia. Fifteen bishops and two hundred priests attended this synod – the year was 1148 – and authority was given to Malachy to return to Rome to receive the pallia for Armagh and Cashel. No time was lost in setting out and by October 1148, he had arrived at Clairvaux on his way to Rome. After a few days there spent in the company of Bernard, it is recorded that Malachy was struck by a fever, from which he did not recover; it was All Souls Day, 2 November, and the following day, 3 November, is celebrated as the feast of Saint Malachy. He lies buried in the monastery at Clairvaux.

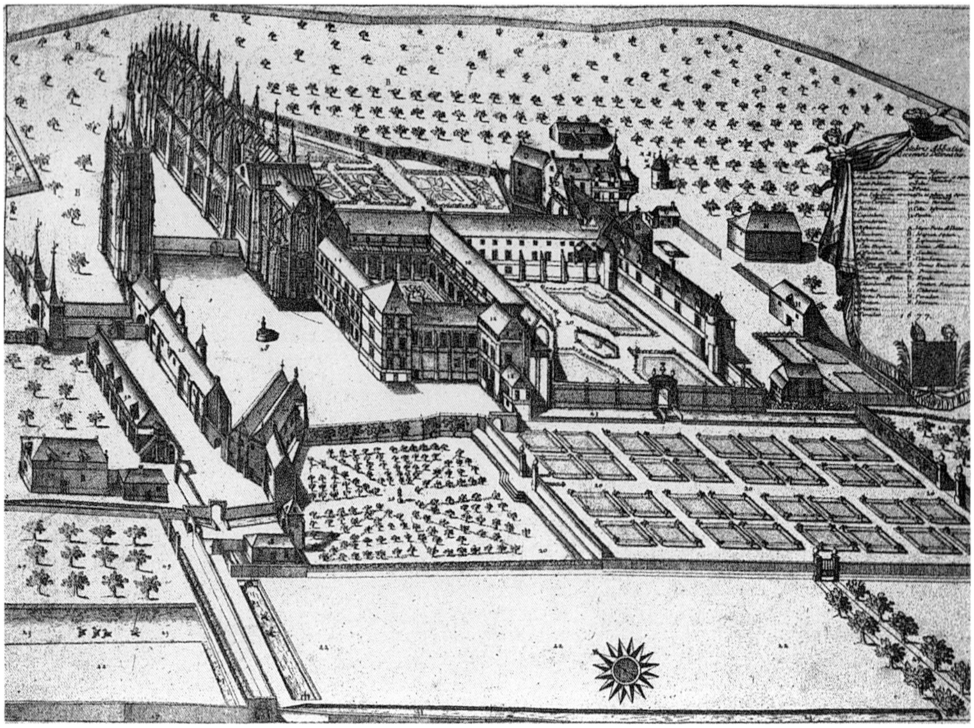

Le Bec Abbey in Normandy as drawn in 1677. Much has survived and it remains a thriving Benedictine House

THREE

JOHN DE COURCY

On the death of *Máel Ísu* (Malachy II) in 1175 (it seems that he held the See for only a few months), his successor as Bishop of Down was another Malachy, who has become known as Malachy III. Malachy was to preside, perhaps unwittingly, over the greatest upheaval which the church in Down had yet undergone.

Some years earlier, in 1169, the English, with a century of interbreeding since William I had arrived from Normandy, attacked Ireland and established a strong foothold along the south-eastern coastal strip around Wexford and Waterford. The ambitious Henry II was on the throne of England; he had already inherited much of France from his mother, Matilda, and his father, Geoffrey, as well as further lands in that country through his marriage to Eleanor, a former wife of the King of France. He was anxious to add Ireland to his possessions, having obtained papal sanction to do so and proceeded to consolidate his foothold, extending his rule inland and northwards towards Dublin. Constant fighting greeted the newcomers as they extended their power and influence and so it was when one of these Anglo-Norman adventurers, John de Courcy, rode north from Dublin in 1177. Not only did de Courcy seek to quell the native Irish, but he intended to conquer new lands for himself. It is said that he took less than a week to arrive at Down from Dublin, reputedly with 24 knights-at-arms and three hundred men. There was never any doubt but that Down was the main target for his assault because of its importance as the former centre of *Dál Fiatach* influence; perhaps, even more importantly, it was the burial place of Patrick.

The battle for Down was an unequal fight; Rory MacDunleavy, the King of the *Dál Fiatach*, was routed by the superior arms and tactics of de Courcy's men:

> ...The valiant knight, John de Courcy, came secretly with a band of knights and archers from Dublin to *Dún da Leathglass,* and reaching it unperceived, they made a dyke from sea to sea about *Dún.* The *Uladh* then assembled, under *Ruaidhri Mac Duinn Shléibhe*, to make an attack on *Dún* against John, but on reaching it, they retreated without striking a blow when they saw the Englishmen with their horses in full battle dress. When the Englishmen saw the *Uladh* in flight, they followed them with their people and inflicted slaughter upon them, both by drowning and by the sword. The *Bachall Finghain* (Finghin's Crozier) and *Bachall Ronain Fhinn* (Ronan Fionn's Crozier) and many other relics were left behind in the slaughter.[1]

It is related by the Norman chronicler, Giraldus Cambrensis, that MacDunleavy returned to the attack eight days later with ten thousand warriors and, in the fierce battle which ensued, de Courcy, in spite of being greatly outnumbered, won the day.[2] Henry granted to de Courcy as much of Ulster as he could conquer by force. Cardinal Vivian, the Papal Legate, had just arrived from Man on his way to Dublin and was taken prisoner by de Courcy, along with Bishop Malachy. Both, however, were released very quickly, no doubt as an act of contrition towards the church.

Who were the Anglo-Normans who came to Ireland in the later years of the twelfth century and who were to cause such sweeping and lasting changes on the native culture? It will be recalled that the ninth and tenth centuries were a period of considerable expansion by the pagan Vikings from northern Europe and we have read of their predatory raids and settlement in Ireland during those centuries. Ireland, however, was not alone in being the object of their attacks; England was also the focus of continual raiding and many place-names in England today bear the hallmark of their Viking roots. The Vikings also attacked and gained a substantial foothold in northern France; in fact they met with less resistance in France than elsewhere and were even granted lands by the local Frankish rulers. These Viking settlements in northern France led inevitably to

Le Bec Abbey

the destabilisation of the Carolingian empire and its eventual collapse in 987, but not before the invaders had been converted to Christianity in return for further grants of land.[3] What was to become Normandy was largely the result of the colonisation of this part of France by the Vikings and its effect on the local population.

ANNO DOMINI 1930
DEO GRATIAS
GLORIAE MAJORUM
CETTE PLAQUE A ETE POSEE PAR DES ANGLAIS POUR COMMEMORER LES RAPPORTS ETROITS QUI UNISSAIENT L'ANCIENNE ABBAYE DU BEC-HERLUIN ET L'EGLISE D'ANGLETERRE AUX ONZIEME ET DOUZIEME SIECLES. LORSQUE TROIS DES FILS DE CETTE ABBAYE OCCUPAIENT LE SIEGE PRIMATIAL DE CANTORBERY. TROIS DEVENAIENT EVEQUES DE ROCHESTER, ET PLUSIEURS AUTRES, EN QUALITE D'ABBES, GOUVERNAIENT D'IMPORTANTES MAISONS RELIGIEUSES.
ILS TRAVAILLERENT TOUS EGALEMENT A FIXER LE CARACTERE DES INSTITUTIONS DE LEUR PAYS D'ADOPTION ET PAR LEURS DOCTES LEÇONS ET LEUR HABILETE DE CONSTRUCTEURS ILS CONTRIBUERENT GRANDEMENT A LA SPLENDEUR DES EGLISES CATHEDRALES ET DES ETABLISSEMENTS MONASTIQUES DE LEUR JURIDICTION.
EN TEMOIGNAGE DE LA RECONNAISSANCE QUE LEUR GARDE L'ANGLETERRE CE MEMORIAL RAPPELLERA LEURS NOMS A LA POSTERITE.
ARCHEVEQUES DE CANTORBERY:
LANFRANC: 1070 – 1089.
PRIEUR DU BEC, 1045; ABBE DE ST ETIENNE DE CAEN, 1063.
ANSELM, ST: 1093 – 1109. ABBE DU BEC. 1078.
THEOBALD: 1138 – 1161. ABBE DU BEC. 1137.
EVEQUES DE ROCHESTER:
HERNOST: 1076.
GUNDULF: 1077 – 1108:
SECRETAIRE DE LANFRANC A CAEN ET A CANTERBURY:
ARCHITECTE DE LA TOUR DE LONDRES.
ERNULF: 1114 – 1124:
PRIEUR DE CHRIST CHURCH, CANTERBURY, 1096:
ABBE DE BURGH, PETERBOROUGH, 1107.
ABBES:
GILBERT CRISPIN: WESTMINSTER, 1085 – 1117
RICHARD: ST WERBURGH, CHESTER, 1093 – 1117.
HENRY: BATTLE ABBEY, 1096 – 1102.
RICHARD: ELY, 1100 – 1108.
GILBERT: COLCHESTER, 1104 – 1119.
HUGH FLORY: ST AUGUSTINE, CANTERBURY, 1108 – 1124.
ALBOLD: ST EDMUND, BURY, 1114 – 1119.

Tablet on the Tower at Le Bec detailing the early relationships between Le Bec, Canterbury, Rochester and other English Abbeys

The role of the church was paramount in this society; whilst the Carolingian empire can never be said to have given birth to the cult of monasticism in western Christianity, it certainly assisted in the development of the more formal ideals of monasticism as laid down by the early saints, in particular Saint Benedict (c.480-550), who has been called the patriarch of western monasticism. Medieval Christianity relied heavily on the doctrine of salvation and the need to make amends for sin and evil in this world and, to this purpose, Carolingian rulers built monasteries and greatly encouraged the practice of monasticism in their kingdom. Such good works ensured the safeguarding of the soul not only of the benefactor but of his family, living or dead, as well. Even among lesser nobles, the foundation and endowment of a monastery were regarded as a sure means of salvation. On a more pragmatic level, monasteries were useful places for the younger members of families who could not be provided for out of the family inheritance; monasticism, as envisaged by the Carolingian rulers, was the prerogative of the upper social classes.

During the eleventh century, when Norman power and influence was at its peak, there was a rapid increase in the number of monastic foundations in Normandy. Many of these houses were endowed by successive Dukes of Normandy although, towards the close of the century, the lesser nobility also added to the endowments. By 1070, there were 33 monasteries in the province of which 26 followed the Rule of Saint Benedict.[4] Among the larger and more illustrious foundations was that of le Bec, founded in the 1030s, whose prior was Lanfranc, one of the brilliant theologians of his day. Originally from northern Italy, he was closely acquainted with the Popes of the period. When Duke William invaded England in 1066 and had himself crowned King William I in Westminster Abbey, it was Lanfranc whom he invited to become Archbishop of Canterbury, thus ensuring the co-operation of the ecclesiastical authorities in his new dominions. Lanfranc was succeeded at le Bec by Anselm, who subsequently followed his predecessor to Canterbury.

Hugh of Avranches, a Norman knight who had accompanied William to England, made his way to Chester and on arrival, had himself created Earl of Chester. Chester was, of course, originally a Roman town and had existed on the River Dee for many centuries; its importance lay in its strategic position on the road to northern Britain and also its commercial attraction as a port at which to embark for Ireland. It was also the site of a monastery of secular canons dedicated to Saint Werburgh, the daughter of a seventh century King of Mercia. The original foundation of the monastery was in 673.[5] Earl Hugh, as was the practice elsewhere, replaced the canons and refounded the monastery as a Benedictine house in 1092, making it a daughter house to le Bec and inviting his friend Anselm to organise and advise on its early years. The first abbot, Richard, was a monk from le Bec and it is recorded that he brought the first community with him. Unlike Cistercians, each Benedictine house was independent and the connection with le Bec was soon severed; the Abbey of Saint Werburgh remained in existence until the dissolution in the sixteenth century.

Saint Werburgh
One of eight saints in the west window of Chester Cathedral.
THE DEAN OF CHESTER

De Courcy, it will be remembered, had overcome the native people in Down by virtue of superior arms and tactics. The Norman principle of propitiation for sin now took effect; de Courcy founded an abbey of Benedictines and invited monks from the abbey of Saint Werburgh in Chester to become the founding community with a prior. There is no reason to suppose, as popular tradition tells us, that he expelled the secular canons of the abbey founded by Saint Malachy 150 years earlier; apart from the uncertainty of the location of the earlier foundation, the evidence would suggest that, rather than antagonising the local population, de Courcy endeavoured to play the part of a model ruler in his chosen capital. No clearer evidence of this can be found than his change of dedication of the Cathedral Church, which was to become the Benedictine Abbey, from the Holy Trinity to Saint Patrick. The Chartulary of Saint Werburgh records a grant in 1183 by de Courcy of

> Hurnach with ten carucates of land within the *thewet* of *Cheuelfernan* in order that they may find him from their house a prior and monks for

[Insp]ex[imus] pro [pri]ore et monach[is] de Dun in Hib[er]n[ia] de confirmac[i]o[n]e

R[ex] Omnib[us] ad quos p[re]sentes l[itte]re p[er]ven[er]int salt[e]m. Inspeximus quasdam l[itte]ras patentes sub sigillo quo utimur in t[er]ra n[ost]ra Hib[er]n[ie] signatas in hec v[er]ba. Edwardus dei gr[aci]a Rex Angl[ie] [dominus] Hib[er]n[ie] et Dux Aquit[anie] Omnib[us] ad quos p[re]sentes l[itte]re p[er]ven[er]int salt[e]m. Inspeximus quandam cartam Malachie quondam Dunensis Ep[iscop]i in hec v[er]ba. Sciant tam p[re]sentes q[uam] futuri q[uo]d ego Malachias Dunensis Ep[iscop]us concessi ad honorem dei et s[an]c[t]e Religionis eccl[es]iam s[an]c[t]i Patricii de Dun cum omnib[us] p[er]tin[entiis] suis ad opus prioris et maior[um] monachor[um] quor[um] ip[s]e Ep[iscop]us est custos et Abbas sicut fit in eccl[es]ia Cantuariensi vel Conventrensi. concessi [e]tiam eis et successorib[us] suis et confirmavi villas ad eccl[es]iam suam p[er]tinentes, scil[ice]t Lachmorne, Messefinecht, Ffynochen, Balinscanlan, Arglothin, Balinrothan, Telagnocossi, Balienkretnagh, Telach, Belen Tiperinem, Balimechecho, Dunnonese, Baliendmach, Balienliznom, Telaghmechan, Balinbechan, Mylach cum p[er]tin[entiis], [Insu]la Chengay, Monemner, Rechendusf, Chemays, Tygore, Grestnuchey, Balioconelb, Clemse, Crock, Balindechanne cum p[er]tin[entiis], Balima, Celenge, Balinangatha, Balinculoy, Balimachell, Ffelig, Balienquith, Balinnyngan, Kellechan, Baliolosan, Lescoman, Korres, Monoch, Lamo, Kapenlinchepi, Grede cum p[er]tin[entiis], Balimagges, Karenescher, Chellemmen, Rathcap, et eccl[es]ias de Killedeth et de Ryrher et Corlhan cum p[er]tin[entiis] suis in Uldebina, Karach, Domenach, Kellaginayo. P[re]dicta ad honorem et reu[er]enciam Ep[iscop]atus mei p[ro]prium in manu mea medietatem oblacionum hiis quatuor festis anni et non amplius, scil[ice]t in Natali d[omi]ni, in Purificac[i]o[n]e s[an]c[t]e Marie, in festo s[an]c[t]i Patricii, in Pascha et Pentecosten. Hui[us] concessionis isti sunt testes. T. Dunelmensis archiep[iscop]us, G. Armachan[us] et multi alii. Inspeximus insup[er] quandam aliam cartam Joh[ann]is de Curci in hec v[er]ba. Sciant tam p[re]sentes q[uam] futuri q[uo]d ego Joh[ann]es de Curci dedi et concessi et hac p[re]senti carta confirmavi deo et s[an]c[t]o Patricio et eccl[es]ie sue de Duno et p[ri]ori et monachis eiusdem eccl[es]ie et successorib[us] suis omnes querelas et omnia placita de omnib[us] hominib[us] suis et de omnib[us] terris suis [illegible] ... de rapina et de [illegible] et de igne et de sanguine et de [illegible] et de omni [illegible] et de omni vi et violencia et de omnib[us] causis [illegible] et negociis et [illegible] ... [illegible]

[illegible] Curci

[illegible] ... Inspeximus etiam quandam aliam cartam Joh[ann]is de Curci in hec v[er]ba. Sciant tam p[re]sentes q[uam] futuri q[uo]d ego Joh[ann]es de Curci dedi et concessi et hac mea p[re]senti carta confirmavi deo et eccl[es]ie s[an]c[t]i Patricii de Dun et monachis ibidem deo servientib[us] passagium de aqua de Strangford [illegible] passagium de aqua de Carlingford et passagium de Carrefergus et passagium de aqua de Banne et omnia passagia tocius conquestus mei in Hibernia [illegible] ... [illegible]

Inspeximus insup[er] quandam aliam cartam H. de Lasci quondam comitis Ulton[ie] in hec v[er]ba. Omnib[us] ad quos p[re]sens scriptum p[er]venerit H. de Lasci comes Ulton[ie] salt[e]m in d[omi]no [illegible] ... [illegible]

Inspeximus etiam quandam aliam cartam J. de Curci in hec v[er]ba. Omnib[us] s[an]c[t]e matris eccl[es]ie filiis tam p[re]sentib[us] q[uam] futuris J. de Curci salt[e]m. [illegible] ... [illegible]

Inspeximus insup[er] quandam aliam cartam Joh[ann]is de Curci in hec v[er]ba. Sciant omnes tam p[re]sentes q[uam] futuri q[uo]d ego Joh[ann]es de Curci concessi et hac p[re]senti carta confirmavi deo et eccl[es]ie s[an]c[t]i Patricii de Duno et [illegible] priori et monachis ibidem deo servientib[us] totam illam donacionem [illegible] ... [illegible]

Inspeximus etiam quandam aliam cartam Joh[ann]is de Curci in hec v[er]ba. Sciant tam p[re]sentes q[uam] futuri q[uo]d ego Joh[ann]es de Curci ex p[ar]te d[omi]ni mei regis Anglie dedi et hac mea carta concessi eccl[es]ie s[an]c[t]e Trinitatis de Dun [illegible] ... [illegible]

Inspeximus insup[er] quandam aliam cartam Joh[ann]is de Curci in hec v[er]ba. Sciant omnes tam p[re]sentes q[uam] futuri q[uo]d ego Joh[ann]es de Curci dedi et concessi et hac mea p[re]senti carta confirmavi deo et eccl[es]ie s[an]c[t]i Patricii de Duno et [illegible] priori et monachis ibidem deo servientib[us] [illegible] ... [illegible]

Nos autem [illegible] ... In cuius rei testimonium has l[itte]ras n[ost]ras fieri fecimus patentes. Teste [illegible] Thoma comite de [illegible] ... anno regni n[ost]ri Angl[ie] vicesimo quinto, regni v[er]o n[ost]ri Ffrancie vicesimo secundo. Nos autem cartas et l[itte]ras p[re]dictas et omnia contenta in eisdem [illegible] ... [illegible] In cuius rei t[estimonium] [illegible] apud Westm[onasterium] xxiij die Novembr[is].

p[er] b[re]ve de p[ri]vato sigillo.

the construction of an abbey of their order in the church of Saint Patrick at Down, to be free of all subjection to their church.[6]

William de Etteshall, a monk from Saint Werburgh, came to Down and was installed as the first prior of the newly erected Benedictine abbey.

De Courcy, meantime, in accordance with the practice of his fellow Anglo-Normans, generously endowed the new community. Several charters are extant which set out in detail the nature of these endowments; each includes a list of witnesses which gives us an insight into the leading civil and ecclesiastical personages of the time and many also record the names of those for whose souls salvation was sought.[7]

An early charter, certainly before 1183 when the dedication was changed, describes a grant by de Courcy on behalf of the King of England to the church of the Holy Trinity (*ecclesia Sancte Trinitatis*) of Down, of the land on the right hand of Saint George's as far as the wall of the house of Saint Columba through the street next to the cross of Saint Moninna as far as the wall, and Mungona with all its appurtenances.[8] The witnesses of this charter are the Bishop of Connor, the Abbot of Saul, William de Courcy, Roger, Seneschal of Chester, Simon of Passeleu, Richard son of Robert, Adam the chamberlain and John the priest who acted as scribe. Moninna was an early saint who died in 517 at Killevy in south Armagh, where she is still venerated. Her reputation has, however, been eclipsed by that of Brigid and by that of Patrick himself.[9] It is tempting to suggest that the cross still extant might perhaps be the cross of Saint Moninna. The other locations mentioned in this charter, Saint George's, Saint Columba and Mungona are now unidentifiable; the fact that the names were recorded gives, nevertheless, a useful clue that there existed rather more than just an amorphous group of houses, no matter how humble.

St John's Point Church

Another charter, possibly in the later 1180s, confirms to God and the Church of Saint Patrick of Down with Prior Andrew and his monks, the tenth cow and the tenth animal from all de Courcy's booties, acquisitions and purchases of animals; this for the peace and salvation of his soul, his mother's soul and the souls of his ancestors and successors and all who will give him help and counsel in the conquest of Ulster.[10] He grants a tenth of the hunting on his lands to the church and monks of Saint Patrick of Down, for the salvation of his soul, his wife Affreca's soul, the soul of his master, King Henry of England, the souls of his father and mother, his ancestors and the soul of Beatrice de Villers.[11]

Ferries are the subject of a further grant; the ferries at Strangford towards the *Duffryn*, at Carlingford, at *Cragfergus* [Carrickfergus], and at the River Bann

Folio from Inspeximus of Charters,
41 Edward III
P.R.O. C66/278
CROWN COPYRIGHT, REPRODUCED WITH PERMISSION OF THE CONTROLLER OF HER MAJESTY'S STATIONERY OFFICE

are granted to the church of Saint Patrick with the exception of that between Lecale and Ards; this for the souls of his father and mother, his ancestors and successors, Beatrice de Villers, his own and his wife Affreca's souls, and of all those who have died or are going to die in his service. This grant, possibly c.1192, was witnessed by M.Bishop of Down (Malachy), R.Bishop of Connor (Reginald), E. de *Ynes* [Inch], G. de *Homo* [Holmcultram] and P. de *Saballo* [Saul], abbots; G de Sancto Thoma [Saint Thomas, another monastery in Down], P. de *Mucmor* [Muckamore] and W. de *Cragfergus* [Carrickfergus], priors; Roger the constable, Richard the seneschal, Stephen the clerk, Master Walter and Robert the clerk.[12] In this grant it will be noted that he personally retained the most lucrative of all the ferries, that across the narrow strait at the mouth of Strangford Lough.

In what looks like an attempt to give a degree of self-government, God and Saint Patrick and his church of Down along with D. the prior and monks of that church and their successors were granted the proceeds of all pleas and actions involving their own people and tenants in cases of murder, plunder, rape, seizure, burning, wounding etc., provided that de Courcy's agent was present to see that justice was fairly done.[13]

Apart from the early grant of what was evidently a small parcel of land within the existing ecclesiastical enclosure at Down and which was probably the proposed site for the building of the monastery, none of these grants relates to farm land or 'real estate'; de Courcy was able to grant services and goods which, whilst to some degree under his personal control, were more difficult to quantify in terms of realisable income to the monastery. This was because much of the land was already in church hands, or more correctly, was the property of the See, a legacy from the old Irish church with its episcopal structures. Thus we find that the charter granting a number of townlands to the monastery was executed not by de Courcy, but by Malachy, the Bishop of Down; it is an attractive hypothesis that Malachy may well have been asked, even compelled, to make these grants by de Courcy. This charter is addressed to the Prior and black monks (Benedictines were called black monks because of the colour of their habit) of the Church of Saint Patrick, of whom he himself would be guardian and abbot.[14] A large number of townlands is listed, many of which have been identified in modern times and almost all of which are spread across the peninsula of Lecale. Along with the lands, the grant included three churches, *Killecleth* [Kilclief], *Brichten* [Bright] and *Stethian* [St John's Point]; the witnesses to this charter were L. (Laurence O'Toole, Archbishop of Dublin), T. (*Tomaltach uá Conchobair,* Archbishop of Armagh) and many others *(multi alii)*.[15] The fact that the Archbishop of Dublin took precedence over the Archbishop of Armagh in this charter indicated that the Archbishop of Dublin, Laurence O'Toole, was acting in his capacity as Papal Legate.[16]

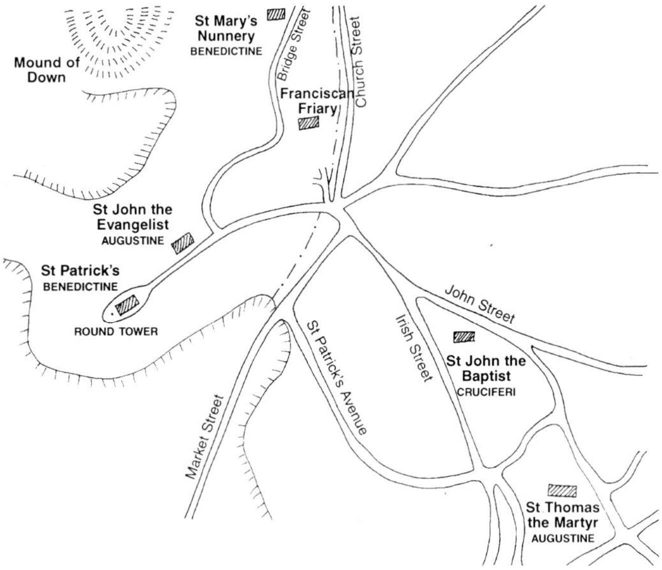

Map suggesting locations of religious foundations at Down c.1300. Modern streets are indicated
– . – . wall 'from sea to sea'

Saint Patrick's of Down was not the only monastery founded by de Courcy; he was, indeed, prolific in this regard. With two exceptions, Carrickfergus and Muckamore, all his foundations were within the modern county of Down. The other foundations were all conceived as daughter houses of monasteries in Britain and surviving records demonstrate the close ties maintained between the daughter house and its parent within the monastic order; at a later period, it will be seen how the Irish possessions were jealously guarded by the mother house in Britain.

Before de Courcy's arrival, there had been a monastery at Erenagh, a few miles south of Down (near Castlescreen), following the Savignac rule, an austere and strict form of the Cistercian order. It was a daughter house of Furness, also under the Savignac rule. The early years of the twelfth century saw the rapid rise of the Cistercians, largely through the efforts of Saints Bernard and Malachy and, by the middle of the century, the Savignacs had been absorbed by the Cistercians. Erenagh did not last long under the Cistercian rule; it was destroyed during the fighting which led to the fall of Down in 1177, reputedly by de Courcy. Possibly in reparation, he made an immediate grant of land at Inch to Furness to build a new abbey; to this day, the ruins of Inch Abbey remain an outstanding example of thirteenth-century Cistercian architecture.[17] Again, at the behest of de Courcy, a Life of Saint

Charter to Inch Abbey
P.R.O. DL25/219
CROWN COPYRIGHT. REPRODUCED WITH PERMISSION OF THE CONTROLLER OF HER MAJESTY'S STATIONERY OFFICE

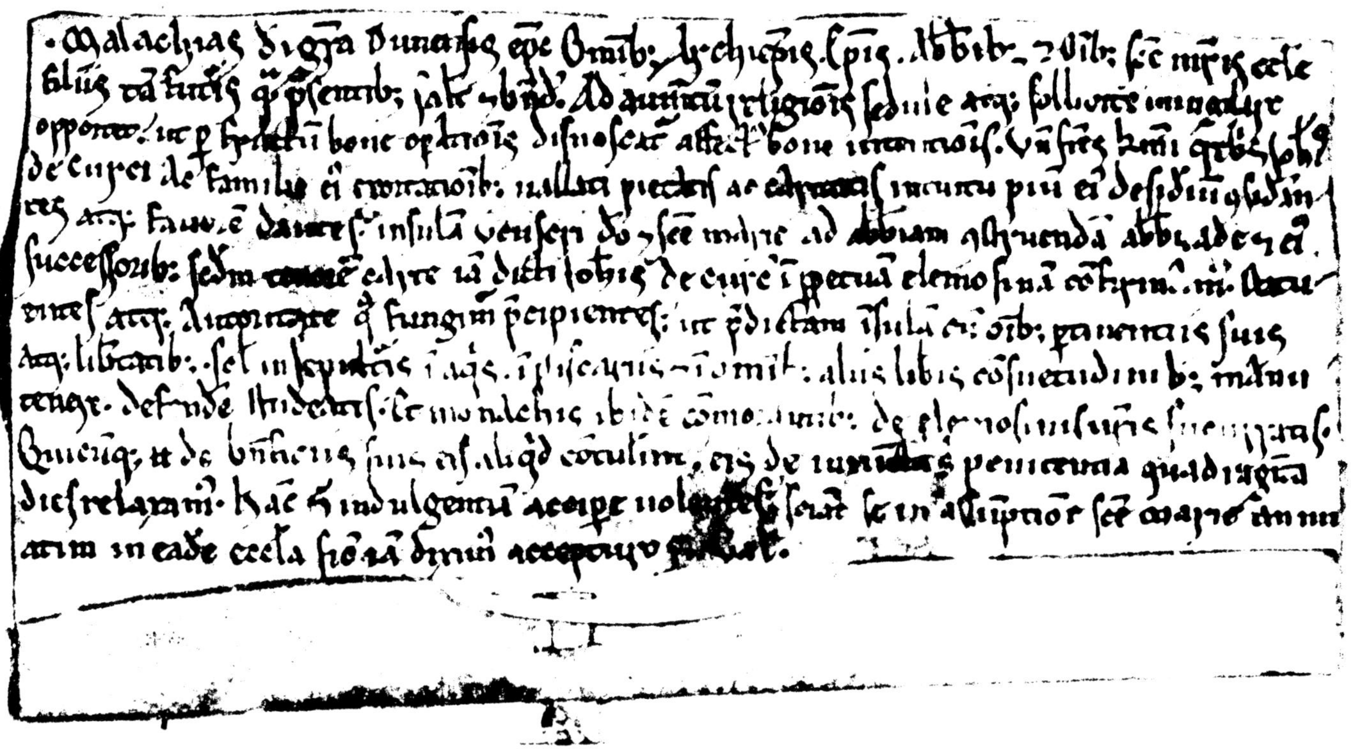

Inch Abbey
W. A. GREEN COLLECTION
ULSTER FOLK AND TRANSPORT MUSEUM

Patrick was written by Jocelyn, a monk of Furness, who may have come to Inch. Although the de Courcy charter to Furness in respect of Inch does not appear to survive, its confirmation by Bishop Malachy survives in the Public Record Office in London.[18] This document refers to the grant to Abbot Adam of the *Insula Venseri* for the building of an abbey to God and Saint Mary; although the place-name *Venseri* is unknown elsewhere and cannot be positively identified with Inch, it is almost certain that we are dealing with one and the same place since we do know that Adam was Abbot of Inch, having been a witness to one of the charters of Saint Patrick's. The passage of centuries has tended to generate a negative view of John de Courcy; he has been represented as a destroyer of monasteries and evictor of their communities. On the contrary, however, there seems little reason to suggest that he was other than generous, within the medieval meaning of that word, to the church and its structures.

John de Courcy married Affreca, daughter of Godred, King of Man; she was responsible for the foundation of *Jugum Dei* [Grey Abbey] in 1193 and made it a daughter house of Holmcultram in Cumbria, under the Cistercian rule.[19] As with Inch, the surviving ruins of Grey Abbey are an enduring monument to the architectural achievements of the Anglo-Norman builders.

Nendrum on Mahee Island in Strangford Lough, whose original foundation is thought to have been by Saint *Mochaoi* in the fifth century, was granted to Saint Bee's, a Benedictine house in Cumbria, itself a daughter house of Saint Mary's in York. The date of this grant from de Courcy was 1179 and included a clause reserving to Malachy the third part of all benefices, lands and easements.[20] In this instance the monastery ceased to exist within a short period, the 1306 taxation recording only a parish church.[21] Stogursey [Stoke Courcy], one of de Courcy's family bases in Somerset, was remembered through the foundation of a Benedictine cell at Saint Andrew in Ards, dependent on Stogursey, itself a daughter of Lonlay, one of the larger abbeys in Normandy.[22]

Nendrum

The next foundation to be noted is the Priory of Saint Thomas the Martyr, on a site at Toberglory which was granted to the Prior and Canons of Saint Mary's of Carlisle, whose home priory was under frequent attacks by raiding Scots. Carlisle and its daughter house, Saint Thomas the Martyr, were houses of canons regular following the Augustinian rule. Toberglory is described as being in a suburb of Down between two roads, that leading to Crems [possibly identified as Killavees] and that leading to Saul Quarter; [23] this community appears to have been quite separate from that founded by Saint Malachy, noted earlier and also following the Augustinian rule, dedicated to Saint John the Evangelist. This latter became known as 'The Monastery of the Irish'.[24]

Finally, de Courcy founded a monastery for an order which cared for the poor and sick: the Priory of Saint John the Baptist of the order of Crutched Friars (*Cruciferi*), following the Augustinian rule. This priory became known as the Priory of the English, in order to differentiate it from the priory of the same dedication by Malachy for the Augustinians.[25] An early charter granted to God, Saint Mary, Saint John, Saint Nicholas, Saint Clement and the brothers who work in the hospital outside the city of Down, one bowl of beer as is the custom in the city of Dublin.[26] Reeves suggested that this priory was located on the east side of what is now Irish Street, the site formerly occupied by the Ebenezer Chapel.[27]

With this impressive list of monastic foundations, what do we know of the man who was the driving force behind such creative activity? Giraldus tells us that he was tall and fair-haired, had immense bodily strength and an extraordinarily bold temperament; a man of courage and a born fighter, always in the front line, eager for battle.[28] Ever an impetuous man, away from the battlefield he was modest and restrained and never omitted to honour the Church of Christ. Devoted to religious observance, he attributed his success in war to God's grace and always gave God the glory and thanks for his victories. It will have been noted that four of his foundations were made dependent to houses in north-western Britain: Furness, Holmcultram, Saint Bee's and Carlisle. Indeed Saint Werburgh's in Chester can also be included in this geographical context but Stogursey in Somerset was clearly the outsider; it being an alien priory (the community were non-native English), its location in southern Britain would certainly have been a matter of greater convenience. A recent study has demonstrated that de Courcy had close family connections in Cumbria and

Grey Abbey. Founded in 1193 by Affreca, wife of John De Courcy
W. A. GREEN COLLECTION
ULSTER FOLK AND TRANSPORT MUSEUM

was, in fact, a grandson of William Meschin, lord of Copeland and refounder of Saint Bee's (originally founded by an Irish saint, Bega); Meschin was the younger brother of Ranulf Meschin, vicomte of Bayeux, who had been granted the earldom of Chester by Henry I in 1120.[29]

De Courcy consolidated his hold over eastern Ulster by the early 1190s and the extent of the Anglo-Norman earldom is marked not only by the geographical spread of its mottes and baileys but also by a number of stone castles still extant in the modern counties of Down and Antrim. These were usually built in defensive positions in marcher districts with the native Irish. He made little or no effort to cross the River Bann with the exception of isolated forays into Derry and Inishowen. Among the tangible artefacts left by de Courcy are coins which, having styled himself King of Ulster, he caused to be minted with his own image; these coins have turned up occasionally in archeological excavations and some are in the possession of the Ulster Museum. Although the Annals tell us that he took part in various campaigns against the native Irish in other parts of Ireland, particularly in Connaught and in Munster, he was back in Ulster by the turn of the century. John had succeeded to the English throne in 1199 on the death of his elder brother Richard. The new King took a closer interest in Irish affairs and seems to have come to the conclusion that de Courcy's activities in Ulster represented a threat to his position as King and Overlord. Indeed it has been suggested that de Courcy refused to do homage to John as King and claimed to rule Ulster independently.[30] Thus it was that King John engineered de Courcy's arrest by Hugh de Lacy – his former ally – in 1201, only to be followed by his release on condition that his followers ceased to plunder de Lacy territory. He returned to Ulster and was offered a safe conduct in order to 'treat of peace'.[31] The next few years saw de Courcy attempting to regain his former territory, being taken prisoner, then released on giving hostages, but he made no effort to keep his side of the bargain. Finally, in May 1205 King John granted all de Courcy's lands in Ulster to Hugh de Lacy and simultaneously created him an earl, which de Courcy had never been.[32] Unbowed, de Courcy appealed to the Pope, but to no avail and even enlisted the help of his brother-in-law, Reginald, King of Man, with whose assistance he landed at Strangford and laid siege to the castle of *Rath*, identified as Dundrum. Again he was defeated by de Lacy.[33]

De Courcy's final years remain obscure. By 1207 he was reconciled with King John and allowed to settle in England.[34] When the King turned on the de Lacys in his Irish expedition in 1210, he brought de Courcy with him and used his knowledge of Carrickfergus to help take the castle there.[35] He surfaced again in 1216 in action when Louis of France was besieging Winchester.[36] He must have been dead before 22 September 1219 as on that date a charter was issued to his widow Affreca to have dower out of the tenements of her late husband. This charter implies that it was de Courcy's wish to be buried at the Augustinian abbey of Canons Ashby in Northamptonshire.[37] It was a twist of history that he outlived King John, but such was the stuff of war in the thirteenth century. Indeed, he would appear to have been granted a posthumous pardon; as late as 1251, Henry III certified that John de Courcy had been ever faithful to King John and was never deprived of any of his lands.[38]

The oft-repeated story of the relics of Saints Patrick, Brigid and Columcille dates from 1186, three years after the foundation of Saint Patrick's; this was, without doubt, a story concocted by de Courcy for political reasons.[39] Saint Brigid of Kildare died in 523 and tradition records that her remains were enshrined on one side of the altar of the church of Kildare, the Bishop, Conleath, who had died a few years earlier, on the other. Some three centuries later, Kildare was plundered by Vikings and the church burned. In order to preserve the most precious relics possessed by Kildare, Down was hastily chosen as their resting place before the advancing Vikings. Similarly, Columcille died at Iona in 594, his remains being removed thence for safe keeping from the pagan Vikings in 824. This was the high summer of the Celtic church and also the period of the ascendancy of the cult of Saint Patrick; it seemed logical, therefore, that Columcille's remains should also be brought to lie in his native soil. Yet the Annals record that the remains were carried to and fro between Iona and Ireland on a number of occasions – no doubt it was a problem to save them from the plundering Vikings – before their final deposition in Ireland in 877.

De Courcy was determined not to let slip the chance to make political capital out of his good fortune; equally it was undoubtedly the reason for choosing Down as his capital city. Whichever way we look at it, he was not the man to turn a blind eye to the fact that Down possessed the relics of the three most important saints in the Irish calendar. But first he had to find the graves of the three in order to have them enshrined to become the focal point of a place of pilgrimage. The story which has come down to us relates that Malachy, the Bishop, prayed earnestly that God would reveal to him the spot where the three saints had been buried. And so on a particular night when he was deep in prayer in the church, a shaft of light like a sunbeam shone over the spot. In great haste, he dug at the place and found the three sets of bones, placed them reverently in boxes and re-interred them. On informing de Courcy, messengers were despatched to Pope Urban III for permission to translate these relics to a more suitable location within the church. Papal permission was readily granted and the legate, Cardinal Vivian, already well-known to both de Courcy and Malachy, was despatched to Down to preside at the ceremony. On 9 June 1196, the Feast day of Saint Columcille, in the presence of fifteen bishops, who must have come from all over Ireland, and large numbers of clergy, the relics of Saint Patrick, Saint Columcille and Saint Brigid were laid in one tomb with great solemnity.

> Hi tres in Duno tumulo tumulantur in uno
> Brigide, Patricius atque Columba Pius

> In Down, three saints one grave do fill
> Brigid, Patrick and Columcille

Modern interpretation of such legend is made difficult by the story, according to the Four Masters, that in 1293, *Nicholas MacMáel Ísu*, at that time Archbishop of Armagh, had a revelation that the relics of the three saints were buried at Saul; he had them disinterred, whereupon great miracles were wrought before they were deposited in a shrine! Again, this legend is probably based in the political rivalry between the Irish and Anglo-Norman parties.

The Mound of Down with Down Cathedral in the distance
R. J. WELCH COLLECTION
ULSTER MUSEUM

FOUR

THE MEDIEVAL BISHOPS

WITH THE SCENE NOW SET FOR the early years of the thirteenth century, this chapter will discuss the men who strode across this stage for the next three and a half centuries. De Courcy had painted the initial backcloth; his legacy was considerable and he is credited with not only the monasteries which have been described in the previous chapter, but also a number of stone-built castles, many of which have survived to the present day. There are, indeed, references in the Annals to the building by de Courcy of a castle at Down; R.E.Parkinson even postulated that this was a stone structure and was, in fact, the tower of the Parish Church, but modern research has proved this not to be the case![1] Many of the Norman castles were, however, wooden structures built on top of mottes and naturally have not survived. The Mound of Down, some distance to the north of Cathedral Hill and assumed by some authorities to be Rathkeltair, is of interest in this context but until archaeological evidence can produce some facts on which to base a judgment as to whether the Mound represents a Norman or pre-Norman structure, or both, the location of the castle must be considered unproven. One school of thought suggests that the Mound may have been the civic headquarters of the *Dál Fiatach* and Cathedral Hill the ecclesiastical centre.

As a reward for his capture of de Courcy, we have seen that Hugh de Lacy was granted the Earldom of Ulster by King John in 1205. In those days of fickle fealty, however, the de Lacy brothers soon fell foul of John, who decided to lead his own expedition to Ireland to oust them. He arrived in Waterford in June 1210 and received the submission of Walter de Lacy a few days later; in pursuit of Hugh, he travelled swiftly northwards through Dublin and Dundalk to Down, where he spent the night of 16 July. De Lacy, however, forewarned of imminent danger, had taken refuge in Carrickfergus Castle, to which John and his troops laid siege for nine days. Among his troops at Carrickfergus was none other than de Courcy, whose knowledge of the layout of the Castle was invaluable. In spite of this, de Lacy nevertheless managed to escape to Scotland and King John, cheated of his prize, retraced his steps, staying at Down for two nights on his return journey. The Irish Pipe Roll of 14 John has this record:

> 10 men-at-arms and 20 foot soldiers who kept guard in the City of Down against the Irish of Iveagh for 20 days after the King's departure were paid 63s 4d. The ferrying of the King's treasure from Down to Carlingford 2s.[2]

The Diocese of Down was in the northern marches of the Anglo-Norman Lordship of Ireland; Ireland was never wholly under Anglo-Norman control and the border between the lands controlled from the Pale and those under native Irish control was constantly shifting. The church, and the clergy who served it, were divided between the two races; it speaks well of the bishops and clergy that, in spite of laws introduced by the newcomers to alienate the natives, by and large they stood together with little obvious sign of friction. In the main, we find that those parts of Ireland under native control retained a succession of Irish clergy whilst within the Lordship, the bishops, if not the lower clergy, were English-born. Laws were promulgated allowing preferment only to English-born clergy, but it was quite impossible to maintain an English succession in the native areas.[3] Down, being in the marcher lands of the Pale, was well mixed; the Benedictine Priory became known as the English House while the other monasteries were mostly known as 'of the Irish'.

Bishops were elected according to a strict procedure laid down by Pope Honorius III at the Lateran Council in 1215, although a similar procedure had already been in use in England under King John. On the death of the previous bishop, the diocesan chapter notified the king, in the case of the suffragan dioceses, represented by the justiciar; a licence to elect was then granted. During the vacancy, the custody of the spiritualities was vested in the chapter, but the temporalities lay with the crown. As long as this division of responsibility prevailed, there was little incentive on the part of the crown to grant a licence. When the chapter had made its choice of a successor the king was informed, as was the metropolitan of the diocese and the pope; the king's assent being given, the new bishop did fealty to him, the temporalities were restored and his election was confirmed by the metropolitan. In spite of this lengthy procedure, the pope was not averse to quashing the election and insisting on the provision of his own candidate. There was much to be gained by taking the trouble to go to Rome to get the ear of the pope and, at the same time, blackening the character of one's rival back home in Ireland.

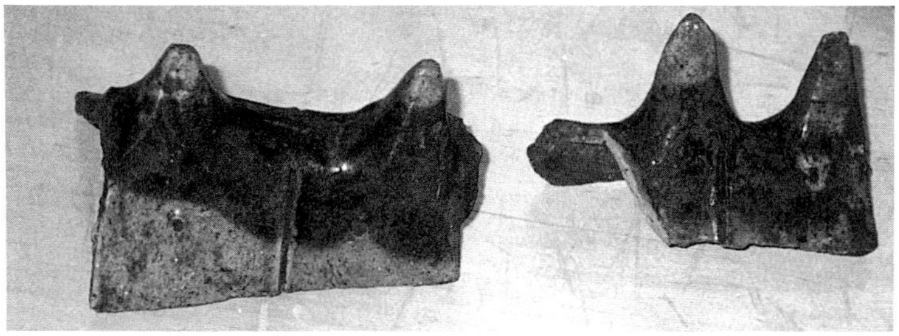

Roof ridge tiles found in the ditch north of the Cathedral. Early Medieval. Excavated September 1997

Malachy III died in 1204 and was succeeded by a Scotsman, Ralph, promoted from the abbacy of Melrose through the influence of the Papal Legate.[4] No records have been preserved of Ralph's episcopate and, on his death in 1213, Thomas succeeded to the See. Thomas was granted an annuity of £20 in payment for losses which he suffered during the wars with Hugh de Lacy, in addition to two carucates of land from the King's demesne in Ards, near the Bishop's manor of Ardquin.[5] He was also granted a licence in 1226, along with Roger Bacon, a clerk, to export corn, flour and other articles for a period of three years.[6] The most interesting document, however, as far as the subject of this book is concerned, is dated 1220, when the Prior and Convent of Saint Patrick of Down addressed themselves to Henry, King of England and Lord of Ireland.[7]

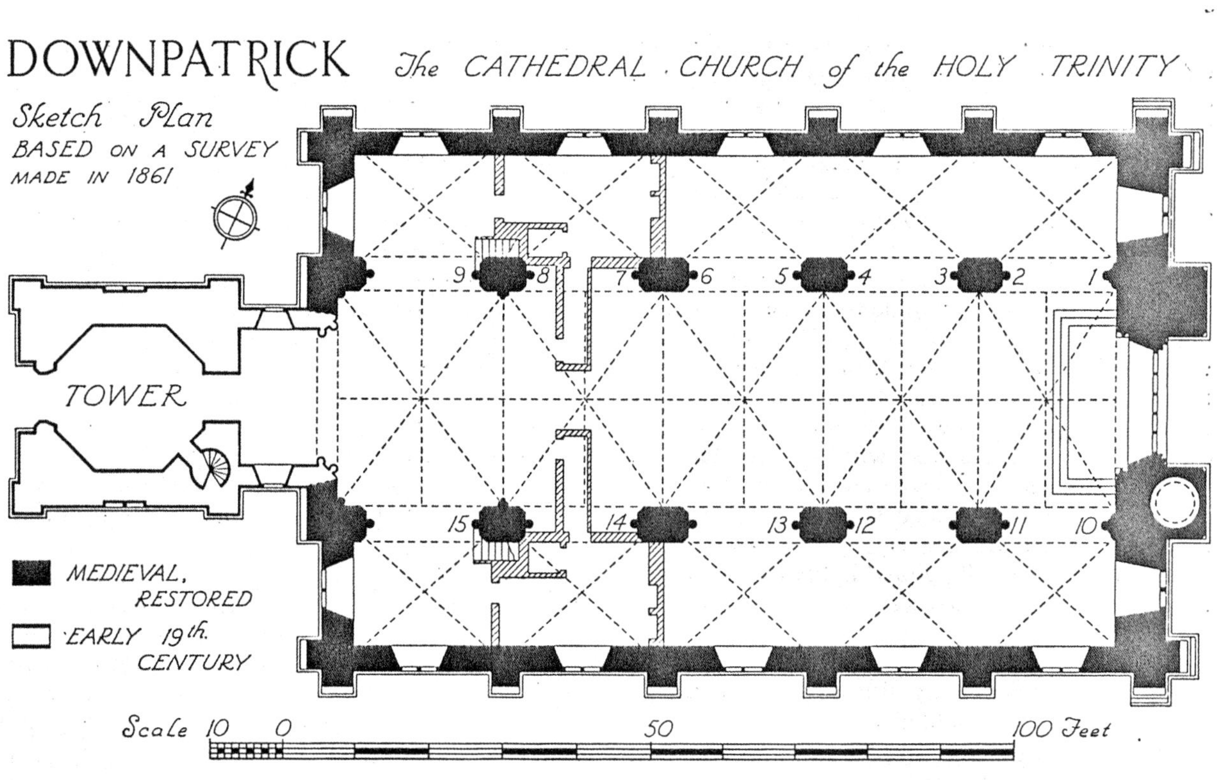

Ground Plan published in *The Archaeological Survey of County Down* 1966.
CROWN COPYRIGHT

> We send across to your Excellency our monk with the bier of the Patrons of Ireland, Patrick, Columba and Brigid with their relics, so that in reverence for them and for the promise which our lord, your father, made, viz., that he would be a benefactor to our church, and in your role as lord of all the land of the patrons of Ireland and its patron, you will, in your charity, give us a small house in England, where we shall be able to give hospitality when need occurs. The house of Saint Patrick has often been destroyed and burned with the church, which is being rebuilt again; hence we are in greatest need of your help.

This document is of vital importance in that it is the earliest Anglo-Norman reference to a church on Cathedral Hill; evidently King John had made a promise to the monks during his stay in Down a decade earlier in 1210. The wording of the petition is equally interesting in that the reference is to a church being *rebuilt* again, implying that there had been a previous church on the site. During the excavation on Cathedral Hill in the 1980s, archaeologists took the opportunity of examining closely the structure of the present Cathedral, which at that time was undergoing major restoration and repair. A trench was excavated on the exterior south wall, revealing a large battered masonry plinth, running east-west; similarly on the north wall, a corner built of stone was found just below the then ground level. These discoveries led the archeologists to postulate that the pre-1220 church may have been cruciform in plan, these excavated remains being the transepts of that building. Should this interpretation be valid, and further excavation to confirm the thesis is now impossible, Down must be one of very few cruciform churches dating from the pre-Norman period in Ireland.[8]

On Thomas's death in 1242, the Abbot and monks of Bangor claimed the right to elect his successor and also to have their abbey established as the diocesan cathedral – shades of Malachy almost a century after his death. The claim of Down, however, was upheld by the Archbishop of Armagh, the Pope, Innocent IV, promoting a bull on 5 March 1244 to the Prior and Chapter of Down of the Order of Saint Benedict confirming their church and not the church of Bangor to be the Cathedral Church of Down and their right to elect the bishop of the diocese.[9] In spite of this, the See remained vacant for a number of years; indeed in October 1246, Innocent IV ordered the Prior and Chapter to send representatives to the Curia within one month with authority to provide to the See or to accept a Papal provision.[10] The name Randal is found in 1251 when he was present at a visitation in Bangor in his capacity as Bishop, but the record is silent as to the date or manner of his election. He died in 1253, when the royal licence to elect his successor was granted.[11]

Ground plan of the Cathedral drawn by Austin Cooper in 1799 from an earlier plan drawn by Gabriel Beranger. To the right are sections through the east window surround and the piers at base and top levels.
THE NATIONAL LIBRARY OF IRELAND

In the ensuing election, agreement could not be reached between the secular clergy and the Irish foundations on the one hand and the English foundation of Saint Patrick – to whom the right to elect had been confirmed by the Pope – on

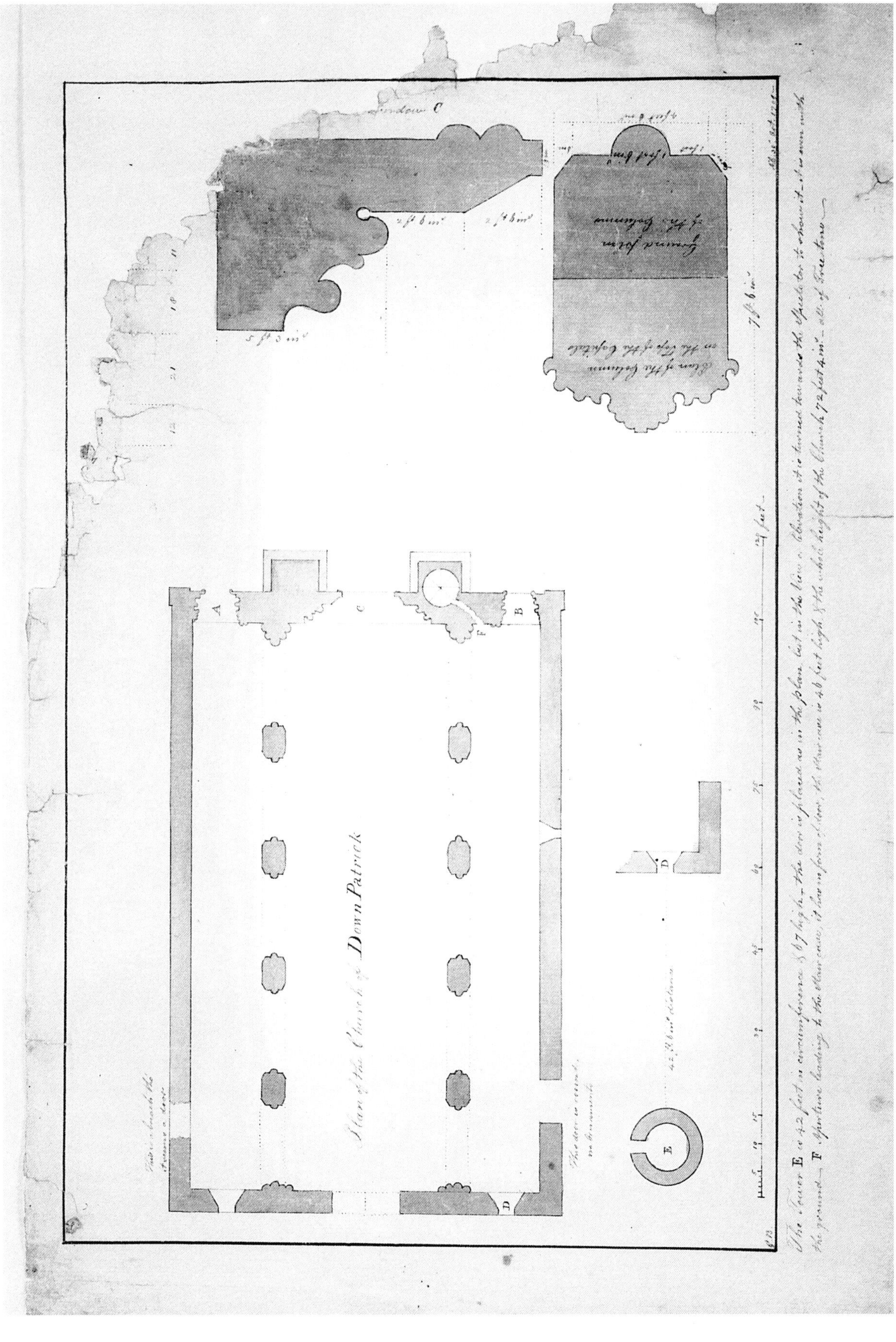
Plan of the Church of Down Patrick

Excavation at the fourth bay (from east) on the North wall shows shallow foundation of the present structure
ENVIRONMENT & HERITAGE SERVICE, DOE NI

Corner of transept excavated on North wall
ENVIRONMENT & HERITAGE SERVCE, DOE NI

the other. The Abbots of Bangor, Movilla, Saul and Comber, together with the clergy of the diocese, with the support of the Primate, elected Reginald, who had been Archdeacon of the diocese; the Prior and Convent of Saint Patrick elected Thomas Lydel, a Rector from the neighbouring diocese of Connor.[12] The King, Henry III, assented to the election of Lydel and ordered the temporalities to be restored to him, but the Primate quashed the election and appointed Reginald, to whom the King then gave his assent; Reginald was consecrated Bishop in 1258.[13] Meantime Lydel and the Chapter of Saint Patrick appealed to the pope and in the following year Lydel went to Rome to stake his claim. The case took several years to decide and judgment was finally given in favour of Lydel; he was declared canonically elected in 1265 and the temporalities were restored to him. Reginald was translated to the See of Cloyne.[14] Lydel had occasion to appeal to the King in 1269 for protection from the harrassment and exactions wrought by Walter de Burgh, Earl of Ulster.[15] It appears that the Bishop would not answer in a secular court and consequently was 'despoiled of his manors' by the Earl. He threatened that, unless the King gave him assistance, he would place his diocese under an interdict and appeal to Rome. Henry dutifully came to the Bishop's aid and commanded de Burgh to desist from such injuries and oppressions, saying that he had no right to interfere in ecclesiastical affairs.[16]

Thomas Lydel died in 1276 and his successor was elected the following year with general consent; Nicholas had been Prior of Saint Patrick's, thus becoming the first Benedictine to be elected Bishop.[17] A posthumous document among the Justiciary Rolls tells us that he was Nicholas le Blound.[18] Ware states that he was also Treasurer of Ulster, an office under the Crown; there does not appear to be documentary evidence of this appointment and in view of Nicholas's litigation with the justiciar, it is extremely unlikely. In June 1279, Bishop Nicholas took a case against the Archbishop of Armagh, whose proctor had carried out a visitation of certain churches in the diocese without his (Nicholas's) consent, exacting procurations 'to the injury of the said bishop and churches'. The Archbishop, *Nicholas Mac Máel Ísu*, a native Irishman, was in frequent trouble with the justiciar, both for keeping to himself temporalities of churches during vacancies and for instituting bishops without licence from the king.[19] Agreement between the two Nicholases must have been reached as almost two decades later we find them commanded to appear before the justiciar to answer why clerks of English origin were not allowed into monasteries in their dioceses 'to

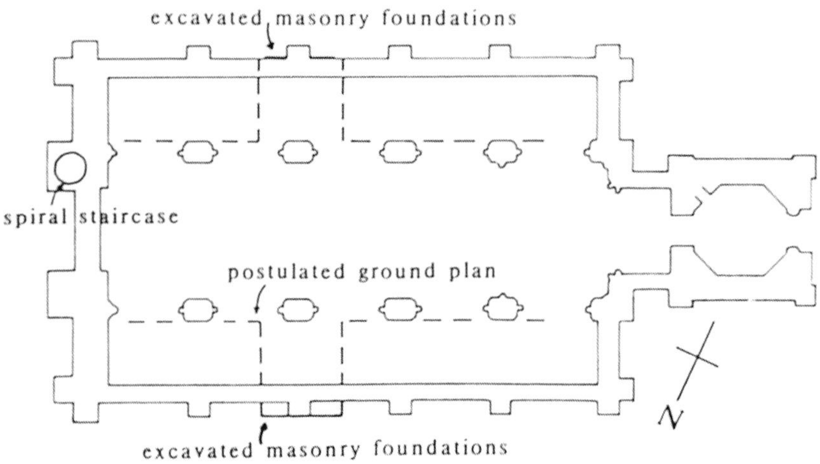

Plan of earlier church with transepts postulated by Nick Brannon
LECALE MISCELLANY NO 5 1987

the prejudice of the crown'. Nicholas (of Down) was also accused of hearing all pleas in his manors and lands except those of treasure trove, rape, arson and forcible entry, again to the prejudice of the crown.[20] Twelve months later, when the Prior and Convent of the Irish house of Saint John of Down requested licence from the King to elect an Abbot, the Bishop maliciously stole the King's letter and himself appointed the Abbot, thereby defrauding the Crown of £1000, the value of the temporalities during the vacancy.[21] There is also a record of a lawsuit brought by the Abbot of Saint Mary's, York against the Bishop concerning lands in Ireland, very probably the possessions of Nendrum, which, it will be remembered, were granted to Saint Bee's by the mother house of Saint Mary. Agricultural land then, as now, was the most valuable asset possessed by a monastery and any attempt to interfere with the Chapter's inalienable right was worth defending at law.[22]

After a stormy episcopate, Nicholas le Blound died in 1305. Following notification to the king of his death, the Prior and Convent of Saint Patrick were granted licence to elect a new bishop.[23] Their choice fell on Thomas Ketel, a priest from the church of Lismoghan, near Ballykinlar, who was duly elected with royal assent.[24] The justiciar, however, refused to restore the temporalities to him, because the election had not been confirmed by the metropolitan archbishop, the See of Armagh being vacant.[25] The spiritualities were indeed restored by the Dean and Chapter of Armagh, custodians of the suffragan dioceses during vacancy, but the temporalities had to await the election of a new Primate. O'Laverty quotes *in extenso* a valuation of the See property taken during the vacancy; the income from the temporalities between 4 March and 2 July 1305 was £67. 9s., a substantial sum when one considers that an even greater sum would be payable during the autumn when the crops were being harvested.[26] Ketel went to England in 1311, attorneys being appointed to act on his behalf for two years; he died in March 1314, whether in England or Ireland is not known.[27]

John, the sub-Prior of Saint Patrick's, was granted licence to elect a new bishop in March 1314, the Earl of Gloucester and Hertford (Gilbert de Clare) being granted the temporalities of the See during the voidance, to hold of the King's gift.[28] In fact, the Prior, Thomas Bright, was elected; it fell to him to govern the diocese during the difficult period of the Bruce wars of 1314-1318, during which Down was ransacked and the cathedral plundered.[29] According to Ware, Thomas Bright died in 1327 and was buried in his own Cathedral.[30] We have a detailed account of the value of the temporalities during the vacancy from the account of the escheator, Walter Wogan, in the Irish Pipe Roll from 17 May 1327 until 21 December 1328:[31]

> Down Bishopric: [The escheator] accounts for £30.1s 9d rent and issues of the lands, demesnes, meadows, pasture, mills, prise of fish, perquisites of hundreds and court, rent of free tenants, farmers, cottars with their works, of the temporalities of the bishopric, in the king's hand by the death of brother Thomas, the late bishop from 11 March 1328 to 21 December the same year, viz., for terms of the Apostles Saint Philip and Saint James, All Saints, Pentecost and the Feast of the Saint Martin. Also increment of £7.16s 8d beyond the extent. Sum £37. 18s 5d.

The Prior and Convent on this occasion elected John of Baliconyngham (Quoniamstown?), the parson from Ardquin, with the king's consent;[32] although he enjoyed the temporalities for a short period, the pope quashed the election and provided Ralph of Kilmessan (Meath), from the Order of Friars Minor, despatching John

Bronze escutcheon (with rivets) in the shape of a swan. Found during 1985 excavation. ENVIRONMENT & HERITAGE SERVICE DOE NI

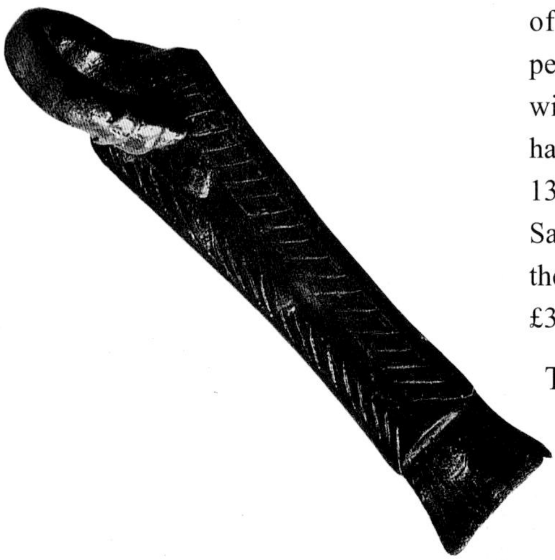

to the See of Cork.[33] As late as 1329, Ralph was granted a faculty to contract a loan of 500 florins, to be repaid within two years; although the reason for the loan was not stated, and a search amongst the Papal petitions has been unsuccessful, it was very probably a loan to restore the abbey after the destruction of the Bruce wars.[34] A number of earlier grants both to Saint Patrick's and to the hospital of Saint John of Down were confirmed during Ralph's episcopate. One of these confirmed the grant by William Fitzwarin to the Prior and Brethren of the Hospital of Saint John of 'four marks of rent out of land called *Cubynhillis* [Kircubbin] in the tenement of *Inchemkargy* [Inishargie], for the sustenance of a brother; as priest, to celebrate mass daily in the oratory of the church in the sight of the sick lying there'.[35] Another confirms the grant by William de Mandeville 'of an acre of land in *le Garth,* to wit that which begins from the common way called *Blacfurd*, leading from the town of *Haye* to the monastery of *Cumber,* and stretches in length as far as the moor called *Ynl*, with the advowson of the church of Saint Mary, *Hayton,* to support a brother, as chaplain, to celebrate mass in their house for ever for the souls of the grantor, Joan de Audeleye, sometime his wife, his ancestors and successors'.[36]

In an idle moment, a monk incised this mask found during 1985 excavation.
ENVIRONMENT & HERITAGE SERVICE DOE NI

The Pope was advised prematurely of Ralph's death and he provided Gregory, Provost of Killala, to the See in February 1353; Gregory was, in fact, consecrated at Avignon.[37] On the discovery that Ralph was still living, Gregory was given a titular bishopric and later translated to the See of Elphin. Ralph died in August 1353.[38] The Chapter elected their Prior, Richard Calf, to the vacant See; he also went to Avignon for consecration – the Primate, Richard Fitzralph, was a keen supporter of the Avignon papacy – but was ordered to return to his diocese under the terms of a mandate of January 1354.[39] Calf died in October 1365.

On this occasion, Robert de Aketoun of the Order of Hermits of Saint Augustine was selected by the Chapter and two proctors were appointed to take the matter to the pope; the selection was not approved.[40] Aketoun promptly resigned and was provided to Kildare, whilst William White was provided to Down from

This excised stone was found by Arthur Pollock during the 1950s. The lettering suggests that it is of 14th century date. Its whereabouts are now unknown.
ENVIRONMENT & HERITAGE SERVICE DOE NI

Kildare, where he had been Prior of the Augustinian abbey of Conall.[41] White had a short episcopate – just thirteen months – and it is probable that the stress engendered by litigation with the Primate may have contributed to his early death. The cause of the litigation is obscure but appears to turn on a letter from the Primate addressed to White, advising him of a metropolitan visitation. The letter was given to him by his Archdeacon, John Logan, whom he had excommunicated; quite properly, the Bishop refused to accept it.[42] White was then cited to appear in Saint Ronan's church, Dromiskin (the Provincial Court) to answer for his contempt and disobedience towards the Archbishop. We do not know the outcome of the case but six months later, by August 1368, White was dead.[43] Nevertheless, in a subsequent letter from Dromiskin, he was referred to by the Archbishop as William 'of good memory'.[44]

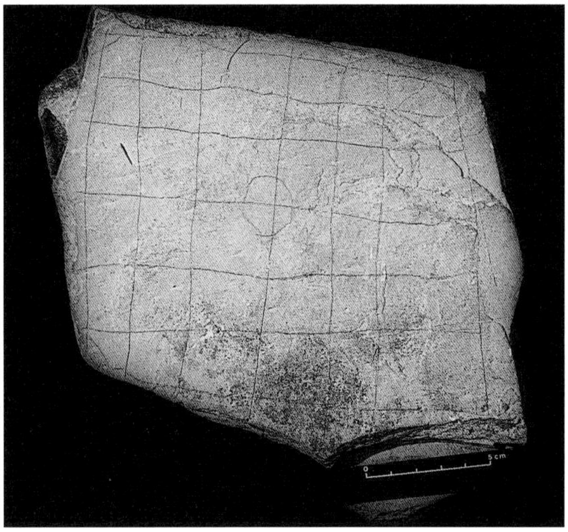

Gaming Board
Pattern excised on flat stone.
Actual game unknown.
12th century. Found during
1985 excavation
DOWN COUNTY MUSEUM

In Sweteman's Register, Document 81, dated 13 December 1368, a dispensation is given to Sir Robert Ogean of the Bishopric of Down from the vacancy because he had carnal knowledge of Matilda Stokys, a professed nun from the House of Nuns at Down.[45] Who was Ogean? Had he been elected and had his election quashed by the Primate? According to Ware, the Archdeacon of the diocese, John Logan, was elected but died before enjoying the fruits of the See.[46] It would appear very likely that Logan and Ogean are one and the same person.

Next in the line of succession came another Richard Calf, also receiving promotion from the Priory of Saint Patrick. He was unanimously elected by the Chapter and was provided by the Pope, Urban V, on 19 February 1369.[47] No documents survive relating to Calf's episcopate, but at this time the Primate, John Colton, issued a decree stating that any cleric of Armagh province who kept a concubine or an harlot should expel her within one month.[48] Evidently there was sufficient scandal in the province to make such a pronouncement necessary! Richard Calf II died in 1386 and was succeeded by John Ross, also promoted from the Priory of Saint Patrick,[49] carrying the succession through until his death in 1394.

Motif piece
Practice interlace excised on stone.
Early Christian. Found during
1985 excavation
DOWN COUNTY MUSEUM

John Dongan succeeded, translated from the See of Sodor and Man in 1395; according to O'Laverty, he had been consecrated for that See in 1374, previous to which he had been Archdeacon of Down and Papal Nuncio for Ireland.[50] His wide experience led to his appointment in 1401 by Henry IV as Seneschal of the Liberty of Ulster;[51] his knowledge of the tensions between the various Celtic peoples around the Irish Sea led to his being asked to make peace terms with the Lord of the Isles, who had carried out pirate raids against merchants in the Irish Sea for many years. Indeed the Annals record another despoilation and destruction of the monastery of *Dún da Lethglas* in 1404, this time by the local Maginnis and MacGillmore families, assisted by Scots.[52] Down was still regarded as a centre of English administration, as also was Coleraine, destroyed on this occasion as well. Dongan died in 1412.[53] At this period, it was the custom for pilgrims to Saint Patrick's Purgatory in Lough Derg – pilgrims who came from all over Europe – to spend a few days at Down on their way from Dublin in order to venerate the relics of the three saints.[54]

When Dongan was appointed to the See in 1395, the choice of the Chapter had fallen on John Cely, one of their number in Saint Patrick's. Cely had to wait a further eighteen years, by which time he had become Prior, before he was to occupy the episcopal throne.[55] John Cely was provided by the Pope in July 1413 and was to become one of the most notorious and colourful characters ever to have occupied the See of Down.[56] For the first decade of his episcopate, he was a model bishop, so much so that in 1425, Henry VI appointed him Chancellor and Treasurer of the Liberty of Ulster.[57] From then on, things began to go badly wrong. The first complaint concerned his refusal to wear the Benedictine habit, which was the canonical duty of all Benedictine monks who had been elevated to the episcopacy, leaving himself open to a charge of excommunication.[58] He was ordered by the Primate, John Swayne, to appear before the Provincial Council of Bishops at Saint Peter's, Drogheda, in October 1427, properly dressed in his sacred clothing and pontifical insignia. This he refused to do and was again ordered to appear before the Archbishop to show

Kilclief Castle
Reputedly built by
Bishop Cely c.1440
F. J. BIGGER COLLECTION
ULSTER MUSEUM

cause why the sentence of excommunication should not be publicly pronounced. He was also warned to settle for procurations within 14 days, 'having been warned long since'.[59]

The real scandal was yet to come; in 1434, it had come to the Archbishop's knowledge that Cely kept a concubine, Letys Thomas, and that he 'publicly and together cohabited with her'. If she was not dismissed within 15 days, Cely was warned by the Archbishop that he would be suspended from the spiritualities of his See and that, if he continued with his contumacy, he would be excommunicated.[60] The incident demonstrates vividly the moral and spiritual depravity of the period, a symptom of the malaise which was affecting not only Ireland, but the entire conventual life in western Europe. Following the Bruce wars of more than a century earlier and the break-up of the Anglo-Norman earldom, usually dated by historians by the murder of William de Burgh, Earl of Ulster, in 1333, there was a rapid decline in prosperity. The havoc caused by the wars together with the lack of orderly government were the principal reasons for a drop in agricultural production, on top of which there was a requirement to ship large quantities of grain and meat to victual the King's armies in his wars in France – this was the Hundred Years War, when the preoccupation with that war left little inclination on the part of the English to look after their colony in Ireland.

These two factors, the decline in agricultural prosperity leading to a reduction in the church's income through tithes, and the moral decline which had swept through the church, can be seen as vital elements in the union of the Dioceses of Down and Connor. In 1438, the respective Bishops, John Cely of Down and John Fossard of Connor, requested licence from Henry VI for a union of the Sees on the next voidance, 'neither See alone being sufficient to maintain the estate of a bishop'. They were granted leave to take the matter to Rome and, on so doing, Eugenius IV promulgated the necessary bull.[61]

Scallop shell on stone. The scallop was the symbol of Saint James of Compostella. Found during 1985 excavation.
DOWN COUNTY MUSEUM

Swayne, the Primate, resigned in 1439 and was succeeded in Armagh by John Prene, who brought matters to a swift conclusion. In September 1440, he cited the Bishop of Down to instruct the Prior and Convent of the Cathedral Church, together with other religious and clergy, to appear at a metropolitan visitation.[62] It is not recorded if Cely was present at this visitation, even though the affair was evidently reaching its climax. Three mandates in December 1440 are addressed, not to the Bishop, but to the Prior of the Cathedral Church along with the Abbot of Saul and the Archdeacon.[63] Cely had been living in Kilclief castle, which he is reputed to have built, with his concubine, Letys Thomas, and had been ordered to go to his official residence at *Lismolyn* [Bishopscourt]. He continued to occupy Kilclief, even after suspension and excommunication; yet again he was ordered to appear at the Provincial Court at Termonfeckin, near Drogheda, on the Monday after Epiphany, and, if unable to justify himself, the case was to be referred to the Pope. Prene passed sentence of excommunication and, at his request, Cely was deprived by the Pope in May 1441.[64] The way was now open for the union of the Sees of Down and Connor, which was to last for over 500 years.

The immediate succession to the union was a matter for dispute; by provision of Eugenius IV, John Fossard, Bishop of Connor since 1432, became Bishop also of Down.[65] But this did not take account of the opposition of the Archbishop of Armagh, John Prene (Archbishop 1439-43), who was not only not in favour of the union, but had his own candidate ready for the bishopric.[66] Prene wrote to the Pope and the King, recommending William Basset, a Benedictine monk and priest, as a fit person to undertake the government of the Diocese of Down, but to no avail; Fossard retained the See.[67] For a number of years the position was, to say the least, extremely confused.

The bottom of the spiral staircase in the East wall buttress. Photograph taken during the 1985 Restoration

In April 1445, Eugenius IV provided Ralph Lederle to Down;[68] he was an Augustinian prior from the Diocese of Winchester, but does not appear to have been consecrated or taken possession. A new Pope, Nicholas V, (Armagh also had a new Primate, John Mey, successor to Prene) made a further provision, in July 1447, of Thomas Pollard, a Carthusian, and had him consecrated in Rome the following month.[69] On arrival in Down to take possession, however, he found the palace at *Lismolyn* occupied by Fossard, whereupon, aided and abetted by the Prior of Saint Patrick's and others, he forcibly entered the palace, injuring Fossard and causing damage to his possessions to the value of £40.[70] As punishment, Mey excommunicated those guilty and put both dioceses under an interdict; despite the sentence, Pollard and his followers persisted in their contempt and Mey was forced to call in the secular arm (the phrase used when the church needed military support).[71] The crisis continued for a further year and was finally brought to a conclusion with the announcement on 1 October 1449 by the Primate that he proposed to hold a visitation in the Cathedral Church of Down on 4 October at which John [Fossard], the Bishop and Thomas Pollard, the pretended Bishop, were to show their respective titles to the bishopric.[72] Following the visitation, a

During the building of the Verger's house in 1935, a wall was discovered. Unfortunately detailed records were not made and it is impossible to tell the extent of the wall from the photograph.
ENVIRONMENT & HERITAGE SERVICE, DOE NI

number of injunctions were issued by the Primate, but no reference was made to the claims of Pollard;[73] it would appear, therefore, that he surrendered his claim and his name thereafter almost disapppeared from the record. The injunction issued to William Stanley, Prior of Saint Patrick's, again reveal the low level of discipline and morality then prevalent; he was enjoined to maintain a sufficient number of persons, in decent dress and tonsure for the celebration of the divine offices and he was further required not to keep any concubines or suspect women and, if any were present, they were to be expelled.[74] Fossard, having endured considerable physical and mental stress, did not live long in the enjoyment of his bishopric; according to Ware, he died early in 1451, following which the King granted the temporalities to Pollard but, as long as Mey was in Armagh, he did not receive the spiritualities.[75]

Mey wrote to Pope Nicholas V on 10 April 1451, recommending Robert Rochford, of the Preaching Order of Friars, for the Bishopric of Down and Connor.[76] The Pope, however, had other ideas; just over two months later, on 21 June, he provided Richard Woolsey, a Dominican Friar.[77] Woolsey was suffragan bishop in the Diocese of Lichfield from 1452 until 1463, thereafter in Worcester and Hereford, and probably never visited his Irish dioceses; he had, in fact, resigned Down and Connor by 1453.[78] In August of that year, the Pope made a further provision; this time it was Thomas Knight, O.S.B., Prior of the Cluniac

House of *Daventre*,[79] but it was not until May 1456 that he was consecrated by Primate Mey.[80] Evidence is extant that both Woolsey and Knight petitioned the Pope for permission to retain other benefices in England in addition to the Sees of Down and Connor as the fruits of those sees were insufficient to meet the needs of their episcopal dignity. The Papal dispensation to Knight, dated July 1463, makes reference to the church in Down and Connor, 'where dwell men untamed and half savage'.[81] Although Woolsey apparently lived until 1502 and was buried in Worcester, Knight died, according to Ware, in 1468.[82]

This confusion is fairly typical of the state of affairs in the more remote Irish dioceses and reflects the loss of control by the Crown over episcopal appointments. Papal provisions, which had become the normal method of appointment by the fifteenth century, were open to considerable abuse, there being no adequate check built into the system to prevent this abuse.[83] The confusion was not helped by there being two popes at this time, one in Rome and one in Avignon. Partly to blame was the rapid spread of the orders of preaching friars, whose life was not centred on a monastery as were the Benedictines and Cistercians; both Irish and English friars, anxious to gain episcopal orders, used the lesser Irish dioceses in order to attain their object. All they had to do was to proceed to Rome and give false news of the death of the incumbent. They had no interest in the spiritualities of the diocese; they were absentee and earned their living as suffragan bishops in one of the larger English dioceses or, as noted above, obtained a dispensation to hold another benefice in England to supplement their income.

Excavated in September 1997, possibly a rubbish chute from the monastery kitchen. A large number of butchered animal bones were found in the pit at its base

Although Knight's career before his Irish appointment can be traced from being a monk at Glastonbury to being intruded as Prior of Gloucester College, the Oxford College founded by the Benedictine order,[84] nothing is known of his period as Bishop of Down and Connor. Indeed it is likely that he did not take possession, remaining an absentee during this time. His successor, consecrated in Rome on 10 September 1469, was *Tadhg Ó Muirgheasa*,[85] Prior of the Augustinian Priory of Saint Katherine in Waterford, of which priory he received a dispensation to hold in addition to his new see.[86] Local opposition in Waterford, however, put a stop to this and, following an appeal to the pope in 1479, he was allowed to hold the Priory of Saint Mary in Kells, in the Diocese of Ossory, *in commendam*, as the *mensa* of Down and Connor was too slight for the maintenance of episcopal dignity.[87] It should not go unremarked that *Tadhg* was the first Irish-born bishop in the diocese since the death of Malachy in 1204. A series of letters from Archbishop Bole of Armagh to *Tadhg* is preserved in Octavian's register, inviting *Tadhg* to meet the archbishop and the other bishops of the province at the forthcoming provincial council. The letters are dated from the latter half of 1470 and assure *Tadhg* of the archbishop's resistance to the claims of Richard Woolsey, recommended by the King, should he arrive from England, as expected(!).[88] On his death in 1486, he was succeeded by an Italian, Tiberius Ugolino. Tiberius, by which name he is known to history, was a parish priest near Rome and appears to have been chosen by Pope Sixtus IV some three years earlier as the next Bishop of Down and Connor. Nevertheless, he was not consecrated until 1489 and, as the consecration took place in Rome, it is reasonable to assume that he did not take possession of his See until after that date. His name is not recorded as among those present at the Provincial Councils in 1483, 1486 or 1489.[89] The choice of an Italian stems directly from the fact that, since 1478, the see of Armagh had also been occupied by an Italian, Ottaviano Spinelli de Palatio (known as Octavian), who had been sent to Ireland with a clear directive to get ecclesiastical finances into some sort of order, a mission with which he appears to have achieved a measure of success.

Decorated stone built into wall at west door, probably 15th century

By this time, the conventual life of western monasticism was so far in decline that the pope issued a bull for the suppression of monasteries with an annual income of less than 3000 ducats.[90] But Tiberius had already forestalled this directive by initiating his own action among the various foundations in Down; a document which he issued at Carrickfergus, dated 20 February 1512, is confirmed in Dowdall's Register:[91]

> ...that we have made certain unions for the Cathedral Church of Down which is suffering ruin both in walls and roof; and for augmenting

> Divine worship in foresaid church; also on account of the relics of the holy Saints Patrick, Columba and Brigid lying there in one tomb; by the consent of the Prior of Down and of the Convent of the same, which formerly, from ancient times, was governed by nuns, which same monastery is at present lying in ruins; and the Monastery of Saint John the Baptist; and the Monastery of Saint Thomas the Martyr; and the Monastery of the Irish; and the Rectory of the Parish Church of Ardglass and the Prebend of Ros; and the Prebend of Ballykilbeg; and the Chapel of Saint Mary Magdalene......all and singular the aforesaid, for the causes already premised, that it is better to endow the Cathedral Church than that both fall to ruin, we have united, annexed and incorporated.

In the summer of 1517, the Papal Nuncio in England, Bishop Chiericati, journeyed to Ireland, staying with Tiberius at Down for three days; he has left us this description of his stay:[92]

> In this place I could not walk in the street because everyone ran to kiss my dress, understanding that I was a Nuncio from the Pope, so that I was almost compelled by force to stay in the house, so great was their importunity, which arose from a strong religious feeling. The good bishop (Tiberius) received us most graciously and procured for me much pleasure in fishing; there for a shilling one can obtain a salmon weighing fifty pounds which in Italy would be of great value and would be very highly esteemed.

Compared with his predecessor and indeed, his immediate successor, it must be acknowledged that Tiberius was one of the more notable bishops to have graced the See of Down and Connor. Perhaps the Pope was right in sending someone who had not been nourished in the internecine quarrels of Ireland and England; someone who was able to govern the Dioceses objectively after centuries of instability, not to speak of corruption. Tiberius died in 1519 after an episcopate of 30 years, almost coeval with the tenure of Armagh by his compatriot who had died in 1513. But the winds of reform were blowing across Europe; Henry VIII on the throne of England was laying preparations for the day when he would be able to pronounce himself Supreme Head of the Church in England and Ireland. The centuries of papal supremacy were coming to a close. However, before that momentous event, we have two more bishops to note.

Robert Blyth, Benedictine Abbot of Thorney in the Diocese of Ely, was provided to the united Dioceses in April 1520; there is no record of his ever having set foot in Ireland. In his absence, the Primate assumed all collations and appointments in Down and Connor, to which Blyth took exception and appointed his own administrator. A number of similar appointments are noted in Cromer's Register but the result was so unsatisfactory that the Primate issued a mandate in 1527 declaring that Bishop Blyth had lost his right to exercise jurisdiction owing to his prolonged absence without licence. The diocese continued to be administered by the Primate until Blyth was deprived by the Pope in June 1539.[93] In his capacity as Abbot of Thorney, he surrendered his abbey to Henry VIII in 1539, conforming to the new religion and receiving a pension of £200.[94]

Eugene Maginnis, a member of one of the most powerful native families in County Down, was provided by the Pope in June 1539, having already been Archdeacon since 1527; he had, in fact, owing to the absence of Blyth, acted as custodian of the spiritualities of the united dioceses since 1530. On renunciation of his papal bull, he was granted the temporalities of the dioceses in September 1541, but this did not necessarily imply conformation to the new faith. O'Laverty suggests that he was a temporizer,[95] at heart remaining faithful to Rome but paying lip service to the King. Certainly during the reign of Queen Mary (1553-8), he was permitted to retain his Sees, whereas many other bishops who had conformed were deprived of their Sees, which would tend to support the view that he swayed with the wind. He lived at Kilclief as an attack on the castle there by the Savage family of the Ards is recorded in 1553, the Lord Deputy ordering the castle to be restored and the bishop to be assisted in the recovery of his rights and possessions.[96] At the beginning of Elizabeth's reign, he was pardoned by the Crown and sat in the parliament summoned in Dublin in January 1559.[97] He died in 1564.

During the centuries covered by this chapter, a number of significant dates stand out which give some substance to the building on Cathedral Hill rather than the people who lived and worshipped there. The first date is, of course, 1220, when the monks petitioned the King, making reference to their House of Saint Patrick being rebuilt after the wars. Much of this building phase is still extant in the nave of the present building and most of the pier capitals have been dated to this period, although subsequently altered or added to.[98] We have also read of the faculty being granted in 1329 to incur a loan of 500 florins; this date is little over a decade after the ravages of the Bruce wars and the proximity of the two dates is too close to ignore. Whilst the petition requesting this loan is no longer extant in the papal archives, it is highly probable that the money was required in order to rebuild or repair the Cathedral (or, indeed, other buildings on the hill).

No further clues can be detected until 1512, when Tiberius closed the other monasteries in Down, thus paving the financial way towards repairing the walls and roof of the Cathedral. Whatever condition it may have been in, and the inference is that it was in poor shape, it was now being effectively restored.

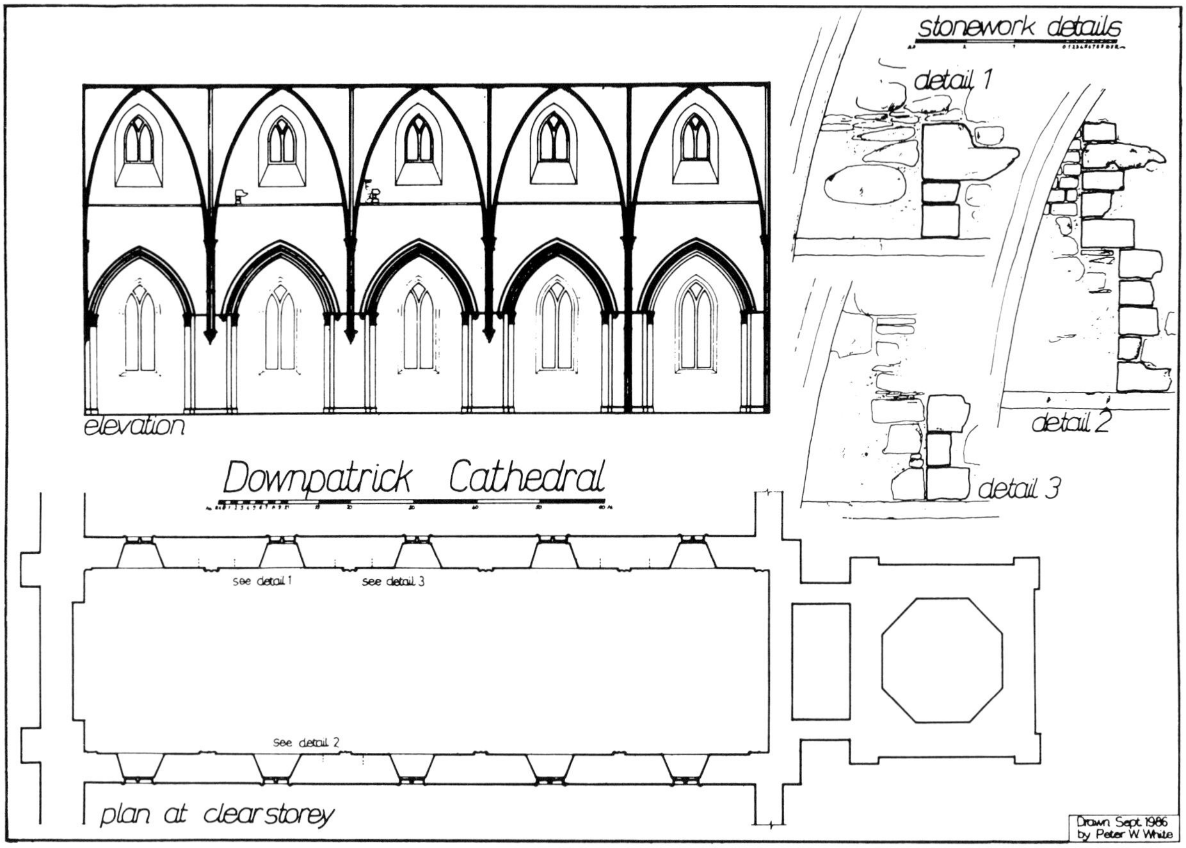

Elevation and plan of the clerestory windows. Indicated in bays 2 and 3 (north wall) the positions of earlier windows over the piers.
ENVIRONMENT & HERITAGE SERVICE DOE NI

When Eugene Maginnis was consecrated Bishop in 1539, a document preserved in the Vatican archives describes the church:[99]

> ...which is dedicated to Saint Patrick, has two doors, one in front and the other at the side. It has a chancel and principal altar and a sacristy with vestments and many chalices. It has a bell-tower, the heretics having removed the bells and a graveyard. It has two dignities, an Archdeaconry and a Priorate. It has monks of the Cistercian (sic) order, whose revenues are greatly diminished on account of the ravages of the heretics, who, at the beginning of this year, removed the relics of Saints Patrick, Brigid and Columba and burnt the bodies.

In a later chapter, we shall discuss the problems surrounding the dating of the dissolution but this Vatican reference is most useful in ascribing a possible date.

The Terrier of Down and Connor, quoted by O'Laverty,[100] and usually dated to the early seventeenth century, includes among the possessions of the Bishopric of Down and Connor a hall and kitchen in the cloister of the Abbey of Saint Patrick, 'towards the parish church on the north side', and also certain gardens.

In the report on the archaeological excavations on Cathedral Hill during the 1980s,[101] it has been suggested that the extent of medieval buildings may have been much greater than previously thought, due to the extensive terracing around the top of the hill to give relatively flat ground for building purposes. Future generations of archaeologists, perhaps with more sophisticated equipment may discover more than is currently possible. During the 1980s, a substantial medieval building was located to the south-west of the Cathedral, outside the graveyard, dated by the discovery of a coin of the reign of Edward III, to around 1400. This had been stone-built, with a slated roof, leaded windows with painted glass and had clearly served an ecclesiastical function. It was not possible, however, to extend excavation sufficiently to determine the existence of an altar at the eastern end and it is therefore not possible to say if the building was used for worship. Perhaps too grand for monks to live in, it may have been the Abbot's house.

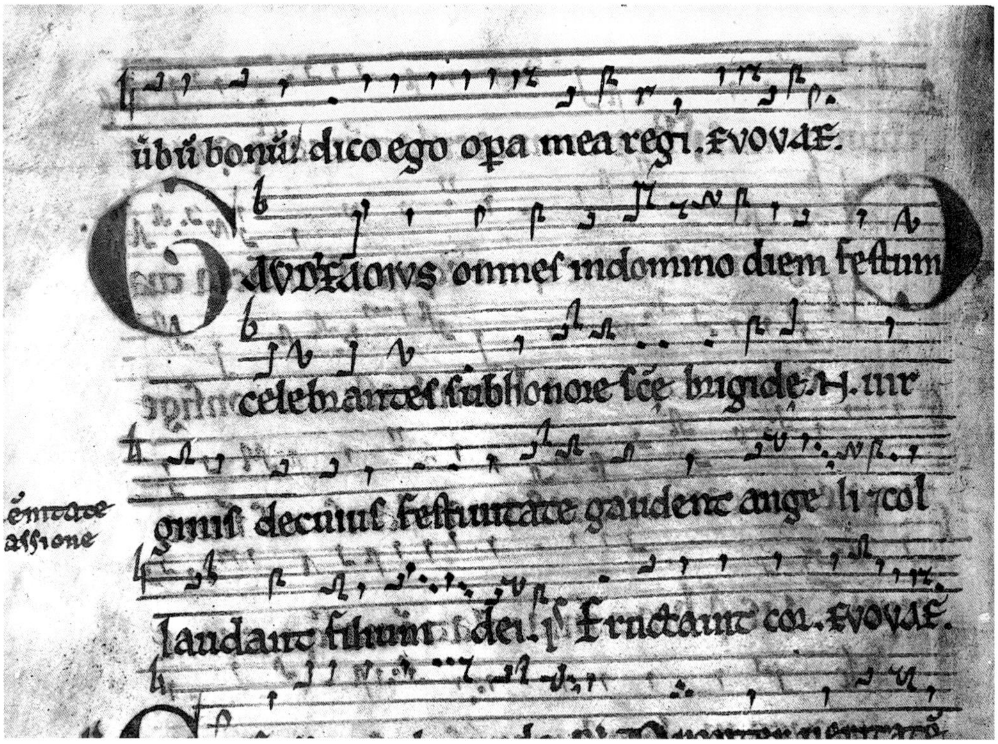

The Down Gradual. Folio 143V the Liturgy for Saint Brigid's day, 1 February.
THE BODLEIAN LIBRARY, OXFORD RAWLINSON C.892

FIVE

THE BENEDICTINE PRIORS

As well as the Bishops of Down, who were, as we have read, the titular abbots of the Benedictine Abbey of Saint Patrick, any survey of the later medieval period would not be complete without documenting what little evidence has come down to us concerning the Priors. Such a succession list, however, presents something of a problem, insofar as the Bishops played a central role in the government of the country and their appointment was ratified by the King or the Pope; consequently their names occur in official documents, either from the Crown or the Vatican. On the other hand, the Prior was elected by his fellow monks and his appointment was not subject to ratification by higher authority. The names of Priors pass across the pages of history as signatories to legal or other documents or if, as happened on a number of occasions in Down, the Prior was subsequently elevated to the Bishopric and it is that appointment which is the subject of record. Reeves was the first to complete such a succession list, making some use of Archdall;[1] he published his work, however, before the Calendars of Papal Letters were published and most of the additions to his list have been culled from that source.

1183 William de Etteshall. Installed by John de Courcy when he brought the first monks from Saint Werburgh's, Chester

1183 Andrew, named in a charter by de Courcy

1183+ D., named in a charter by de Courcy

1224 W.[2]

1237 R. Witness to the Charter of the Abbey of Newry. In 1251, Robert, Prior of the Benedictine Abbey of Down was present with other monks, at a visitation in the monastery of Bangor, at which they recommended the deposition of the Abbot there.[3]

1266 R. is mentioned in the Papal Letters in connection with the election of Thomas (Lydel) as Bishop. May be the same R. as previous.[4]

1277 Nicholas le Blound, Prior, was elected Bishop.[5]

1301 Roger.[6] Also mentioned in Justiciary Rolls in February 1308,[7] called Robert in same source, June 1305.[8]

1314 Thomas Bright, Prior, elected Bishop.[9]

1317 John, mentioned with other abbots in Patent and Close Rolls of the Irish Chancery;[10] in the Pipe Roll of 3 Edward III (1329), brother John Sarazin, Prior of the Church of Saint Patrick of Down, acounted for £4 for trespass.[11]

1336 Roger, witness to a grant to the Prior of the Hospital of Saint John of Down.[12]

1353 Richard Calf, Prior, elected Bishop.[13]

1366 Nicholas Langtoun mentioned in Sweteman's Register (85, 93) in connection with the election of Robert de Aketoun as Bishop.[14]

This register (219)[15] also details a case of some interest between the Archbishop of Armagh and the Prior and Convent of Down, when a citation was issued to the Prior, who had gone into hiding in order to avoid it being personally served on him. The citation was thereupon entrusted to a chaplain and a messenger, who, on finding the Prior and his followers, were beaten and wounded, put into fetters, subjected to torture and compelled to eat the citation, including its wax seal. The Archbishop appointed a day on which the Prior and his followers would acknowledge their offences, but evidently the Prior would have none of this; he gathered a band of clerics and laymen from almost the entire diocese and appeared 'armed as for war'. Two men, who had been sent in advance by the Archbishop to provide food, were intercepted and killed, whereupon the Prior and his companions were excommunicated. This case should be read in the context of the diocese in 1368. Bishop William White, by all accounts a sick man, was clearly out of touch with his clergy and, in fact, died in August of that year. Logan, the Archdeacon was so corrupt that he had already been excommunicated! It became necessary to cite separate dates for metropolitan visitations on the Bishop and Chapter in the Cathedral and the Archdeacon and clergy of the Deanery of Lecale. Although the Statute of Kilkenny, perhaps the most notorious statute passed by the medieval parliament in Dublin, which, *inter alia*, forbade religious houses among the English to receive any of Irish birth, had been passed the previous year, it is difficult to read into this incident anything more than a domestic upset within the diocese, but nevertheless typical of the absence of discipline which permeated religious life at this time.

1369 Richard Calf II, Prior, elected Bishop; presumably he had been elected Prior on Langtoun's excommunication.[16]

1380 John Ross, Prior, elected Bishop.[17]

1395 Walter Calfe. In this year, the Papal Letters record that John Cely, the Bishop, complained that Walter Calfe had 'put off the habit of his order, left the church and gone to Scotland and lands occupied by schismatic adherents of the antipope'. The Pope, through the Archbishop, ordered Cely to summon Calfe and, if the case was proven, to deprive him; alternatively, if found fit, he was to be collated to the Priory which was valued at 60 marks.[18] Cely was not, in fact, Bishop at this date, although he had been elected by his fellow monks; he was not provided by the Pope until 1413, having in the meantime become Prior.

1413 John Cely, Prior, elected Bishop.[19]

1419 William Perkyn. The Papal Letters record a mandate to the Abbot of Bangor to collate William Perkyn, a monk of Down, O.S.B., if found fit, to the priorship of the same, void by the promotion of John Cely to the Bishopric. The priorship was a major dignity with cure and was valued at 50 marks.[20]

1434 William Stanley. Swayne's Register has an entry of a complaint against William Stanley, Prior of Saint Patrick's of Down, that he rarely celebrated masses and other divine offices and that he kept a concubine, the daughter of Shane Boyd Macshymym, to the scandal of the church.[21] Stanley remained Prior of the Abbey over the period of the union of the Dioceses of Down and Connor and took Pollard's side in the succession dispute. The reader will recall his attack, in company with Pollard and others, on John Fossard, the Bishop at his palace at *Lismolyn.* Stanley's name disappears from the record after 1449.

1470 Thomas Brekway O.S.B. There are two entries in Octavian's Register (613, 614) requesting Thomas Brekway, Prior of Down Cathedral, to receive Thadeus (*Tadhg Ó Muirgheasa)*, the newly consecrated Bishop of Down and Connor.[22] However, as far back as 1449 in Mey's Register, the Abbot of Saul is named as Thomas Brekway, at which time he was the addressee of Mey's citation in the Pollard affair, when Stanley, the Prior, had sided with the intruder against the incumbent.[23] Whilst it cannot be said with certainty that these are one and the same person, a reasonable assumption might be made.

1474 Oliver Walsh, O.S.B., monk of Down, was collated to the Priory, worth 30 marks sterling, by default of Thomas Brecnay (sic), whom Oliver could not safely meet in the city and diocese of Down.[24]

1478 On Oliver Walsh's death, the Priory was granted by the Pope to Thomas, Bishop of Annaghdown, *in commendam.* Although on this occasion it was stated to be worth 80 marks, this is an extraordinary increase in value in a relatively short space of time. Rather does the plural appointment signify the decline in the revenues of the Benedictine house at this period.[25]

1484 Robertus Breanus is first mentioned as Prior. Ten years later, Robert is the addressee of a document in Octavian's Register (230) in which Saint Patrick's, both church and revenue, are stated to have been greatly impaired by wars and exactions of nobles.[26] In April 1495, Robert Brechne (sic) was ordered to be deprived in favour of *Gelasius Magaengussa*, a cleric of Dromore, the value of Saint Patrick's being 40 marks sterling.[27] Eight months later, he was ordered to be reinstated as he had been unlawfully deprived.[28]

1496 Although he does not appear to have occupied the office of Prior, Senequinus Suerdus gets a mention in the Papal Letters on 24 November. He was a monk of Saint Patrick's of Down, O.S.B., and he asserted that the resources of the monastery, on account of several suits which the Prior and Convent had had with several clerics and laymen, had been made so meagre that he could not sustain himself suitably from them and be present at divine offices. A mandate was granted in his favour, collating him to the perpetual vicarage of the Parish Church of Saint James, Ramaylyn, [Rathmullan ?], Diocese of Down, value 2 marks sterling, which was vacant.[29]

1501 William Mangan was collated to the Priory of the Church of Saint Patrick O.S.B.; Robert Brechimay (sic), Prior, lately dead. *Gelasius Magnyssa* has detained the priory without title or support of law. Annual value 24 Marks sterling [30]

1519 Gelasius Magennis is back in office. In Cromer's Register, he failed to appear at the hearing of a case of excommunication at the Vicar-General's court at Termonfeckin, for which he was found contumate and fined the expenses.[31] At the date of this document he was custodian of the spiritualities of the Diocese of Down, owing to the recent death of Tiberius. The Four Masters place his death in 1526 when he was slain by the sons of Donal Magennis in what was clearly a family feud. He was said to have been the Prior of Down and Saul.

The continued absence of the Bishop, Robert Blyth, upset the succession on this vacancy. John Swerds (possibly Senequinus Suerdus) was appointed by the Primate but Blyth, through his administrator, the Bishop of Clonmacnoise, appointed Conacius Magennis. Swerds' appointment was eventually confirmed whilst the evidence put forward by Magennis was declared a forgery, for which he was excommunicated. The charges included falsification of a Papal Bull, causing public scandal and disturbing the peace of the Prior and Brethren of Saint Patrick's of Down.[32] Nevertheless, Magennis had Papal support, as he bound himself to pay the annates of Saint Patrick's, not exceeding thirty marks.[33] It will be recalled that the Magennis family, which included the Bishop, Eugene, was perhaps the most powerful dynastic family in south Down at this time.

The office of Prior ceased to exist at the dissolution and the Cathedral Church of Down remained without a Chapter until 1609. The only other diocesan dignitary whose name occurs occasionally in the record is the Archdeacon; his function was quite unconnected with the abbey. In a monastic foundation, the monks collectively formed the Chapter and spoke with one voice. Thus, in the late medieval period, we find no reference to cathedral appointments such as would be found at a secular foundation. It is difficult to estimate the number of monks in the community of Saint Patrick, as no reliable Irish figures have ever been published. In the early thirteenth century, an outside estimate might be forty or fifty religious, but the number had undoubtedly dwindled to twenty or less by the time of the suppression.

Occasionally, we read the names of the Priors of one or other of the remaining monasteries in Down, but the record would not be complete without the known references to the convent of nuns, also following the Benedictine rule. Anne de Mandeville was the Benedictine Prioress and Margaret de Mandeville a nun in 1353.[34] In Prene's register (392), Alice, the Prioress was deprived by the Archbishop's commissary for incontinence on 16 March 1463. The Bishop, Thomas Knight, and Prior were ordered to denounce her, although she was allowed to remain in the nunnery at the discretion of her successor, Christiana, from Sodor Diocese.[35] The Nunnery was dedicated to the Blessed Virgin Mary.[36]

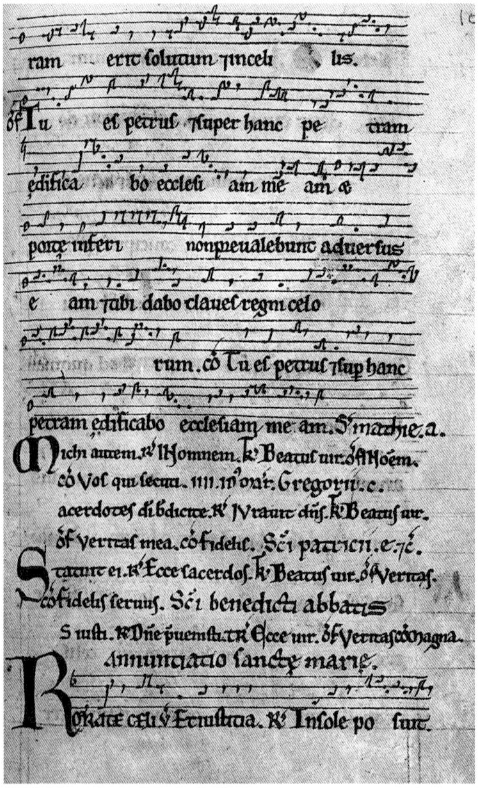

The Down Gradual. Folio 106R. The liturgy for the Annunciation of the Blessed Virgin Mary in which Saint Patrick is prayed for along with Saint Benedict.
THE BODLEIAN LIBRARY, RAWLINSON C.892, OXFORD

We would be wrong to overlook the part played by music and liturgy in the life of the Benedictines, who lived and worshipped here for something over 350 years. The central core of the Benedictine Rule was the *Opus Dei*, the celebration of the daily offices in the oratory, at which attendance of all the brothers, unless they were ill, was obligatory. A typical day consisted of eight separate visits to the oratory, usually relatively short except on Sundays and Feast Days, when they would have lasted up to two hours. In the Anglo-Norman period, as in the earlier Celtic church, the possession of the relics of important saints acted as a focus for pilgrimage and consequent source of wealth through the alms of the pilgrims. A visit to Down *en route* was obligatory for all pilgrims to Saint Patrick's Purgatory at Lough Derg in order to venerate the relics of Patrick, Brigid and Columcille. Each of these saints would have been celebrated on their Feast Days – 17 March, 1 February and 9 June – and considerable numbers of the faithful were undoubtedly attracted to Down on these occasions. Liturgical celebration was, of course, associated with elaborate processions, just as in the church to-day; indeed, the Anglo-Norman observance greatly increased the number of processions in the liturgical year, a factor said to be responsible for the building of long naves in order to accommodate them.[37]

Before the thirteenth century, different parts of the Mass and Office were copied into separate books, thus no single book contained all the liturgy for any one office. It was not until the thirteenth century that complete service books came into use. Fortunately a number of these early books, possibly associated with Down, survive in various libraries. The most notable and the one most likely to have been used in Down is in the Bodleian Library at Oxford.[38] It is a gradual, a book containing chants for the Mass throughout the year, dating from the second half of the twelfth century. Palaeographers have so dated it because of the red stave lines and capitals, alternating between purple and red. The clues which point towards its association with Down are its inclusion of Feasts for Saint Brigid, *(fol.143v)*, Saint Patrick, *(fol.106r)*, and Saint Benedict, *(fol.114r)*, suggesting that the book was copied for use in Ireland and most probably in a Benedictine monastery. Internal evidence also suggests that it was intended for use in a Cathedral. There is a strong probability, therefore, that this gradual is a surviving example of a book actually used by monks at the Benedictine Abbey of Saint Patrick in Down.

The Gradual commences with the Introit for the first Sunday in Advent, *Ad te levavi animam meam,* continuing with the offices for the remainder of the liturgical year; this part of the book is called the *Temporale.* At fol.101v commences the *Sanctorale,* which includes the Offices for Saints' Feast Days, beginning on Saint Andrew's Day – 30 November. The major festivals are marked with richly ornate and coloured capitals; Christmas, *Puer natus est, (fol.9r);* Easter Day, *Resurrexi et adhuc tecum, (fol.68v);* and Pentecost, *Spiritus Domini, (fol.81r).* The Palm Sunday procession, the most elaborate in the liturgical year, can be read in considerable detail on fol.44r. The liturgy for Holy Saturday is followed by one of the earliest known examples of polyphonic music written down on two staves, signifying the rejoicing for Easter Day, as opposed to monophonic singing or plainchant for the rest of the year. Saint Brigid, whose Feast Day is celebrated on 1 February, can be found on fol.143v: *Gaudeamus omnes in domino diem festum celebrantes sub honore Sancte Brigide.*

The Down Gradual. Folio 67.V
The Polyphonic Chant for Easter Day.
THE BODLEIAN LIBRARY, OXFORD
RAWLINSON C.892

Two scribes were responsible for copying this gradual; in a total of 149 folios, scribe A copied the larger number from fol.1 to fol.108 and from fol.132 to fol.149. This scribe began each of the gatherings with the invocation *O Emmanuel* in the right hand top corner of the first folio. Scribe B, responsible for folios 109-131, wrote in a markedly insular hand, which could be ascribed to Ireland. Can it be that we have here a gradual brought from Chester by the founding community and subsequently added to by a scribe who had been taught at an Irish scriptorium, perhaps even Down? When establishing daughter houses the practice was to introduce, as far as possible, the customs and observances of the mother house.[39]

In the National Library of Scotland is a manuscript, widely known as The Rosslyn Missal;[40] the missal came into use somewhat later than the gradual and contained the texts only for the Mass, without music. H. J. Lawlor, Dean of Saint Patrick's, Dublin and a leading ecclesiastical historian, made a critical edition of this Missal for the Henry Bradshaw Society in 1898;[41] in his introduction, he argued that the provenance of the Rosslyn Missal was the Cathedral Church of Saint Patrick of Down. Dating it to the late thirteenth century (about one hundred years after the Bodleian Gradual), his argument was based on a number of clues. The Missal was evidently in use in a church which claimed to be the burial place of Saint Patrick; in addition, de Courcy's change of the Cathedral dedication from Holy Trinity to Saint Patrick led to accusations of heresy in some quarters. A simple way to rebut this charge would have been to institute frequent masses to the Holy Trinity and this Missal demonstrates that the *Missa de Sancte Trinitate* was in frequent use. The book includes masses for both the Bishop and Archbishop, suggesting its use in a diocesan cathedral rather than at Armagh, where one would expect to find a Mass for the Archbishop only. Perhaps the most interesting and most determining clue is to be found in the liturgy for the blessing of candles on 2 February; this particular liturgy was largely confined to the Benedictine order and was known to have been used frequently in the province of Canterbury, which, at this period, encompassed the southern half of England as far north as the Diocese of Chester. It is probable, therefore, that the Rosslyn Missal was copied from service books brought to Down by monks, or even by one of the Bishops of the period, who had come from England.

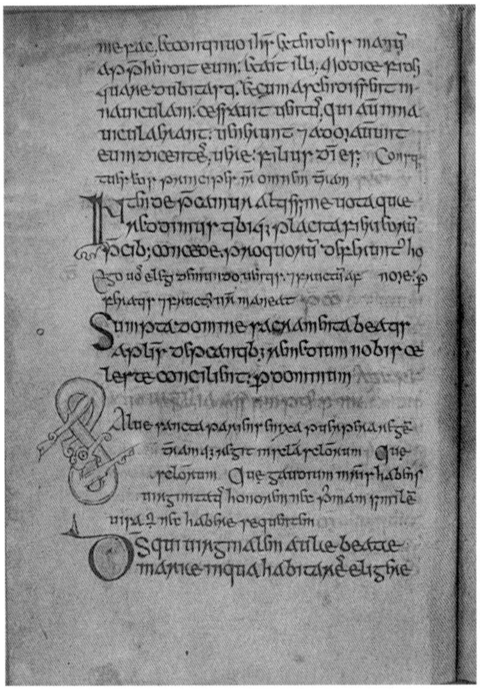

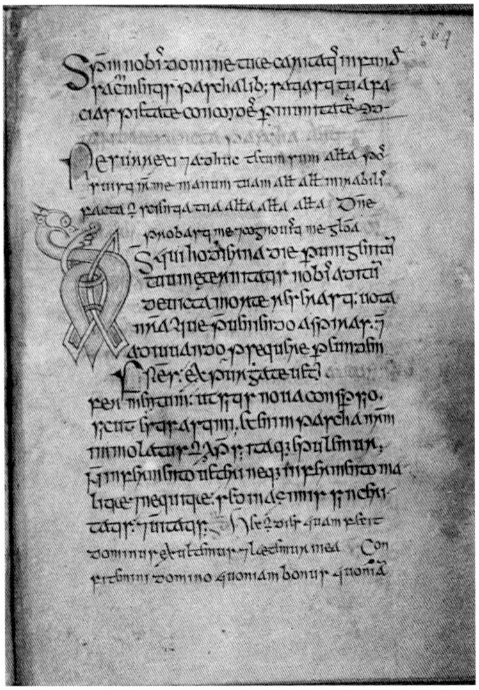

Two folios from the Rosslyn Missal
THE TRUSTEES OF THE NATIONAL LIBRARY OF SCOTLAND

How the Rosslyn Missal reached Scotland is purely conjectural; it is thought that it may have been carried by a Scottish follower of Edward Bruce and returned to that country by a homeward bound soldier and most likely deposited in a monastic library. We know that the Abbey of Down was plundered during the Bruce wars and this Missal might well have been one of the spoils of war. It was rescued by Henry Sinclair, Bishop of Ross, on the dissolution of the monasteries in the sixteenth century and passed to his nephew, Sir William Sinclair, who had established a library at Rosslyn Castle, Midlothian. This library was dispersed in 1630 and the book came into the hands of Sir James Balfour, on whose death, it was purchased by the Advocates' Library in Edinburgh for the sum of three shillings; from there it passed to the National Library of Scotland.

This review of pre-Reformation service books associated with Down would not be complete without a short reference to another book to be found in the Bodleian Library.[42] This is a Sarum breviary which, because it includes offices for Patrick, Brigid, Columcille and Finnian, has come to be associated with Down. However, as the offices include only nine lessons and responsories, it must have been for secular, rather than monastic use, otherwise twelve lessons would have been included. It may have been used in one of the parish churches associated with Saint Patrick's, where it would have been the duty of a member of the community to celebrate Mass on Sundays.

It would be idle to think that life in the cloister remained immune to the changing scene in the world outside as the centuries passed; claustral life evolved but slowly, in Down as elsewhere in Ireland or, for that matter, in Europe, in order to meet the changing environment in which

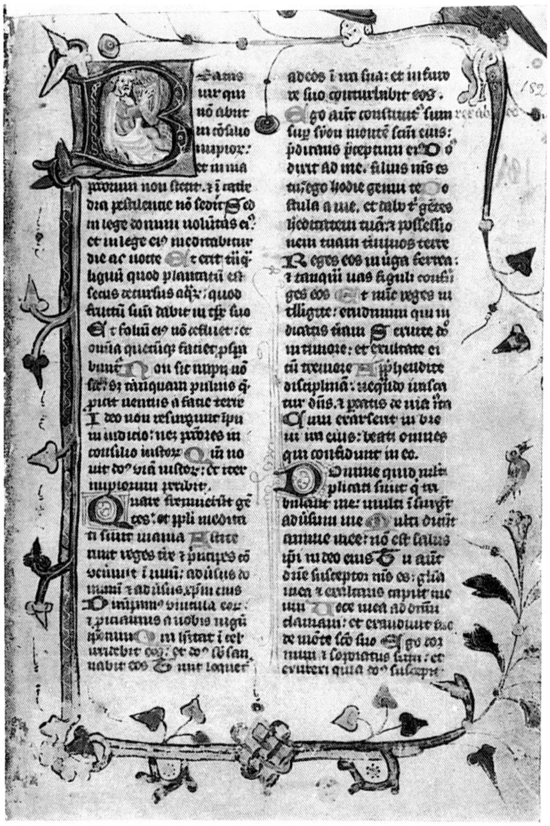

Folio 211V

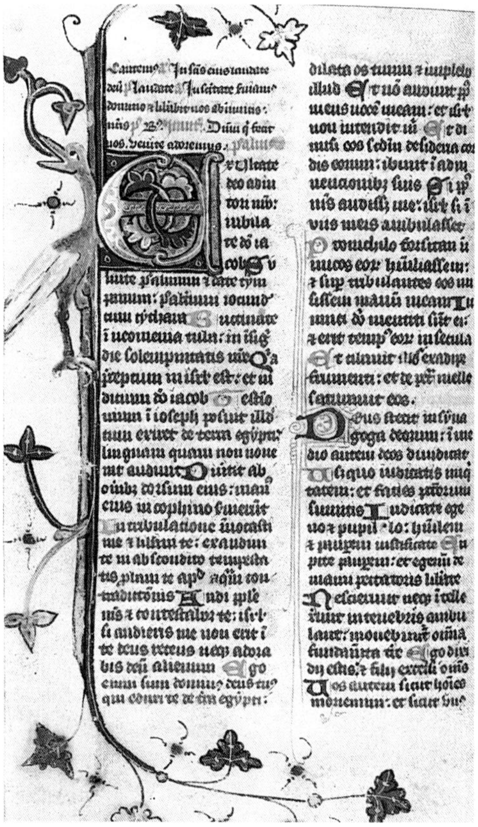

Folio 182R

Sarum Breviary.
THE BODLEIAN LIBRARY, OXFORD
CANON LITURG. 215

the monks found themselves. The Black Death of 1349-50 swept through Europe, sparing no country, causing mortality of up to 50% in some places; the enclosed nature of monastic life made the monasteries particularly vulnerable to the spread of the plague. Gradually the introspective, communal life of the enclosed orders became less attractive, their numbers dwindling in favour of the mendicant or preaching orders. Changing circumstance brought some relaxation of Benedictine discipline, even to the point of having a shortened form of liturgy approved by the Pope. Absentee abbots, in our case the diocesan bishop, were another problem; even if they did cross the sea to visit their diocese and many, indeed, saw no necessity to do so, they were non-resident in the monastery. Whilst the prior was technically responsible for the spiritual life of the community, the bishop, in many cases, appears to have had scant regard for his flock, having more concern for his temporalities. Such was the formalised structure of the medieval church; the bishops were virtually feudal magnates in their own right, enjoying a seat in parliament (as also did the Prior of Saint Patrick's), close to the seats of power and authority in the land and deriving a considerable income from estates entirely separate from the monastic demesnes. Little wonder, therefore, that a degree of corruption set in; the pages of history speak for themselves and leave the reader in no doubt that the century prior to the union of the Dioceses of Down and Connor marked the nadir of the church in the north-eastern corner of Ireland.

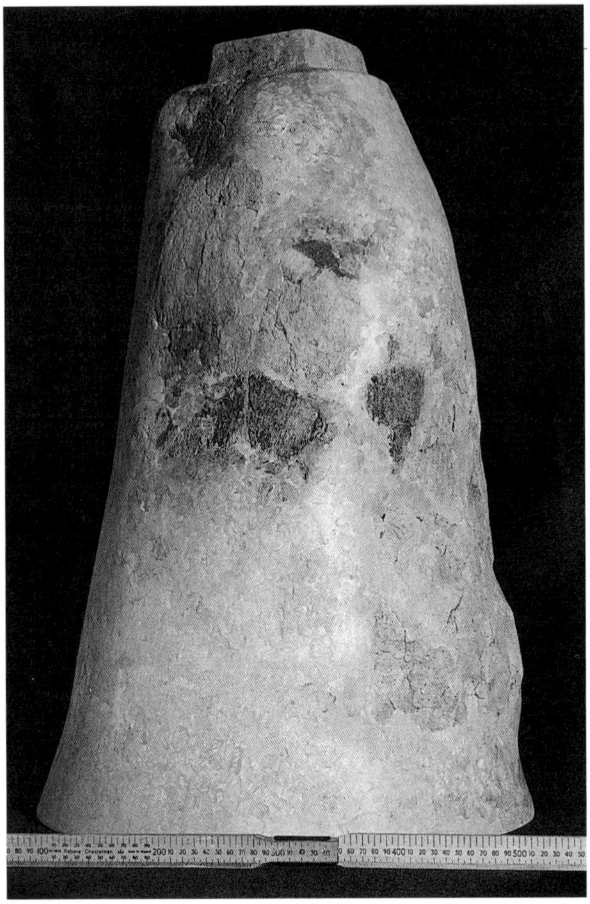

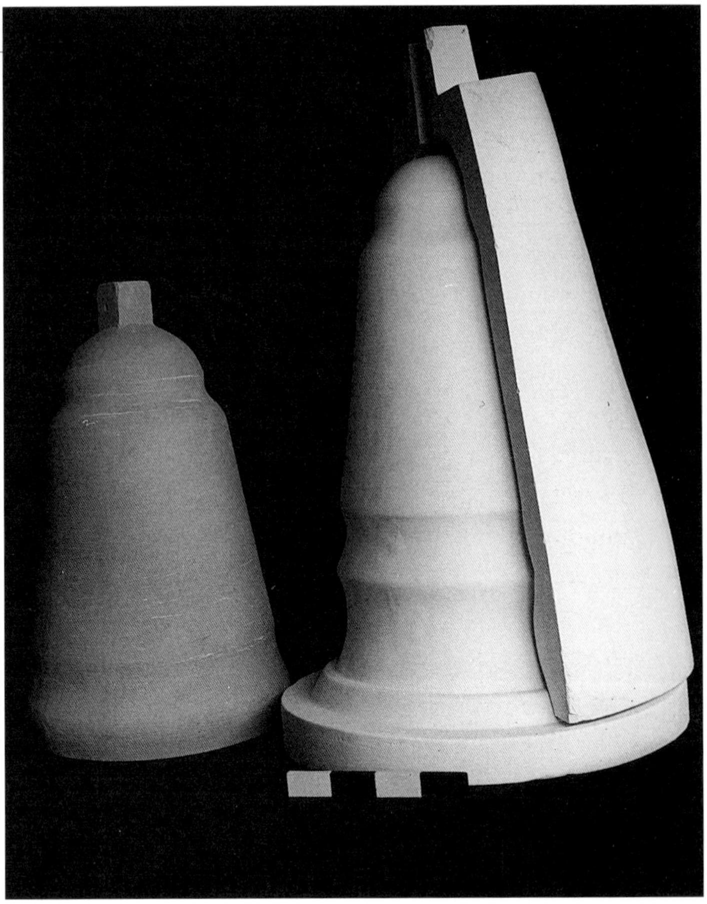

Fragments of a bell mould were found during the 1985 excavation.
These were pieced together and a new mould made from which a new bell shape was made.
ENVIRONMENT & HERITAGE SERVICE
DOE NI

Hand-bells are emblematic of the early Irish church. Their use can reasonably be traced to the earliest days of organised Christianity or to the 6th-century flowering of monasticism. Bells of sheet iron, bronze-coated, and bells of cast bronze were certainly made in parallel, but it seems that the former is the older category.

Iron bells were made to a standardized method from a single sheet and their loop-like handles alone admit of variation. A C-sectioned form is typical, but the handle from Cathedral Hill (now incomplete) is a square-sectioned bar to which three twisted iron wires have been applied, one on each face and another as a kind of minimalist crest. Crests appear in an equivalent position on 11th- and 12th century bell-shrines and the Downpatrick handle is likely to be contemporary. However, this is not to rule out the possibility that it replaced the lost or damaged handle of an *older* bell, perhaps an ecclesiastical heirloom.

CORMAC BOURKE

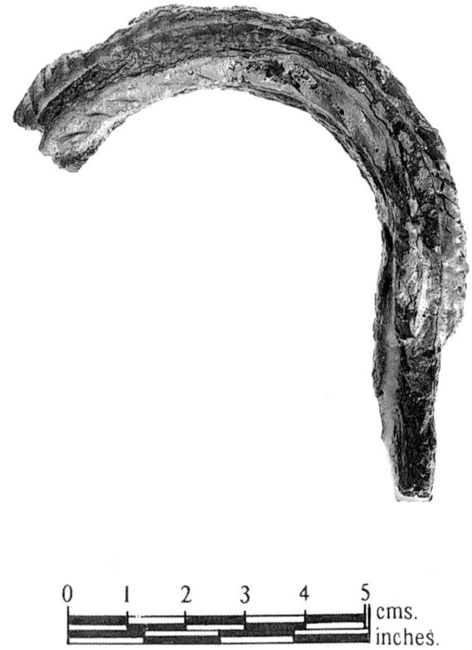

Handle of a bronze-coated iron bell discovered in 1986 in an unstratified context during excavations on Cathedral Hill.
11th-12th century.

But to read the pages of history with the cold clinical eye of the twentieth century is to distance oneself from the world in which these fourteenth and fifteenth century people were living. Could the sins for which interdict and excommunication were pronounced so frequently be all that sinful? Doubtless some offences caused some stir in the community and doubtless, as in all communities, there were bad apples in the barrel, but to view these incidents in isolation is to take an unnaturally simplistic view. Just as in the present day, the chronicler – the daily recorder of events – often noticed the scandal, the bad news, as this was what everyone wanted to know. Despite these pressures, the everyday spiritual life of the monastery carried on unnoticed and unrecorded. In fact, the half century before the suppression was a period of considerable building activity, both new and additional, by both the enclosed and preaching orders and the builders of that period have left a remarkable artistic and architectural legacy. Tiberius, the late fifteenth-century Bishop of Down, appears to have lent his support to this movement and indulged in what was the last major building exercise at Down Cathedral before the Reformation which was only 30 years away.

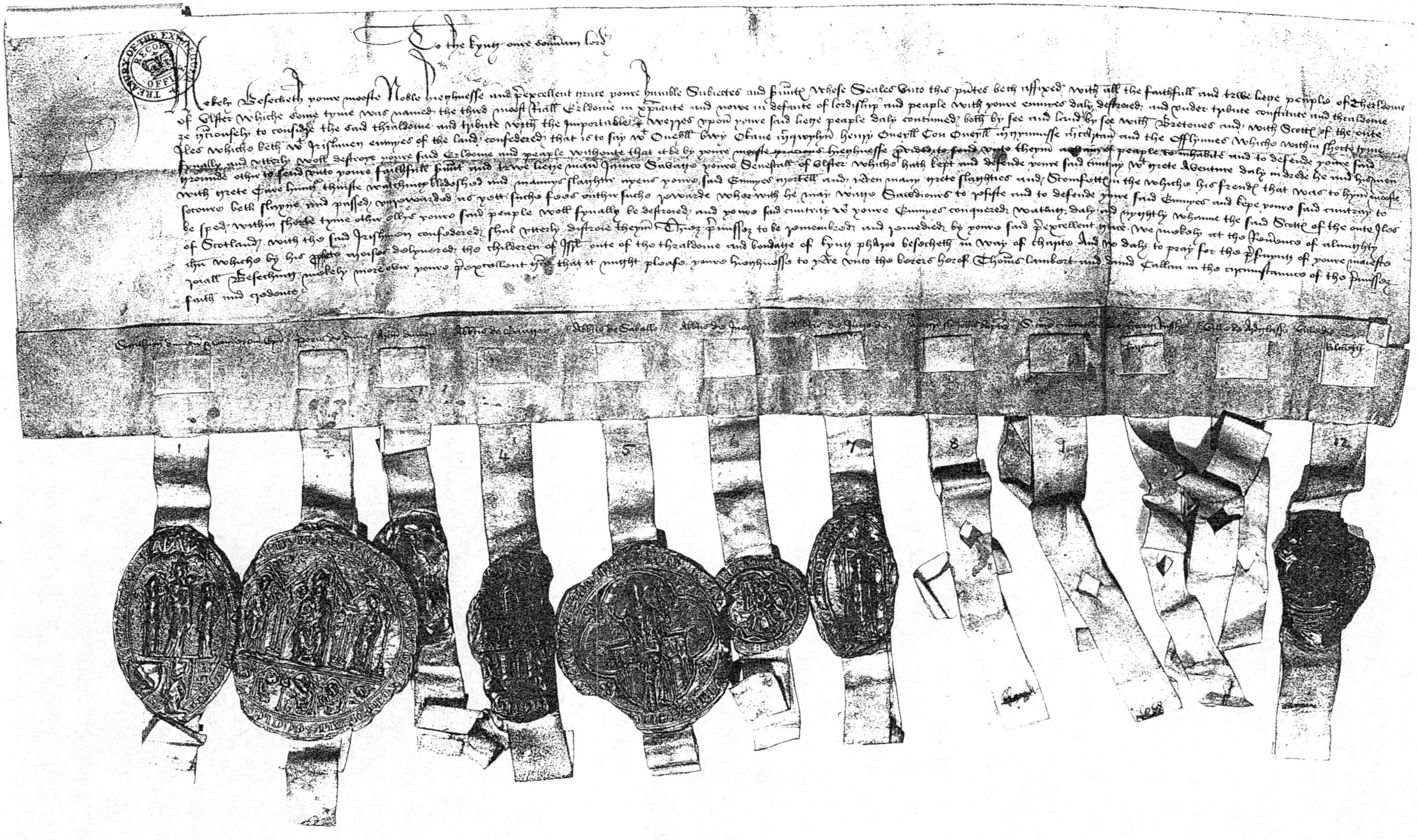

To the kyng oure souerain lord

Mekely besecheth youre moste noble hieghnesse and excellent grace youre humble subiectes and liege whose seales vnto this presentes beth affixed with all the faithfull and trewe liege peoples of the Erldome of Ulster whiche some tyme was named the third most riall Erldome in cristiante and nowe in defaute of lordship and peaple with youre enemyes daily destroied and vnder tribute constitute and thraldome ye gracionsly to consider the said thraldome and tribute with the importable werres vpon youre said liege peaple daily continued bothe by see and land by see with Bretones and with Scottes of the oute Iles whiche beth with Irishmen enemyes of the land confedered that is to say with Onell boy Okane Magwylyn Henry Onell Con Oneyll Magynnysse [illegible] and the Offlynnes whiche within short tyme fynally and vtterly woll destroye youre said Erldome and peaple withoute that it be by youre moste gracious hieghnesse provided to send vnto theym an army of peaple to inhabite and to defende youre said [illegible] other to send vnto youre faithfull seruant and trewe liege man Janico Savage youre Seneschall of Ulster whiche hath kept and defende youre said cuntrey with grete aventure daily in dede he and his men with grete travaill thurgh watching bloodshed and many slaughter ayens youre said enemyes mortall and yeven many grete slaughtres and discomfitures in the whiche his frendes that was to hym moste sorowe beth slayne and passed vnrewarded as yet suche fees outher suche rewarde wherwith he may wage souldiours to resiste and to defende youre said enemyes and kepe youre said cuntrey to be sped within short tyme outher elles youre said peaple woll fynally be destroied and youre said cuntrey with youre enemyes conquered wherfore daily and nyghtly whanne the said Scottes of the oute Iles of Scotland with the said Irishmen confedered shal vtterly destroie theym. Thes premisses to be remembred and remedied by youre said excellent grace. We mekely at the reverence of almyghty god whiche by his [illegible] delyuered the childeren of Israel oute of the thraldome and bondage of kyng Pharao besecheth in way of charite And we daily to pray for the prosperite of youre maieste roiall Besechyng mekely moreouer youre excellent grace that it myght please youre hieghnesse to yeve vnto the berers herof Thomas Lambert and [illegible] Callan in the circumstances of the premisses faith and credence

SIX

THE ENGLISH COLONY AT DOWN

THE YEARS FROM THE ARRIVAL OF de Courcy until the union of the Dioceses of Down and Connor, a period of just over two and a half centuries, were a time of considerable political upheaval. In fact, the turmoil continued throughout the late medieval period until the Tudor monarchs were able to assert a greater measure of authority over their neighbouring island, an island which the English had attempted to colonise with varying degrees of success in the wake of the Anglo-Norman conquest of the late twelfth century. Whilst Down was far removed from the seat of power in the Pale – situated in what was referred to as a marcher, or border area – it was nevertheless subject to a pattern of continual warfare between the Irish and the English and between the native Irish families themselves. The large land mass covered by the Mourne mountains was under the control of the powerful Macartan and Magennis families and, as a consequence, communication with the Pale administration was mostly by sea; it was therefore imperative to keep those sea routes open. It is not the purpose of this book to rehearse the political history of medieval Ireland; the interface between church and state, however, was so blurred that it is necessary to take a brief look at the overall picture insofar as it touches on our subject. We left Hugh de Lacy taking refuge in Scotland with King John in hot pursuit and John's subsequent more leisurely return to the Pale, the chiefs of which had pledged him their allegiance. He gave orders for Dublin Castle to be built and laid the foundations of government which were to last for many centuries.

The enlarged seal of the Bishop of Ergal.
P.R.O., LONDON
E/30/1744

Following King John's death in 1216, de Lacy made a determined attempt to recover Ulster; he created havoc for many years before the government finally gave in and restored him to the earldom in 1226. During the succeeding decades, de Lacy consolidated his hold on Ulster and even managed to make the local native chiefs subordinate to him. This was the period during which the mendicant orders were in the ascendant across Europe, partly as a reaction to the enclosed orders; de Lacy is credited with the foundation of the Franciscan Friary at Down in 1240. Among the charters granted by de Lacy was one in which free

The Down Petition
P.R.O., LONDON
E/30/1744

fishing in the River Bann was granted in perpetuity to the Prior and monks of Saint Patrick's in Down; the witnesses included Thomas, Bishop of Down, which therefore dates this charter to earlier than 1242.[1]

Involved so closely as it was in feudal society, the church was subject to feudal contributions. The record contains many references to payments of tenths being required of clergy to support the King in his wars, be they in France, Scotland or the more distant Crusades. Needless to say, the lower orders of clergy resented this encroachment and it is a moot point if the collection of tenths was ever really effective. In addition, there was papal taxation which had to be collected; this was carried out by a highly organised network of Italian merchant bankers which operated in medieval Ireland. The papal revenues took various forms of which the best known and most widely effective was that known as Peter's Pence. It is the tax known as *census*, however, which concerns us at Down. *Census* was a tax paid to the pope by protected and exempt ecclesiastical foundations in return for which the See of Saint Peter protected that foundation against encroachment by lay landlords. Theoretically the Pope had absolute ownership over the property but, in practice, he had no authority to dispose of it. The monastery paid an annual sum – in modern days it would be called an insurance premium –which came to be known as the *census*. In the thirteenth century, only three institutions in Ireland were subject to *census*; the Church of Saint Patrick at Down which paid half an ounce of gold; the Cathedral Church of Saint Mary in Louth which paid twenty *solidos* and the Hospital of Saint John in Dublin which paid two *solidos*.[2] The payment by the Church of Saint Patrick of *Dundaleglas* of half an ounce of gold is recorded in March 1281.[3]

By the end of the thirteenth century, the system of ecclesiastical taxation had become regularised and it was for this reason that valuations of ecclesiastical property were prepared; this was to take the form of a triennial tenth of which half was due to the Pope and half was due to the King. The 1306 taxation is familiar to students of ecclesiastical history since its rediscovery in the nineteenth century and the publication by Reeves of that portion of it relating to the Dioceses of Down, Connor and Dromore in his *Ecclesiastical Antiquities*. In this taxation the church of Saint Patrick at Down was valued at five marks of which the tenth was 6s 8d; in view of the not inconsiderable estates which we know belonged to the monastery, this was a remarkably low valuation in relation to other churches in Lecale; Saul and Ballyculter were together valued at 25 marks, Ballee at 20 marks and even Kilclief at 12 marks. It is probable that Saint Patrick's was subject to some partial exemption from this taxation, being already subject to *census*.

Nowadays one might be permitted to ask where the money came from to pay the different levels of taxation; whilst there were small amounts of coinage in circulation, a feudal society from the lowest level upwards paid by rendering service. We tend to overlook the fact that, by this time, agriculture had become highly developed and, within Lecale, the ports of Ardglass and Strangford carrried on a thriving export trade both to Britain and to Europe. No monastic leases for Down are extant; one such lease from the Prior of Holy Trinity, Dublin in 1352 has, however, been published. The lease was for a period of 16 years and in return the tenant was to pay 30 shillings for the first eight years and 40 for the remainder; in addition, he was to:[4]

> ...plough with his plough for one day at winter seed time and for one day at Lent seed time upon the land of the demesnes of the Priory; to reap with one man for one day the corn there in harvest; to carry with his cart the corn for one day, or with a car for two days or with two cars for one day; to give two gallons of ale as often as he brewed; to render suit to the manor court as often as he is summoned.

In addition to arable farming, beef and wool were also exported. Much of the produce of monastic demesnes was destined for the mother houses in England; in 1289, the Abbot of Saint Mary's in York, mother house of Nendrum through Saint Bee's, brought a lawsuit against the Bishop of Down concerning the lands of his monastery in Ireland.[5] The Irish possessions were jealously guarded. Down was also the home of a pottery industry, located close to what is now the Down County Museum. Excavations were carried out in 1960, the kilns discovered suggesting that Down was an industrial centre of some importance.[6] Sherds of Down pottery have since been identified at many widely scattered sites.

Hugh de Lacy died in 1243, leaving no heir; the earldom therefore passed to the Crown and it was not until 1264 that Walter de Burgh, already Earl of Connaught, was created Earl of Ulster as well. For some years prior to this, almost continuous warfare had been carried on by Brian O'Neill (of the Tyrone family) with the O'Connors of Connaught and the O'Briens of Thomond. Henry III, preoccupied elsewhere, had little interest in Ireland and O'Neill, supported by O'Connor, took the opportunity of launching an attack on the isolated English colony in Down in 1261. In the ensuing battle, at Drumderg just outside the town, the Irish were hopelessly defeated. O'Neill himself was slain – it was recorded that his head was taken to London – together with many other Irish chiefs who had joined him in support.[7] This defeat of the Irish in what was a determined attempt to restore the O'Neill dynasty to power, gave much encouragement to the English colony and certainly paved the way for Walter de Burgh's appointment. By way of reward for their victory, the citizens of Down were excused from the annual payment of 100 shillings to the King in order to build a wall around their town.[8]

Whilst on the one hand it can be said that the Anglo-Norman Lordship reached its zenith under Richard de Burgh (Walter's heir – the Red Earl) and that he was undisputed Lord of Ulster, it is also true that the increasing disinterestedness of the English Crown led to a succession of feuds among the magnates. Not only was the Irish exchequer impoverished by progressively increasing taxes and exactions, particularly during the reign of Edward I, but considerable numbers of men were conscripted to fight the king's wars in Scotland and Wales. This led, during the remaining years of the thirteenth century, to a gradual resurgence of Irish power and a diminishing area of the country under the control of the Pale. The division of the country into two nations became more marked and nowhere was this demonstrated more clearly than in ecclesiastical affairs; the church became markedly *inter Anglicos* and *inter Hibernicos.* In spite of this there is little evidence of the spread of tribal feuding into the affairs of the church and the clergy of each area appear to have co-existed on terms of mutual respect.

For many hundreds of years, a close affinity had existed between the Irish of the north-eastern coastal strip of the country and those who lived across the narrow channel in Scotland; following the success of the Scots against the English at Bannockburn in 1314, the Irish requested the assistance of King Robert Bruce of Scotland in an effort to repeat that success on Irish soil. Edward Bruce, brother of the King, landed at Carrickfergus on 25 May 1315 and, in the course of the next three years, made two extended predatory excursions across Ireland, plundering and laying waste the countryside through which he travelled. Eventually he fell in battle near Dundalk in October 1318, but not before he had had himself crowned High King of Ireland and received the tribute of many Irish chiefs, particularly those from Ulster. The descriptions of the Bruce wars which have come down to us reveal a picture of intense plundering and pillaging of property and crops and livestock. The casualties included the monasteries of Saint Patrick at Down and at Saul which, along with many others, were plundered. They also burned the church of Bright, 'full of persons of both sexes'.[9] The Bruce wars heralded the end of the Anglo-Norman lordship and the seal was put on it by the murder of William de Burgh, grandson of the Red Earl and last of the line, near Carrickfergus in 1333. Whilst the English retained control of a diminished area around the Pale and clearly a foothold, if no more, in Lecale, the remainder of Ulster was quickly regained by Irish families, of whom the most powerful were the O'Neills of Tyrone. The supremacy of the Irish in Ulster was complete by 1375 when Niall O'Neill defeated the English at *Dúndalethglas*, among those slain on that occasion being the then Lord Deputy, Sir James Talbot of Malahide.[10]

Ireland was not immune to the effects of the great schism in the church. During much of the fourteenth century, there were two Popes, one at Rome and one at Avignon, a situation which gave rise to conflicting allegiances throughout the church. Whilst England remained faithful to the Roman See, Scotland gave allegiance to the antipope in Avignon. Ireland, in general, remained faithful to Rome although the Avignon papacy was able to intrude a number of bishops, particularly in the western dioceses. In 1395, Walter Calfe, Prior of Saint Patrick's, defected to the schismatics in Scotland.

As early as the final years of the thirteenth century, a parliament was assembled in Dublin, consisting of both temporal and spiritual peers. Parliaments were held every two or three years and at various locations for a short period of weeks, just as long as was necessary to transact business in hand. In a feudal society, the church was expected to play its part and could not claim exemption from taxation and service; as the Crown held the right to the temporalities during a vacancy, by inference the Bishops held their temporalities of the Crown. Lists are extant for the attendance at many of the Irish parliaments and councils of the late medieval period; we do not know how many bishops were summoned, but the lists show that the attendance consisted largely of the bishops *inter Anglicos* and that the bishops from the native areas had little interest in the assembly. Failure to attend was marked by a fine, or amercement. The Bishops of Down were regularly summoned, although the records show that on occasion they were able to relegate their duties to a proctor. The condition upon which priors of religious houses were summoned to parliament is unclear. The prior of Saint Patrick's was regularly summoned but whether this was because Saint Patrick's was an 'English' house or for reasons of valuation or numbers in the community is not known. Abbots and priors across the country objected to the summons, various reasons being put forward and exemptions were obtained with comparative ease. In the parliament of November 1380, the Prior of Saint Patrick's asked that a summons should not be addressed to him or his successors, thus establishing exemption in perpetuity.[11]

Throughout the fifteenth century, the English power and presence continued to decline; the same period was marked by ongoing feuding amongst the great native families, of whom the O'Neills of Tyrone laid claim to supremacy in Ulster. The English colony in Down maintained a precarious foothold against the many incursions from the natives, both by land and sea. Ever since Reeves brought it to the attention of the Royal Irish Academy in 1851, a remarkbale document has excited historians.[12] It was then in the Chapter House of Westminster Abbey but is now preserved in the Public Record Office in London.[13] The parchment document, 19° inches long by 5 7/8 inches deep, bears no date and is a petition to an unnamed king from the 'faithfull and trwe liege peaple of Thealdome of Ulster' for help in the wars against a number of Irish families led by the O'Neills. Janico Savage is named as the king's faithful servant and pendant from the petition are a number of seals of leading ecclesiastics and laymen. The first seal, of which the superscription is *Sigillum Dunens et*

Connerens Epi (Seal of the Bishop of Down and Connor), reveals on close examination quite different lettering: *Epi Scopi Ergaliensis Miseraciona Divina.* (Bishop of 'Ergal', by divine compassion).

Dating this petition involves correct interpretation of the clues contained in it. Whilst it can be broadly dated to the middle of the fifteenth century, the precise dating is more problematical. Although another possibility has been put forward,[14] the most probable date is 1453 when the Four Masters record a battle at sea off Ardglass. It is, however, the apparent confusion between the Bishop of 'Ergal' and the Bishop of Down and Connor which is of paramount interest to historians. Ergal was the latin form of Oriel, a barony within the diocese of Clogher; in earlier centuries, the diocesan name was taken from the name of the dynastic family within its boundaries, in this case *Airgialla.* Lawlor has pointed out that the latest annalistic reference to the Bishop of Oriel is in 1218.[15] In 1453, Down and Connor had an absentee bishop, Richard Woolsey, for whom there is no record of any visit to Ireland. Nevertheless, it would have been necessary for Woolsey to appoint an administrator of equal rank to carry out his official duties and to approve official documents by attaching his episcopal seal.

The political scene in Ireland from the later years of the fifteenth century was dominated by the rise of the powerful Fitzgerald family, the Earls of Kildare. The eighth Earl, Garret More, had successively held the office of Lord Deputy, been deposed, attainted of treason, imprisoned in the Tower of London, restored and re-appointed Lord Deputy, in which office he remained on the accession of Henry VIII in 1509. On his death in 1513, his son Garret Oge succeeded to the Earldom and to the Lord Deputyship. The ninth Earl remained loyal to the King and managed to reverse the tide of events in Ireland by marching against the native Irish and extending the area nominally under English rule. It is said that the Kildare estates in Lecale date from this period, when Garret Oge was given land by the Magennis and other families, to whose aid he had come when they were under attack by the Savages of the Ards and Lecale.[16] He also received a royal grant of the customs of Ardglass and Strangford, fishing in Strangford Lough and the salmon fishery on the Bann.[17]

Over the next two decades, however, Kildare was at the centre of charges and counter-charges of high treason, a term which carried a somewhat different meaning under the Tudor monarchy than it does now. In Tudor times and earlier, the state was embodied in the person of the monarch and any instance of disloyalty or disobedience to the monarch was a treasonable offence. In the south, the Butlers and Desmonds and in the north, the O'Neills and O'Donnells occupied the political stage, all vying for supremacy with the Kildares. On two occasions, Kildare was accused by his rivals and was forced to travel to London to plead his case before the King and on each occasion he was temporarily replaced as

Lord Deputy; on the first occasion he took the opportunity to marry Lady Elizabeth Grey, a sister to Lord Leonard Grey and cousin to the King. On his second visit, in 1534, he pleaded in vain against the accusations of the Irish chiefs and the Council in Ireland and found himself committed to the Tower.

During his confinement in the Tower, a false report was put out that he had been executed, which caused his son, known to history as Silken Thomas, to gather the Irish chiefs together in revolt against the English. All those sympathetic to the Geraldines threw in their lot with Silken Thomas. The rebellion was short lived, but the fact that it took place at all and the circumstances surrounding it contributed to the Earl's death, still in the Tower, in December 1534. William Skeffington was sent to Ireland as Lord Deputy with troops to quash the rebellion, which finally collapsed with the surrender of Maynooth Castle, the Fitzgerald stronghold, in March 1535. Silken Thomas was sent to England and despite pleadings from his uncle, Lord Leonard Grey, he was hanged at Tyburn with five of his Fitzgerald uncles, the object clearly being to extinguish, once and for all, the house of Kildare.

Shortly after the fall of Maynooth, Skeffington died; Grey, who had come to Ireland as Marshal of the Army, was appointed Lord Deputy in his stead, taking up residence in Maynooth. Grey was a soldier first and a politician second; he spent much of the next few years penetrating those parts of the country still under the rule of Gaelic chiefs and receiving their submission. His kinship with the Kildare family ensured that he could move easily among the Irish but that kinship created a deep suspicion amongst the English officials of the Pale. It was still a member of the Kildare family who was the object of much of the English activity. Young Garret Fitzgerald, half brother to Silken Thomas, spent these years in the care of his aunt Eleanor, the widow of MacCarthy Reagh of Cork. Young Garret was widely believed by the Irish to be their future leader and, as such, his pursuit and capture were of paramount importance to the English. In the State Papers, Grey frequently makes mention of his attempts to capture him, but the prize always eluded him for what seemed to be the flimsiest of reasons. This lack of success, indeed, became one of the indictments against Grey when his opponents accused him of connivance and the furthering of the Geraldine cause.

By 1539, Fitzgerald was in Ulster – his aunt had married an O'Donnell – and Grey was there also in the hope of his capture. He described how he was cheated of his prize yet again in a letter to Cromwell, Lord Privy Seal.[18] Grey concluded the letter by requesting a meeting with Cromwell, at which time he would disclose his plans both for the apprehension of his nephew and the subduing of the Irish rebels. The treasurer, Brabazon, who accompanied Grey on this expedition, in a separate letter to Cromwell, pointed out the close alliance between the O'Neills and the O'Donnells with the Scots and Alexander McDonnell; this Gaelic alliance was in constant war with the people of Lecale and Brabazon made the suggestion to Cromwell that two ships of war, of 80 tons and 50 tons, should be deployed between Ireland and Scotland in order to prevent the Scots coming to the aid of the Irish.[19] This advice went unheeded and Fitgerald eventually escaped to Scotland and thence to France; he stayed there until 1547, when he returned to Ireland, following the death of Henry VIII. He was eventually restored to the Kildare estates in 1552.

Meanwhile, Grey remained active in the field. Not only did he harass the border lands of the Pale, but he campaigned as far afield as the Shannon and Galway, showing great skill in manoeuvring his cannon across the boglands of central Ireland. As a politician and parliamentarian, however, his skill was less in evidence and his overbearing manner at meetings of the Council lost him many friends among the English officials in the Pale, in particular Archbishop Browne of Dublin and Piers Butler, Earl of Ormonde, both of whom were at the forefront of the movement towards the acceptance of Henry VIII as supreme head of the church. Whilst Grey presided over the parliament which enacted the statutes for the abolition of papal authority and the establishment of Henry VIII as head of the church, and also the statute for the suppression of the monasteries, many of his actions in the field gave rise to strong suspicions that his motives were allied towards personal aggrandisement and the accumulation of wealth and booty, much of which found its way to his residence at Maynooth Castle. The extent of the booty may be gauged from this extract from a letter from Robert Cowley, Master of the Rolls in Dublin, to the Duke of Norfolk, following Grey's departure in 1540:[20]

> ...to make serche for suche coyne plate and goodes as the lord Leenard Grey late the Kinges Deputie had here and the same to seyse to bee furthcomyng at the Kinges pleasure, with as litil rumore as might be; Accordingly the said lord Justice and the said Archebisshop furthwith went to Maynothe there seysing all suche stuff and jewelles as there was founde, making thereof an inventary; and I repayred to Saint Mary Abbey and toke an inventary of suche stuff as there was, And we examyned Arlond Ussher, who by his othe hathe deposed that a litill before the said lord Leonardes departing, the said Arlond had in his kepyng a stele casket locked, full of mony as he supposid, golde, and divers bagges of money sealyd; which casket and bagges oon Lewte toke from him; and how mouche mony was in the casket and bagges the said Arlond could not tell, but it is thought to bee a very greate thing....

There are many instances quoted in the State Papers when Grey's vile temper surfaced if he did not get his way at the Council table; indeed he frequently seems to have gone his own way, ignoring council decisions. The Bishop of

Derry, who had refused to accept Henry as head of the church, appealed to the pope, saying that the Deputy had burned houses, destroyed churches, ravished maids and killed innocents.[21] Butler asserted that Grey remained at heart a Papist and, as such, sheltered papists from punishment;[22] Cowley declared that, through his negligence, the progress of the reform was everywhere held in check.[23] There was certainly more than a grain of truth in both these statements.

In October 1539, during the campaign to capture Fitzgerald in Ulster, Grey went to Lecale in order to repulse the Scots. The following month he reported to Cromwell:[24]

> ...And to Dundalk came Mr Thesourer [Brabazon], with hys companye to me. And seing that my purpoos was lettyd as towching Oneyll, and for soo myche as Mr Thesourer was fermour of the Kinges countre of Lecayll, and that Savage, chyeff capitayn of his natyon, wolde not pay his ferme unto the Thesourer, and besydys the sayd Savage browght into the sayd countre dyverse Scottys, whyche had myche of the sayd countre in theyr subjection, then yt was concludyd betwyxt the said Mr Thesourer and me, that we showlde have gone towardes the sayd Lecayll; and so, with the ost, we sett forward, and entred into the sayd coiuntre, and tok all the castells theyr, and delyvered them to Mr Thesourer, who hath warded the same. I toke another castell, being in McGynons countre, called Doundrome, whych I assure your Lordeship, as yt standyth, ys one of the strongyst holtes that ever I saw in Ireland, and moost commodios for the defence of the hole countre of Lecayll, both by see and lande; for the sayd Lecayll ys invyroned rounde abowte with the see, and noo way to goo by lande into the sayd countrey, but only by the sayd castell of Dundrome. Owt of whyche countre the sayd Scottys fled, and left mych corne, butters, and other pylfre, behinde them, whyche the ost hade. Besydys this, I toke a castell that the sayd Scottys had, and other castelles in Ard bordering to the sayd Lecayll, whyche lykewyse I delivered to the Thesourer, who hath warded theim; in nombre 8 castelles, I assure your Lordeship I have byn in manye placys and countreis in my days, and yet dyd I never see for so myche a plesaunter plott of grounde, then the sayd Lecayll, for comoditie of the lande, and diverse ilandes in the same, ynvyroned with the see, whyche were sone reclaymed and inhabited....

Despite the apparent confidence evident in such letters, time was running out for Grey. The accusations made against him by his enemies in Ireland forced the King's hand and he was finally recalled to London in April 1540.[25] The letter, from the hand of Henry VIII, gives little clue as to the fate which awaited Lord Leonard; instead of appearing at court, as he fully expected to do, he found himself committed to the Tower on charges of high treason. The principal officers of the Dublin administration were also called to London to give an account to the King of the Lord Deputy's activities; with them went a book 'of diverse abuses and enormities, among others, noted and collected by the Kinges Counsell of Irland', a book which included no fewer than 90 counts.[26] In December of that year, 1540, the Privy Council, meeting at Westminster, found Grey, because of the affection he had borne towards the Geraldines through his sister's marriage to the Earl of Kildare, guilty of high treason on five counts.[27] None of these five counts relates to the destruction of Down Cathedral, laying to rest the age-old myth that his desecration of the Cathedral was one of the reasons for his execution. The five counts were: firstly, the entertainment of certain of the King's enemies who had not been pardoned; secondly, the destruction of Maguire, who had been the King's friend; thirdly, the release of Fitzgerald and the Dean of Derry, both of whom had been committed for treason; fourthly, inciting O'More's sons to spoil the King's subjects and finally, the entertainment of one Edmund Ashbold after he had been indited for treason.

Lord Leonard Grey was executed at the Tower of London on 28 July 1541.

Lord Grey beheaded 1541

There is a widely held tradition that Grey plundered and destroyed Down Cathedral during an expedition to Lecale in 1538; this legendary tale has been in circulation, and been repeated by successive authors, for so long that one might be forgiven for believing in its authenticity. The *Annals of Ulster*, which, at this period, were a contemporary compilation, record in the year 1538:[28]

> A hosting by the Saxon Justiciary to *Leth-Cathall* and the monastery of Down was burned by them and the relics of Patrick and Columcille and Brigit and the image of Catherine were carried off by them. And the Saxon captain took the image with him to the green of his castle of Dun-a-droma and he himself went into the castle and there was a hole in the castle and that man fell into it through the miracles of God and Catherine, without tidings of him from that to this.

The Four Masters, writing perhaps a century later, make no reference to the event, but Richard Stanyhurst, the author of the Irish volume of Holinshed's *Chronicles,* first published in 1577, embellished the story a little further:[29]

> In this journey he razed Saint Patricke his Churche in Doune, an olde auncient Citie of Ulster, and burnt the monuments of Patricke, Briged and Colme, who are sayd to have been there entumbed, as before is expressed in the description of Ireland.

Stanyhurst then lists the articles with which Grey was charged, including the destruction of Down Cathedral, and concludes with this further information:

> ...that, without any warrant from the King or Counsaile, he prophaned the Church of Saint Patrickes in Doune, turning it to a stable, after plucked it downe, and shipt the notable ring of belles that did hang in the Steple, meaning to have them sent to Englande, hadde not God of his justice prevented his iniquitie, by sinking the Vessell and passengers wherein the sayde Belles should have bene conveyed.

Stanyhurst was a member of a patrician family in Dublin, his father having been Recorder of that city. They remained true to the Roman faith, as did many of their class until the harsher regime under Elizabeth in the later years of the century. Stanyhurst, in fact, sought refuge in Belgium in later life rather than conform to the reformed faith.[30] From where did Stanyhurst get his information which accords very closely with the record in the Vatican archives quoted by Costello and Coleman?[31] Was he quoting within the memory of a generation, a memory of the unpopularity of Grey and the desire to blacken his name?

No-one has ever questioned the destruction of Down Cathedral by Grey; the story has been perpetuated by every writer from that day to the present. But was he responsible? His own letter to Cromwell, quoted above, is the only report in the State Papers wherein he mentions visiting Down or Lecale; on the other hand, Dundrum Castle, originally built by de Courcy and enjoyed by the Knights Templar until their dissolution in 1313, was the property of the Prior of Down, who at this time was a Magennis. Was Grey so thoroughly dishonest – and his general conduct would suggest that he was a scoundrel – that he did, in fact, plunder the Cathedral and not admit to the deed, as he must have been aware by this time that his recall was not far off? Was he the opportunist adventurer, living for the moment without any thought for the morrow? We shall never know. What we can say without any shadow of doubt, however, is that he lost his head on the block (not before his master, Cromwell, the Lord Privy Seal, had lost his) for reasons quite unconnected with Down Cathedral.

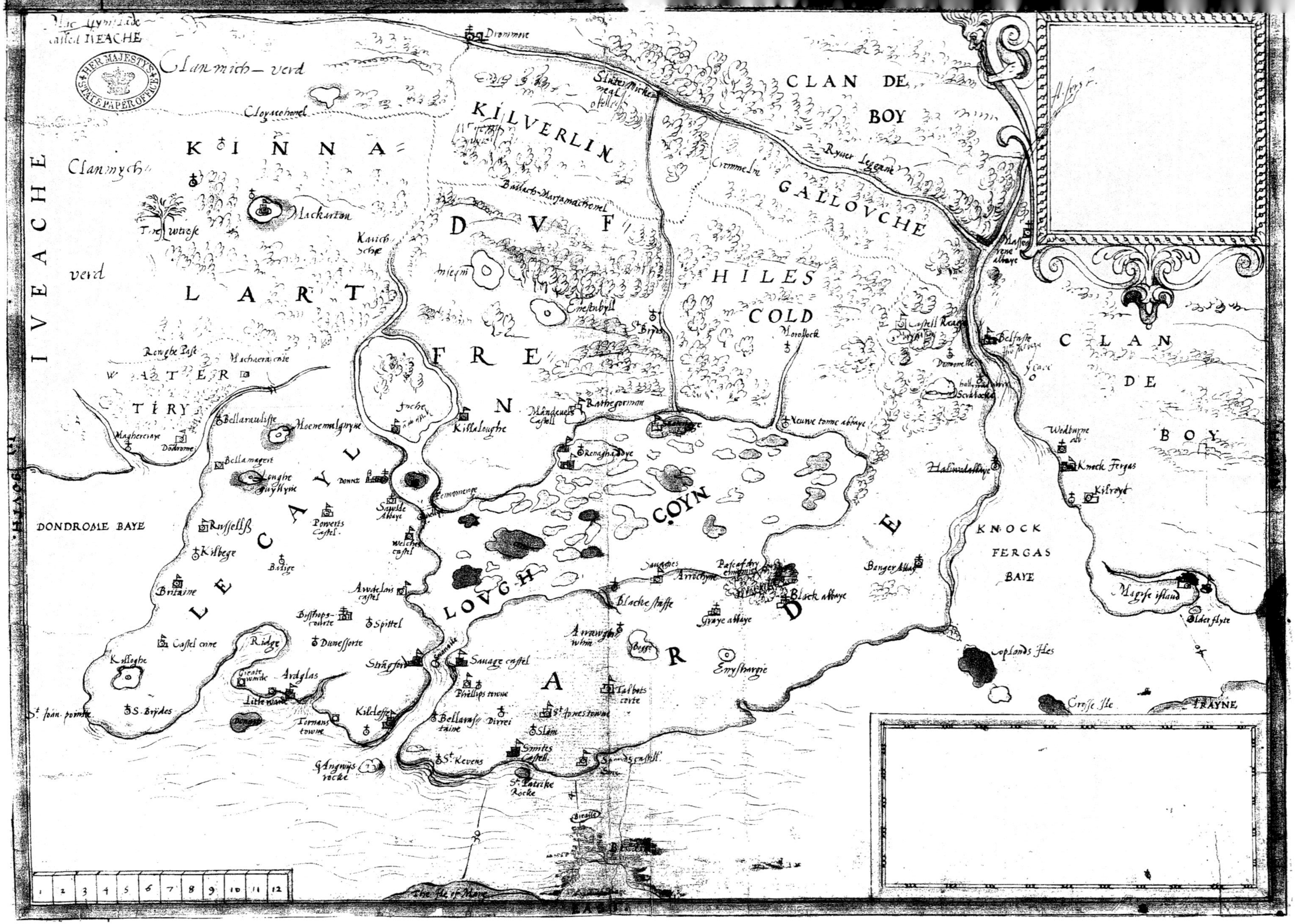
HER MAJESTYS STATE PAPER OFFICE
IVEACHE
Clanmich-verd
Clanmych
verd
KINNA
LART
WATTER
TIRY
Cloyacehonel
Mackarton
KILVERLIN
DVF
FRE
N
CLAN DE BOY
GALLOVCHE
HILES
COLD
Ryuer Legane
Dromore
Belfaste
Knock Fergas
Kilroyt
Magyse island
KNOCK FERGAS BAYE
Coplands Iles
Crosse Ile
TRAYNE
Banger Abbaye
Black abbaye
Graye abbaye
Blacke staffe
Arrochyne
LOVGH
COYN
LECAYL
ARD
E
DONDROME BAYE
Russells
Kilbege
Britaine
Castel cone
Ridge
Ardglas
Litlewarde
S. Brydes
St. Joan pointe
Dunesforte
Spittel
Bisshops-courte
Powerts Castel
Welches castel
Sawle Abbaye
Stranfort
Sauage castel
Phillips towne
Bellawsy taine
Dirrei
St. Kevens
Smites castell
Slain
Talbots corte
Emysharge
St. Patrike Rocke
The Ile of Mane
Angwys rocke
Kildeffe
Tornans towne
Killaloughe
Renaghadaye
Rathegorman
Neuwe towne abbaye
Halinwddaye
Castell Reagh
Bellamagert
Loughe Gylly
Dondrome
Magheresaye
Hoenemalgryne
Rowghe Paste
1 2 3 4 5 6 7 8 9 10 11 12
SOVTH
EAST

SEVEN

THE SUPPRESSION AND ITS LEGACY

THE READER WILL FIND ELSEWHERE the political background leading to the decision by Henry VIII to declare himself Supreme Head of the Church in England and to break the bond which bound that church to the See of Rome; the fact is that the political reasons were foisted on, as far as England was concerned, a ready and willing body of clergy which had largely come under the influence of Lutheran teaching. The natural sequel to this new situation was the suppression of the religious houses, bearing in mind that Henry VIII and those who surrounded him, of whom the most notable was Thomas Cromwell, were to a degree greedy, materialistic and opportunist, utterly devoid of any empathy for the inner life of the religious. During the two years before the general suppression commenced in 1536, commissions of visitation under royal warrant were made to all the monastic houses in the length and breadth of the land, reporting on all aspects of the religious life, both spiritual and temporal. Many abbots and priors, of course, with the foreknowledge of their inevitable doom, sequestrated monastic property in advance, but any property thus disposed of was relatively minor compared to that which was confiscated in due course by the commissioners. David Knowles describes the English picture graphically:[1]

> As they [Cromwell's commission] rode over the rainswept English countryside in the late summer of 1535, the life of some eight hundred religious families, great and small, was continuing, at least in external show, to follow that rhythm that had endured for centuries....When, five years later, their work was done, nettles and fireweed were springing from the dust and the ruins of Hailes and Roche and Jervaulx were already beginning to wear the mantle of silence that covers them to-day.

Events in Ireland ran parallel to those in England with minor variations because of local reaction and at a somewhat later date. Indeed the suppression might not have taken place in Ireland at all had not the Tudor monarchs chosen to exercise their authority over the neighbouring island; nevertheless the royal writ ran over a limited area of the country and the majority of the native Irish along with large numbers of those who called themselves Anglo-Irish continued to give allegiance to Rome. Many of the more remote religious houses were not, in

Opposite:
County Down c.1580
P.R.O., LONDON
MPF 87

fact, formally suppressed by a commission acting under warrant – they just drifted into oblivion. Robert Cowley, Master of the Rolls, wrote to Cromwell in October 1536:[2]

> The abbayes here doo not kepe soo good Divine service, as the abbayes in England, beeing suppressid, did kepe; the religeous personages here lesse contynent or vertuous, keping no hospitalitie saving to theyne silves, theire concubynes, childerne, and to certain bell wedders, to eclypse theire pernycious lyevinges and to beare and pavesse theire detestable deedes; whych rynge leaders have good fees, fatte profitable fermes, the fynding of their children, with other daily pleasures of the abbayes; and fearing to loose the proffit thereof, repugne and resist the suppressing of abbayes, swinysing it should bee prejudiciall to the comon weall; which is otherwise.

Surprisingly, the first Suppression Bill placed before the Dublin parliament in 1536 failed to pass, but a second bill, promoted the following year, found the necessary majority and became law. The King himself brought extreme pressure to bear on Grey and Brabazon, the Lord Deputy and Treasurer; he wrote to the Lord Deputy and Council on 25 February 1537:[3]

> ....you have not yet proceded to the suppression of the monasteries and that you have had no more regarde to our sundry letters written unto you for thalleviating of our charges there...

To which the Lord Deputy replied on 20 April:[4]

> ...As to the suppression of certen monasteries, expressed in a commission under your Greate Seale, we shall procede theirunto with souch convenient speade, as shalbe moaste for your Hignes profecte...

The actual pattern of suppression followed closely that in England, with the exception that it was not preceded by a visit from the commissioners under royal warrant; the rebellion of Silken Thomas had so occupied the attention of the Dublin executive that there was neither time nor opportunity for such a visit. However, the chronology of events can be pieced together from various sources, the chief of which are the accounts of Treasurer Brabazon. These were returned to the Exchequer in some detail, much of which is recorded in the Letters and Papers of Henry VIII. Brabazon and Cowley, together with Thomas Cusack and John Alen, Archbishop of Dublin, were appointed by letters under the King's privy seal:[6]

> to deface and remove all images or relics within Ireland to which simple people have used superstitiously to resort in pilgrimage, or otherwise to kiss, lick or honour, also to take voluntary surrenders of religious houses, to sell, for payment of debts and servants, all moveables, except plate, jewels, lead and bells, and to assign part of these to the heads of

> the same religious houses by way of reward and put the rest in safety to the King's use...

The years 1538-40 were occupied in taking surrenders of the monasteries in the Pale; although Grey found time to make an expedition to the north and Lecale in 1539, the object of this trip appears to have been the capture of young Fitzgerald rather than carrying out the King's instructions towards monasteries. On the confiscation of a monastery, its property and estates escheated to the Crown and were subsequently regranted to someone in the Crown's patronage. In fact, most of the houses in the Pale and its border lands had their lands regranted to those in parliamentary favour, in the hope of strengthening the English administration in those areas with men well disposed to Cromwell.

Information on the suppression of the monasteries in Ulster is virtually non-existent. Despite an exhaustive search among all the probable record depositories, it has not been possible to trace any documentation relative to the suppression of any monasteries in east Down and Lecale. The probable sequence of events can only be pieced together by analogy with what is known to have happened elsewhere. Following Grey's recall to London in 1540 and the caretaker appointment of Sir William Brereton for a few months, the Lord Deputyship was held by Sir Anthony St Leger. Whilst St Leger's reputation has not been tarnished by historians to the same extent as that of Grey, it must be understood that he was at all times in the service of the King and held the senior office in the Dublin executive. Only the understanding of this position can explain a postscript in his own hand to a document recording the suppression of a monastery in Wexford:[6]

> Take ane oblygatyone for asmyche stone off the churche ther as schall suffyce for the repayr off the kyng's castell ther.

When the Lord Deputy arrived to take the surrender of a monastery, everything movable and of any value would have been taken out and either sold for immediate profit or melted down for use as base metal; this applied to statues, ornaments, bells, jewels and anything else which the commissioners thought could be realised for cash. The lead from the roof would have been removed and sold for cash and it is this fact, more than any other, which led to the ruination of the building. We can assume that this scenario represents the events on Cathedral Hill in Down. Surprisingly, a number of relics are known today which may have been among the possessions of Saint Patrick's, perhaps removed before the commissioners arrived, although it is impossible, of course, to be certain of this. The Roman Catholic Bishop of Down and Connor possesses a gilt silver shrine of Saint Patrick's hand,[7] the artwork on which dates it to the fourteenth or fifteenth century and is typical of Irish metal work of that time; it is inlaid with studs of rock crystal and glass and the cuff has panels with

The Shrine of St Patrick's hand.
DIOCESE OF DOWN AND CONNOR. ON LOAN TO ULSTER MUSEUM

Madonna at Dunsford Roman Catholic Church 14th/15th century

engravings of lions, griffins and stags. This shrine is currently on loan to the Ulster Museuem. Built into a niche in the east gable wall of Dunsford Roman Catholic Church is a very fine statue of a Madonna and Child, carved from Scrabo stone and also datable to the same century.[8] Both the Down County and Ulster Museums have in their collections a number of medieval earthen tiles which have been provenanced to Down Cathedral; they have various inlaid patterns similar though not identical with tiles found in other parts of Ireland or for that matter any published designs from England.[9] No analytical work has been carried out to establish if these might have been made at the nearby kiln which flourished in the latter half of the thirteenth century.

The absence of documentation leaves us without a firm date for the dissolution of these monasteries; it is possible, however, from the State Papers to trace the expeditions of the Lord Deputy and his entourage around the country. In May 1541, St Leger endeavoured to settle a dispute between two members of the Magennis family and left Prior Magennis of Down to arbitrate on the matter;[10] this is the final reference to a monastic official. By October 1542, the possessions of the suppressed religious houses in Ulster had become 'parcel of the King's revenue, no profit yet because no perfect order [i.e., inquisition] taken'.[11] We can thus narrow the probable date of surrender to a period of eighteen months. A study of the Papers within that period reveals a letter from St Leger on 9 October 1541 in which he states that he had been in O'Neill's country for 22 days.[12] '...have burnid grete parte of the same...have also slayne dyverse of his people'. During a later expedition in December of the same year, O'Neill submitted to the English crown. Late September, therefore, would seem to be the most probable date for the surrender of Down and the remaining monasteries in East Ulster.

The final submission came in 1543 when the Bishop of Down and Connor, Eugene Magennis, surrendered his Papal Bull and accepted his bishopric from the King.[13]

The removal of the monasteries from the Irish countryside left a gaping void which the English administration was in no hurry to fill. In earlier days, the monks and friars had acted as pastors to the local community, providing not only pastoral oversight but also education and care of the sick as well; the sudden destruction and desecration of the religious houses removed at one stroke the parochial nucleus without making any provision for the celebration of Divine Service in its place. In medieval Ireland, the

Glazed tiles from Down Cathedral found by Mr Albert Colmer
DOWN COUNTY MUSEUM

ordinary people were closely bound to the old faith and many saw the new faith as a tool of conquest by the English government. The new religion had great difficulty establishing itself in Ulster as there were no clergy trained to take the leadership; the old religion continued to be practised underground.

For the remaining years of the sixteenth century, the record is silent about Down Cathedral. Bishops continued to be appointed to the United Dioceses and, with one remarkable exception, they were all Englishmen and there is no evidence that they even visited their dioceses, preferring the relative peace of Dublin and the social life surrounding the Crown's representative. Ulster and the tiny colony of Lecale were lost to the English; north Down (Clannaboy) was ruled by the powerful O'Neill family whilst south and west Down were under the control of the Magennis and Macartan families. In the early 1570s, a new form of colonisation was devised by the English; instead of sending over crown forces to conquer and hold the land, the country was parcelled out to private adventurers to conquer and hold at their own expense on the Crown's behalf, at a considerable saving to the Exchequer. In County Down, the first of these adventurers was Sir Thomas Smith who, with his son and a force of 100 men, landed at Strangford in 1572. Once more, the country became a battlefield as Smith tried to secure his position against the O'Neills but, after two years and the death of his son in battle, he gave up the unequal struggle.

Glazed tiles from Down Cathedral
ULSTER MUSEUM
SKETCHED IN ARCHAEOLOGICAL SURVEY OF COUNTY DOWN HMSO 1966

With the exception of an abortive incursion by the Earl of Essex, there was little further organised attempt by the English to settle in east Ulster but, in their stead, a large influx of Scots took place in Counties Down and Antrim; the Scots were, of course, equally hostile to the English. The final years of the century and indeed, of the reign of Queen Elizabeth, were to become the Nine Years War, as the three-cornered conflict was fought in Ulster. A letter, written by an English officer in August 1596, describes the chaos in Lecale:[14]

> Brian McArt [O'Neill] and others with all their forces preyed all the savages and tenants of Strangford and killed two or three. Then they came back to Down which they threatened to assault. They cut down all Captain Fitzgerald's wheat to his utter undoing and left never a cow from Down to Strangford.

Another version of events was given by Father McCana, a Franciscan friar who, in the course of a journey through east Down in 1643, had this to say about the Cathedral:[15]

> The impiety of an Englishmen whose name was Cromwell deserves to

be mentioned in this place with abhorrence. This son of earth, and foul spot on the human race, having been sent to Ireland by Queen Elizabeth in command, came with an army to the City of Down and set fire to the noble church and monastery of Saint Patrick, where even the reliques of Saints Patrick, Columba and Brigid were exposed to the fury of the flames. And there cannot be a doubt that many other sacred monuments, and very ancient writings, as I was told by old men who were alive at that time, perished in that conflagration.......I have been told by my grandfather that he was an eyewitness of that sacrilegious incendiarism and further that all churches, previous to that consumption, were lightly roofed and highly adorned with sacred statues and things.

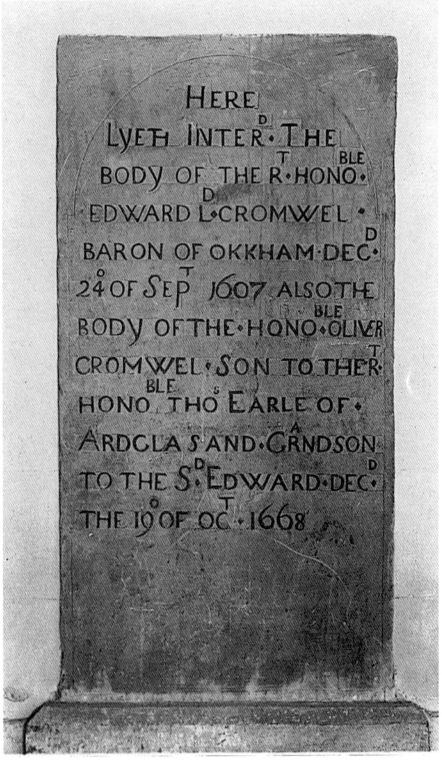

Cromwell's tombstone

The Cromwell on whom Father McCana lays the blame was Edward, a great grandson of Thomas Cromwell, who had been the principal architect of the suppression of the monasteries more than half a century earlier. He had come to Ireland with the Queen's forces in 1599 and was active in the north under Mountjoy, who was appointed Lord Lieutenant in 1600. If we are to believe Father McCana, the destruction which was blamed on St Leger in 1541, or by others on Grey in 1538-9, may not have taken place until the Nine Years War. On the cessation of the war, Cromwell exchanged his English property for the Barony of Lecale, owned by Mountjoy, who in turn held it from the Kildare estate.[16] Cromwell died in 1607 and was buried in the ruined cathedral; his tombstone has been relocated in the vestibule.

With the exception of successive episcopal appointments, the church is scarcely mentioned in the State Papers during the second half of the sixteenth century; none of these bishops is recorded as having visited their dioceses and were presumably occupied in court circles in Dublin. Sir William Russell, Lord Deputy 1594-7, records in his journal three Sundays in 1596 when the Bishop of Down preached in Dublin.[17]

This chalice (130mm in height, 70 mm across base) was dug up at Inch Abbey in 1866 and presented to Rt Rev. Dr Denvir, Roman Catholic Bishop of Down and Connor. It is dated 1632
COURTESY OF MONSIGNOR DR J. J. MAGUIRE

Eugene Magennis, the Bishop who had conformed to the reformed faith, died in 1564. Some years earlier, the powerful O'Neill family had tried to intrude a prior, even though the Priory no longer existed! This was in 1558, when Edmund O'Coyne, chaplain to Con, the Earl of Tyrone, obtained Papal Bulls for the priory of the Cathedral Church of Down. He was 'a man of good disposition and well learned in canon law'.[18] Following Magennis's death, James McCawell was nominated by the Crown but does not appear to have been consecrated or taken possession. Two months later, in the confusion which surrounded the appointments, the Pope provided Miler Magrath, a one-time Franciscan friar who, like O'Coyne, was a protege of the O'Neills, this time Shane. However, on Shane's death in 1567, Miler took the easy option of conforming and accepted his bishopric from Queen Elizabeth; he must have made a considerable impression on the Queen as, almost immediately, he was translated first to

Clogher in 1570 and then a year later to the archbishopric of Cashel, a benefice of much greater wealth and substance than Down and Connor and where he lived to a ripe old age.

John Merriman was Bishop from 1568 until 1571 and was followed by Hugh Allen, who probably came over with Sir Thomas Smith in 1572. Allen held the diocese for ten years until his translation to Ferns. The diocese then lay vacant for over eleven years, no doubt because of the unsettled state of the district with the consequent inability to attract a candidate. Eventually Edward Edgeworth, a 'learned grave man', was nominated by the Crown in 1593 on the recommendation of the Lord Deputy.[19] He died two years later and was followed by John Charden, who himself died in 1600. The Earl of Ormonde, Lord Lieutenant, recommended Mr Meredith Hanmer, his chaplain, for the vacancy, along with Dromore, Kilmore and Clogher [20] but, before he could be appointed, Mountjoy was in the Castle and recommended Robert Humpston, preacher to the garrison at Carrickfergus.[21] Humpston was consecrated in 1602 and was followed by John Todd in 1607.

It is customary for a newcomer to take stock of his possessions and so it was with the English in Ireland after the suppression of the monasteries. The collective estates of the monks probably represented the greatest single asset accruing to the English Crown. In May 1553, the Lord Chancellor, Sir Thomas Cusack, in his report on the state of Ireland, had this to say about Lecale and the Ards:[22]

> ...Lecaill, where McBrerton is farmer and captain, which is a handsome, plain and champion country of 10 miles long and 5 miles breadth, without any wood growing therein, The sea doth ebb and flow round about that country, so as in full water no man may enter therein upon dry land but in one way, which is less than two miles in length. The same country for English freeholders and good inhabitance is as civil as few places in the English Pale. The next country to that and the water of Strangfourde is Arde Savage his country, which hath been mere English, both pleasant and fair, by the sea, of length about 12 miles and 4 miles in breadth, abouts; which country is now in effect for the most part waste.

An inquisition was held at Greencastle under the chairmanship of Cusack on 10 August 1549 to determine the possessions of the monastery of Saint Patrick of Down.[23] Subsequently William Brabazon, the Treasurer, was granted the Manors of Lecale, Ardglass and Strangford.[24] Although Fitzgerald had been pardoned after the death of Henry VIII and returned to Ireland from exile, the regrant of his lands in 1552 related only to lands in Meath and Kildare.[25] A further commission was appointed in 1558 to determine the possessions in County Down of the late Earl of Kildare, father of the eleventh Earl.[26] The lands were regranted to him by Philip and Mary and were finally confirmed by Queen Elizabeth in 1570.[27]

8 versions exist of the ruins of the cathedral pre-1790. This one is in the British Library K.TOP.52.47.2A (Note east door)

EIGHT

THE CATHEDRAL IN RUINS

THE UNSETTLED STATE OF ULSTER during the reign of Elizabeth culminating in the Nine Years War left a trail of devastation, which for the the church meant inadequate leadership and few places of worship. In January 1607 the Lord Deputy, Sir Arthur Chichester, reported to the Earl of Salisbury on the death of Robert Humpston, Bishop of Down and Connor; by the same letter, he recommended Doctor Todd, Dean of Cashel as his successor, 'well known to my Lord of Canterbury',[1] and suggested that the relatively poor Bishopric of

The ruins, as drawn by the architect, Charles Lilly.
REPRODUCED IN CATHEDRAL GUIDE BOOK 1872

Dromore, worth £20, should be annexed to the Sees of Down and Connor which together were worth £120. Chichester also pointed out that these Sees had neither Deans nor Chapters and that the livings were disposed of by the Bishop and clergy. It was clear that a very unsatisfactory state of affairs existed and Chichester's advice on placing the Established Church on a firm footing was timely. Since the dissolution of the monasteries almost seventy years earlier, the Established Church of Ireland, as an organised institution, had virtually ceased to exist and equally certainly, as far as its pastoral role was concerned, meant little or nothing to the people. In the more remote parts of Ireland there was still, no doubt, a pastoral role being carried on by the Friars but the acceptance of the reformed faith by the people was achieving little success even in those parts of the country which were under English rule. The problem in the north east corner, Counties Antrim and Down, was compounded by the large influx of settlers from Scotland, adherents of Presbyterian orthodoxy and as equally uncompromising towards the Established Church as to Rome. James I, in spite of his Scottish ancestry, was shrewd enough to realise that he had to make some pretence of support for the Established Church in order to prevent the country sliding into an even more chaotic state. As part of this programme of stabilisation, a charter, dated 20 July 1609, was granted to the Dioceses of Down, Connor and Dromore, creating a cathedral church in each of the three, with four dignitaries and a number of lesser dignitaries known as prebendaries.[2] Together the persons holding these offices formed the chapter of the cathedral and spoke with one voice, an echo of the former monastery when the prior and his monks formed the chapter and spoke as one.

The charter pronounced another major change for Down Cathedral; henceforth it would be called the Cathedral Church of the Holy Trinity,[3] thus removing the dedication to Saint Patrick which had been given it over four hundred years earlier by de Courcy and reverting to the earlier dedication of the cathedral prior to the arrival of the Benedictines. John Todd, a Jesuit before his appointment as Dean of Cashel and subsequent elevation to the Sees of Down and Connor, was declared to be the first Bishop and was granted the See of Dromore *in commendam*. For their support, each member of the chapter was granted a number of rectories and vicarages i.e., the tythes arising from them but it also became their responsibility to provide a curate with pastoral oversight for each parish.

The first Dean named in the charter was John Gibbson; to the Deanery were attached the rectories and vicarages of Down, Saul, Greencastle [Castleskreen] in Bright Parish, Killemochan [unidentified], Kilbriditche [Kilbride, near Killough], Bright [alias Braten] and Ballyrichard [part of Comber parish].

The second dignitary was the Archdeacon, surprisingly, as the Archdeacon was not usually a capitular appointment. The Archdeacon so appointed was John Blakeborne and the Corps of the Archdeaconry comprised the rectories and vicarages of Killcliff [Kilclief], Killbeg, alias Kilbert [Ballykilbeg], Rosglas [near St. John's Point], Drumbo, Drumbegg and Capella Saint Malachiae [now Hillsborough].

The Chancellor was William Worsleye and to his office were appropriated Philipston [Ballyphillip, Portaferry], Troston [Ballytrustan, near Portaferry], Slane [in Ards], Rathmullan, Arglas [Ardglass] and Ardthuayle [Ardtole,near Ardglass].

John Marshall was the first Precentor and to his office were appropriated Kinles [Ballykinlar, part of Loughinisland], Stion [St. John's Point], Drumcadd [in Loughinisland], Racatt [now Clough], Boriston, Balliraga and Villa Bilesa [all unidentified] as well as Ballintympany [Magheratympany, near the Spa].

The Bishop, John Todd, reserved the Treasurership to himself and to the office were annexed the rectories and vicarages of Kilkaill [Kilkeel], Taulaght [a daughter church of Kilkeel in the townland of Lisnacree], Killmighan [Kilmegan] and Killcudua [Kilcoo], both daughter churches of Kilkeel.

The ruins of Killandras Church in the townland of Toye and Kirkland near Killyleagh. The prebend of Saint Andrew is named after this church

The Chapter of Down had three prebendaries appointed by the charter, Saint Andrew's, Talpestone and Dunsporte, thus preserving the geographical areas of the three adjacent baronies, Dufferin, Ards and Lecale. The first prebend of Saint Andrew's, to which John Christian was appointed, had appropriated to it Saint Andrew's [Killandras or Killarsey near Derryboye], Rosse [in Kilclief parish, near Ardtole], Killseaclan [a townland in Bright parish now called Carrowdresagh], Inis [Inch], Syth [now Ballygalget in Ards], Earchin [Ardkeen] and Killinseach

[Killinchy].

The second prebend, Talpestone, was granted to Patrick Hamilton and appropriated to it were Talpestone [Ballyhalbert], Ruda [near Inishargy],

Ruins of Down Cathedral.
Pencil drawing by Samuel Wooley,
later painted by Dr James Moore

Iniscarrge [Inishargy], Drumornan [probably near Balligan], Clontagh [Cluntagh, in Killyleagh parish], Leirg [in Loughinisland parish] and Ballekehulte [Ballyculter].

Dunsporte was granted to James Hamilton and to it were appropriated Dunsporte [Dunsford], Whitechurch [Ballywalter], Donoghdie [Donaghadee], Balleristard [probably Ballyrichard in Comber parish], Powley [Pawle Island?], Balleneskeans [Ballyskeagh, near Newtownards], Balleoran [in Dundonald parish], Knockcolumkill [Knock] and Bredagh [Breda].[4]

Thus were disposed almost all the rectories in the diocese among eight dignitaries. Many are now forgotten and remembered only by their names being still in use as townland or placenames. Reeves, in his invaluable *Ecclesiastical Antiquities,* takes us through each one, identifying it with a place on the map, where a church, or the memory of one, once existed and with the various occurrences of the name in medieval documents. Whilst it is certain that many of these churches had already ceased to exist by 1609, the incorporation of their names into the charter preserved the knowledge of their existence in medieval times when the countryside must have been dotted with tiny churches or chapels of ease, each surrounded by its burial ground. Lecale alone must have supported upwards of twenty churches although it is impossible to say now if they were all in use at the same time.

The Prebend of Saint Andrew's is of interest in that in recent times it has become associated erroneously with the Norman foundation of Black Abbey in the Ards, also dedicated to this saint. This is not so; the ruins of the church of Killandras [Church of Saint Andrew] still exist in the townland of Toye and Kirkland. The framers of the charter were also conscious of the geographical spread of the three prebends. The Parish of Saint Andrew's in the Ards was formed by a union of Ballywalter, Inishargy and Ballyobekin, as a result of a Regal Commission in 1693; the move was brought about through the dispersal of the parishes forming the corps of the prebend of Talpestone which ceased to exist in that year.[5]

The charter was modelled on that granted to Saint Patrick's Cathedral in Dublin in 1555, where the chapter also included the Archdeacon (until Disestablishment). A clause in the charter ordained that the chapter shall be 'in deed, fact and name, one body corporate and shall have perpetual succession and shall behave, have and occupy themselves according to and in conformity with the ordinances, rules, statutes, indulgences and privileges granted, ordained or made or hereafter to be granted, ordained or made to the Dean and Chapter of Saint Patrick's of Dublin in our Kingdom of Ireland'.[6] Nevertheless it is difficult to understand why this should have been thus, as the Down (and Connor and Dromore) Charter is, in essence, quite different from that of Saint Patrick's in Dublin. The latter quite properly abides by the Sarum Rite in the precedence accorded to its dignitaries i.e., Dean, Precentor, Chancellor, Treasurer, Archdeacon. The Down Charter provides for a somewhat different order of precedence: Dean, Archdeacon, Chancellor, Precentor, Treasurer.

There is an intriguing explanation for this extraordinary situation; the 1609 charter was framed on the precedence which then existed in Saint Paul's Cathedral in the City of London. The customary precedence in Saint Paul's depended on the date of collation to the dignity and consequently was (and is) never static. At the date of the charter, James I had just arrived from Scotland and there is reason to believe that he was favourably disposed towards Saint Paul's; thus, when he granted a new charter to the three Irish dioceses, he was anxious that they should emulate his Cathedral of Saint Paul in the city of London. Unfortunately the seventeenth century records of Saint Paul's are no longer extant, but that this peculiar situation existed there is no doubt, from an examination of Crockford's Clerical Directory over a period of years.[7]

If the grant of this charter went a long way towards the stabilisation of ecclesiastical affairs and the provision of pastoral care, it did not provide any funds with which to build or rebuild the cathedral which was lying in ruins. Nevertheless the intention on the part of parliament to rebuild the cathedral was not far away. By 1611, there was a proposal to bring forward an Act in the Irish parliament for the re-edifying and repairing of cathedral and parochial churches;

Down was among those listed for re-edification.[8] But the financial resources were not forthcoming and the proposal was dropped. Again in 1637, the Bishop of Down, Henry Leslie, wrote to the Archbishop of Canterbury:[9]

> Since I came here I have had many troubles and may say I have fought with beasts. I have now almost settled the rights of my See and brought my people to conformity but the greatest work of all, the building of the cathedral, has not yet been done and cannot be without some general purse or his Majesty's favour in granting some part of the fines of the Court of High Commission.

Archbishop Laud consulted with Wentworth, the Lord Deputy, on the practicability of this proposal and then gave his consent but wrote that it would be a charge on the whole diocese 'to be raised upon the abler sort, not upon the poor people'.[10] Although the proposal was brought to the King's notice, no further action was taken.

Thus, for almost two centuries, the history of the cathedral becomes in reality the story of the deans and chapters who continued to hold office, as provided in the charter, in spite of not having a cathedral in which to worship. In fact, with two exceptions, the Bishops of the United Dioceses during this period appear to have had little or no concern with Down. Firstly, Henry Leslie, noted above, made some effort to have the cathedral rebuilt – but he had been Dean for eight years before his elevation to the episcopate, the only Dean to have been so elevated within his own diocese. The other exception was Francis Hutchinson who was enthroned within the cathedral ruins on 1 February 1721. There was, however, an understandable reason for this lack of interest on the part of the Bishops. In 1662, when the country was recovering from the effects of the Commonwealth and Jeremy Taylor had been brought over from England by Viscount Conway of Kilultagh, initially as a private chaplain and then to occupy the Sees of Down and Connor, Charles II, with whom Taylor had considerable influence, granted a patent erecting the parish church of Lisburn into the Cathedral of the United Dioceses on the grounds that the Cathedrals of Down and Connor were 'not only ruinous and waste but were also built in inconvenient places'.[11] Henceforth the Bishop's seat was in Lisburn and for the most part they resided there; the likelihood of rebuilding Down seemed further away than ever.

Many of the deans, and indeed other members of the chapter, have left their mark on history, even though they had little to do in the way of formal duties at the Cathedral. Appointed in the 1609 Charter, the first Dean was John Gibbson, who served the cure of Bangor and was maintained by James Hamilton, later Viscount Clannaboy. Gibbson was a Presbyterian minister brought over from Scotland by Hamilton, conforming to the Established Church simply in order to avoid the hardships then the lot of the non-conformists. When on his death bed,

Gibbson requested another Presbyterian, Robert Blair, to preach in his stead. Blair later wrote:[12]

> Likewise the dying man did several ways to encourage me. He professed great sorrow for having been a Dean. He condemned episcopacy more strongly than ever I durst do. He charged me in the name of Christ, and as I expected his blessing on my ministry, not to leave that good way wherein I had begun to walk; and then drawing my head towards his bosom with both his arms, he laid his hands on my head and blessed me.

Gibbson died in 1623 and was buried in Bangor Abbey where a tablet to his memory can still be seen.

Robert Dawson, 'a man of discretion, learning and integrity', held the Deanery for a short time[13] and on his elevation to the See of Clonfert, Henry Leslie was appointed Dean; the year was 1628 and he was concurrently Prebendary of Connor in that Diocese and Treasurer of Saint Patrick's in Dublin. Leslie laboured to promote episcopalianism, unlike his Bishop, Robert Echlin, who often turned a blind eye to the Presbyterians, even to the point of ordaining certain of them. In 1633, the Lords Justices wrote to the English Privy Council:[14]

> recommending Dean Leslie going to England. He has done much to keep down the schism in his Diocese and at his own expense recovered the rights of the church and has built manses and chancels for the good of his successors.

Henry Leslie
Dean of Down 1627-1635

Bramhall, then Bishop of Derry, wrote to Laud, Archbishop of Canterbury, on 20 July 1635:[15]

> The United Bishopric of Down and Connor is vacant since last Friday when the Bishop [Echlin] died. If a Disciplinarian should succeed him, farewell hopes of better order and revenue. . . . People wholly Scottish, no man so well acquainted with it as Dean Leslie, nor more capable, if it please you to commend him.

And so Leslie was elevated to the Bishopric of Down and Connor; with almost the entire Irish bench, he fled the country in 1641 on the outbreak of the rebellion. A sermon, preached at Breda in the Low Countries, in 1649 before Charles II, also in exile, is extant.[16] At the Restoration, however, he returned to Ireland and, for his loyalty to the Royalist cause, was rewarded with the Bishopric of Meath.

The new Dean was an Englishman, William Coote, a Cambridge graduate.[17] It is thought that he favoured the parliamentary party and probably remained in Ireland during the Commonwealth period as a consequence. The 1657 inquisition states that in 1640 he served the cure himself, but he must have been dead by 1657 as Down, in that year, was only served by a Preacher in Salary every second Lord's Day. There were no appointments in the Established Church until the Restoration and Down did not have another Dean until 1662; he was Thomas Bayly, again a Cambridge scholar but in addition he held a TCD doctorate. Bayly had come to the notice of Jeremy Taylor in England as a highly-learned man and it was Taylor who invited him to Ireland. Not only was he secured in the Deanery of Down by Taylor, but he was also Pro Vice-Chancellor of TCD, while Taylor himself was Vice-Chancellor. Concurrrently he also held the Archdeaconry of Dromore, a dignity also in Taylor's gift. His tenure of these offices, however, was short lived as his learning marked him out for the bench; by 1664 he was elevated to the Sees of Killala and Achonry.

Daniel Wytter succeeded, through the influence of the Lord Lieutenant, the Duke of Ormonde, to whom he had acted as Chaplain, enjoying the Deanery (along with the Chancellorship of Dromore) until 1669 when he became Bishop of Killaloe.

William Sheridan was installed in the Deanery in 1669. He was the son of a Roman Catholic priest, who had been converted by Bishop Bedell. Sheridan occupied the Deanery until 1682 when he, too, was elevated to the bench as Bishop of Kilmore and Ardagh; he was an ancestor of the Dufferin family of Clandeboye. His successor was Benjamin Phipps, who also held prebends in both Christ Church and Saint Patrick's Cathedrals in Dublin and in addition was Dean of Ferns. His death took place less than 12 months later.[18] John McNeale, a son-in-law of Archbishop Francis Marsh of Dublin was presented in 1683, largely as a result of Marsh's influence. His brother, Archibald, was installed as Chancellor of the diocese two years later. The Vestry Book of Down Parish is still extant;[19] at the first recorded meeting on 15 April 1704, John McNeale signed as Rector of Down. He died in 1709 and a tablet to his memory was erected by his son in the parish church.

Ralph Lambert succeeded, again through the influence of the Lord Lieutenant, the Earl of Wharton, to whom he had acted as Chaplain, prior to which he had occupied the precentor's stall in Down, which carried with it the rectory of Loughinisland. The vestry book, already referred to, gives us more glimpses of the chapter's activities, insofar as they impinged upon the parish church, (although it is clear that the vestry felt responsible for the site of the old Abbey) from this period and it is possible to learn more about them than heretofore. Dean Lambert was instrumental in raising money to build a belfry in the parish church; although he was no

William Sheridan
Dean of Down 1669-1682
Bishop of Kilmore 1682-1693

Ralph Lambert
Dean of Down 1709-1717
Bishop of Dromore 1717-1726
Bishop of Meath 1726-1731/2

longer Dean, his efforts were crowned with success – a minute in the book reads: *the bells were hung 27 August 1718.*

Lambert was elevated to the Bishopric of Dromore in 1717 and was succeeded by Benjamin Pratt. Pratt had been Provost of Trinity College Dublin, one of the various steps available for preferment in the Established Church. A friend of Swift, who described him as a man of wit and learning, he frequently absented himself from college in order to mix in London society. He was a victim of political circumstance, a Tory who fell out of favour with the accession of the Whigs in 1714 and the departure of his patron, the Duke of Ormonde, from Dublin Castle. It is said that he had hoped for at least a Bishopric and was disappointed to be awarded only the Deanery of Down![20] Nevertheless, in the few years before his death in 1721, he took an active interest in parish affairs and left a legacy of £50 to the parish as well as £200 to found the diocesan school.

Although his successor, Charles Fairfax, was to be Dean for only two years before his death, he carried forward a project, initiated by Dean Lambert, of having a residence near the cathedral and for this purpose summoned a meeting of the chapter to make the necessary arrangements with Edward Southwell, the proprietor of the Manor of Downpatrick, for the exchange of the present glebe lands with other lands more beneficial to the Dean and his successors.

Benjamin Pratt
Dean of Down 1717-1721
THE PROVOST AND FELLOWS, TRINITY COLLEGE, DUBLIN

Vestry books are perceptive sources for illuminating customs of the period; none more so than Down. At a meeting of the Vestry presided over by Dean Fairfax, the purchase of a velvet pall for the use of the poor was authorised, the following rates to be charged for its use: in the town 16s 3d and in the country 16s 6d; for the use of cloaks in the town 1s 6d and in the country 2s; for the use of the cloth pall in the town 2s 8°d and in the country 3s 6d. Under Dean Fairfax, it was also agreed to raise 40 shillings cess off the parish in order to enclose the churchyard of the Cathedral. Fairfax died in 1723 and was succeeded by William Gore who had been Dean of Saint Macartin's Cathedral in the Diocese of Clogher. Gore carried on the fund-raising efforts of his predecessor towards the complete rebuilding of the parish church but he did not live to see its completion.

Among the Leslie MSS in the Public Record Office of Northern Ireland is an interesting document giving the value of the Deanery of Down in 1723, the year of William Gore's appointment.[21] The great and small tythes were valued at £1253 17s 6d and the charges against that sum were

Rev Mr Brett's salary	£20.0.0	Curate of Rathmullan
Rev Mr Gregory's salary	£50.0.0	Curate of Down
Rev Mr Kelly's salary	£42.10.0	Curate of Ballee and Ballyculter
Rev Mr Brown's salary	£20.0.0	
Rev Mr Carson's salary	£40.0.0	
King's rent	£8.18.8	
Port Corn	£10.0.0	
Latin schoole	£3.0.0	
2 English schools in Ballee and Ballyculter	£4.0.0	
2 English schools in p'ish of Down and Saul	£4.3.4	
Proxies	£5.7.5	
Sequestration fee	£97.0.0	
	£304.19.5	
Neat proceeds to be divided between present Dean and widow of late Dean	£948.18.1	
	£1253.17.6	

Richard Daniel was installed in the Deanery on 13 March 1732. He had been Dean of Armagh but owing to a lawsuit involving the Primate, was obliged to seek another preferment. His litigious nature is evident from an extensive correspondence still extant between Dean Daniel, the landlord Edward Southwell and the latter's agent, Trotter.[22] Southwell had founded the school which bore his name in 1733, using his own money as well as Dean Pratt's legacy of £200. The schoolmaster, Butler, had been appointed by Dean Gore and, in 1738 was summarily dismissed by Trotter, acting on orders from Southwell. He was allegedly more often drunk than not and had been chastised by the Dean with his cane, who, nevertheless, was under the impression that he could not dismiss him because of possible interference from the Bishop or the landlord. But when Trotter dismissed him, the Dean took exception to this usurpation of his authority and wrote to Southwell making his point very clear. Southwell penned a reply in which he stuck to his decision, not giving in to the arrogant and haughty Dean, but before forwarding it, decided to take legal advice. One of the Dean's objections was that the new schoolmaster appointed by Trotter, a Mr Day, did not have the Bishop's licence to teach. Eventually Southwell conceded most of the Dean's wishes, but it is not clear if Butler was re-appointed. Dean Daniel's tenure of office saw the building, not only of the Southwell schools, but also the Southwell almshouses and the completion and consecration of the new parish church in 1735, to which he personally subscribed £100.

On his death in 1739, his successor was Thomas Fletcher, an Englishman, Chaplain to the Lord Lieutenant, the Duke of Devonshire. Whilst we know that he was installed in the ruins of the Cathedral, it is probable that this was his only visit to Down. There is no further record of him and Mrs Delany, the wife of his successor, wrote that the good people of Down told her that, during six years, Dean Fletcher spent only two days in the Deanery.[23] He became Bishop of Dromore in 1744.

The next Dean to be appointed to Down was perhaps the best remembered, certainly of those who served in the eighteenth century: Patrick Delany, or, as his signature in the parish vestry book shows simply, Pat Delany. He had a brilliant career at TCD and was a member of the literary circle which included Swift and Sheridan. Whilst in Down, where it seems he only spent the summer months, he lived initially at Mount Panther, then the home of the Rev Edward Mathews, Precentor of Down, and latterly at Hollymount. Prior to his arrival in Down, he had been Chancellor of both Dublin Cathedrals where his future second wife, Mary Granville, heard him preach:[24]

> Last Sunday I went to hear Dr Delany preach and was extremely pleased with him; his sermon was on the duties of wives to husbands, a subject of no great use to me at present! He has an easy pathetical manner of preaching that pleases me mightily!

Patrick Delany
Dean of Down 1744-1768
Enamel on Copper
THE NATIONAL GALLERY OF IRELAND

When they eventually married, it was her ambition which sought promotion for her D.D., as she called him, and he was presented to the Deanery of Down on 16 July 1744, a living evidently worth more than some of the smaller bishoprics. Although he still had commitments in Dublin, where he was Rector of Glasnevin, Delany undertook his new duties with enthusiasm, building the new church at Bright at his own expense and contributing to the rebuilding of the church at Ballee, in addition to re-roofing Down parish church, which apparently had not been built to last! Again, the vestry book of the parish church shows that the vestry was not unmindful of the needs of the cathedral as we find an item in the accounts of 7 June 1756 for the payment of ten shillings for a five bar gate at the old abbey.

Not only did Dean Delany carry out his administrative duties assiduously but he was appalled to find the pastoral care of the poor and sick had been sadly neglected by the resident curate; indeed members of the Established Church had been attracted to other churches. He set himself the task of visiting every home in the parish and, although his visits to the town were seasonal, a marked improvement was noted in church attendance.[25] In 1767 he took part in the annual distribution of carcases of beef to the poor.[26] His last years were marked by increasing illness and he died at Bath in 1768 at the age of 83; he was buried at Glasnevin. Mrs Delany, so well known to later generations for her writings and observations on contemporary society, survived her husband by twenty

Opposite:
Page from Vestry book of Down parish showing installations of Cathedral dignitaries 1721-1742
THE RECTOR OF DOWN PARISH

ye Revd Father in god Fran: Hutchinson Bishop of down and Connor was installd in down ye first day February in ye year 1720/21 of our Lord god 1721

ye Revd dean of down Charls fearfax was installed ye 3 of march in ye year 1721/22

Francis Hutchinson Lord Bishop of Down and Connor was Enthron'd in ye Cathedral of Downpatrick The First day of February Annoque Domini 1720/1

Benjamen Pratt Reverend dean was Installd the 10th June in ye year 1718 but died ye 6th decemr 1721

Charles Fairfax was Install'd Dean of Down The 3d of March 1721/2

& died ye 27th of July in ye year 1723

The Revd William Gore was Installed Dean of down ye 29th day february in ye year of our Lord god 1723/4 & Dyed ye 7th Janry 1731/2

The Revd Mr Samuel Hutchison was Enstalld chancellor of Portafery the 2d August Ano Dom 1728

Samuel Huchenson was Installed in ye cathedral of down ye 24th of march ye in ye year 1724

The Revd Henry Daniel was Installd Prebendary of Dunsport in the Cathedral of Down July 27th 1728

ye Revd Henry Daniel of Dunsport was installd in the Cathedral July 27th 1728

The Revd Dr Anthony Rogers Parish Minist of Lisburn was Installd in the Cathedrall Chancelor of Portifery Novemr the 21 1731

The Revd Richard Daniel was Installd Dean of Down March the 13th 1732 and Died the 1 May 1739

The Revd Francis Hutchinson was Installd Arch Deacon of Down the 10th Day of September 1733

The Revd Vear Essex Lenorgan Parish Minister of Saintfield was Installed Prebend of Dunsport in the Cathedrall the 2th June Anno 1736

Saturday 23rd June 1739 Died the Rt Revd Francis Lord Bishop of Down & Connor at his Seat at Portlehone

Saturday 20th October 1739 The Revd Doctr Thomas Fletchar was Installd Dean of Downe

Novemr 1739 The Rt Revd Carew Reynolds Was Enthroned Bishop of Down & Connor by Proxey of ye Revd Doctor Mathews

28 March 1741 The Revd Benjamin Barrington Was Enstalld Chancellor of Portaffery

years, moving easily in London society in the circle of George III.

James Dickson, Rector of Seapatrick (Banbridge), was next appointed Dean but he does not appear to have taken up residence in Downpatrick although his signature appears in the vestry book. James Dickson was the father of both William, appointed Bishop of Down and Connor in 1783 and of John, who became Prebendary of Dunsport in 1782 and later Archdeacon.

On Dickson's death in 1787, the Honorable and Reverend William Annesley, from the Castlewellan family, became Dean and took up residence in Downpatrick almost immediately. Two years later, he purchased Oakley, a mansion and large estate in the townland of Ballydargan, employing the architect and builder, Charles Lilly, to carry out improvements to the house.[27] To Annesley, together with Wills Hill, the Earl of Hillsborough, is due the credit for the restoration of the Cathedral over the next decade.

During these two centuries when the Cathedral lay in ruins and roofless, it would appear that a number of Deans and other dignitaries and at least one Bishop were installed within the walls of the building. A list of these installations is given in the vestry book of the parish church.[28] Although the surroundings must have been somewhat unusual, there was clearly a symbolic significance in carrying out these ceremonies in the old Cathedral. The graveyard was, of course, still in use and the building would still have been regarded as consecrated and hallowed ground. As with all church ruins, burial within the walls came to be highly prized – an echo of earlier times when Cathedral Hill was regarded as the burial place of Saint Patrick and people were eager to be buried alongside him. Two important burials took place within the walls during this century (apart from the Cromwell family in the previous century) which afford a glimpse of the position which the Cathedral occupied as a national shrine. Thomas Jackson, the Presbyterian minister (not the curate of the parish as quoted by Pooler),[29] was interred in 1708 and the inscription on his tombstone is quoted by Harris.[30] Dr Edmund O'Doran, the Roman Catholic Bishop of Down and Connor died on 18 June 1760 and was interred in the ruins of the Cathedral.[31] According to O'Laverty, when the Cathedral was being rebuilt thirty years later, 'his bones were carted outside' and his tombstone broken.[32] Aynsworth Pilson, writing in the *Downpatrick Recorder*, tells us that, at the time of rebuilding, 'it was necessary to remove a large quantity of soil which had accumulated round the building, the result of extensive burials for 250 years. Coffins were heaped upon coffins with little earth to cover them; the space within the walls was equally crowded. Large quantities of soil were drawn away to the adjacent fields which were used to cultivate onions. The local wags proclaimed that the onions were the soil of decomposed bodies, with the unfortunate result that the sale of onions ceased in Downpatrick market, driving the onion sellers out of town'.[33]

Vine-leaf ornament
A. R. HOGG

Space does not permit a detailed account of the succession in each dignity in the Chapter; a full list can be found in appendix 4. Nevertheless, a close examination of the lists tells us much about the state of the Church of Ireland in the seventeenth and eighteenth centuries. He would be blind who would not admit to a considerable degree of nepotism; one's appointment all too frequently depended on family connections or marrying into the right family. Having been Chaplain to the Lord Lieutenant was also a useful step on the ladder of preferment. The 1723 statement of the value of the Deanery demonstrates that the senior members of the Chapter were in receipt of considerable emoluments but the poor curate existed at a very lowly level, perhaps for his entire career. Such was the concern over money that even Dean Leslie complained in 1630 that the King had usurped the rectories of Ballee, Ballyculter and Tyrella;[34] the case was ultimately settled in court and the rectories granted to Leslie although Ballee was still in dispute in 1664.

Grotesque ornament
A. R. HOGG

At the beginning of this chapter, it was noted that each member of the Chapter was granted a number of rectories; in practice, of course, only one rectory could have a resident rector and whilst he enjoyed the tythes of the other parishes in his prebend, he had to provide a resident curate in those in which he did not have the cure of souls. In some cases, the prebendary did not even reside in his parish and had to provide a curate there also; in other words the job was a sinecure. After the 1609 Charter, the Dean was normally the Rector of the parish of Down and with few exceptions, appears to have lived in the town. Perhaps the most notable exception was, in fact, the first Dean, John Gibbson, who was obviously Rector of Bangor, although, having been appointed by Sir James Hamilton, it was quite evident that he was of the Presbyterian faith.

In the early years, the Archdeaconry does not appear to have been tied to any particular parish, but following the rise of the Hill family, the principal county

Capitals
A. R. HOGG

family with its seat at Hillsborough, it became the custom for the Rectors of Hillsborough to occupy the Archdeacon's stall. In 1762, the Earl of Hillsborough, Wills Hill, gave a house and land to the Archdeacon, Francis Hutchinson, and from then until Disestablishment in 1870, the Archdeacon lived in Hillsborough.[35] There was one exception; Ralph Ward, Archdeacon 1782-4, was Rector of Knockbreda.

The Chancellors were Rectors of the parish of Ballyphilip [Portaferry]; in fact, the installations recorded in the Down vestry book refer to those being installed as 'Chancellors of Portaferry'. A study of the biographical details in Leslie's succession list would suggest that few, if any, of the Chancellors ever set foot in Portaferry.[36] The office of Precentor was linked to the parish of Loughinisland and with the exception of Bernard Ward, Rector of Knockbreda 1730-70, it would seem that, during their period of office, each of the Precentors lived in the parish. Edward Mathews, in fact, lived at Mount Panther within a mile or two of Loughinisland parish church and it was here that Dean Delany and his wife made their home during their early years in Downpatrick.

The first two Treasurers held dual office; they were also the Bishops of the Diocese, Todd and Echlin. Todd was deprived of his bishopric for selling off much of the See property and for unlawful separation from his wife;[37] Echlin farmed the office out to a layman.[38] Thereafter is a long gap in the succession

Conjectural plan of original 13th century Benedictine Abbey by J. J. Phillips
THE IRISH BUILDER VOL XXI No 470 15 JULY 1879

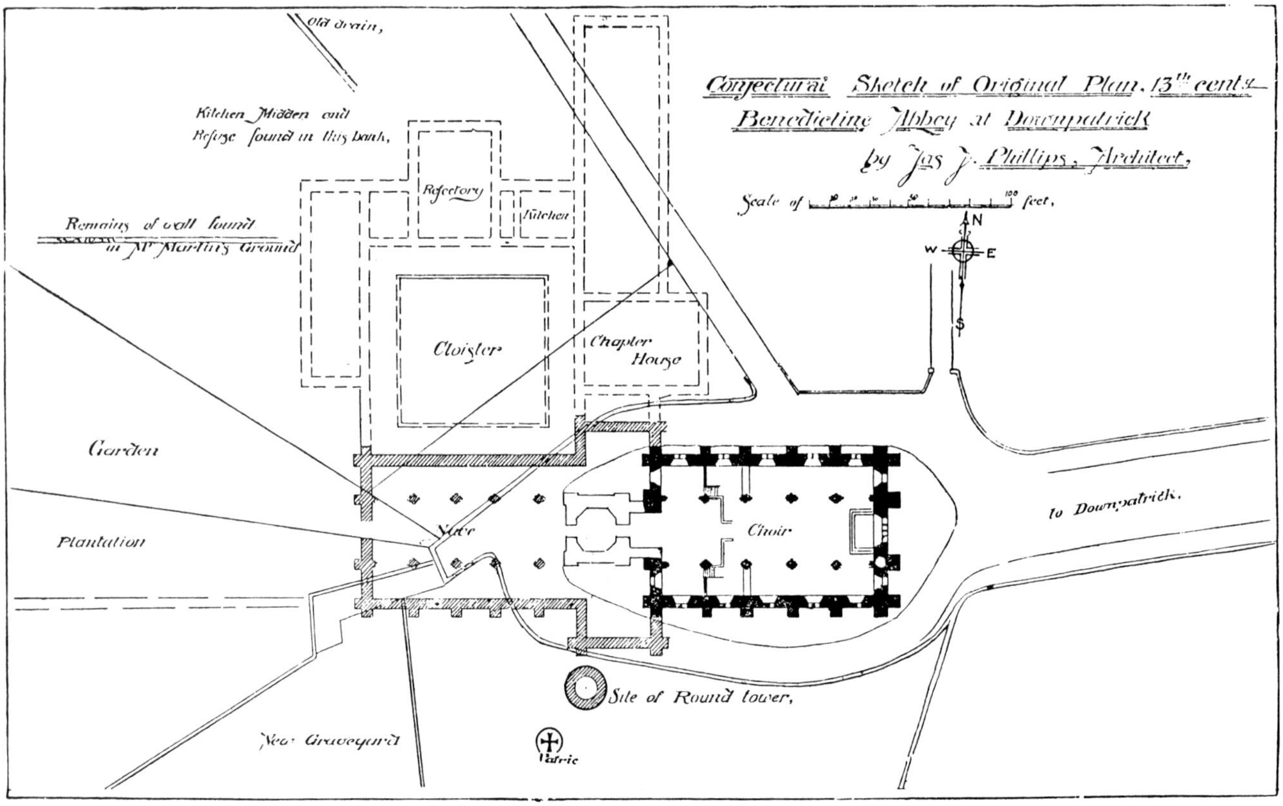

until 1693 and of the five treasurers between then and 1790, at least three were Rectors of Kilkeel, a parish in the prebend. A dispute lasting several centuries between successive Bishops and successive Earls of Kilmorey, who held jurisdiction over the Exempt Jurisdiction of Newry and Mourne, made the appointment of a Treasurer by the Bishop hardly worth while as the tithe income from the parishes of the prebend was retained by the lay proprietor. This anomalous situation was terminated at Disestablishment in 1870.

Although the parish of Inch was nominally attached to the prebend of Saint Andrew's, Edward Benson was the first prebendary to serve the cure himself (he was responsible for building the present church at Inch); the remainder employed curates. A matter of some curiosity is that five consecutive prebendaries 1745-1842 were Connor men, four of these being granted faculties to hold the parish of Ballintoy concurrently with the prebend. The first three, Ryder, Lodge and Trotter, employed curates at Ballintoy; the fourth, Anthony Traill, resigned the prebend on his appointment as Archdeacon of Connor but the fifth, Robert Trail, brother of Anthony, (spelling his name with one l) resided at Ballintoy (he built the rectory, Mount Druid, and died there, at an advanced age in 1842) and employed curates at Inch. The second prebend, Talpestone, has had a chequered history. It is thought that the first occupant of the stall, Patrick Hamilton, never came to Ireland and may have been a brother of Sir James; in any case, he was deprived by the Primate in 1622 for non-residence.[39] The stall remained vacant for over 70 years when we find John Francis instituted in 1692. Less than a year later, however, a Regal Commission declared him not to have been properly elected and he retired immediately, the parishes in his prebend being redistributed. Although not included in Leslie's published succession list, amongst the MSS which he left is the name of Stafford Lightburne, installed as Prebendary of Talpestone in 1691.[40] Dunsport does not seem to have been linked to any particular parish although Ardglass would have been the obvious central point. Only one prebendary, Henry Leslie, was Rector of Ardglass and Ballyculter although, to be fair, Vere Essex Lonergan was Rector of Saintfield, not very far away.

The student of ecclesiastical preferment will find much of interest in the chronological comparison of each of the Cathedral dignitaries; nepotism was the order of the day. Francis Hutchinson, Archdeacon 1733-68, was a nephew of the eponymous Bishop, 1721-39, and brother of the Archdeacon of Connor, later Bishop of Killala; Trevor Benson, Archdeacon 1768-82, son of the Prebendary of Saint Andrew's 1706-41, was a brother-in-law of Archdeacon Hutchinson.

John Dickson, Archdeacon 1790-1814, was the Dean's son and the Bishop's brother. Edward Trotter, Prebendary of Saint Andrew's 1761-77, was Dean Dickson's son-in-law and therefore brother-in-law to the Bishop and the

Archdeacon, although, to be fair, his was the first appointment.

John McNeale, Dean 1682-1709, was a son-in-law of Francis Marsh, Archbishop of Dublin and grandson of Jeremy Taylor. John Ryder, Prebendary of Saint Andrew's 1745-59 was the son of the Diocesan Bishop 1743-51; Robert Trail, who held the same prebend 1782-1841 was the nephew of the Diocesan Bishop 1765-83; Sir Richard Wolseley, Precentor 1791-1823, was a son-in-law of his predecessor, Jeremiah Symes, another of whose daughters was the wife of Bishop Dickson.

There are other cross relationships but this short list is sufficient to prove the point that the word preferment meant just that. If the lowly curate could not get his foot on the first rung of the preferment ladder, his lot remained a bleak one. Relationships between members of the Chapter were not always as cordial as one might expect. During Dean Dickson's period of office (when he was also Rector of Seapatrick), Rev Edward Trotter held the Prebend of Saint Andrew's (he was also Rector of Ballintoy in the Diocese of Connor). Trotter had, in additon, inherited from his father the office of agent to the Southwell estate. In 1770 he wrote to his master, Lord de Clifford:[41]

> You have gratified to the full the unreasonable vanity of our absurd Dean, who shows your letter with the plume of self-importance. You will smile when I tell you that tho' I dislike this man much, his daughter and I have settled the preliminaries of a bargain for life; she is not handsome, but entirely to my taste. . . . . her father received my proposal very graciously but when we came to talk of her fortune, he bitched, as I have heard you call it, and I am convinced means very unhandsomely – I am determined, however, that I will have the girl tho' without one shilling.

The marriage took place on 20 December 1771.

NINE

THE CATHEDRAL RESTORED

Panoramic view of Downpatrick showing the cathedral with the spire which was never built. A cartouche from Williamson's map, 1810. The original is in the Linen Hall Library
DOWN COUNTY MUSEUM

ON THE DEATH OF DEAN DICKSON in 1787, the Honorable and Reverend William Annesley was appointed Dean; his previous incumbency had been in the parish of Drumgooland. Annesley was a brother of both the first and second Earls Annesley, sons of Viscount Glerawley; on his maternal side, he had Beresford blood. He came to live in Downpatrick almost immediately, throwing himself into the work of the Deanery and two years later purchased Oakley, in the townland of Ballydargan, which was to remain his home for the rest of his life. Within the same space of time, he had made plans to restore the Cathedral and had enlisted the support of Wills Hill, the Earl of Hillsborough, without whose help and contacts at the highest level, the project could never have got off the ground. The earl, now in his 71st year, had held high public office in both the Westminster and Dublin parliaments and in this same year, 1789, was created first Marquis of Downshire as a reward for his long career of public service. Some 16 years earlier, he had built the beautiful church at Hillsborough as well as being instrumental in building the parish churches of Clonduff [Hilltown] and Drumbo. Downshire evidently cherished the idea of making Hillsborough the Cathedral Church of the Diocese and carried his ideas into effect to the extent of incorporating therein a Bishop's throne, but the proximity of Lisburn as the Cathedral Church of the United Dioceses of Down and Connor made that proposition difficult to sustain and, in any case, Down was the historic diocesan Cathedral. It is to his everlasting credit that he threw his considerable weight and influence wholeheartedly behind the plans to restore Down. Charles Lilly, the architect and builder, was a Dubliner and appears to have been in the employment of Downshire or, at least, in the position of being recommended by him. Little is known of his background, although by the turn of the century he was to take a lease of a farm on Downshire's Wicklow estate at Blessington. He was employed by Annesley to remodel Oakley and is also known to have been responsible for a number of other houses and public buildings in County Down around this period, notably Ballykilbeg House, Portaferry House, Downpatrick Gaol and Drumbo Parish Church. [1]

Lord Hillsborough's first duty was to inform the Lord of the Manor, but as the new Lord de Clifford was still a minor, he wrote to his guardian, Lord Vernon, on 21 June 1789. Referring to the state of the Cathedral, he wrote:[2]

> . . . the economy of it has been lost and there is no support for the service; the Chapter consists of a Dean, Archdeacon, Chancellor, Treasurer, Precentor and two Prebendaries and the Dean is willing out of his own income to establish a choir to consist of a Chaplain, two Vicars Choral, eight Choristers, an Organist, a Verger and a Housekeeper at £200 a year and £100 a year for repairs to the Cathedral, provided the gentlemen of the county will, by subscription, build a new Cathedral Church. It is my opinion that such a subscription may be easily obtained as will complete a proper edifice for this purpose which will indeed be honourable and decent for the county and very much tend to bring the inhabitants of Down to the Established Church who are now misled by Popish priests and fanatic preachers. The sum we propose to raise is £5000 and as everybody is particularly fond of the scheme, I have no doubt of it's being easily done.

A few weeks later, the Dean and Chapter, meeting at Downpatrick, passed a number of resolutions which got the project under way:[3]

> We the said Dean and Chapter having taken into consideration the ruinous state of our Cathedral and having long hoped and wished from

the assistance of well disposed men that the same might be repair'd so far as to shew a convenient Church without expecting ever to restore the splendour and magnificence of the ancient building, have until lately despaired of carrying our wishes into execution. We are however called upon from the duty we owe to ourselves, to our successors, to the Publick at large, and to posterity to embrace and lay hold of the generous offers that have lately been made to aid this undertaking and we lament that from the troubles and confusions that many years have disturbed this Kingdom, the Economy of our ancient Cathedral have (sic) been lost without a fund equal to support such an edifice and discharging the duties relating to it, all attempts heretofore to rebuild the same has (sic) been ineffectual, but the present Dean has generously proposed to remove that difficulty and appropriate tyths (sic) from his Deanry (sic) equal in value during his incumbency to £300 p annum provided this plan shall take effect and be settled by Act of Parliament to bind his successors, his schemes for the support of the Cathedral and choir, service to be administered therein all Sundays and hallidays (sic) and every Wednesday in the year as soon as £5000 shall be paid into the hands of, or received from subscriptions to be gather'd for that purpose.

To allow for a Chaplain	£50. 0. 0
Two Vicars Choral	£50
An Organist	£40
Eight choristers at £4 each	£32
a Schoolmaster	£10
a Verger	£8
Organblower and Bellringer	£5
Housekeeper	£5
for repairs of the church, elements	£100
	£300

We are further encouraged in the prosecution of this scheme by a Nobleman of this County having laid our plans before the Lord Lieut. who has promised to recommend to his Majesty to grant £1000 to assist us in case we compleat (sic) subscriptions for this purpose. We are also informed that on application to the Board of First Fruits, £500 may be had for what we call so laudable an undertaking.

We have had a survey and estimate from a skilfull (sic) architect who proposes to execute the work for £5000 and as upwards of £3000 has already been engaged for previous to this solemn Act of Chapter, we have no doubt from the assistance of a noble Earl who through the whole Tenor of his life has given undented and convincing proofs how much he has at heart the good of our Establishment in Church and State and also in the present instance pointed out to us the method

> leading us into the way to carry our scheme into execution that our Cathedral may be rebuilt and restored and we agree to perform our part. . .

John Brett was appointed Actuary and Receiver for the subscriptions and a later entry in the Chapter Book reported that Mr Charles Lilly was to be paid five pounds by the hundred for the money expended in the work and fifteen pounds a year to enable him to pay a clerk to state his account

> provided Mr Lilly shall from time to time and at all times hereafter during his continuing in our employ render when required a just, true

Wills Hill, the First Marquis of Downshire: PORTRAIT BY POMPEO BATONI THE ULSTER MUSEUM

> and satisfactory account of his several disbursements and expenditures and in every other account conduct himself as a faithful agent as a true accountant ought to do.

Senex, writing in the *Downpatrick Recorder* on 19 October 1861, some 70 years later, remembered seeing the Marquis of Downshire in Downpatrick in 1790, along with the architect, Mr Charles Lilly, inspecting the works. Besides restoring the fabric of the church and erecting two octagonal spires on top of the turrets at the east gable, pinnacles were also erected on top of the twelve buttresses on the north and south sides of the building. By 1792, the Marquis was able to write that the ruins had already been reroofed,[4] but apart from these bare facts, we have little record of the progress of the work. Where we do have abundant record, however, is in the matter of raising subscriptions to enable the work to be carried on. As even to-day when raising money, it is useful to have a big name behind the appeal and in this capacity it is very evident that the Marquis acted not only with outstanding generosity himself, but personally wrote solicitous letters to all the Irish Archbishops and Bishops as well as to many of his parliamentary colleagues and the nobility in general. The subscription list survives, with blanks for the insertion of future subscriptions; this fact dates it prior to 1792, as much of the correspondence from and to the Marquis, dated 1792, also survives both in the Public Record Office and in Down County Museum.

Not only was it useful to have an influential nobleman to write the appeal letters, but when that nobleman wrote with a degree of wit and twist of phrase unparalleled to-day, it must have been extremely difficult to refuse. But refuse some of the recipients of these letters did and the modern reader will find a trifle amusing some of the excuses given by certain Bishops as to why they could not or should not subscribe. This series of letters is of such interest that it is proposed to quote extensively from them.

In March 1792, Downshire wrote to Robert Fowler, Archbishop of Dublin:

> My Lord,
> I take the liberty at the desire of the Dean and Chapter of the Cathedral Church of Down to inform your Grace that the Cathedral has for many years past been in almost a total state of ruin and that the Diocese, County and Neighbourhood of it's situation feel mortified and ashamed at its appearance and this has induced the Bps and Clergy, the Nobility and Gentry to offer themselves as subscribers to raise such a sum as may enable them to repair this Cathedral in such a manner as may do honour to them and to the established Church of Ireland, and the Dean and Chapter have requested me as Govr of the County of Down that I would presume to transmit to your Grace a list of such subscribers whose subscriptions we have already rec^{d} & also of such as we may, I think depend upon receiving, tog^{r} with such as upon solicitation will

be inclined to patronise and support an undertak^{g} which cannot but do honour to this part of the Kingdom; your Grace will observe that next to the gracious approbation that his Majesty has been pleased to give by his Royal subscript^{n} of £1000 and the generous deduction that the Dean has granted to arise out of his Deanery to constitute an oeconomy during his incumbency and that of his successors which is confirmed by Act of Parliament, my Lords the Bps are placed at the Head of our subscribers and are certainly those from whom we should hope and expect support and assistance in a work which seems partarly (sic) to claim their Lps protection. The Primate has been pleased to give the sum of £113. 15s upon hearing that such a subscription was intended and my Ld. Bp. of Waterford and my Ld. Bp. of Cloyne without solicitation have subscribed also £50 each and my Ld. Bp. of Down £113. 15s. This application to your Grace is the first that has been made and your Grace will forgive me as being employed by the Dean and Chapter humbly to solicit your Grace's goodness to support and assist their undertaking with such a subscription as you may think proper to confer upon them; which will lay the Dean and Chapter under the greatest obligation and be considered as a further mark of your Grace's favour and goodness

My Lord, with the utmost respect
Your Grace's
Most Obed^{t} and Most
Hble Servt

This letter brought forth a reply from his Grace, dated 12 March 1792:[5]

I have the honour of an obliging letter in your Lordship's name of March 7; I am glad to find by it that the subscriptions for rebuilding the Cathedral of Down amount to so large a sum. I should be very happy could a sum equal to it be procured for my Cathedral of St Patrick, but although repeated applications have been made to different administrations not a shilling has been granted to save it from destruction. The consequence therefore must be that that venerable fabric in a very few years to the disgrace of the Kingdom, will be an entire ruin. Two of my parish churches in Dublin, St. Michael and St. Nicholas Without, have also been in ruins for many years and as no aid can be procured from government, they are likely to continue in that deplorable state. I have lately subscribed to the building of an elegant church in Merrion Square and as I never had estate or patronage in the very wealthy County of Down, and as my Diocese wants every assistance I can give it, your Lordship must excuse me from complying with your request.

Opposite:
Original Subscription List 1789-1793

Downshire to Charles Agar, Archbishop of Cashel, March 1792:

1789 – 1792

This list came out of the custody of the Downshire Office Muniment Room to be placed amongst the Records of Down Cathedral. Edward Sclater Agent for The Marquis of Downshire Nov. 7. 1911

A LIST,

PREPARED by the Governor of the County of DOWN, and the Dean and Chapter of the Cathedral Church thereof, of the Archbishops and Bishops, Nobility, Clergy, and Gentry, who have already subscribed towards the Repair of the said Cathedral;—and a List of such of the Archbishops and Bishops, Nobility, Clergy, and Gentry, as the said Governor, Dean, and Chapter most humbly solicit, and hope will be pleased to add their Subscription in Support of so great an Undertaking.

HIS MOST EXCELLENT MAJESTY has been graciously pleased to signify his Royal Approbation and Support of the Reparations intended to be made of the Cathedral Church of Down, by subscribing towards the same the Sum of One Thousand Pounds.

The Honourable and Reverend WILLIAM ANNESLEY, Dean of Down, has subscribed the annual Sum of Three Hundred Pounds, to constitute the Œconomy of the said Cathedral, and to issue out of the Tythes of the Deanery for ever—which is confirmed by Act of Parliament.

The Sums that are already subscribed and paid, are set opposite to the name of each Person who has so subscribed, and Blanks are left for the inserting of future Subscriptions.

	£.	s.	d.
His Grace the Lord Primate of Ireland	113	15	0
His Grace the Archbishop of Dublin			
His Grace the Archbishop of Cashel			
His Grace the Archbishop of Tuam			
The Right Revd. and Right Honourable the Lord Bishop of Meath			
The Right Revd. the Lord Bishop of Kildare			
The Right Revd. the Lord Bishop of Elphin			
The Right Revd the Lord Bishop of Waterford	50	0	0
The Right Revd. and Right Honourable the Earl of Bristol, Lord Bishop of Derry			
The Right Revd. the Lord Bishop of Raphoe			
The Right Revd. the Lord Bishop of Clogher			
The Right Revd. the Lord Bishop of Killaloe			
The Honourable and Right Revd. the Lord Bishop of Ossory			
The Right Revd. the Lord Bishop of Cloyne	50	0	0
The Right Revd and Right Honourable the Lord Bishop of Limerick			
The Right Revd. the Lord Bishop of Dromore	22	15	0
The Right Revd. the Lord Bishop of Killala			
The Right Revd. the Lord Bishop of Down and Connor	113	15	0
The Right Revd. the Lord Bishop of Clonfert			
The Right Revd. the Lord Bishop of Leighlin and Ferns			
The Right Revd. the Lord Bishop of Kilmore			
The Right Revd. the Lord Bishop of Cork and Ross			
The Right Honourable John, Lord Fitzgibbon, Lord High Chancellor of Ireland			
The Right Honourable John, Lord Viscount Clonmel, Lord Chief Justice of his Majesty's Court of King's Bench			
The Right Honourable Hugh, Lord Carleton, Lord Chief Justice of his Majesty's Court of Common Pleas			
The Right Honourable Barry Yelverton, Esq. Lord Chief Baron of his Majesty's Court of Exchequer			
The Right Honourable John Foster, Esq. Speaker of the Honourable House of Commons			

	£	s.	d.
The Right Honourable John Hely Hutchinson, Esq. his Majesty's Principal Secretary of State and Provost of Trinity College			
His Grace William Robert, Duke of Leinster			
His Grace Francis, Duke of Bedford	108	6	8
George de la Poer, Marquis of Waterford			
Wills, Marquis of Downshire	597	3	9
His Lordship likewise engages to give the Organ, estimated to cost from 300l. to 500l.	300	0	0
Arthur, Marquis of Donegall			
The Right Honourable Lord Charles Fitzgerald			
The Right Honourable Lord Henry Fitzgerald			
John, Earl of Ormond			
James, Earl of Clanbrassill			
John, Earl of Moira			
John, Earl of Milltown			
John, Earl of Clanwilliam, and Theodosia, Countess of Clanwilliam			
Francis Charles, Earl Annesley	113	15	0
Francis, Earl of Hertford			
Arthur, Earl of Hillsborough	341	5	0
Arthur, Earl of Belfast			
William Wildman, Lord Viscount Barrington	113	15	0
Arthur, Lord Viscount Dungannon			
Thomas, Lord Viscount Northland			
Francis, Lord Rawdon			
Edward, Lord de Clifford			
George, Lord Macartney			
Robert, Lord Londonderry			
The Reverend Richard Dobbs, Dean of Connor			
The Reverend William Digby, Dean of Clonfert			
The Reverend Dr. Hugh Hamilton, Dean of Armagh			
The Reverend John Hume, Dean of Derry			
The Revd. Dr. William Craddock, Dean of St. Patrick's			
The Revd. Raphael Walsh, Dean of Dromore			
The Revd. Dr. Edmund Leslie, late Archdeacon of Down	20	0	0
The Revd. John Dickson, Archdeacon of Down	22	15	0
The Revd. Stewart Blacker, Archdeacon of Dromore			
The Revd. Anthony Trail, Archdeacon of Connor			
The Revd. Dr. Henry Leslie, Rector of Tanderagee	56	17	6
The Revd Hamilton Trail, Vicar General of Down	22	15	0

> . . . Do not, I beg of you, my Lord, make me unhappy by refusal. I think to flatter myself you will not & therefore boldly presume to subscribe myself. . .
> P. S. A kind word of recommendation to your Grace's brethren of the Bench cannot but have a good effect.

Downshire to Lord Clonmel, Lord Chief Justice of the King's Bench:

> I do not wish to say anything that may tend to lessen your goodness in contributing to advance what we have in view but I think it right to mention that our expect^{ns} do not extend to be very troublesome but we shall be extremely thankful and grateful to receive whatever your Lp may incline to give in support of what we humbly think will be an honour to the country and to the subscribers. . .

Earl of Clonmel, Dublin to Lord Downshire, 13 March 1792:[6]

> . . . a matter that so highly redounds to your magnificence and zeal for the splendour of the church and the ornament of that part of the Kingdom which owes so much of its civilisation to your exemplary residence and spirited exertions. . .

Ten days later, Clonmel sent a 'minikin' subscription.[7]

Downshire reserved his most mendicatory tone for the local nobleman, the Marquis of Donegall:

> . . . For my own part I flatter myself your Lordship will excuse the liberty I take in laying this matter before you, being humbly of opinion that you would not be pleased to have an inscription of the names of the subscribers exhibited in the Cathedral without <u>the Marquis of Donegall's name making a most considerable appearance among them</u> and I should have accused myself of want of respect to your Lordship if I had made any difficulty in yielding to the Dean and Chapter's request to present it to you. . .

To Downshire's initial letter, the Bishop of Kildare, George Louis Jones, replied on 20 March, writing from Rutland Square:

> I am honour'd with your Lordship's letter, inclosing a list of benefactors to the restoration of the ancient Cathedral of Down, it is an undertaking worthy of your Lordship's beneficence & well approved affection to the Establish'd Church, to whose fostering care & support it is largely indebted.
>
> Happy, my Lord, wou'd it be for the Dean & Chapter of Christ Church, if that ancient structure, the Church of State, situated in the metropolis of the Kingdom, were so powerfully patronised – to support a repair & additional improvements, the Chapter has engaged in a plan, which, on an estimate, amounts to upwards of £7000 and without other aid or

support than the slender one directed to this purpose from its annual oeconomy & the private benefactions of its members, we entred (sic) upon this work last year & have expended already upwards of two thousand pounds.

Here we pause, but the stream is small, yet as it flows perpetually, we flatter ourselves that we shall be able to resume our work in the course of a year or two.

I do not advance these facts from a disinclination to follow where your Lordship leads – I am proud of such a conductor – but the consideration of these facts will, I hope, plead my apology for not pressing so forward in this business, as otherwise I should have done for in proportion as I quicken your Lordship's operations, I retard my own.

The calculations of expense, which might serve to guide the liberality of the subscribers, is not mentioned in the paper transmitted to me, nor do I see any sum affix'd to the name of any Bishop, the Primate and the Bishop of the Diocese excepted. I would not wish to stand in the front rank, not solely from modesty, but lest, as my present abilities are contracted, my example should damp the liberality of others.

May I therefore be permitted, my Lord, to wait the motions of these Gentlemen. Crippled as I am, I cannot reconcile myself to withdraw entirely from your Lordship's service, for no one more sincerely wishes the accomplishment of all your undertaking than

My Lord,
Your Lordship's ever faithful
& most obedient humble servant,
Geo Louis Kildare

Downshire penned a second letter to the Bishop of Kildare on 3 May:

. . . as I have waited a consible (sic) time in the hopes of receiving answers to all the applications made to my Lords the Bps, without receiving any that I could consider as favourable from, I am sorry to say, at least seven of them, I think it right to enclose to yr:Lp ano^{r} General List of the Subscribers, by which yr Lp. will be able to determine the sum you will think proper to bestow upon the Dean & Chapter. . .

James Hawkins, Bishop of Raphoe, to Downshire, 14 March:[8]

I hope it will be a sufficient proof of the value I put on any notice from your Lordship when I acknowledge pleasure from your putting a pistol to my breast and demanding my money. Were I to plead a small poor charge, your Lordship, like other collectors, would laugh and tell me of the capacity you were under of discharging a Debt of Honour. I allow your Lordship's to be a debt of very high and real honour, so spare my life and take what I have though at this instant I have a church capable of being made as handsome as ever I saw, in danger of falling for want of attention which I shall ever require from Parson and Parishioners previous to my own roar. Last Post Day would have given me more pleasure had it brought information of continuance or increase of health and happiness of your Lordship, self and family. I hear little but hope much, thank all for kind entertainment, I have taken leave of the world (though I was quite alive personally to have given a Not Content to the Herculean Bill could it have been of any use); age and a comfortable, nay a fine retreat here are, I hope, rational motives so here I remain but as elsewhere.

William Bennet, Bishop of Cork, sent 20 guineas:[9]

> . . . the expenses of my late preferment (including near £5000 for my See house) and those of my marriage have left me in a situation in which it is not possible for me to answer the expectations of the Dean and Chapter in the manner I ought. . .

Charles Dodgson, Bishop of Elphin, 26 March:

> I was prevented by a gouty complaint in my right hand from answering your Lordship three posts ago as I wished to do, that the exigencies of my own Diocese have required, and still do, so many contributions towards the building of our churches and steeples that I cannot consistently with those and many other duties send any more than a mite towards the rebuilding of the Cathedral of Down, which your Lordship has had the goodness to promote with a laudable attention and munificence. In consequence of your Lordship's letter, I shall order a friend in Dublin to send twenty guineas to Mr Brett the Secretary as soon as he can find a proper opportunity. . .

Euseby Cleaver, Bishop of Ferns, 20 March

> I have received the Honor of your Lordship's letter relative to the Cathedral of Down and am very sensible how much the Church of Ireland is indebted to your Lordship in every respect as well as for your attention in an hostile neighbourhood to give form and grace to our Establishment.
>
> I assure your Lordship, that there is no-one more anxious than myself to introduce here, as far as I can, the habits and practices of our sister country, and from inclination as well as propriety should most readily contribute towards the undertaking so liberally patronised by your Lordship, if the peculiarity of my situation had not disabled me.
>
> I have not yet, my Lord, been a Bishop three years; it was my lot to be placed in a diocese in which there had been no establishment for a Bishop since the Reformation.

> I found a See house begun by a Predecessor on so large a scale, that in my endeavours to complete it, exclusive of furniture, I have already been under the necessity of expending three years income and have yet much to do. Under the weight of this burthen, which perhaps too liberal an attention to my successors has increased beyond my duty to my children, I am sorry to say that it is not in my power to become a subscriber to a plan, which under different circumstances, I should have been proud to have promoted.

William Cecil Pery, Bishop of Limerick, 12 March

> . . . I am much concerned that I cannot contribute my mite to so good and laudable a work, as I am already deeply engaged in building a church in my own diocese which has already cost me £400 & also in repairing others, which have been most shamefully neglected. Besides my state of health is so bad, that I am scarce able to write these few lines to acknowledge your Lordship's favour. . .

These extracts from letters to and from the Marquis of Downshire afford a valuable insight into the art of eighteenth-century fund raising, particularly when the appeal fund was headed by someone as outstanding, both locally and nationally, as he was. As his own generosity towards the fund was second only to his Majesty's, he could afford to be aggressive, but despite his persuasion, it proved quite difficult to elicit subscriptions from many of the bishops.

In addition to soliciting subscriptions throughout the length and breadth of the land, the Marquis was influential in having passed in parliament *'An Act for the more effectual Application of the Sum of One Thousand Pounds, granted by King's Letter, for the Support and Repair of the Cathedral Church of Down, and for defraying the Expences of the Celebration of Divine Worship therein'*. This Act, which was passed by parliament in 1790, not only provided for the gift of £1000 from King George III, as soon as a like sum had been raised by subscription, but gave formal recognition to Dean Annesley's generosity in providing an annuity of £300 out of the tythes of his Deanery, which provision would be binding on his successors.

AN

ACT

FOR

The more effectual Application of the Sum of One Thouſand Pounds, granted by King's Letter, for the Support and Repair of the Cathedral Church of *Down*, and for defraying the Expences of the Celebration of Divine Worſhip therein.

DUBLIN:

Printed by GEORGE GRIERSON, Printer to the King's Moſt Excellent Majeſty. MDCCXC.

Act for the grant of one thousand pounds, 1790

By April 1792, Lilly had carried out work to the value of £3311 14s and the actuary, John Brett, was authorised forthwith to apply to those persons who had promised subscriptions to pay the amount of their subscription. In the Chapter account book, there now follows a list of the subscribers together with the amounts promised and a note against each whether that amount had been paid or not; whilst the majority were paid and blanks remain against only a few, we find 'refused' beside the name of Lord de Clifford. There was a political feud behind this; in 1790 there were elections for both the borough of Downpatrick and the County of Down. De Clifford sponsored the Whig candidate whilst Downshire had controlled the Tory representation in the County for many years; the two noblemen were on opposing sides. [10] Tempers were at fever pitch, each side accusing the other of malpractice; evidently de Clifford took offence and withdrew his promise of a subscription. His name disappears hereafter from Cathedral records. It is also probable that Downshire's considerable involvement in Cathedral affairs in the town where de Clifford was, after all, Lord of the Manor, caused resentment.

On the debit side, payments began in January 1790 to Matthew Gamble, who acted as overseer of the work on behalf of Lilly. By the end of 1792, over £5000 had been expended and the roof was in place. During late 1793 and early 1794, four payments totalling £33. 13. 4d were recorded to Mr Filmar, the organist. Some form of divine service was taking place but what sort of instrument was Mr Filmar playing? Lord Downshire had died in October 1793 and it is extremely unlikely that he had anything to do with this instrument; indeed, it was probably a small chamber organ. Bearing in mind that little interior construction work had been carried out and that there was evidently little more than a roof on the building, it would be surprising if anything more elaborate had been installed. The payments at this period are principally for brick and stone, although there are substantial amounts for timber, no doubt required for the roof.

There are grounds for suggesting that funds ran out during 1795. The Marquis had died in October 1793, leaving very considerable liabilities and encumbrances;[11] his heir, Arthur, the second Marquis, was rarely seen at Hillsborough. Apart from a few minor payments in March and April 1795, no cash was paid out between September 1794 and March 1796; building was at a standstill, nor does there appear to have been any activity inside. Matthew Gamble, the overseer, had occasion to write to the absentee Marquis on 19 December 1795:[12]

> My Lord,
> Having lately received a letter from Mr Lilly informing me your Lordship is rather displeased with me for having taken steps of law against the Rev[d] Dean of Downe for the recovery of money due me from the Cathedral Church, I humbly presume your Lordship will not be offended at my thus laying a fair and judicious state of the whole before you as my character and support of my family entirely depends on the result. In the year 1790 I was employed to direct and carry on the entire works of the Cathedral, to receive and pay all the money then necessary for carrying on the same. My salary for which I was

entered in the Cathedral books was £50 per year and at the rate of which sum I regularly received until the 20 August 1791 from which time I have not received anything neither had I any benefit from my Contract not even for the stonecutters who were employed in finishing the pinnacles and east window but was even at that very time laying out what ready money I had in taking bills on me to a considerable amount. In the latter end of the year 1792 I could not get money to enable me to support the stonecutters but the late Marquis then coming desired me to carry on the east window assuring me I should be honourably paid under which promise I endeavoured to enlarge my credit and forwarded the work with every expedition until December 1793, but unfortunately for me, I did not again see the Marquis as I am well assured, had he seen the work finished, he would have seen my account settled to my satisfaction. I before the last term made every submission possible; offered to take what was due to me at 3, 6 and 12 months with which the Dean would not comply. In March last when my Creditors were very pressing I begged for £40 to satisfy them but was also refused; the Dean even then paid everyone (myself excepted) the one half of their demand, he well knowing my distressed situation and that I had not only faithfully and honestly attended the work but laid out my whole substance on it. As the publick works here are all finished and no expectation of further employment, my situation at present is very distressing, nor can I leave this until the disagreeable affair is settled, having a large family to support and my creditors pressing. I know not well how to act, but from your Lordship's well known goodness, humbly presume to hope you will take the premises into consideration. I am willing to stop proceedings, I will be satisfied with whatever your Lordship may think fair and equitable.

Your Lordship will please forgive the length of this statement and your consideration and interference in having the affair settled shall be ever remembered with every sentiment of gratitude and respect by your Lordship's most obedient and very humble servant

Matthew Gamble

Gamble's legal action against the Dean met with some success, but it took some years for recompense to be made. As far ahead as April 1799, there is an entry in the account book 'paid James Wallace, Attorney for Mat. Gamble, the amount of the damage and cost due to him in full £112. 1s. 2°d'. Gamble carried out his threat to leave the Cathedral; his name disappears from the record. It would be interesting to learn the other side of this unhappy episode; if we are to believe Gamble, the Dean acted in a most high handed and uncharitable manner, which is out of character considering his personal generosity towards the rebuilding project. The new overseer was Peter Daly.

During these years – years, incidentally, of upheaval in the countryside leading

Barrel organ by Robert Woffington c.1810
NATIONAL MUSEUM OF IRELAND

to the 1798 rebellion – Dean Annesley's annuity of £300 was used to keep what construction work was possible going, as subscriptions had virtually ceased to come in. The annuity was obviously not being used for the purpose for which it was originally intended. Nor did the second Marquis show any interest in the work, and it was not until after his death in 1801 that a revival in building work took place. When the third Marquis inherited the title, he was but twelve years old; his mother, the Dowager Marchioness, is known to history as a very formidable lady and is also known to have had great admiration for her father-in-law, the first Marquis. She was created Baroness Sandys in her own right, having succeeded to very considerable estates on the death of an uncle in 1797. With her encouragement and indeed determination, the young Marquis set out to clear the Downshire estate of the debts and encumbrances inherited from both his father and his grandfather.

Aynsworth Pilson, a well known Downpatrick merchant, has left a diary recording day-to-day events in the town covering approximately the first half of the nineteenth century; this diary is an invaluable source in dating events, which are not elsewhere noticed.[13] For instance, he tells us that, on 10 April 1800, the east window was being glazed and the interior flagged. On 17 February 1801, we read that workmen were putting up the seats in the cathedral. An organ arrived on 9 July 1802 and was first played on 3 August in the same year. An entry in the Chapter account book records a payment of £21. 10. 8d to Edward Morgan for 'freight of organ' and a corresponding entry in a Downshire ledger on 4 November 1802 records the cost: 'Robert Woffington, for an organ erected at Downpatrick, £190. 7. 6d'.[14] Not only was an organist being paid regularly but singing boys received fifteen shillings each quarter. Regular Sunday worship was taking place.

Little is known about Robert Woffington; he lived (or his workshop was situated) at 9 William Street, Dublin and he was in business from c. 1780 until his death in 1819. He was best noted for the construction of barrel organs (there are three examples in the National Museum, Dublin), a form of instrument which enjoyed great popularity in church music at the close of the eighteenth century.[15] They had the advantage of not requiring a trained musician to play them, the only dexterity required being the ability to turn a handle for a limited number of tunes. One Francis Holden played the organ for some months, while Samuel Hall was the bellas (*sic*) blower but on 11 August 1803 Robert McCune was paid the first quarterly amount of £15 as organist, a position which he held until 1817.

Weekly payments continued to be made to the workers although it is difficult from the payees' names, to tell whether they are construction workers, suppliers of materials or persons in the employment of the cathedral. By September 1804, Pilson was able to record that the cathedral had been cleaned out and slaked; this tells us that the interior walls had been limewashed and that the place was usable, if no more. As corroboration of Pilson's statement, the account book records expenditure of 16s 3d for lime and 2s 2d for a brush at this date. Sundry payments continue for the next few years, mostly to the choir men and boys, but also fairly constant payments both to Charles Lilly and Peter Daly. Lilly wrote to the actuary, John Brett, on 20 February 1806 to ask for the balance of his account £315. 3s to be paid;[16] this was subsequently paid in instalments and the final payment not made until 8 September 1808. Lilly's name thereafter disappears from the record, although he was still living at Merrion Row in Dublin in November 1812.[17]

Architectural historians have referred to the architect, Robert Furze Brettingham, as having had plans for a new choir in Down Cathedral exhibited at the Royal Academy in 1795.[18] Brettingham was responsible for Hillsborough Castle, commissioned by the first Marquis and completed in 1797, as well as other work for the Downshire family in England, but his name does not occur anywhere in the Cathedral records. There is no question of him having been responsible for the exterior restoration as that was quite clearly the responsibility of Lilly, but there is just a possibility that he may have designed the interior seating and pulpitum; unfortunately the plans in question have not survived.

The young Marquis attained his majority in October 1809, having been educated at Eton and Oxford. Just down from Oxford, his mother despatched him on a tour of his estates, the management of which was to become his life's work. No doubt as he travelled to his property at Dundrum, he took the opportunity of visiting Downpatrick and the subsequent letter which he wrote to the Bishop of Down, Nathaniel Alexander, in July of that year, is without doubt the most detailed description which has survived of the progress or, more correctly, the lack of progress, in the restoration of the Cathedral:[19]

> My Lord,
> I beg leave to acquaint your Lordship that upon coming round to this town, I have to-day visited the Cathedral, the restoration of which had been promoted by my ancestors and that I am much concerned to observe it still continues in an unfinished state. I have since conferred with Hon & Reverend the Dean upon this subject and have taken the liberty

to suggest that in my opinion some means ought to be speedily adopted for the completion of it so that it may be opened as soon as may be for Divine Service in such manner and subject to such regulations as your Lordship may be pleased to recommend; and with a view to ascertain what may be requisite to be done, I have since directed a letter to be addressed to the Dean of which I enclose a copy for your Lordship's information. After he shall have received the Report and Estimates to which it alludes, I humbly conceive it might be proper to call a meeting of the Chapter and of those who were entrusted by the Act of Parliament for rebuilding the Cathedral, for the purpose of taking into consideration the Architect's report, the state of the Receipt and Expenditure and the most proper measures for procuring a fund sufficient for concluding this laudable undertaking after which I should suppose it might be proper to have a statement presented to be addressed to such persons as may be likely to subscribe towards the accomplishment of an object so important as this is; and I hope your Lordship will believe that in presuming to make this suggestion, I am solely actuated by a desire to express my readiness to concur in whatever may be approved as the most proper mode to complete the designs of those who undertook this great work & by no means to interfere in the management of those with whom the subject more properly rests. As, however, the restoration of the Cathedral originated with my family, and it may be considered to be in some degree answerable to those whose subscriptions it solicited, I trust your Lordship will forgive my introducing this matter to your notice, nor doubting your desire to see the design of the promoters carried into effect.

Mary, Baroness Sandys, wife of the second Marquis of Downshire.
LORD SANDYS

The concurrent letter from Downshire's agent, Handley, to Dean Annesley adds some further detail; evidently Lilly was still considered to be the architect in charge:[20]

. . . His Lordship desires me to request that you will have the goodness to direct Mr Lilly, the architect, forthwith to draw up and transmit to you a report upon the present state of the Cathedral – what remains to be done to finish it according to the plans heretofore adopted (including, of course, the making of a suitable altar, pulpit, reading desk, Bishop's Throne, a bell or bells etc., etc. , and every other work proper for having the Cathedral opened for Divine Service) and an estimate of the sum of money necessary to carry all this into speedy effect. Lord Downshire supposes such a report would in the first instance be necessary to ascertain what funds may be wanted for the purpose, after which he has no doubt suitable means for raising them may be speedily

> devised and his Lordship will be happy to concur with the Lord Bishop, yourself, the Chapter and Clergy in carrying the work into execution.

There is no record of a subscription list having been opened nor does the chapter book record any receipts other than the annual £300 from the Dean. Nevertheless, considerable impetus was given to the work as urged by the Marquis. The Communion Rails were purchased from Clark of Dublin in 1811 for £59. 8s 1°d; during 1813 and 1814 there were two payments of £50 each to Nevin, Sayers & Co. for oak,[21] as well as various lesser amounts, alongside regular weekly payments to Richard Cairns, suggesting that Cairns was the carpenter responsible for the interior of the cathedral as we now know it. Richard Carleton was paid regularly for masonry work. By 1818 we see the finishing touches being put to the work; there are payments to stuccoplaisterers and whitesmiths and also for cushions (including one for the Bishop's seat), mats and branches (candelabra). Serge for the verger's gown was paid for as well as surplices for the singing men and boys. Aynsworth Pilson was able to write in his diary on 23 August 1818 'that the Cathedral was opened for Divine Service being the first time for centuries past. Dean Knox preached and the organ was played by McCune'.[22] One might suppose that the consecration of the cathedral would have been a matter for considerable rejoicing among the people of Downpatrick and particularly those who claimed membership of the Established Church. But no, the vestry minutes of the parish church are silent on the event, as indeed they are during the entire restoration period! Nor does the Cathedral Chapter consider it worth a mention; it was left to the local diarist to record the event for posterity. The total sum of payments between 1790 and 1818 amounted to over £13,000 although, to be fair, the later years included amounts unconcerned with the actual fabric of the building.

Arthur Hill, Third Marquis of Downshire
ETON COLLEGE: PHOTOGRAPH COURTAULD INSTITUTE OF ART

During the month prior to the consecration of the cathedral, the account book records the first payment to William Hull, organ builder; over a period of 18 months, Hull was paid a sum of over £623, virtually on a weekly basis. Here we have an organ builder of whom less is known than of Woffington. What little we do know is that he lived in Dublin and died there c. 1820 so it is is quite possible that Down was his last commission. In those days, it would not have been unusual for an organ builder to spend such a long time on site, far away from his workshop and there is little doubt that Hull was also responsible for the oak case which houses the organ. There is some evidence that he was in straitened circumstances; with this in mind, the Chapter could have been exercising a degree of prudence in making weekly payments.[23]

Sadly Dean Annesley did not live to see the completion of the cathedral; he died in June 1817, in his seventieth year. The new Dean, Edmund Knox, was appointed almost immediately. At the same time, a chaplain, Rev Richard Maunsell, was appointed to carry out the weekly duties; his stipend was the princely sum of £50 per year and when he applied for an increase to £60 the Chapter refused, 'being of the opinion that £50 was sufficient.'

And so the Cathedral, whose restoration had been undertaken almost 30 years earlier through the initiative of the first Marquis of Downshire, was at last consecrated for Divine Service, the task being completed as a matter of family honour and pride under the enthusiastic aegis of his grandson, the third Marquis. History has credited Dean Annesley with the restoration and, whilst his voluntary surrender of a small portion of his not inconsiderable income undoubtedly kept the work going, the part played by the Downshire family has been largely overlooked. It was, without doubt, the strong sense of family honour, inherited by young Arthur through his mother from the great Wills Hill, which created the climate which spurred the Chapter on. To him must go the credit for the beautiful box pews with their elegant bow fronts, for the imposing Bishop's throne and its opposing Judge's seat, so called because it was used by the judiciary, the Crown's representative, when they visited Downpatrick on assize. We have in Down Cathedral one of the finest examples in the British Isles of early nineteenth-century adaptation of medieval choir stalls, with the *decani* on the south side and the *cantori* on the north, leaving a broad central area to accommodate ceremonial processions.[24] To him also must go the credit for the superb organ case set on top of the pulpitum, which divides the choir from the narthex. Although they can also be seen in the small Cathedral of the Diocese of Achonry, the chapter stalls, facing east under the pulpitum, i.e., against the west wall of the choir are most unusual; such stalls are known as *return* stalls. On the south side of the entrance through the screen are the stalls of the Dean, Chancellor, Treasurer and Prebendary of Talpestone, whilst north of the entrance are the stalls of the Archdeacon, the Precentor and the Prebendaries of Saint Andrew and Dunsport. This layout reproduces exactly the medieval layout as detailed in the Sarum *Consuetudinarium*.[25]

TEN

TOWARDS DISESTABLISHMENT

Down Cathedral before completion of the Tower. Lithograph by Robert O'Callaghan published in *Picturesque Views of the Antiquities of Ireland Drawn in Stone* by J. D. Harding, 1830.
DOWN COUNTY MUSEUM

THE NEW DEAN, THE HONOURABLE Edmund Knox, like his predecessor, came from noble stock; he was the son of Viscount Northland of Dungannon and his elder brother was created Earl of Ranfurly. Another brother was Bishop of Derry. As soon as possible after his appointment, he came to live in Irish Street where he remained for some years before moving to Rostrevor and subsequently to Ardglass.[1] Mindful of the influence the young Marquis of Downshire had on the restoration, Dean Knox wrote to him early in 1819 saying that he had appropriated the best pew for his Lordship but as he lived some distance away, he did not expect him to use it;[2] the Marquis thought otherwise, however, his reply indicated that he needed the pew for himself and requested the Dean to have the pew 'fitted up in such manner as may appear to you befitting of the place and consonant with the beauty of the interior of the building'.[3] We cannot be sure to which pew the Marquis referred, but it was probably the pew nearest the sanctuary on the north side, which has traditionally been used by the gentry and would be analogous to the Downshire pew in Hillsborough which was the front pew in the north transept. As we might expect, music played an important part in worship in the Cathedral. Henry and William McNamara were paid £5 per quarter as choir members, although Henry doubled as Parish Clerk, earning him a further £2.10s. Among the boys after 1820 can be found the name of John Carroll, surely the lad who would later become Cathedral organist. The boys earned fifteen shillings per quarter but this was withheld occasionally for misbehaviour. A letter survives from the organist, William McCune, to Lord Downshire, asking for support for his application for a degree at Trinity College.[4] Lord Downshire duly complied; his letter to the provost of TCD in support of the application for a MusDoc degree states that McCune had been organist of Down Cathedral for 20 (sic) years and had a choir of four men and six boys; 'the state of his choir and the manner in which church service is performed does him great credit'.[5] Dean Knox was also well pleased with the choir's performance; in a letter to Lord Downshire in 1825, he wrote: 'I am quite delighted with the chaunt you have sent us and I think the choir does it great justice. I was so much pleased with it in the "Jubilate" that I sent up to the organ loft to have it continued in the "Te Deum"'.[6] Can we infer from this letter that Lord Downshire had a sufficiently keen musical ear to send to McCune the latest service settings for his appraisal and use?

Richard Mant
Bishop of Down and Connor
1823-1848
(and Dromore from 1842)

Dean Knox's first task was to complete the planned work on the Cathedral, sufficient to open it for public worship. Whilst this was speedily achieved, the tower remained unfinished; an engraving of the building at this time shows a rough stump. A new Bishop came to the diocese in 1823; Richard Mant, translated from Killaloe, to which diocese he had been appointed three years earlier from England. Mant was a tireless worker for church extension; years later he founded the Church Accommodation Society and was responsible for building several new churches in Down and Connor, necessary for the rapidly increasing urban population of the early nineteenth century. To this day, these churches are known as 'Mant' churches. He threw himself energetically behind the efforts to complete the Cathedral tower. In October 1825, a letter was addressed to 'the Nobility, Gentry, Clergy and other inhabitants of the County of Down', pointing out the desirability of completing the tower, 'set on a hill, where it of necessity attracts the attention, not of the neighbourhood only, but of the surrounding country; it presents an object both unsightly in itself and altogether unworthy of the otherwise handsome and venerable fabrick to which it is appended'.[7] A meeting was called for the following month at which subscriptions of £1183 were announced; the meeting was chaired by the Bishop and Lord Downshire was among those present. Mr William Farrell, the architect to the Board of First Fruits for the Province of Ulster, was requested to draw up plans for the tower and Mr Lynn, the contractor responsible for building the new County Gaol, was requested to furnish an estimate for carrying the design into effect. Lynn was also asked to report on the expense of surmounting the tower with a spire, which may have been Lilly's original intention, as is shown by the cartouche on Williamson's map of 1810! Mant wrote to Downshire at the end of 1825 saying that Lynn's estimate amounted to £3825 including £750 for the spire and £660 for the tower, but still the subscriptions amounted to only £1450.[8] The committee, recognising an insurmountable deficiency, decided to enlist the King's 'gracious assistance' and prepared a memorial to the Lord Lieutenant, the Marquis of Wellesley, describing the situation in which it found itself and requesting assistance to meet the deficiency. At the same time, Farrell was asked to draw up fresh plans, the carrying of which into effect would not exceed £2000. The committee worked through until May 1828 when Farrell was again asked to revise his estimate and then to recommend any builder who would be willing to undertake the completion of the work on that estimate.

Eventually the contract was awarded to Messrs Cobden and Sands for a figure of £1890. The plans of the tower survive and are in the possession of Down County Museum; they are accompanied by an agreement dated 27 April 1829 between the Chapter and T. A. Cobden of Carlow and James Sands of London. The vast reduction from the original estimate was achieved by allowing the existing walls of the tower to remain to a height of 64 feet from the ground, rather than rebuilding from a lower level. The upper storey of the tower can be seen today in regularly dressed stone as opposed to the random coursing of the lower storeys. Mr Sands's final balance was not paid until March 1838.

Dean Knox was appointed Bishop of Killaloe in 1831 and three years later was translated to the United Dioceses of Limerick, Ardfert and Aghadoe. The new Dean was the Honourable Thomas Plunket, son of Lord Plunket, Lord Chancellor in the Irish parliament. Dean Plunket took up residence in Dundrum and employed two curates, Revs W.Leahy and J.F.Gordon, to take care of his duties.[9] The Church Temporalities Act came to the Statute Book in 1834; this measure had far reaching effects for the Established Church, including a radical reorganisation of the dignities attached to cathedrals and consequently to the working lives of the chapter clergy. Dean Plunket was understandably concerned about his income; he prepared a memorial to the Lord Lieutenant, Wellesley, on 1 March 1834, in which he detailed his income as £2827.13s 8d with deductions amounting to £1099.12s 5d.[10] This was made up as follows:

Tythe composition of Parish of Down	1078	11	3
Tythe composition of Parish of Ballee	491	14	3
Tythe composition of Parish of Ballyculter	259	12	6
Tythe composition of Parish of Bright	468	5	8
Tythe composition of Parish of Saul	358	18	3 °
Tythe composition of Parish of Tyrella	164	15	9
Rent of Glebe, Parish of Down	6	6	0
	2827	13	8 °

The necessary expenses of the Deanery added up as:			
To Dean & Chapter for support of the Cathedral pursuant to Statute 30 George III, Chapter 43	276	18	5 °
To the preachers' fund	8	8	0
For proxies, exhibits and visitation fees	12	16	0
Quit Rent	7	9	4 °
Diocesan School Master	6	0	0
Parish School Masters	8	0	0
A licensed curate	100	0	0
Chaplain of the Cathedral	10	0	0
A residence, there being no house	105	0	0
Expense of collection & management at 5%	141	17	7
Deduction for landlord at 15%	423	3	0
	1099	12	5

In a further letter to Wellesley, dated 19 April, the Dean expressed great anxiety: '...the uncertainty as to the amount of income to be reserved for the Dean of Down places me under great embarassment'.[11] To which Wellesley made the comment: 'It having been stated in Parliament that the present Dean was an absentee, he thinks it right to add that he has no glebe house nor could he procure one within the deanery. He however rented one as near to it as he could at £105 pa & there resided during the 2 years he held the preferment ending November last & during that time he preached 68 sermons in the Cathedral & Parish Çhurch and occasionally in the church of Bright and adjoining parishes'.[12]

It is apparent that the Dean was under considerable pressure to reside within the parish; in a letter from Dundrum to the Primate at Armagh, dated 13 January 1836,[13] he referred to the order made by his Grace at the triennial visitation at Lisburn: 'that the Dean of Down shall provide a residence within the parish of Down, or build a glebe house on his glebe taking the usual proceedings by memorial etc'. The letter outlined the reasons why he was unable to do so, principally because of his large family, and offered to have his benefice sequestered, should his Grace consider it necessary. The reason for the Dean's anxiety was the passing of the Church Temporalities Act in 1834 which disappropriated all the parishes from the Corps of the Deanery except for Down and Tyrella; indeed the recommendation of the Ecclesiastical Commissioners was to remove Tyrella as well, but Plunket seems to have had some success in retaining it. Henceforth the Dean of Down was, by right of office, only Rector of the parishes of Down and Tyrella.

Meantime, the Chapter was suffering from a serious lack of funding for the upkeep of the Cathedral; some entries from the chapter book illustrate how serious the situation had become.

> 2 November 1830: £250 lent to Lagan Navigation Company called in to assist with tower debt

> 9 August 1832: Dean requested to write to the Marquis of Downshire on the practicability of raising a sum of money sufficient to defray the expenses of the tower and at the same time mention to his Lordship the additional sums that have been subscribed.

> 3 November 1835: This was the day for the half-yearly meeting; the members of the Chapter were noticed accordingly (a week previous) for the hour of 12 o'clock, but one o'clock passed and no-one attended, the Actuary waited no longer. The day was exceedingly wet and stormy.

2 pencil sketches by William Batt probably c.1840
THE ULSTER MUSEUM

> 16 August 1842: A sum not exceeding £10 to be expended in procuring and putting up a baptismal font. (A further entry two years later informs us that Messrs Kelly & Co. were paid £20 for a font).

Half a century had now passed since the commencement of the restoration programme, although a much shorter time had elapsed since the installation of much of the interior furnishing. The chronic shortage of funds undoubtedly led to the use of much cheap material; it is clear that the Chapter was at its wits' end to keep the Cathedral open at all. By the late 1830s both the roof and windows were giving trouble and the Chapter tried every way open to it to raise revenue to carry out repairs. Application was made to the Ecclesiastical Commissioners and following their grant, work commenced in 1835 by replacing the sashes of the lower windows with metal sashes.[14] The Commissioners were indeed ready to undertake the renovation of the entire building when they came to the opinion that, in law, they were unable to grant assistance to a Diocesan Cathedral; only parochial churches could claim assistance. At the last moment an attempt was made to insert a clause in the Church Temporalities Act to enable the Commissioners to meet the wishes of the Dean and Chapter, without success.[15] It had been calculated that a sum of £700 was necessary to carry out repairs caused by damp and to install a heating system in order to prevent future trouble. And so the Cathedral was plunged into continuing financial difficulties.

Theophilus Blakely
Dean 1839-1855

Dean Plunket was elevated to the Bench as Bishop of Tuam in 1839, being replaced as Dean by Theophilus Blakely, who had successively been Dean of Connor and of Achonry. Dean Blakely's tenure of the Deanery was not an easy one, a situation which was not helped by the fact that he was already 70 years of age at the time of his appointment. He had strong sympathies with the Oxford Movement and Puseyism, sympathies which he shared with his Bishop, Richard Mant; indeed Mant had some influence over his appointment, as is clear from his previous appointment in Connor. Unfortunately the Downpatrick of the period was not the most comfortable place in which to hold these sympathies and the contemporary press contains many reports of meetings held specifically to denounce Puseyism. During his visits to Downpatrick, Blakely lived with the Rector of Killyleagh, Rev. Edward Hincks,[16] but it is evident that he was absent for long periods, particularly in his later years, when ill health forced him to spend long periods in Cheltenham. The state of the cathedral was such that he had no option but to carry on with the programme of repair initiated by his predecessor. A new heating system was installed by Messrs Gardner of Armagh; the nave and 'porch' were replastered and coloured (painted) along with the ceiling and the nave and chapter room were flagged.[17] The contract for total replacement of the roof and window sashes survives among the cathedral records; the cost quoted was £353 11s 6d although, in fact, the payments totalled over £445. The old slates were disposed of by auction. Some rearrangement of the pews was proposed but thankfully there was no money left over to carry out these plans. The pulpit and reading desk were to be moved; the seat against the second pillar, known as the Dean's seat was to become a seat for the Reader (this must refer to the Judge's seat); the Bishop's throne was to be moved to the pew nearest the Communion Table on the north side and the pulpit was to be moved to the position of the Bishop's throne with a canopy over it. It must be acknowledged that Blakely, in spite of his age, accomplished more in the first few years of his tenure of the Deanery than Plunket had during his entire term; Plunket was more concerned with his own income and security than he was in maintaining the fabric of the cathedral.

In Dean Blakely's absence, much of the administration of the cathedral was carried out by other members of the Chapter, in particular by Walter Bishop Mant, the Archdeacon and son of the Bishop; indeed by 1850, he signed himself

After completion of the Tower. Painted by Dr James Moore from a drawing by Samuel Wooley.
PHOTOGRAPH BY ALAN JOHNSTON

as sub-Dean, having been formally appointed as such by Dean Blakely. But trouble was looming on the horizon; an entry by Aynsworth Pilson in his diary, dated February 1845, records a meeting by Protestant parishioners to take action against the Puseyite doctrines pursued by some of the chapter clergy; the Dean denied them entrance to the Cathedral. In the following month, he tells us that Rev. J. Ford, the cathedral curate had discontinued the prayer for the Church Militant, thus giving way to Protestant opinion which had been insulted by the

Bishop and the Dean. A study of the pages of the *Downpatrick Recorder* at this time reveals the depth of anti-Puseyite feeling in Lecale; scarcely a week passed without meetings being held in schools or Presbyterian churches to mark the protest. Bishop Mant, Dean Blakely and the other members of the chapter were completely out of touch with the ordinary people of Lecale.

As a corporate body, the Chapter was extremely jealous of its position; in 1848, as a result of doubts expressed concerning the obligations, privileges and powers of the Dean and Chapter, a copy of the Charter of Saint Patrick's Cathedral in Dublin (upon which the 1609 Charter had been modelled) was requested. The Actuary, Rev.J.F.Gordon, drew up a long list of questions to be put to Dr Radcliffe, the eminent ecclesiastical lawyer in Dublin. The main thrust of his reply was that the Dean was individually responsible to see that Divine Service was duly and regularly performed and that the Dean, Dignitaries and Prebendaries were bound to attend and preach in their turn; the payment of a substitute preacher should be borne by the member of the Chapter, whose turn it was to preach on a particular day and that no part of the annuity should be appropriated for this purpose. On the other hand, the appointment of Reader was vested in the Dean and his salary could come from the annuity. The Actuary was requested to prepare a cycle of preaching turns in which the Dean would preach for one quarter of the year and the other members of the Chapter would divide the remaining three quarters between them. Any member not preaching in turn would pay a fine of £1 to a fund from which substitute preachers would be paid, which suggests that substitutes were on duty fairly often. Rev Horatio Moffat was appointed both Reader and Substitute Preacher. There was clearly a fine distinction between the two offices; when his successor, Rev.J.S.Eager, arrived in 1853, the Dean appointed him Reader. He also proposed to appoint him Preacher, but this appointment had to be ratified by the Chapter; there being no members of the Chapter present, he affixed his own seal, *pro hac vice,* 'the Chancellor, (Rev. J.L.M. Scott), having refused to give up the common seal to the Dean'.

Bishop Mant died in 1848. Echoing across the centuries to the Papal Bull of 1244, the Actuary reported that the Dean and Chapter were guardians of the spiritualities *sede vacante*. Counsel's opinion was sought in order to clarify the position: '...that by Canon Law the Dean and Chapter were guardians during the vacancy but that this privilege had been altered by custom and they are now vested in the Archbishop of the Province'.

Apart from small items of maintenance, no further major repair work was undertaken over the next number of decades; the Chapter was able, therefore, to devote funds towards the purchase of two items very much overdue. A bell was purchased from Hodges of Dublin at a cost of £323. The bell was inscribed: ECCLES: S.S.TRIN: AP: DUNUM: ROBTO: KNOX: EPISCO: THEOPHILO: BLAKELY:

DECANO: MDCCCLV:[18] The organ, installed by William Hull in 1818, had been deteriorating over a number of years; although a Trumpet stop was purchased from Mr Walker in 1837 at a cost of £10, Dean Blakely, on his arrival in 1839, remarked that the organ was almost useless.[19]

William McCune ceased to be organist in 1848, having occupied the organ loft for 31 years; his place was taken by another Robert McCune, perhaps another generation of the same family. There is a curious entry in the chapter book in March 1850, when we read that Frederick Barnby, Vicar choral from York Minster was paid £2.5s travelling expenses on coming to Down; he sang in the choir for about eighteen months when his name drops from the record. In March 1854, the Chapter placed an advertisement in *The General Advertiser* for a new organist; John Carroll secured the job and took his place almost immediately. Aynsworth Pilson wrote that 26 April 1854 was a day set apart by authority for humility and prayer, beseeching Almighty God to strengthen the effort of our armies [in the Crimea]; '...large congregation. The singing by the Cathedral choir was good, very much improved since Mr Carroll, the new organist, came, although scarcely three months. Service lasted 2˘ hours'.

The urgent repairs to the fabric of the building had prevented any thought of a new organ for almost two decades, although the desirability of doing something about it must have occupied the attention of the Chapter for some time. The Archdeacon, the Venerable Walter B.Mant, chaired a meeting on 16 October 1854 which authorised the Actuary 'to communicate with Mr Telford of Dublin for the purpose of ascertaining the expense of providing a new organ or placing a complete set of new pipes etc., in the case of the present organ and if necessary to arrange for Mr Telford visiting the Cathedral and meeting some members of the Chapter. His expenses to be paid, if not engaged to perform the work'. William Telford, perhaps the most noted Irish organ builder of the nineteenth century, lost no time in responding. His report to the Chapter of 2 November, is here reproduced in full:

> Gentlemen,
> We have carefully examined the organ in your Cathedral and respectfully beg to report that we found the bellows of the old construction, known as the 'vertical bellows', which can never give an equal or steady pressure of wind to the organ, the action throughout is in a very bad state both from construction and decay. The pipes are greatly injured from bad treatment, damp and poor materials – those in the fronts of the case being beyond repair, the metal of which they are composed being too soft to carry its own weight;[20] the Swell Organ is in every respect useless, the compass being too limited and the whole in a bad state – the Trumpet of the Great Organ has only six small pipes left out of fifty seven. Under these circumstances we cannot advise a repair of the present instrument for though a new bellows of modern

construction, new front pipes, new action, a good new Swell Organ, new pedals and pedal pipes and a general repair of the remainder of the organ would very greatly improve the instrument, we are of the opinion that the improvements would not be of such a permanent and satisfactory nature as to warrant the necessary outlay which could not be less than £270. 0s and although the new portions might be all that could be wished for, yet there would be imperfections and inequalities in the parts repaired that would ever be a source of regret and annoyance.

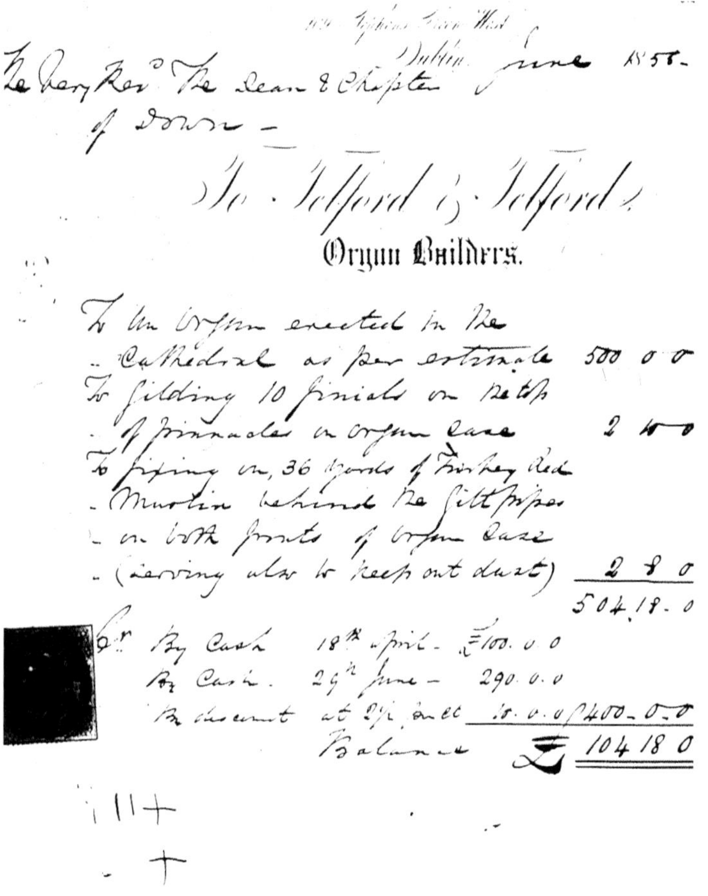

109 Stephens Green West
Dublin June 1855
The Very Revd The Dean & Chapter of Down –
To Telford & Telford
Organ Builders.

To an Organ erected in the Cathedral as per estimate	500 0 0
To gilding 10 finials on both of pinnacles on Organ case	2 10 0
To fixing on, 36 yards of Turkey Red Muslin behind the Gilt pipes on both fronts of Organ Case (serving also to keep out dust)	2 8 0
	504.18.0
Cr By Cash 18th April – £100.0.0	
By Cash. 29th June – 290.0.0	
By discount at 2 p ct 10.0.0	400.0.0
Balance	£104 18 0

1855 Telford Organ Receipt

We would therefore respectfully suggest the purchase of a new instrument as the most advisable course and we would propose to erect an organ that we have at present on hands in the case new in the Cathedral, making new pipes in the towers in both fronts and newly gilding the entire of both fronts, and varnishing and repairing the case. We enclose a specification of the instrument and we are willing to stake our professional characters on its excellence and suitability.

We would propose to erect it in the Cathedral complete including all expences (sic) of packing, carriage, removal of the present interim and erection of the new organ, gilding and new front pipes for the sum of Five hundred pounds, using the interior portions of the present instrument,

We have the honour to be your most obedient servants,

Telford & Telford
Organ Builders.
109 Stephen's Green, Dublin

We also engage to keep the instrument in good repair for twelve months from the time of erection, injuries arising from accidents or damp or abuse excepted, and to allow 2° per cent disc^t for cash payments, on the completion of the erection in the Cathedral.

Telford attended the chapter meeting at which his report was presented; without apparently inviting advice from any other quarter, the sub-Dean and Chapter accepted his estimate and ordered him to supply a new organ, whilst preserving the existing case. Within the remarkably short space of six months, the

Downpatrick Recorder was able to report on 5 May 1855 that '...a magnificent organ built in London and shown at the late exhibition in Cork is in progress of erection'. The Cathedral was, in fact, closed for several months whilst the work was being carried out but was reopened on 23 July of that year with a Confirmation Service at which the Bishop confirmed no fewer than 170 people.[21] The press references, however, pose two questions which have proved very difficult to answer; why did Telford & Telford of Dublin supply an organ which had been built in London and secondly what was it doing at a recent exhibition in Cork? Certainly it is difficult to envisage an organ being built from scratch in the period of time which elapsed from the date of the order in November 1854 until the following July, a period of some eight months. Indeed, the whole tenor of Telford's letter to the Chapter and in particular the phrase *to erect an organ that we have at present on hands* would suggest that he had an organ almost ready, if not completely finished, in his workshop. The price quoted would also seem to suggest pointedly that he wanted, indeed needed, a quick sale with discount for prompt settlement. Following the Crystal Palace exhibition of 1851, every provincial city tried to follow suit and show off its local industrial prowess. The movement came to Cork in the following year but, in spite of extensive enquiries, no catalogue of this exhibition can be traced; the opening ceremony is, however, reported in *The Cork Examiner* of 11 June 1852. From this we learn that Mr Telford of Dublin was responsible for the construction of the exhibition's principal organ. Furthermore, a small volume entitled *The Industrial Movement in Ireland as illustrated by the National Exhibition of 1852* by John Francis Maguire M.P., published in Cork the following year, has this to say:[22] '...Organ making is a branch of industry which has been steadily growing up in Ireland of late years. Indeed, the organ for which the Executive Committee applied and which had been made by Mr Telford of Dublin for the Catholic Cathedral of Armagh is one of the noblest instruments in the country....that sent by Mr Telford in its place, and because of the difficulty of removing the other, is a very fine instrument and added greatly to the attraction of the Exhibition'.

It is difficult to discover any link between the organs of the Roman Catholic Cathedral at Armagh and Down Cathedral. The two buildings were conceived on quite different scales and an organ specified for Armagh would have been quite out of place at Down. The London reference remains a mystery; Telford never built organs in London to the best of anyone's knowledge nor was he known to be an erector of instruments made by builders other than himself. In spite of the lack of conclusive evidence of its original destination, Down now had a Telford organ, which was second to none in Ireland. The newly appointed organist, John Carroll, who had scarcely played the old organ before its removal, was evidently delighted with the new; the *Recorder,* in its issue of 22 September 1855, reported that the organ led the sacred music in a most delightful manner and again on 4 July 1857: '...Mr Carroll, who performs on the magnificent organ, lately erected, does his part most creditably'.

On the suggestion of the Archdeacon, the Ven. W. B. Mant, the Chapter considered opening a subscription list in order to install a new east window in the cathedral as a memorial to his late father, Bishop Richard Mant, and it was agreed to spend a sum of £50 from funds at the Chapter's disposal for this purpose. However, Dean Blakely died in December 1855 at the age of 86 and shortly afterwards, the Chapter decided to install a 'painted' glass window in the east wall as a memorial to him. Preaching his funeral sermon in Killyleagh on 9 December, the Rector, Rev. Dr Edward Hincks, spoke of the late Dean's zealous attachment to his church; 'Whatever appeared to him to be done out of hostility to the Church, excited his displeasure.....and if the opinions which he entertained on matters of church polity were sometimes erroneous, it must be admitted that he was entitled to have great allowance made for his mistakes'.[23] The writer of the obituary in the *Downpatrick Recorder* also made an interesting comment: 'As to religion, he was what is commonly called a High Churchman.....though warmly attached to his own peculiar views and perhaps too far advanced in years to fall in with new religious agencies as they arose'.[24]

In spite of the well attested popular view of the late Dean, the Chapter pressed on with its plan to install a window portraying 'pictures of our Saviour, the Virgin Mary etc.,'[25] no doubt spurred on by the Archdeacon. For several weeks, both the *Downpatrick Recorder* and the *Downshire Protestant* carried voluminous editorial and correspondence, the correspondence on the whole supporting the design but the editorial in both newspapers opposing the design in a most vitriolic manner. The matter quickly became a *cause célèbre* in Downpatrick and one can imagine the citizens waiting eagerly for the next instalment as the drama unfolded. The principal supporters were William Keown of Ballydugan and Captain Hamilton of Killyleagh, but the opponents, with the exception of William Beers of Newcastle, chose to remain anonymous. The *Recorder* was, of course, still in the ownership of the Pilson family; the *Downshire Protestant*, which had a short life from 6 July 1855 until 20 September 1862, was owned by William Johnston of Ballykilbeg. Perhaps not surprisingly, the cathedral records are silent on the entire affair and it is only through the contemporary local press that one can appreciate the depth of concern on the part of the citizenry of the town. In that age of sectarianism, even the Roman newspapers took up the cudgel; again the *Recorder:* '...we find that the Popish organ in Belfast has heaped the most virulent abuse upon ourselves and taken the window and its special promoters under its special patronage. The *Ulsterman* was in its element at such work'.[26]

The people of Downpatrick took the matter into their own hands; on the night of Friday 26 September 1856, a person or persons unknown hurled a brick through the window.[27] As if that was not enough, someone fired a gun into it the following week, causing additional damage. '...Various rumours are afloat as to the quarter from which the breaking emanated. The general impression is that it proceeded from the parties who originated the window. They may have sought an excuse for removing it, when they found that they had run counter to the feelings of the Protestant community and that removed it must be. Of one thing we are almost certain: that the window was not broken by any who deserve the name of true Protestants'.[28]

In spite of its Protestant ethos, the *Recorder* printed this imaginary conversation between the three Saints in the cathedral graveyard, supposedly from a waggish priest:[29]

St Patrick	Bridgit dear, do you not hear, some lurking villain prowling near? Old Columb! Rise, lift up your eyes – the night is cold and dark the skies
St Bridgit	Why, Pat, you fool! lie kind and cool, you're now too old to go to school The heretics, that's in a fix, must pay the piper for his tricks
St Columb	My second sight in this dark night beholds a scowling Orange wight, He's slight and tall, behind the wall, he grasps a stone that's round and small
St Bridgit	Holy Mother! I hear a dash – I hear a rattle – I hear a smash. The stone is through the window sash.
St Patrick	I'm sorry but I cannot cry; the fragments all in ruin lie. *Gloria transit sic mundi*
St Columb	Puseyites have now before 'em, what is sure to rattle o'er them: *In secula saeculorum*
St Bridgit	Now to slumber, till again, boys shall break a painted pane: in darkness, wind and rattling rain
St Patrick	*Pax cum vobis:* Columb, Bridgit, better sleep than endless fidget: My blessing on the boy who did it.

A reward of £100 was immediately offered for the prosecution of the perpetrators of the crime; the letter offering the reward in the *Downshire Protestant* was signed by no less than 43 people but the *Recorder* was careful to point out that not all of the 43 people were necessarily in favour of the window. The *Downshire Protestant*, in a leader entitled *Should there be a Blakely Monument* in its issue of 21 November, emphatically said 'No.....we believe that the smallest possible memorial, in any corner quite out of view, would have been more than sufficient'. The episode left such an impression on the people of Downpatrick that it was to be 40 years before the Chapter had the will to replace the window.

Dean Blakely had died on 1 December 1855 and, before the month was over, both local newspapers carried long editorials as to the character of the man whom the people of Downpatrick expected as a replacement. The *Recorder,* in its issue of 15 December, declined to mention names, preferring to concentrate on principles: 'The Protestants of the Parish of Down want for their Dean a pious, faithful, working, evangelical resident clergyman....No Oxford theology for them. They want a sound gospel minister who will live among them and do his duty'. As may be expected, the *Downshire Protestant* was somewhat more outspoken; the issue of 14 December suggested the name of Rev I.G.Abeltshanser (*recte* Abeltshauser), Professor of French and German at T.C.D., Prebendary of Saint Andrews (*recte* Saint Audeons), Dublin and one of the editors of the *Irish Church Journal.* '...While we acknowledge Mr Abeltshanser's claims as a scholar and as a gentleman, we cannot imagine what he has done to entitle him to the living of Down. Another arrangement than this the Protestants of Ireland have a right to expect; perhaps not, however, from the government of Lord Carlisle'. Elsewhere in the same issue is a report from *The Limerick Chronicle* that Dr Tighe, Dean of Ardagh, would succeed and in the following issue it was rumoured that Rev John Gregg had been offered the Deanery by the Lord Lieutenant. Rev Gregg was described as an eloquent and able divine, well-known and loved as a popular preacher in Dublin; 'though taking no great part in the great Protestant movement which is a matter for regret, would still be a faithful minister and zealous pastor'. By the end of the month, speculation and rumour were at an end; Rev Thomas Woodward, Rector of Mullingar, had been appointed. The *Downshire Protestant*: 'It is not in our power to state what the Rev. Gentleman's views are on doctrinal and educational questions; but of this we are persuaded, that no man will be acceptable to the Protestants of Down unless he is a thoroughly evangelical minister'.

Thomas Woodward
Dean 1856-1875

The *Recorder*, by 5 January 1856, had had time to carry out an extensive search into the new Dean's background and credentials; the editor concluded that his views on the Gospel, on Education, on the enemies of the Church, be they Romish, Infidel or Puseyite, concurred with its own; 'We cordially welcome such a minister to this parish. We wish him God Speed'. Dean Woodward read the Communion Service and preached for the first time in his Cathedral on 17 February. The *Recorder* reported 'that the Very Rev. Gentleman's enunciation was clear, distinct and emphatic... not so long as to fatigue the audience. The new Dean has made a good impression and the reasonable expectation prevails that he will make a good active working clergyman. That he has at once taken up residence among us is a good symptom. The Very Rev. Gentleman is daily occupied in visiting his parishioners'.

Before the end of his first year, Dean Woodward had, of course, to cope with the upsurge of anti-establishment feeling associated with the affair of the window. Although Queen Victoria was to remove it from the Book of Common Prayer three years later, there still existed in the Prayer Book a Service of Thanksgiving on 5 November, *for the happy Deliverance of King James I and the Three Estates of England, from the most traiterous and bloody-intended Massacre by gunpowder; and also for the happy Arrival of His Majesty King William on this day, for the Deliverance of our Church and Nation.* The Down Protestant Association had been accustomed to hold an annual service in the cathedral on this day, but, as feelings in the town were running high, the Dean refused to allow the cathedral to be used on this occasion. The offending window was finally removed later that month; 'The Protestants of Down have gained a signal victory.....May temporary animosities cease with its departure and peace and union prevail among protestants'.[30]

Dean Woodward's early years were spent taking stock of the situation and pursuing the appeal for funds. A personal letter to the Primate, Lord J.G.Beresford, brought the response regretting his inability to help Down Cathedral as he already had two cathedrals and had already given pretty large assistance in the Diocese of Down in the way of augmenting incomes of clergy who held benefices of which he was the patron.[31] The Chapter, at its meeting on 7 March 1856, asked Mr Henry Smyth, the County Surveyor and regular worshipper at the Cathedral, to make a plan of repewing the Cathedral, putting the chapter seats and choir towards the east end, forming a chancel there screened off from the other part. Thankfully, funds were insufficient to enable this to be carried out. Yet an ongoing programme of maintenance and repair went ahead, necessitating closure of the Cathedral for a prolonged period. By January 1863, the Cathedral had been closed for over two years, causing considerable anxiety among the parishioners, especially those who did not have accommodation in the parish church. A special clause had been included in an Amendment to the Church Temporalities Act in 1860, granting power to the Ecclesiastical Commissioners to contribute to the repair of the Cathedral Church of the Holy Trinity of Down, though non-parochial.[32] In spite of this sudden availability of funds, the only structural work done on this occasion was the erection of a new pulpit on the south side of the chancel and the removal of the old one from the north side; in addition, the Cathedral was totally refurnished and painted. Two accounts survive among the archives; one from R. & J. Quail, Upholsterers of Irish Street for £283 7s 10d covering cushions, carpets and stools and another from James Girdwood of 44 High Street, Belfast for £121 6s 4d covering large quantities of cocoa matting, velvet, silk fringe and silk tassels, grey calico, amber cord, pulpit tassels and the like.

The Cathedral was eventually reopened on Thursday 10 December 1863 with Morning Prayer at half past eleven o'clock at which the Preacher was the Bishop of Killaloe, Rt Rev. William Fitzgerald and Evening Prayer at seven o'clock at which the Preacher was Rev. W. Alexander, Rector of Camus in the Diocese of Derry and Chaplain to the Lord Lieutenant. The following week, the *Recorder* published an extensive history of the Cathedral together with details of the work which had been carried out.[33] On the exterior, there was considerable work done to the walls and pinnacles; in the interior, the centre aisle was fitted up with open seats (presumably the centre pews which were removed in 1987) and a row of seats was placed along the walls of the side aisles. On the walls behind these seats, R. & J. Quail had erected richly carved wooden shields carrying the arms of the families to whom the seat had been appropriated. The new pulpit was the gift of Conway Pilson and had been carved in oak by Mr George Stockdale who was, in fact, the contractor responsible for the entire contract.

The remarkable series of heraldic achievements on the walls are not mentioned in the press reports of the period; with the exception of the two original examples of 1801, they were erected by the Belfast firm of Marcus Ward in 1864. The two exceptions are those in the centre of the north and south aisle walls, the former being the arms of the See of Down and the latter the double achievement of the Downshire and Sandys families, erected by the wife of the second Marquis of Downshire, who, as we read in an earlier chapter, was Baroness Sandys in her own right. These two are of Coade stone, signed by the London firm. The entire series has been described in detail by Lt Col. J. R. H. Greeves, who made a detailed description of these achievements and which has been printed in Appendix 5.

By all accounts, the new Telford organ was not entirely trouble free; Telford had continued to tune the organ regularly until 1860 but, thereafter, for upwards of a decade, the Chapter must have fallen out with him. In January 1863, Mr Carroll was paid ten shillings expenses for travelling to Belfast 'about the organ' and subsequently we find J. C. Combe tuning the instrument. Carroll's salary was raised from £40 *per annum* to £60, but he had to find the bellows blower out of his salary. The payroll was also extended at this time to accommodate five singing girls, joining the boys for the first time.

During the prolonged period when the Cathedral was closed, J. C. Combe, the local representative of William Hill & Son, was requested by the Chapter to report on the organ and give an estimate for 'improving and lightening the touch'. Combe suggested that the cause of the touch being so immensely heavy was due to the bad construction of the pallets in the Great Organ Sound Board, the pressure of wind upon their extraordinarily large surface accounting for the tremendous resistance to the touch on the keys. In order to remedy this, he proposed to introduce a pneumatic lever to the Great organ, a device which he claimed to have invented. His proposals also included a new swell box of solid deal to replace the existing 'wretchedly ill-contrived box' and recovering the keys with new ivory. A new German circular (sic) pedal board was also added.[34] It is not clear if the Chapter acted on Combe's advice, which, in the event, could not be taken seriously. Pneumatic action had been in use for at least twenty years; it was something of an overstatement to say that he had invented it!

It may be appropriate here to relate some press reports concerning Rev. Thomas Drew. After 25 years as the first Incumbent of Christ Church, Belfast, he was appointed Rector of Loughinisland, which incumbency carried with it the Precentorship of the Cathedral. Drew was notorious for his ultra-evangelical views and was an outspoken preacher; his daughter, Arminella, was the wife of William Johnston of Ballykilbeg, the owner of *The Downshire Protestant* (although she died six months after the marriage), a circumstance which ensured full press coverage of all his public pronouncements. On his appointment to Loughinisland, the newspaper had this to say: 'It is well known that, on many subjects of public interest and public policy, the views of the Reverend Doctor and his Diocesan are directly antagonistic'.[35] His first sermon preached in the Cathedral was 'full of that pathos for which the Rev. Gentleman is so deservedly popular'.[36]

Thomas Drew
Precentor of Down
1859-1870

In its issue of 20 July 1860, *The Downshire Protestant* printed an address to the Dean from the Downpatrick Loyal Orange Lodge, thanking him for the use of the cathedral on 12 July at which service between two and three thousand people (sic) were present; the sermon had been preached by Rev. S.G.Potter of the Diocese of Leighlin, Deputy Grand Chaplain of the Grand Orange Lodge of Ireland. In the following month, Mr Potter was invited to preach in the parish church of Belfast, even though the Bishop had written to the Vicar of Belfast prohibiting Mr Potter from preaching. 'There is a good deal of religious hypocrisy going these days but we fairly award the palm to the Lord Bishop of Down and Connor'.[37] Three months is a long time in popular memory. By November, the Orangemen of

Lecale were in an incipient state of insurrection against Dean Woodward because he had refused to celebrate Divine Service in the Cathedral on 5 November,[38] (Of course, he was perfectly entitled to do so as the service in question had been removed from the Book of Common Prayer in 1859). The Orangemen had all their arrangements made and engaged Rev. Dr Drew to preach one of his usual meek and charitable sermons when the Dean coolly informed them that the cathedral doors would remain closed. However, all was not lost; they all went to hear Rev. Hugh Hanna in the Presbyterian Church instead!

The case between the Bishop and Rev. Potter was eventually tried by the Consistorial Court in Dublin. Again *The Downshire Protestant*: '.....the Bishop of Down deserves a Cardinal's hat and we should not be surprised to hear that there is one in store for him in the Old Curiosity Shop in Rome'.[39] The outcome of the case was in favour of the Bishop, leading to a placard being carried around the town of Downpatrick:

> PROTESTANTS OF DOWN BEWARE
>
> On 12 August next, a Confirmation will take place in your Cathedral. Bishop Knox, the inhibitor of Honest Miller and Brave Potter will be the officiating prelate. On no account permit him to confirm the children of loyal fathers and warm hearted protestant mothers. Keep your children at home on that day. Send the renegade Bishop home to Holywood, there to concoct another speech on behalf of Sabbath desecration.[40]

The events of which we have read in this chapter represent a microcosm of the general resentment felt in the community concerning the privileged position of the Established Church. Disestablishment in 1870 brought profound changes to the Church of Ireland, not least in the management and support of its Cathedrals. Seen through the eyes of the local clergy, the effect was virtually cataclysmic and the uncharted waters ahead seemed to offer no future. Looking back across the intervening years, we can marvel at the spirit of those clergy who built bridges into the new era. But one who steadfastly refused to cross that bridge was Dean Thomas Woodward.

View looking west from the Chancel, probably pre-1899
THE LAWRENCE COLLECTION
THE NATIONAL LIBRARY OF IRELAND

ELEVEN

SEEKING A NEW ROLE

This day is a memorable day in our country's history. This morning, the first day, the first Sunday of 1871, the ancient Church of Ireland, the Church of our fathers, the Church of Bedell, Ussher, Taylor, Berkeley and Magee, with all its time-honoured memories is at an end, as far as it can be destroyed by any human power. By a faithless set, unparalleled in the records of legislation, the Church, which the British Government was bound by every principle of honour, by every sacred obligation, including the solemn oath of the sovereign, to nurture and defend, has been degraded from its position of Establishment and sacrilegiously plundered of all that prosperity which was never given her by the state, but was hers for centuries before parliament itself existed. Of the

> treatment which we Irish Churchmen have received from those towards whom our only failing was too implicit faith, too enthusiastic loyalty, I shall not trust myself to speak, lest language unsuited to this sacred place should escape my lips...I see in that unrestricted liberty of self-government which we now possess not the glorious privilege which some think it, but the unhappy dissolution of that connection between the Church and the civil government which is essential to the very idea of a Christian community, and necessary to the well-being of both, for a disestablished church implies a Godless state.

So spoke Dean Woodward in his sermon in Down Parish Church on 1 January 1871.[1] Here was a man, not just apprehensive of the future, but of such limited vision, that he was quite unable to take the step forward and lead the cathedral into the uncharted waters of the Disestablished Church; that task he was compelled to leave to others with greater vision than he. To be fair, he had some justification for adopting such an uncompromising stance; in its report leading to disestablishment, the Irish Church Commission had proposed the closure of Down Cathedral as soon as Belfast Cathedral should be built.[2] Although this

View of interior prior to 1899 when the present east window was installed.
THE LAWRENCE COLLECTION
THE NATIONAL LIBRARY OF IRELAND

proposal was dropped from the legislation, the position of Down Cathedral was nevertheless very unclear during the disestablishment debate. Not being a parochial church, it did not appear to come under the appropriate legislation, even though the small measure of support it had received in recent years from the Ecclesiastical Commissioners was now removed.

The Diocesan Synod, acting through the Diocesan Council, in fact became the controlling body.[3] At its meeting on 4 January 1871, the council appointed a committee to make temporary arrangements for the cathedral and to provide for the continuation of Divine Service in it. A week later this committee met for the first time; neither the Dean nor any member of Chapter was present as they considered themselves to have been dissolved at the end of 1870. Dean Woodward, however, sent word that he would be at home should the committee wish to consult him. Mr W. N. Wallace, a well-known citizen and life time worshipper at the Cathedral, was appointed convener. Throughout these months, the Dean was under considerable misapprehension as the general Convention of the Church of Ireland which met in Dublin during 1870 had, in fact, passed a statute confirming cathedral dignitaries in the continuance of their offices with the same rights, powers and privileges until the General Synod made alternative arrangements.[4] He even went so far as to publish a letter in the *Irish Ecclesiastical Gazette,* dissenting from anything decreed at the 1871 General Synod which altered the doctrines or formularies of the Church of Ireland.[5]

After much deliberation and consultation with the Dean and Chapter of Cork Cathedral, the committee recommended the appointment of a Provisional Board to be comprised of the Chapter and an equal number of laymen. Dean Woodward agreed to attend its meetings on condition that he would not be put in the position of surrendering any rights which he held for the benefit of his successors.

The first meeting of the General Synod, held in April 1871, was much too early to have legislation framed for the management of cathedrals; there was more important work to be done. More delicate negotiation was necessary among the various parties before a consensus of opinion could be reached. In early March 1872, Bishop Knox addressed an open meeting in the Cathedral at which he emphasized that the Cathedral could not look for support from the townspeople of Downpatrick but that its upkeep should be a diocesan responsibility. The financial support necessary, which he had estimated should be around £400 *per annum*, should be forthcoming from the nobility, gentry and clergy of Down. The Bishop also announced that Dean Woodward had unreservedly placed in his hands all his special privileges and had agreed to the appointment of a Board of Management. One of the early actions of the Provisional Committee was to issue an appeal for funds; this took the form of an 'Historical Notice of the Cathedral of the Holy and Undivided Trinity at Down: Its past and present state, and the efforts for its improvement and restoration'. This little volume, in

East window shortly after its installation in 1899. Note the absence of the brass plaque recording the donors names and the Londonderry Arms on the North Pier before removal to their present position to make way for the McCammon Memorial. The Central Pews, removed in 1986, can also be seen
THE R. J. WELCH COLLECTION
THE ULSTER MUSEUM

an orange cover and printed by the Belfast firm of Marcus Ward, was the first of many such appeals over the years, each of which took the form of a short history of the Cathedral.

The Down Cathedral Bill, which was placed before General Synod in April 1872 bears the stamp of Mr W. N. Wallace, a solicitor by profession, in its framework. His close association with the Cathedral all his life coupled with his undoubted vision for the future of the Disestablished Church gave him a penetrating view into the nature of lay involvement in church affairs which he considered desirable. But he went too far. The Bill, in its original form, provided for the appointment of the Dean and two minor canons by the Cathedral Board as well as the determination of the duties of the Chapter and minor canons, but, in the committee stage, the appointment of the Dean reverted to the Bishop of the Diocese and the lesser appointments reverted to the Dean and Chapter. In its final form, the Bill was passed by General Synod on 7 May 1872.

The principal clauses of the Bill included the separation of the Deanery from the incumbency of the Parish; the Ordinary of the Cathedral should in future be the Bishop of the Diocese and the appointment by him, in his capacity as

Ordinary, of the members of the Chapter consisting of a Precentor, Chancellor, Treasurer, Archdeacon,[6] and two Prebendaries, Saint Andrew's and Dunsport; the creation of Vestrymen who in their turn would elect Synodsmen and Cathedral Wardens and the constitution of a Cathedral Board to consist of the Chapter together with eight laymen elected every third year.

On the last day of February 1873, the Vestrymen held their first meeting and, after considering a number of points carried over from the provisional committee, proceeded to elect the lay members of the new Board. In the event, the Bishop suggested all eight names which were accepted by those present without dissent. They were the Earl of Dufferin, Colonel Forde M.P., John Mulholland D.L., Major Maxwell, William Keown M.P., W. N. Wallace, Conway Pilson J.P. and Henry Smyth C.E., Mr Wallace continued to act as secretary and treasurer and, indeed, it is to him that we are indebted for a very full record of cathedral business, both in reports and minutes, until his death 20 years later.

There was still considerable difficulty over the position of Dean Woodward. He absented himself from all Board meetings and, although he had moved his residence from Downpatrick to Newcastle, surviving correspondence is addressed both from Richmond, Surrey and from the English Club, Pau, France. Although he had resigned his rights in a letter to the Bishop at the end of 1871, the passing of the statute by the General Synod in 1872 required that he should do so in writing again; in the meantime, he had taken legal advice. His stance was that any rights conferred on him by the Royal Charter of 1609 could only be removed by Act of Parliament; under that Charter, the Dean was created Ordinary of the Cathedral, this position now being held by the Bishop under the new disestablishment legislation. Woodward was now at loggerheads even with the Bishop. Legal counsel was sought on both sides and eventually, by January 1874, Dean Woodward gave the necessary authority to the Bishop regarding the Board's management of the Cathedral, whilst he was permitted to retain his dignity as Dean. At one point he even attempted to bargain with the Bishop in return for the re-creation of the Prebend of Talpestone, but the Bishop was unable to respond, even if he had so wished, as the recent statute provided for only two prebends.

The name of Dean Woodward effectively disappeared from the record at this point although he was present at a meeting of the Down Clergy Widows' Fund, i.e., the Chapter in October 1874. He died in London in September 1875 at the comparatively early age of 61. In its obituary, the *Down Recorder* said nothing of the controversy of recent years, rather it referred to his excellence as a preacher and the strong voice with which his carefully prepared sermons were delivered. His oversight of the cathedral restoration a decade earlier was also noted saying that it would remain a monument to his industry and zeal.[7] There is little doubt but that Woodward was a casualty of Disestablishment; whilst the vast majority of clergy accepted the challenge of the new order, Woodward's world collapsed around him and he was quite unprepared for the sacrifice of dignity and position which the upper echelons of clergy had undoubtedly held in the predisestablished church. With his death, Down Cathedral could look forward with a clearer, if not altogether unclouded vision, to the future under a new Dean, strongly supported by William Nevin Wallace.

The new Dean was the Rev. E.B.Moeran, Rector of Killyleagh, who, in his capacity as Treasurer of the Chapter, had effectively been carrying out the duties of the Dean for the previous five years. Moeran was of a more tolerant and liberal spirit but, as one peruses the Board and Vestry minutes, one is left in no doubt that the real power behind the scene was Wallace. His industry and diligence were prodigious and it would not be an exaggeration to say that the very survival of the Cathedral in these early years, when it was desperately trying to seek a role in the Diocese, was in no small measure due to his advocacy. Around this period, just 20 years after that fateful accident to the east window, the Board felt it opportune to re-open the subject of installing stained glass, believing that a number of well-known persons would be prepared to subscribe towards it. Accordingly designs were asked for, although the minutes do not specify from whom; at a subsequent meeting a design was presented representing Saint Peter with his keys, with Saint Paul, ten apostles and our Saviour on His throne and a dove descending with holy fire. Bishop Knox was apprehensive if such a design would be favourable to the people of Downpatrick, bearing in mind what had happened at an earlier date, which was still fresh in the memory of many people. Someone took exception to the representation of our Saviour, someone else did not like Saint Peter with his keys. Saint Andrew is normally represented with a saltire cross but it was requested that this be omitted. Finally it was felt that it would be better to have select illustrations from Scripture 'such as were in other churches'. A sub-committee, in whose hands the matter was left, presented a revised design at a subsequent meeting; this was defeated on the motion of Mr Wallace, seconded by Henry Smyth, on the premise that approval had not been unanimous. The revised design took the form of scenes from the life of our Lord and the parables. Nevertheless, no further action was taken towards replacing the window until after Mr Wallace's death in 1894. Such was his control over the business of the Cathedral coupled with his evangelical outlook that no member of the Board was prepared to override him in such a fundamental issue. The window was eventually installed in 1899, to the design of Ballantyne of Edinburgh, who had apparently prepared the original design; it was made by the well-known firm of Meyer of Munich at a cost of £350, which was generously subscribed by a number of clergy and gentry of

Edward B. Moeran
Dean of Down 1876-1887

Opposite:
View looking east from entrance porch, probably pre-1899
THE LAWRENCE COLLECTION
THE NATIONAL LIBRARY OF IRELAND

the county, headed by Lord Dunleath.

The Rector of Down Parish at this period was Rev. Townley Blackwood Price; he was also Treasurer to the Chapter and subsequently Archdeacon of the Diocese. On the whole reasonably harmonious relations were maintained with the parish church, many of whose parishioners attended evening service in the Cathedral. As early as 1882, Bishop Knox suggested to the trustees of Hollymount Church that the incumbency of their church should be combined with the minor canonry in the Cathedral; Rev Stephen Campbell, whose wife belonged to the Mulholland family of Eglantine and later Ballywalter, took up the position and was installed as Prebendary of Dunsford a year later. Rev. Campbell, on his own initiative, prepared plans for the enlargement of the Cathedral and asked for them to be placed before the Board for consideration. The Board must have thought otherwise, however, and the matter was quietly dropped; Canon Campbell resigned as Minor Canon although he retained Hollymount until 1889. He was a man of not inconsiderable independent means; in his will, very substantial sums were bequeathed to various charities connected with the church both in Ireland and in England, including £5,000 to the Representative Church Body and over £10,000 to the building fund of Saint Anne's Cathedral in Belfast.[8]

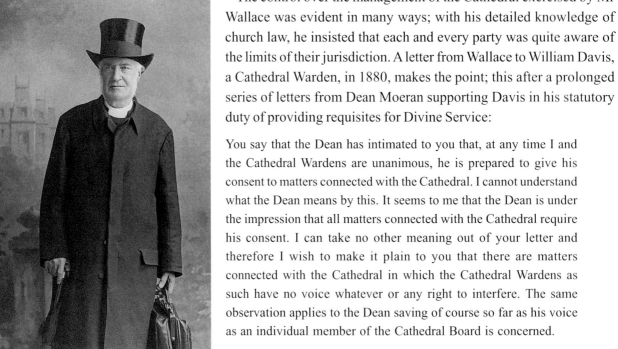

Edward Maguire
Dean of Down 1887-1912

The control over the management of the Cathedral exercised by Mr Wallace was evident in many ways; with his detailed knowledge of church law, he insisted that each and every party was quite aware of the limits of their jurisdiction. A letter from Wallace to William Davis, a Cathedral Warden, in 1880, makes the point; this after a prolonged series of letters from Dean Moeran supporting Davis in his statutory duty of providing requisites for Divine Service:

> You say that the Dean has intimated to you that, at any time I and the Cathedral Wardens are unanimous, he is prepared to give his consent to matters connected with the Cathedral. I cannot understand what the Dean means by this. It seems to me that the Dean is under the impression that all matters connected with the Cathedral require his consent. I can take no other meaning out of your letter and therefore I wish to make it plain to you that there are matters connected with the Cathedral in which the Cathedral Wardens as such have no voice whatever or any right to interfere. The same observation applies to the Dean saving of course so far as his voice as an individual member of the Cathedral Board is concerned.

Dean Moeran died in October 1887 at the age of 78; his obituary in *The Down Recorder* described how he was accustomed to walk from Killyleagh to Downpatrick throughout the winter in order to preach at the cathedral.[9] He was succeeded before the end of the year by Edward Maguire, who had been Chancellor to the Chapter for the previous two years. Dean Maguire was Rector of Bangor Parish, where the magnificent church in the centre of the town, dedicated to Saint Comgall, stands as a monument to his incumbency there. So long as he did not interfere with the week-to-week running of the Cathedral, and from which he was sufficiently distant, the new Dean appears to have kept a low profile. To Mr Wallace's credit, the cathedral finances were in a very satisfactory state.

In 1889, some consternation was caused among Board members by a press reference to the opening of a new chancel in Lisburn Cathedral, wherein that edifice was described as the Cathedral of Down and Connor. The chairman of the Board, no less a figure than Bishop Reeves (Bishop of Down, Connor and Dromore 1886-1892) stated that this title was perfectly correct under the Charter granted by Charles II. Nevertheless, the Board decided that something ought to be done in order to reassert the position of their Cathedral as the Cathedral of the Diocese but it was not clear as to the most appropriate way to approach the subject, nor, in fact, if any action was actually taken. On Reeves's death, the new Bishop was T.J.Welland, Rector of Saint Thomas's in Belfast. Dean Maguire immediately wrote to Mr Wallace suggesting that there should be a special service at the Cathedral on the occasion of the first visit of the new Bishop.[10]

Rt Rev. William Reeves

> If the Dean and Chapter should arrange to hold such service, it would add much importance to the function if the Board, as such, would co-operate. The united action of Board, Dean and Chapter and Clergy would in itself be a protest against the perpetration of the Charter of Charles II, and would lay a foundation for future synodical (or even parliamentary) action...However gratified we would be to you for any personal aid in the matter, we would not wish to impose on you any unnecessary trouble. The Dean and Chapter would, I have no doubt, undertake all responsibility with the service in case it should be decided to hold such. I am sure it would gratify and greatly encourage our new Bishop if all the Cathedral authorities would unite in giving him a welcome to the only Cathedral in the United diocese.

In spite of the Chapter's wish, the service did not take place owing to the fact that the 1662 Charter was still legally in place, requiring the enthronement for both Dioceses to take place in Lisburn. By way of consolation, Dean Maguire read the mandate from the Primate at the service in Lisburn.[11]

William Nevin Wallace died in January 1895 at the age of 77; no-one had done more for the cathedral than he. As Secretary and Treasurer to the Board in the formative years since Disestablishment – a period of 25 years – he had guided the business affairs of the Cathedral as an extension to his own legal practice of Hugh Wallace & Co. He did not miss a meeting of the Board or

Vestry and not only did he write the minutes of each meeting in the appropriate book, but he sent a report to each member in addition to the formal notice convening the next meeting. A public spirited man, he had been appointed High Sherriff for the county in 1891 in addition to his duties as Deputy Lieutenant. In passing a resolution of sympathy at the first Board meeting after his death, the Board made mention of the tirelessness of his efforts for the benefit of the Cathedral as well as his numerous acts of generous liberality. At the same meeting his son, Major Robert Hugh Wallace was appointed Secretary and Treasurer in the room of his late father; as he took on his father's mantle, he was not to know that his term of office would exceed by many years that which had just closed.

William Nevin Wallace
DOWN COUNTY MUSEUM

The Board now met much less frequently, sometimes only once a year and indeed on occasion, only in alternate years. This may have been partly due to a change of secretary but was principally due to the efficiency of management of the Cathedral by the Minor Canon, Rev. L. A. Pooler. He had been appointed to the position in 1889 and took a deep interest in the Cathedral in addition to his duties at Hollymount. By 1896, he was able to report an increase in the number of communicants, a total of 615 during the year. The portrait of Primate Knox in the Chapter Room was a gift from Rev. Pooler and the Board purchased the companion portrait of Bishop Reeves. On the resignation in 1899 of Archdeacon Townley Blackwood Price from the incumbency of Down at the age of 74, Rev. Pooler was appointed to succeed him, thus removing him from the minor canonry; he retained Hollymount, however, which has remained united to Down since that date.

Col. R. H. Wallace
DOWN COUNTY MUSEUM

The High Cross at the east end of the Cathedral was re-erected in 1897 through the instigation of Mr F. J. Bigger of the Belfast Naturalists' Field Club; in addition he personally paid all the expenses.[12] It had been taken down presumably in the early eighteenth century during the early growth of modern Downpatrick, from its original position at the foot of English Street. However, before it could be erected, it had to be assembled from its constituent parts. The arms and head were in Col.Wallace's yard; the shaft was behind the chancel of the Roman Catholic Church and the base was being used as a horse trough in McEvoy's (now Denvir's) hotel.[13] It was Rev. Pooler's suggestion to have the cross erected in its present position, his 'only fear being that the R.C.s may object to giving their part of it to be placed under the shadow of our Cathedral'. To which Col.Wallace added: 'Let the Naturalists [BNFC] get the shank first from the Priest'.[14] Bigger succeeded in persuading the Roman priest and the cross was erected without any trouble.

Bigger next turned his attention to the provision of a new memorial stone near the cathedral to mark the reputed grave of Saint Patrick. The Cathedral Board readily agreed but the fact that the local Roman Catholics were not consulted

Before F. J. Bigger placed the Patrick Memorial Stone in 1900, the site was occupied by an earlier stone commemorating Patrick, Bridget and Columba.
THE LAWRENCE COLLECTION
THE NATIONAL LIBRARY
OF IRELAND

occasioned some bitterness. The local parish priest, Rev.P. O'Kane, wrote to *The Irish News* protesting against non-Catholics assuming to themselves the right to erect such a memorial.[15] The same newspaper also published a letter from no less than Monsignor O'Laverty of Holywood, supporting the parish priest of Downpatrick, not so much in the provision of the memorial, but objecting to the decision being taken by those who were not the heirs of Saint Patrick. In the following issue of *The Irish News,* Bigger published a rejoinder in which he stressed that the memorial was being provided by Irishmen and that no question of Catholic or Protestant had arisen; the Cathedral Board had not provided any funds and he was now taking the opportunity of inviting subscriptions from all creeds and classes of Irishmen at home and abroad. In the event both Monsignor O'Laverty and Father O'Kane did send subscriptions (along with Lord Dufferin, Colonel Sharman Crawford and Dean Maguire), although the letter accompanying Father O'Kane's subscription asked for his name not to be published nor did he wish to be publicly associated with it.[16] The stone is a large slab of Mourne granite from Slieve-na-largie, near Castlewellan, with the name 'Patric' deeply cut on it along with an early form of Celtic cross. It took 12 men 14 days to move it from its original site to the country road and it was then transported to its present site by rail and road.[17]

The Patrick Memorial stone.
W. A. GREEN COLLECTION.
ULSTER FOLK AND TRANSPORT MUSEUM

Shortly after Disestablishment and the appointment in 1872 of a new organist, a Mr Stevenson, Telford was brought back to report on the unsatisfactory state of the organ. In his letter to the Board of 14 October 1873, he reported that the instrument required a thorough cleaning and overhaul; all the pipes and action needed taken out, repaired, regulated, reclothed and rehung; new steel pull downs in the wind chests were needed along with new pins in the blowing action and new valves on the feeders of the bellows. The entire instrument needed regulated and tuned. The pedal organ must have been in a bad way as he could not use the 'pneumatic action' but recommended that it should be repaired or removed completely as he should decide on examination. The estimate for the work was £45 (in fact, it cost £65). Telford was determined to return the organ to where it had been prior to Combe's work of 1863.

Mr Stevenson's tenure of the organ loft was short as a sub-committee was appointed in 1877 to select a new organist. Four years later (!) the sub-committee reported that there had been twenty applicants for the post, of whom three had been short-listed: Mr Crowe of Lichfield, Mr O'Shaunessy of Galway and Mr Wilson of Gilford. On a vote being taken, Mr Wilson was appointed at a salary of £50.

William Telford died in 1885 at the age of 75 and, although his sons carried on the business for another half century,[18] the Cathedral Board had to look elsewhere for regular tuning and maintenance. Hart & Churchill of Belfast undertook to tune the instrument three times a year at an annual cost of £4. In the cathedral report for 1885, the names of the choir are quoted; they total 15 gentlemen and 8 ladies in addition to the organ blower and Mr C.M. Wilson. Among the gentlemen is the name of Albert Coulter, who offered his services as organist at a salary of £35 in 1898 on Wilson's resignation. Thus began the most remarkable tenure of the organ loft, perhaps only equalled by that of C.J. Brennan in Saint Anne's Cathedral in Belfast; Albert Coulter presided there until his death in 1957. To be fair, he asked for an increase in salary twelve months after his appointment, but the Board felt unable to grant it owing to the state of the finances, although they did increase it to £40 the following year. In spite of his threatened resignation in 1906, his initial years were trouble free – the organ was in fair shape. By 1908, however, the Telford firm was called in to advise on repair and estimates were also sought from Evans & Barr of Belfast and Conacher of Huddersfield, a firm which was particularly active in Ulster at this period. Nevertheless, no action was taken and the condition of the organ continued to deteriorate.

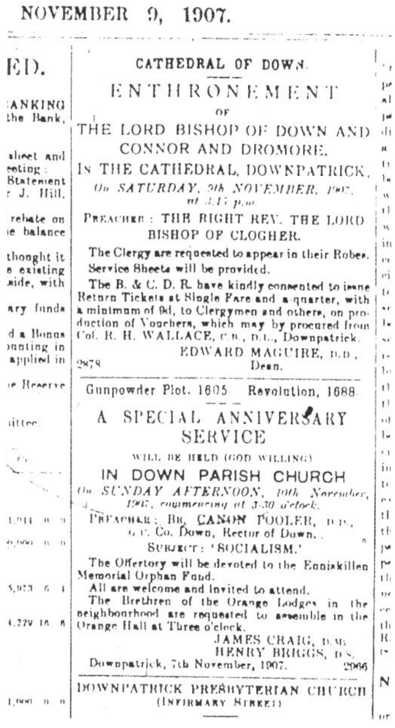
NOVEMBER 9, 1907.

CATHEDRAL OF DOWN.

ENTHRONEMENT

OF

THE LORD BISHOP OF DOWN AND CONNOR AND DROMORE.

IN THE CATHEDRAL, DOWNPATRICK,

On SATURDAY, 9th NOVEMBER, 1907, at 3.15 p.m.

PREACHER: THE RIGHT REV. THE LORD BISHOP OF CLOGHER.

The Clergy are requested to appear in their Robes.

Service Sheets will be provided.

The B. & C. D. R. have kindly consented to issue Return Tickets at Single Fare and a quarter, with a minimum of 9d, to Clergymen and others, on production of Vouchers, which may by procured from Col. R. H. WALLACE, C.B., D.L., Downpatrick.

EDWARD MAGUIRE, D.D., Dean.

2878

Gunpowder Plot, 1605 Revolution, 1688

A SPECIAL ANNIVERSARY SERVICE

WILL BE HELD (GOD WILLING)

IN DOWN PARISH CHURCH

On SUNDAY AFTERNOON, 10th November, 1907, commencing at 3.30 o'clock.

PREACHER: BR. CANON POOLER, D.D., G.C. Co. Down, Rector of Down.

SUBJECT: 'SOCIALISM.'

The Offertory will be devoted to the Enniskillen Memorial Orphan Fund.

All are welcome and invited to attend.

The Brethren of the Orange Lodges in the neighbourhood are requested to assemble in the Orange Hall at Three o'clock.

JAMES CRAIG, D.M.
HENRY BRIGGS, D.S.

Downpatrick, 7th November, 1907. 2966

DOWNPATRICK PRESBYTERIAN CHURCH (INFIRMARY STREET)

Enthronement of Bishop J. B. Crozier
November 1907
DOWN RECORDER

After a prolonged period of ill-health, Bishop Welland died in 1907; the new Bishop was Rt Rev. J.B. Crozier, translated from the Diocese of Ossory. On this occasion, after enthronement services at both Saint Anne's Cathedral in Belfast and at Lisburn Cathedral, Bishop Crozier was enthroned in Down Cathedral, the first time such a ceremony had been held in Down since the eighteenth-century restoration. The service took place on Saturday afternoon, 9 November, and the Belfast and County Down Railway offered return tickets from Belfast at single fare and a quarter with a minimum of 9d to clergymen on production of vouchers obtainable from Colonel R.H.Wallace.[19] The special preacher at the service was Rt Rev. Dr C.F. d'Arcy, Bishop of Clogher and Bishop-elect of Ossory; in addition to the Chapter, over 60 members of the clergy were present. Following the service, the new Bishop was presented with an address in the narthex by the Archdeacon whilst, in the evening, Lord and Lady Dunleath hosted a reception in the Assembly Rooms.[20]

J. P. Brown
Dean of Down 1912-1923

Dean Maguire resigned from the incumbency of Bangor in 1903, when he was 81 years old; although he no longer attended Cathedral Board meetings, he retained the Deanery until 1912, a year before his death at the age of 91. In his absence, the Archdeacon, the Venerable J. P. Brown, presided at Board meetings in his capacity as sub-Dean. On Dean Maguire's death, Brown was appointed Dean, although he had already reached the age of 69. Dean Brown had been Rector of Loughinisland since Disestablishment, a parish sufficiently close to Downpatrick to enable him to keep in close touch with the cathedral, although the effective management still appears to have been in the hands of Colonel Wallace.

The new Dean's first priority was to address the problem of the organ; in

September 1912, a special meeting of the Board was called, which Coulter was invited to attend, at which the state of the organ and the necessity for immediate repairs were discussed. A report and estimate had already been received from Telford; further estimates were sought and, by November, it was clear that a decision had been taken to build a new organ as Coulter was authorised to hire, with the option of purchase, an American organ or harmonium, 'as the organ in its present state might give out at any moment'. Whether the new organ should be powered by gas or oil was also discussed. The decision taken, estimates and specifications were invited from five other organ builders in addition to that received from Telford. The estimates ranged from £650 quoted by Megahey of Cork to £1240 quoted by Harrison & Harrison of Durham. Indeed the latter estimate and one from Norman & Beard at £1243 were eliminated owing to their being so expensive in relation to the remainder. Coulter evidently had reservations, for various reasons, about certain details of the specification and it was eventually decided to accept Megahey's offer provided that enquiries from churches and cathedrals, in which he had worked, proved to be satisfactory. It is apparent that Coulter, being still relatively junior, was unable to influence the verdict and Canon Armstrong, of the Diocese of Derry, an acceptable expert on organ matters, was asked to confirm the Board's opinion.

Harrison & Harrison Account for rebuilding the organ 1914

Telegrams: "AUTUMN, DURHAM."

PRIZE MEDAL, EDINBURGH, 1890.

Durham, 26th May 1914.

Down Cathedral,

Downpatrick. Per G.T.Harley, Esq.

Dr. to HARRISON & HARRISON, ORGAN BUILDERS.

AND AT LONDON AND GLASGOW.

To three-manual organ as per specification and estimate.	1018	5	-
CREDIT.			
By By Cheque March 25th, 1914.	510	-	-
To Balance.	£ 508	5	-

E. & O. E.

With great good fortune for posterity, enquiries into the firm of Megahey turned out to be such that the organ committee felt unable to recommend their estimate. Coulter, in the meantime, having formed a personal friendship with Mr and Mrs Arthur Harrison, suggested that their firm be again requested to inspect the organ and advise on a rebuild along the lines which he (Coulter) would suggest. Arthur Harrison seized the opportunity and spent the morning of 7 February 1913 in the cathedral; that afternoon he reported to the organ repair committee, saying that there was a considerable amount of 'Green' work in the organ, with additions having been made from time to time.[21] He gave an account of what needed to be done and suggested a figure of £900 exclusive of mechanical blowing apparatus. Following a written report a week later, the committee awarded the contract to Harrison & Harrison.

Little more than a year later, on Ascension Day, 21 May 1914, the rebuilt organ was ready for dedication at a service at which the preacher was Rt Rev. Dr C.F. D'Arcy, now Bishop of Down and Dromore; the guest organist was Coulter's close friend and contemporary, C.J. Brennan. In a letter preserved among the Cathedral archives, Mr Brennan congratulated the Board on the success of the rebuild and in particular the manner in which the tonal tradition of the old organ had been carried on being quite masterly. The organ was a delight to play.

The Down Recorder, in its subsequent report of the service, commented that 'Worshippers of the wealthier class used to drive from distant outlying places in carriages. Now for the most part they come in motor cars. So on Thursday afternoon nearly the whole length of the Mall was lined with such vehicles, indicating in a striking way the change which has been effected in means of locomotion'.[22] The Cathedral was filled and a large number of clergy, in addition to the Chapter, took their places in the procession. The anthem "Lift up your heads" was written by Coulter as also was the chant used for one of the psalms. The late Lord Dunleath wrote that Harrison's preservation of the original chorus work was almost without parallel at that time; although perhaps regrettable, the conversion from tracker to tubular pneumatic action has stood the test of time insofar as the organ remained trouble free for almost another half century.

In spite of the fact that the organ was paid off by 1919, Colonel Wallace complained that financially the cathedral was living a hand-to-mouth existence. In his report to the Board in May 1918, he said that, in spite of Down being the Cathedral Church of the Diocese, no benefit or support was forthcoming from that source. He begged for a small annual contribution from each parish in the Diocese; such an appeal was in fact sent to the parishes the following year. A subscription of not more than £1 per parish was suggested!

CATHEDRAL OF DOWN.

SERVICE OF DEDICATION

OF

THE NEW ORGAN

BY THE

RIGHT REV. THE LORD BISHOP OF DOWN AND CONNOR AND DROMORE,

ASCENSION DAY, 21st MAY, 1914,

3.15 P.M.

Anthem, 'Lift Up Your Heads' (Soloist, Mr. JAMES NEWELL).

Hymns, 205, 90, and 'Hark, Hark, the Organ Loudly Peals' (John E. West).

PREACHER: THE LORD BISHOP.

Collection in aid of Organ Fund.

ORGAN RECITAL.

Organist, Mr. C. J. BRENNAN, Mus. Bac., F.R.C.O., Organist of Belfast Cathedral.

JOHN PIERCE BROWN, M.A., Dean.

3182

THE EVANGELISTIC SERVICES

Conducted in the Large Room of the

ANNESLEY ARMS HOTEL, NEWCASTLE,

Will (God willing)

BE CONTINUED

From SUNDAY, 17th MAY, 1914,

And until Further Notice, Nightly (except Saturday) at Eight, by Lieut.-Colonel BEERS (formerly of 26th Cameronians), Mr. H. B. THOMPSON (formerly of Central Africa), and Mr. J. RANKIN, from Scotland.

All Seats Free. No Collection. All Welcome. Come. 3191

Dedication of organ, May 1914
DOWN RECORDER

At the end of the first world war, a number of memorials were erected or otherwise provided. A new Holy Table, carved in oak, together with mosaic tiling in the Sanctuary was given by Mr & Mrs Stephen Perceval Maxwell in memory of their son Nigel, Lieutenant in the 16th Queen's Lancers, who had fallen in France. A tablet was also erected on the eastern pier of the north arcade by the officers of the Royal South Down Militia in memory of their commanding officer, Lt-Col. T. V. P. McCammon. The arms of the Londonderry family were formerly in this position and the then Lord Londonderry gave permission for them to be moved; these are now on the south aisle wall.

W. P. Carmody
Dean of Down 1923-1938

At the close of 1923, when he was aged 80, Dean Brown resigned. The Board minute recording his resignation reminds us that he was the last link which bound the cathedral to the years prior to Disestablishment, having been ordained in 1868, appointed Precentor in 1870, Archdeacon in 1899, succeeding to the Deanery in 1912. 'Beloved by all, a most generous contributor to the funds, devoted to its interests and welfare for over half a century, he now leaves behind him a splendid record of work nobly done and a memory ever to be venerated'. He died barely two years later at Newcastle.

William Patrick Carmody was installed as Dean on 5 December 1923. In a letter to Colonel Wallace concerning the appointment, the Bishop, Rt Rev.C.P.Grierson wrote:[23] 'Canon Carmody is not young but then I could not make a young clergyman Dean and he is full of vigour and a man of great goodness and wisdom'. He was, in fact, already 60 years old (a youngster compared to some of his predecessors) and had had a very distinguished career, not only in the church but as a member of various learned societies, where his contribution to and knowledge of ecclesiastical history made him second only to Bishop Reeves. Carmody was also instituted to the incumbency of the Parish Church and took up his duties immediately. His historical interests surfaced early; he wanted to have the eastern tower, which was known to contain a spiral staircase, opened as he believed that valuable information on the Cathedral's past might be forthcoming. In the event this could not be achieved. In 1928, Colonel Wallace presented the Cathedral with the old Norman font, thought to be the socket of a High Cross although Dean Carmody believed that it was the original font.

The 'new' font alongside the 'old' font 1930
THE A. R. HOGG COLLECTION
THE ULSTER MUSEUM

The Board was ever eager to keep the Cathedral in the forefront of diocesan affairs, having been requested by the Easter 1929 meeting of the Vestrymen to enlist the support of the Lord Bishop and other dignitaries in bringing the claims of the Cathedral for support and encouragement before members of the Church of Ireland in the Diocese. The Vestrymen had passed a resolution to the effect

St Patrick (Rev. Cuthbert Peacocke) landing at Saul

1932 Patrician Pageant. Saint Patrick – alias Rev. Cuthbert Peacocke later Bishop of Derry and Raphoe – coming ashore near Saul

that 'apparently no interest whatever is being taken by the Diocese in the Cathedral which is rapidly losing its character as such and assuming that of a small local church'.

Colonel Wallace died in December 1929; he had been secretary and treasurer for 35 years. Educated at Harrow and Oxford, he trained as a solicitor and, indeed was the principal partner in the family practice, but he looked back on his years as a soldier with enormous pleasure.[24] For fifteen years, he commanded the Royal South Down Militia and indeed led the regiment in the Boer War of 1899-1902, for which he was awarded the C.B. and after which he penned the famous ballad entitled "The South Down Militia". This tells of the exploits of the regiment during the Boer War, in rather humorous form, each verse ending with the refrain 'For the South Down Militia is the terror of the land'. In the first world war, he raised and commanded the 17th Battalion R.I.R. and then transferred to the 19th Battalion; for his services he was awarded the C.B.E. Prominent in the Masonic and Orange Orders, he was Deputy Lieutenant and High Sherriff for the county in 1908; although selected as Unionist candidate for East Down at Westminster in 1902, he failed to be elected. Two years after his death, the Freemasons of Ireland installed a memorial window in the cathedral to his memory (the eastern window in the south aisle).

The year 1932 was commemorated throughout Ireland as the 1500th anniversary of the reputed arrival of Saint Patrick. As well as the rebuilding of the little church at Saul, which was consecrated by Primate D'Arcy the following year, the United Dioceses of Down, Dromore and Connor marked the occasion by mounting a most colourful and ambitious pageant illustrating his coming. No fewer than 200 players and 100 singers took part. The pageant, which took place on Saturday 11 June was preceded by a special service in the cathedral on the previous evening at which the Primus of Scotland preached to a packed congregation which included the Bishops of Down, Cashel and Birmingham in addition to over 80 clergy from all over Ireland. The programme which was published for this event would suggest that this was the most extraordinary event of its kind ever organised by the Church of Ireland. The finest talent in the country was harnessed; the script was written by local poet Richard Rowley, the costumes were designed by William Conor and Lady Mabel Annesley, both foremost names in the art world, the producer was A. S. G. Loxton and the musical director was C. J. Brennan.

The backdrop for the pageant was the field at Audley's Castle, near Castleward. The part of Patrick was played by the young Rev.Cuthbert Peacocke, who was later to become Bishop of Derry and Raphoe; Lord Bangor of Castleward skippered his own boat for the occasion and the Roman legionaries were played by the mounted North Staffordshire Regiment, then stationed at Ballykinlar. Particular tribute was paid in the programme to Dean Carmody, without whose initiative and historical research, the event could not have taken place.

The Archbishop of Armagh, the Most Rev. Dr C. F. D'Arcy, retained much affection for Down after his elevation to the Primacy as his daughter was the wife of the third Lord Dunleath. Archbishop D'Arcy dedicated the window in

The six Queens and the soldiers of King Laoghaire, together with Patrick. Audleystown Castle in background

St Patrick's parish church, Saul. A general view during the foundation -stone laying by the Primate of All-Ireland (the Most Rev. Charles F. D'Arcy, D.D.)

THE FOUNDATION STONE OF THIS CHURCH
BUILT ON THE SITE GIVEN TO
ST PATRICK, A.D. 432.
WAS LAID BY
CHARLES F D'ARCY D.D.
ARCHBISHOP OF ARMAGH,
ON ASCENSION DAY 1933.

Archbishop C. F. D'Arcy laying the foundation stone of the new church at Saul, Ascension Day 1933

the north aisle depicting Saint Patrick to the memory of the second Lord Dunleath on Saint Patrick's Day 1937. The window was designed by Mr C. C. Powell, a Fellow of the British Society of Master Glass Painters.

Dean Carmody was an active member of a number of learned societies of which the most prestigious was the Royal Irish Academy; he was president of the Belfast Natural History and Philosophical Society and the Belfast Naturalists' Field Club; chairman of the Ancient Monuments Advisory Committee and of the committee which launched the third series of the Ulster Journal of Archaeology. Surviving correspondence with well-known figures such as Harold Leask and H. C. Lawlor [25] indicates that he had a deep interest in the history of the Cathedral, although this knowledge seems not to have been committed to print. Needless to say, he was of considerable assistance to Canons Leslie and Swanzy with the compilation of the clergy succession lists, published at this time. In 1931 he was appointed Select Preacher to Cambridge University, where he delivered a lecture on Saint Patrick. In spite of this breadth of interests, he

View of Cathedral showing pre-1935 Verger's house.
THE LAWRENCE COLLECTION NATIONAL LIBRARY OF IRELAND

yet found time to take an active part in the life of Downpatrick. A glance through the newspaper scrapbooks which he kept, reveal that he was a frequent attender at school prize givings, hospital boards and missionary meetings.

In 1935, a new verger's house was built on a new site some few yards to the north of the previous house, which was at the entrance to the new graveyard. During removal of the old house, several old stones, thought to be of archaeological interest, were discovered. The diocesan architect, Seaver, was called in; he, in turn, did not feel able to advise and called Dr D. A. Chart, from the ancient monuments advisory council of the Ministry of Finance, for advice. Chart suggested that the 'stones' should be photographed and their position recorded before covering them up again.

Ill health forced Dean Carmody to offer his resignation in February 1938 and he died the following month. His funeral took place from the Cathedral to Knockbreda parish church where he had previously been Rector. In paying tribute to his 46 years in the ministry of the United Dioceses, Bishop J.F.McNeice referred to his numerous publications in historical journals as well as his histories of Lisburn Cathedral and Knockbreda Parish Church.[26] His work for the 1932 pageant was recalled with gratitude as also was the part he took in the rebuilding of Saul church.[27]

Canon R. C. H. G. Elliott, hitherto Prebendary of Saint Andrew's and Rector of Saint Patrick's, Ballymacarrett, was installed as Dean of Down and Rector of the parish of Down in the following May, at a service which also included the installation of four other members of the Chapter. Dean Elliott remained at Downpatrick throughout the second world war but the cathedral record is silent for this entire period. When he moved to Belfast as Dean in 1945, Canon Frederick Hatch was appointed Dean in his stead. Over the next few years, it became apparent that the ravages of time had taken their toll on the fabric of the Cathedral and that urgent repairs and maintenance had to be carried out. In 1952, the Bishop, Rt Rev. W. S. Kerr, along with Dean Hatch launched an appeal for £20,000 in order to replace the clerestory windows, carry out repairs to some of the pinnacles as well as extensive replastering of the interior. The roof of the tower also required attention. Mr A. F. Lucy was retained by the Board as Consultant Architect, although it was felt that the work should be carried out in stages as money became available. Intensive fund-raising was undertaken with frequent appeals through the press and radio both from Bishop Kerr and Dean Hatch; among the unusual events (in ecclesiastical terms) were the two film premieres held at the Royal Hippodrome in Belfast in aid of the Cathedral Restoration Fund. In May 1954, the Duchess of Kent and Princess Alexandra were present at the premiere of 'The Maggie' and, two years later, the premiere of 'The Battle of the River Plate' took place at the same theatre. Eventually sufficient funds were raised to enable the work

R. C. H. G. Elliott
Dean of Down 1938-1945

A. J. H. Coulter
Cathedral organist 1898-1957

to proceed and the Cathedral was closed for much of 1956; as well as the removal and re-instatement of the windows and belfry opes in the tower, faulty stonework in the aisle windows was replaced and the roof beams were strengthened. The old heating system was replaced as also was the reredos, the old one having decayed so far that replacement was felt to be necessary. The Cathedral was re-opened on Trinity Sunday, 16 June 1957 with a service at which representatives from each of the parishes in the diocese presented their gifts towards the restoration and at which the guest preacher was the Dean of Chester, Very Rev. Michael Gibbs. In his sermon, the Dean referred to the link between the Cathedrals of Chester and of Down, going back to 1183 when monks from Saint Werburgh's of Chester were sent to found the Benedictine Abbey of Down. The Governor of Northern Ireland, Lord Wakehurst, with Lady Wakehurst and the Lord Chief Justice, Lord MacDermott along with Lady MacDermott were among the distinguished guests present – a representative gathering of church and state.[28]

Frederick Hatch
Dean of Down 1945-1954

A. J. H. Coulter retired from the organ loft in June 1957,[29] and died some months later, on 18 November 1957, aged 90.[30] He had joined the choir as a boy chorister at the age of 8, remaining for 22 years before becoming organist, a post which he held for 60 years. He saw the enthronement of nine Bishops and the installation of seven Deans, ten Archdeacons and over 50 Canons. A familiar figure in Downpatrick, he spent his career in the office of Martin & Henderson, a firm of solicitors; he was sometime chairman of the Downpatrick branch of the East Down Unionist Association. Among his chief interests was Down High School, of which he was a founder. Coulter was replaced at the organ by W.R.Harrison, formerly organist of Hillsborough Parish Church.

The death of Dean Hatch in 1954 occasioned no reference in the Board minute book; there had been an unfortunate climate of unfriendliness and non-cooperation between him and the Love family, who occupied the offices of Secretary and Treasurer to the Board, as well as having been Cathedral wardens for very many years.

TWELVE

BISHOP MITCHELL AND HIS SUCCESSORS

DEAN HATCH'S DEATH WAS FOLLOWED in 1955 by that of Bishop W. S. Kerr; both had worked tirelessly in their efforts to raise funds towards the repair and maintenance programme which had been commenced some years earlier. Under the direction of the diocesan architect, Mr A. F. Lucy, this was to last another decade and incur a total cost of almost £50,000, a very considerable sum at that period.

Canon W. H. Good, rector of Bangor, became the new Dean and the new Bishop was F. J. Mitchell, enthroned in the Cathedral in December 1955. Dean Good was also instituted to the parish of Down. The position of the cathedral in both the life of the diocese and the wider church was a priority with Bishop Mitchell. He quickly captured the post-war mood of the people and, with a glance back through history at the medieval cathedral as a place of pilgrimage for Irishmen to the shrine of Saint Patrick, he decided to re-instate the annual pilgrimage service on Saint Patrick's Day, 17 March. The first service was held in 1958 and attracted crowds such as had not been seen for a long time. The pilgrimage service has remained the principal event in the cathedral calendar ever since. It has become the usual practice to invite notable preachers to take part; over the years these have ranged from Archbishops Fisher and Ramsay of Canterbury to, in more recent times, Cardinal Ó'Fiaich and Bishop Walsh from the Roman Catholic Communion.

W. H. Good
Dean of Down
1955-1963

In a different context, Bishop Mitchell revived a dormant prebend from the 1609 Charter of the Cathedral; he restored the Prebend of Talpestone. This prebend, based on the medieval parish of Saint Andrew's in the Ards, had lapsed in the final years of the seventeenth century and had not been subsequently revived. Indeed, at Disestablishment, the Down Cathedral Bill provided for only two prebends and the re-creation of the third necessitated a Bill being passed by General Synod; this was enacted at the meeting of Synod in 1958.[1]

Alongside the ongoing repair work on the exterior of the fabric, a new bell was installed and dedicated on Trinity Sunday, 24 May 1959, at a service at which the special preacher was the Bishop of Croydon, Rt Rev. J. T. Hughes.[2]

F. J. Mitchell,
Bishop of Down and Dromore 1955-1969

A new bell was installed in April 1959.
Dean W. H. Good with members of the Cathedral Board

The old bell, installed in 1855, was cracked and had not been in use for many years; in fact, the verger, Mr Arthur Pollock, believed that it had last been rung on Armistice Day in 1918. Eighteen months earlier, the Ulster Operatic Company had given a Gala performance of 'White Horse Inn' at the Grand Opera House in Belfast in aid of the Cathedral Restoration Fund. As a result, Lord Brookeborough, Prime Minister of Northern Ireland was able to hand Bishop Mitchell and the Treasurer, Mr Hugh Love, a cheque for £205.[3]

Dean Good retired through ill-health in 1963 and the new Dean, appointed by Bishop Mitchell, was Rev. Canon A. W. S. Mann, Rector of Kilwarlin, who had been Precentor. The Board also accepted the resignation of Hugh Love, secretary and treasurer since 1951, a post to which his brother Samuel was then appointed; Samuel had, in fact, been cathedral warden since 1940, to which post Hugh along with another brother Clifford were now appointed! At the same time Canon R. W. T. H. Kilpatrick was appointed Rector of Down Parish and Precentor of the cathedral. Although beset by many difficulties during his time as Dean, Dean Mann played host to the Archbishop of Canterbury, the Most Rev. Dr Michael Ramsay, at the televised pilgrimage service in 1964 and in the following year, to the Bishop of London, Rt Rev. Dr R. W. Stopford.

The programme of restoration was ongoing; the screen and pulpitum were found to be unsafe and required to be completely rebuilt. It was thought necessary to consult Sir Albert Richardson, President of the Royal Academy, who suggested that the organ console might be relocated on the ground floor, with the screen being glazed so that there would be an uninterrupted view from the west door to the sanctuary. With great foresight, the young Lord Dunleath decided to enlist

St Patrick's Day, 1959
Bishop F. J. Mitchell leads the procession to the Cathedral followed by the Archbishop of Wales, Most Rev. A. E. Morris

the moral help of Sir John Betjeman; before his untimely death, Lord Dunleath kindly allowed me to quote from the correspondence which passed between them. Sir John Betjeman wrote to Sir Albert Richardson in February 1962:

> My dear Professor
> With thrilled and trembling hand I take up my biro to write to you to say how overjoyed I am to learn from our friend Lord Dunleath, that sweet and cultivated Irish peer, that you are taking a hand in the proposals for the re-arrangements inside Down Cathedral. I have long considered this the prettiest small cathedral in these islands and the only vaulted example of 18th century Gothick in the world. Being pre-disestablishment and pre-Tractarian, it is 18th century high church which is why, I am sure, the restorers retained the old medieval plan with an enclosed quire and return stalls and those glorious curved box pews as extra stalls facing N. & S. and left the nave bare and open.
>
> I think the idea of doing away with those hideous and out of scale Victorian pews in the middle of the choir so good a one, that I can even partly reconcile myself to the opening of the choir screen so that people in the nave can see through. But the screen must still be there and the canopy of wood above the stalls and any backs to the stalls must be designed in 18th century Gothick. And only you, my dear Professor, could do this. As to the pulpit, don't you think it should be high or with lectern below – a 2 decker – in Strawberry Hill Gothick and stand in the middle of the choir at the E end and be rolled back on tram lines as at Newgate Parish Church or St. John's, Hoxton, when the altar was to be used.

A. W. M. S. Mann
Dean of Down
1964-1968

St Patrick's Day, 1964
The Archbishop of Canterbury, Dr Michael Ramsay, in procession to the Cathedral (no 125)

God bless you, dear Professor, fight on against the Lord Bridgeses and the grey men of the world.

Yours ever

John Betjeman

Plans survive for the proposed alterations, prepared by Mr Lucy, presumably at the behest of Sir Albert Richardson, but with hindsight, one can only be eternally thankful that the wiser counsel of John Betjeman prevailed. The screen and pulpitum were replaced just as they had been, with the aid of a generous gift of £8000 from Mrs M. B. Brown of Pasadena, California, whose parents, Dr & Mrs Adam Orr, had originally come from Killyleagh. Also replaced were the two east end aisle windows as a memorial to the 3rd Lord Dunleath.

Harrison & Harrison of Durham were again called in to carry out a major rebuild of the organ at the same time that the structural repairs were being carried out. The Cathedral was closed for over twelve months and, just as we have Sir John Betjeman to thank for retaining the pulpitum and screen, we have the late Lord Dunleath to thank for drawing up the specification of the rebuilt organ. His specification enabled the organ to be used as a recital organ, on which organists of international repute were able to perform, in addition to its capability as accompaniment to cathedral worship. Kenneth James, the organ voicer of Harrison & Harrison, thought the organ was the finest three manual instrument in Britain. Cecil Clutton, of the Organ Advisory Committee to the Council for the Care of Churches, wrote:[4]

R. W. T. H. Kilpatrick
Dean of Down 1968-1980

> If the 1914 rebuild was a model, that of 1966 is a triumph of good taste....so perfectly are its modest tonal forces deployed that there is hardly any musical contingency to which it is not equal which is more than can be said for many cathedral organs more than twice its size. In the proportioning of its parts and the sheer beauty of its tone, it may well come to be regarded by competent judges as exceeded by few, if any.

In the unavoidable absence of the Archbishop of Armagh, Most Rev. J. McCann, Bishop Mitchell preached at the re-opening service in October 1966, which was attended by the Governor and his wife, Lord and Lady Erskine, along with many representatives from Down Council. Evensong was sung by the Minor Canon, Rev. J. H. R. Good. The Bishop said that the programme of restoration, begun by his predecessor in 1952, and which had cost £48,000, was now complete. On this occasion the contractor had been F. B. McKee Ltd.; Gillespie & Woodside were responsible for the interior furnishing and the new light pendants, five in all, were supplied by Best & Lloyd of Birmingham.[5]

The organ was formally opened on 3 December by Gillian Weir, then on the threshold of a brilliant international career as a recitalist. Among the early visitors were the Campbell College Choir, with their choirmaster, Donald Leggatt, who was the local representative of the Royal School of Church Music and the Trinity College singers from Dublin.[6] Peter Hurford, then organist of St Alban's Cathedral, gave a recital in 1968; Hurford has since become an organist of international repute, who has recorded, amongst much other music, the complete organ works of J. S. Bach.

J. H. R. Good
Dean of Down 1981-1987

The organ continued for another 20 trouble-free years and would have continued to do so had not the Cathedral itself required major restoration work; polythene sheets, of course, enveloped the instrument whilst the work was in progress and, as soon as was possible, the opportunity was taken to carry out some modifications. Entrusted with the work and now with the ongoing maintenance of the organ was the local firm of Wells-Kennedy Partnership.

Ill health forced Dean Mann to retire in 1968, although he remained rector of Kilwarlin; the new Dean was Canon R. W. T. H. Kilpatrick, Precentor of the Cathedral and rector of Down parish. The re-uniting of the two offices of Dean and Rector of the parish acted as a spur to the Diocesan Council to consider the union of the two parishes, involving the closure of the parish church. Apparently the parishioners of Down parish were willing to accede to this arrangement but, although there was considerable discussion on the organisation of such an amalgamation, nothing was achieved in the end; a typical Church of Ireland conclusion of leaving the matter to another generation! Bishop Mitchell retired the following year, to be followed as Bishop by the Venerable G. A. Quin, who had been Archdeacon of the diocese and most recently Rector of Bangor. Although primarily occupied with the civil unrest during the seventies, in which he played a major pastoral role, particularly among the parishes of east Belfast, Bishop Quin took great interest in the missionary work of the Cathedral, appointing Rev. J. Mehaffey (subsequently Bishop of Derry and Raphoe) as the Canon Missioner of the Diocese, installing him in the Prebend of Saint Andrew's. On Dean Kilpatrick's retirement in 1981, Canon J. H. R. Good, Rector of Carryduff and a previous Minor Canon of the Cathedral, was appointed Dean and found himself superintending the most radical restoration of the building since 1790. As with Dean Annesley in 1817, sadly he did not live to see its completion and the re-opening in October 1987 was the responsibility of Dean Hamilton Leckey, but the courage with which he took the decision to proceed with the restoration, supported by his Bishop, Rt Rev. Dr R. H. A.Eames, will remain as a memorial to his foresight.

G. A. Quin. Bishop of Down and Dromore 1969-1980

It became apparent during the early 1980s that the Cathedral, in spite of extensive work being carried out over recent decades about which we have read, required considerably more attention in order to allow it to remain in use as a place of Christian worship. Large pieces of plaster had fallen off the walls and professional advice was sought by the Board; Mr Stephen Leighton, well-known for his similar work in Armagh Cathedral, recommended closure for a more thorough investigation. In the event, much of the lath woodwork behind the plaster on the walls and vaults, was stripped and replaced. It has, of course, been replaced to the identical design but with modern materials now being used, hopefully no further work will be necessary until well into the twenty-first century. At the same time, some of the pinnacles were rebuilt and the entire exterior including the tower was repointed. The work was originally estimated to cost £250,000 but eventually almost three times that amount was spent, a massive sum when one considers that the cathedral has only a tiny congregation and relies almost entirely on voluntary support from visitors and the diocese. Through donations and many other fund raising events, the money was found and the Cathedral is now free of debt. The Cathedral was re-opened and re-hallowed at a magnificent service in October

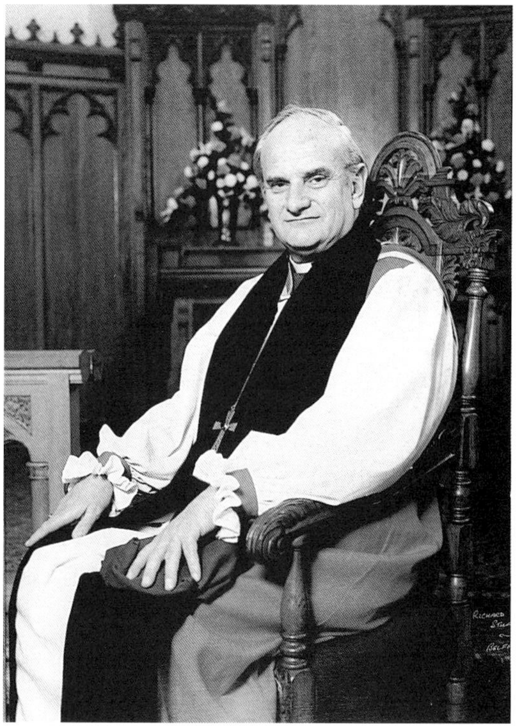

R. H. A. Eames
Bishop of Derry and Raphoe 1975-1980
Bishop of Down and Dromore 1980-1986
Archbishop of Armagh 1986-

The catwalk under the vaulting photographed during the 1985-87 restoration

Scaffolding erected during the 1985-1987 restoration

The Mall from the spiral staircase
photographed during the
1985 Restoration

The 1985 Pilgrimage service attended by leaders of the four churches. From the left: Rev. Paul Kingston, President of the Methodist Church, Cardinal T. Ó Fiaich, Roman Catholic, Rt Rev. Dr H. Cromie, Presbyterian Moderator, Most Rev. J. W. Armstrong, Archbishop of Armagh
DOWN RECORDER

1987, at which Rt Rev. Dr Gordon McMullan,a former Archdeacon of the diocese but now being translated from Clogher, was installed as Bishop and Very Rev. Hamilton Leckey, Rector of Bangor Abbey, was installed in the Dean's stall. Both appointments had been made while the Cathedral was closed. More recently, it was found necessary to replace the verger's house, as the previous house, built in the 1930s, was beyond repair. The cost of this has also been covered by gifts from parishes throughout the diocese and a substantial sum from the Diocesan Council. Both Bishop McMullan and Dean Leckey have recently retired and, as contemporaries, it would be wrong to give an objective assessment of their careers; that is better left to posterity. Their impact on the life of the Cathedral and consolidating its position as the mother church of the diocese will survive as a fitting memorial to their work. To the new Dean, Dean John Dinnen, Rector of Hillsborough and the new Bishop, Rt Rev. Harold Miller fall the task of bringing the Cathedral into the twenty-first century and guiding it through the years ahead.

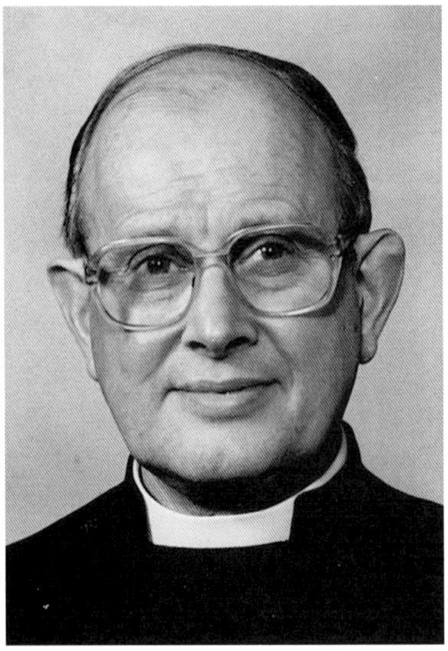

Hamilton Leckey
Dean of Down
1987-1996

It was fitting that, as part of the re-opening celebrations in 1987, Gillian Weir was again invited to take part, on this occasion accompanied by the Ulster Orchestra conducted by John Lubbock. Since then, the cathedral organ has been regularly used for recitals by leading contemporary organists, including Thomas Trotter of Birmingham, John Scott of Saint Paul's Cathedral and Christopher Robinson of Cambridge. Little wonder, therefore, that the late Lord Dunleath, whose love and enthusiasm for organs was unbounded, and who had made himself responsible for Down Cathedral organ for something like 30 years, shortly before his death, wrote:

So here we have an organ which is really far better than it has any right to be. It has been de-mythologised and is no longer the 18th century heirloom which we thought it was....but the proof of the organ is in the hearing and also in the playing. This one produces one of the most beautiful and thrilling sounds known to me....but it is the acoustic, the building and the organ's position therein which make it so successful both visually and aurally.

Saint Patrick's Day, 1987
Saint Patrick, alias Bishop McMullan, disembarking near Saul, from where, accompanied by the Cathedral Canons, he walked to the Cathedral for the pilgrimage service
BELFAST TELEGRAPH

By a happy coincidence, a team from the Archaeological Survey was excavating on Cathedral Hill just outside the perimeter of the graveyard while the cathedral restoration was being carried out; the opportunity was taken to examine the interior walls behind the vaulting which had been part of the eighteenth century work. A number of remarkable discoveries was made.[7] The original east window was much larger than the present one; its outline is represented by a stone arch on the inside (the present window is arched in plasterwork) and a faint difference in stonework is discernable on the exterior. The internal spiral staircase in the south eastern tower was entered but found to be deep in rubble and terminated without revealing any exit. At clerestory level, a number of sills were discovered suggesting that the opes of the present clerestory windows are not original (see p.53). There are a number of versions extant of the engraving of the ruins c.1790, all of which show the windows in their present positions over the arcade arches; the position

Group at the welcome to the new Bishop 1 May 1997.
Archdeacon G. McCamley
Dean J. F. Dinnen
Bishop H. C. Miller
Rev. Dr A. W. McCormack
Canon J. A. B. Mayne, Precentor
REV. H. LONG

of the sills indicated that there were windows above the arcade piers but we cannot say at which period in the history of the Cathedral this change took place. Perhaps the most striking discovery was the massive arch over the west end, which was almost a mirror image of the east window arch; the existence of this arch has proved an enigma to archaeologists, suggesting that the original building terminated at this point, thus disproving the long held theory that the present building represents only the choir of the Benedictine abbey. This arch is, of course, again out of sight behind the new vaulting but a detailed record was made by members of the Archaeological Survey while it was visible.

Bishop Miller giving the traditional knock on the door, requesting admission to his Cathedral, 1 May 1997
REV. H. LONG

Interior view showing the new aisle seats installed in 1987
ALAN JOHNSTON

EPILOGUE

WHAT OF THE FUTURE? Is there a future for Cathedrals like Down in the life and witness of the church in the twenty-first century? Some years ago, the Archbishops of Canterbury and York appointed a Commission on Cathedrals in the Church of England, 42 in number. This Commission, chaired by Lady Howe of Aberavon, presented its report '*Heritage and Renewal*' towards the end of 1994. Although primarily addressed to the Cathedrals of the Church of England, the comments expressed in the report are no less relevant to the Cathedrals of the Church of Ireland.

The report addresses the role of the Cathedral in present day society and makes the point that to-day, when secularism is becoming progressively more evident, paradoxically cathedrals are more popular than ever before. Cathedrals mean different things to different people. To some, they represent an expression of what they are unable to understand, the numinousness of the place; to others, they have an historical context as repositories, not just of the bones of saints, but of great episodes in the nation's history and yet to others they are paragons of artistic achievement, aesthetically satisfying. To all of these people, they are great centres of evangelism and education; they must cater for and fulfil each person's need in his or her own particular way. The experience of visiting the

Cathedral, for whatever reason, must be an enriching one so that the individual, no matter how humble, feels the presence of God.

Cathedrals have evolved, not just within the structures of the Church, but within the wider context of society, without having a particularly well defined role. It is this role which we must seek to define for the future, if in fact the Cathedral is to maintain its position at the centre of church life. Their primary role must be that of mission, but in contemporary society that mission can take many forms. It is up to the Chapter and the lay members of the Board to ensure that a full and varied programme is available to sustain this missionary role. In all these activities, the Cathedral should be seen to be, not only the seat of the Bishop of the Diocese, but the centre where great diocesan events can take place. The Cathedral, by virtue of its place outside the normal parochial structure should be seen as a resource centre, a place where experiment in worship can take place. It should be seen as a centre of excellence, in music and in art, on a level which perhaps cannot be attained by some parish churches. To enable it to achieve all these aims, it must retain a measure of independence from the diocesan structure, although in a sense both structures are complimentary in their mission. The Cathedral must not be seen as an expensive luxury to be maintained by parishes with already pressing financial demands on their resources, but it should nevertheless be recognised as having a vital role to play in the life of the diocese.

Increasingly in years to come, tourism will be seen as part of the mission of the cathedrals. Tourists who visit cathedrals are giving modern expression to medieval pilgrimage, when ordinary folk went on pilgrimage to the shrines of the saints. Those folk, centuries ago, did not understand the theology which informed the buildings, theirs was a simple faith and it was told to them in iconographic form which they could understand. The modern tourist is no different; he may be better educated and informed than his predecessor but he is still very much a pilgrim at heart. In Down, there is a very precious asset in that the Cathedral is the centre of the Patrick story and whilst many of to-day's tourists come to see and photograph the memorial stone, they come for basically the same reason as did the medieval pilgrims.

In order to meet the demands and pressures on the Cathedral, pressures of the rapidly-changing environment in which it must express its mission, the management structure of the Cathedral must bring expertise of a wide variety to bear. In order to do this, the General Synod of the Church of Ireland passed a Bill in 1985, enabling Down Diocesan Council to appoint six extra members to the Cathedral Board, thus giving the wider diocese a voice in the management of the Cathedral. Under the leadership and wise counsel, in recent years, of Bishop Gordon McMullan and Dean Hamilton Leckey, together with the enlarged Board, Down Cathedral now plays a vital role in the life of the diocese as host to many diocesan functions and in return, the parishes of the diocese give substantial financial help to the Cathedral, as indeed does the Diocesan Council of Down and Dromore. There is an active body of 'Friends of Down Cathedral' which sponsors events each year in aid of cathedral funds and each parish has two link correspondents, whose duty it is to raise awareness of the needs of the Cathedral in their parishes. Indeed, the necessity to co-ordinate all these functions led the board, in 1994, to appoint a full time Cathedral Administrator. The first holder of this post is Mrs Joy Wilkinson. With Downpatrick's place on the tourist map assured through the association with Patrick, an acknowledgment must also be made to the Northern Ireland Tourist Board, which has given significant recognition to the role of the Cathedral in promoting the tourist potential of both Lecale and Downpatrick.

The Cathedral of the Holy Trinity of Down occupies a unique position in the Christian heritage of Ireland. The fortunes of history have placed responsibility for its upkeep on the Church of Ireland, but it is, and will always remain, a place of pilgrimage shared by all Christians, of whatever denomination. It is the focal point in the town of Downpatrick, as it sits on top of the hill, beautifully floodlit by night, visible for miles around. But it is a centre first and foremost of living Christian witness, where men of all faiths or none can come and pray or sit quietly, just to *be* there. The modern tourist, no less than the man seeking peace, is treading the pilgrim path just as pilgrims have done ever since Saint Patrick trod these steps.

APPENDIX 1

THE GRANT BY BISHOP MALACHY III
1183

This grant, copied in an *inspeximus* in the Patent Rolls of 41 Edward III and dated 1368-9, (Public Record Office, London, C 66/278, illustrated p.26), was first published by Reeves in *Ecclesiastical Antiquities, p.163.* It was subsequently transcribed by Professor Gearoid Mac Niocaill in *Seanchas Ard Mhacha, Vol.5, No.2, 1970.* In it, a substantial number of villas (settlements) were confirmed to the Church of Saint Patrick of Down. Many of these names may be identified alongside their modern equivalents, but equally many remain unidentified. Reeves himself attempted a number of identifications and the late Deirdre Flanagan, in a lecture entitled *The Place Names of Lecale*, added a few more. These lands were probably termon lands belonging to the pre-Norman monastery of Down along with parcels of episcopal see lands. The full list follows:

Lochmonne	Loughmoney
Messesareth	
Ferrochen	Ballyfrooke
Balinscanlan	
Arthgothin	
Balinrothan	
Telagnocrossi	Tullynacross
Balienbrethnaghe	Ballybranagh
Belgach	Ballee
Delen	Dillin
Tipermeni	Tobermoney
Balimechethe	
Dumonere	
Balienlemath	
Balienlirnoni	Roneystown (DF)
Telaghmethan	Castlemahon ?
Balinbothan	Ballywoodan (Reeves:p.38)
Molrath	Myra (DF)
Kno Chengar	Walshestown (Reeves:p.40)
Monenmor	
Nochenduf	
Chemard	Killard ?
Tirgore	Gore's Island (DF)
Tirestrucher	Struell

Balioconewi	in Demesne of Down (DF)
Cremse	Killavees
Croch	
Balindethdume	Ballydugan ?
Balima Celendre	Ballyclander
Balinangatha	
Balinculter	Ballyculter
Balimackelli	Ballykeel
Kloker	Clogher
Balienstruthi	Ballystrew
Balinrimurgan	Ballyorgan
Kelleiohan	St John
Baliowosan	Ballyvaston
Lesconam	
Kortef	
Cronoch	Crannagh (DF)
in Demesne of Down,	
Lanne	
Karenlatheri	
Feod	
Balimagereg	Cargagh
Karennesche	Carrownacaw
Chellemimen	Killavees
	Killyneeny (DF)
Rathcop	Raholp
Ecclesia de Killecleth	Church of Kilclief
Ecclesia de Brichten	Church of Bright
Ecclesia de Stethian	Church of St John
cum pertinenciis suis in Dalebinn	Dalboyne
Latrach	
Donenach	
Kellagkinere	

APPENDIX 2

THE POSSESSIONS OF SAINT PATRICK'S AND OF OTHER RELIGIOUS HOUSES IN OR NEAR DOWNPATRICK AT THE DISSOLUTION

THERE ARE COPIES EXTANT OF TWO separate inquisitions into the monastic possessions at the dissolution. The first, a copy of which is amongst the Reeves MS (PRONI:DIO/1/24/26/5), took place at Down on 13 August, year unknown, but assumed to be 1549, and appears to be an *extent* of the Rectories belonging to Saint Patrick's of Down. It was taken by Thomas Cusack, Patrick Barnwell and Henry Draycott and the jurors were Richard Walsh of Walshtown, John Audeley of Audeleystown, Edward Dowdall of Ballydergon, Thomas Benson of Kylcliff, Brian Ogone of the same, Killedoe McCartan of Ballydonyll, Patrick McRooll of Strangford, Christopher Russell of Rathmolyn, Patrick Balding of Kilbride, Richard Russell of Rathmolyn, John Jordan of the same, Walter Oge Fitzsimon of Killard, William Duff of Sheplandbeg, John Savage of Saul and Everi Magennis of Loghconill. The list of properties follows, together with their modern form of spelling; values have been omitted:

Site of the Cathedral Church of the Bishop of Down; a dormitory, cloister, other buildings and a garden.

RECTORY OR CHURCH OF BRETT

Ballybretton (Ballybrytten)	Bright
Ballyorgan	Ballyorgan

RECTORY OR CHURCH OF DUNNESFORTH

Dunnsford or Dunnesforth	Dunsford
Ballyhornan	Ballyhornan

RECTORY OR CHURCH OF BARRESTON OR BALLINARY

Bareston	
Ballinary	Ballinary

RECTORY OR CHURCH OF BEALGAGH OR BEALY

Bealgagh	Ballee
Huseston or Ballyhussey	Ballyhosset
Ballyclinder	Ballyclander
Ballybrenaghe	Balllybranagh

Ballycroter	Ballycruttle
Ballyelliny	Ballylenagh
Ballycrosse	Ballynagross
Ballyenosbery	
Ballytrostan	Ballytrustan
Ballyanrlton ?	Ballyalton
Ballybaltir	Ballywalter
Ballyreigna or Ballyrenna	Ballyrenan
Loghmonon	Loughmoney
Ballyfrooke	Ballyfrooke
Ballisallagh	Ballysallagh
Crone	

RECTORY OR CHURCH OF KNOCKAZAR OR BALLYWALSH

Knockazar	
Ballywalsh	Walshestown

RECTORY OR CHURCH OF TAGHRYOLLY

Ballybiffin	
Ellanemocke	
Ballyfrassae	
Taghyrolly	Tyrella
Blountebeg	Ballyplunt

RECTORY OR CHURCH OF LYRGE

Lyrge	in Loughinisland (Reeves:p.31)
Bolloes or Crevysse	Creevy in Dunnanew
Branye in McCartan country	

RECTORY OR CHURCH OF SHENKYLL IN THE COUNTRY OF BRIAN FERTAGH

[O'Neill] in Cloneboy

RECTORY OR CHURCH OF BALLYFUNERAGH OR BALLYNHYMMERAGH IN ARDS

Ballyfuneragh or Ballynhymmeragh	Ballyfinragh
Ballygalgett	Ballygalget
Ballycoller	
quarter of Kerronka or Ballygalga	
quarter of Ballycoos	
quarter of Ballymollin or Wiltbyton ?	

Access could not be gained to the Shankill and Ards Rectories and no value could therefore be ascertained.

[In the inquisition taken at Antrim on 12 July 1605, the Prior of Down was found to be seised of the Rectory of Shankill in Tuogh Cinnament and also the Rectory of Derrykeighan in the Route. An abstract from this inquisition is given in the 26th

Report of the Deputy Keeper of the Records (Ireland). It is tempting to assume that the Rectory of Shankill is the same property as that in Dalboyne in the Malachy grant, quoted in Appendix 1]

The copy of the second inquisition is to be found among the Irish Record Commission lists in the Public Record Office, Dublin. It was taken at Grencastell [Castlescreen] on 10 August in the third regnal year of Edward VI [1549] before Thom' Cusack. After a reference to the former monastery of Saint Patrick of Downe, together with the circuit and precinct of the same and of the walls of a castle in the same and of the waters called Loghdowne and the river of Strangford in which salmon and other kinds of fish are caught, the inquisition lists a number of vill' in which the monastery possessed one or more carucates or one or more balliboes. Vill' might be interpreted as settlements but many of the names can be identified as modern townlands. In a lecture to the Lecale Historical Society in 1979, the late Deirdre Flanagan put forward probable modern equivalent spellings for many of them; these interpretations are listed in the right hand column:

Rossenagh	
Karrykenekenlye	Carricknabregie ?
Ballydonyly	Ballydonety
Beanston or Ballywhae	Ballyvange
Dromquellan	Drumcullen (Hollymount)
Ballynecashall or Marstralston	Marshallstown
Kylcaghnas	in Carrowdressex (Reeves:p.32)
Ballyogalme	Ballygallum
Tobbervynne	Tobermoney
Delyen	Dillin
Ballensroghe	Struell
Han...? (Ardmyn/Ballisroill) [in Grant:1 James I]	Ardmeen
Ballyfrohyll	Ballyfrooke
Ballincrosse	Ballynagross
Ballynegreyley or Slyvenegroley	Slievenagriddle
Loghinoge	
Ballyalton	Ballyalton
Balreynole	Ballyrenan
Ballyrostan	Ballytrustan
Ballyvcrane	Ballycruttle
Ballyvolynory	Ballymurry
Ballenebrenagh	Ballybranagh
Ballyshallagh	Ballysallagh
Ballyverghe [in Grant:1 James I]	Veally ?
Ballyhossyn or Possewykeston	Ballyhosset
Clynder or Ballyclynder	Ballyclander
Ballyvorett or Baretteston	Ballinary

The old walls of a chapel of St Mary Magdalene [Ringreagh, Reeves:p.32] and the Rectory of St Patrick of Down with the chapels of Carnull and Kylsaghlyn [in Carrowdressex, Reeves:p.32], the Rectory of Dromcath [Drumcaw] with the chapel of Rathan from the country (*patra*) of Maghthan (assumed to be a scribal error for Magennis)

The Rectory of Dromgolyn in Sriagh	Drumgooland in Scrib
The Rectory of Brecon	Bright
The Rectory of Duneford or Dunesforthe	Dunsford
The Rectory of Barrestonne or Ballynary	Ballinary
The Rectory of Bealgagh or Bealy	Ballee
The Rectory of Kirrorcagoe or Ballywalsshe	Walshestown
The Rectory of Thogryolley	Tyrella
The Rectory of (blank)	
The Rectory of (blank) in the country of Brian McFertagh in Clonboye	
The Rectory of Ballyfuneragh or Ballywhyegmeragh	Ballyfinragh

The inquisition continues with the possessions of the Abbey of Hughe, clearly a scribal error for Inch. After references to the Narrowewater of the river of Strangford, the vill' are listed:

Ballorenaley	Ballyrenan
Ffaghnebroghe	Finnebrogue
Ballymycuegall	Ballygally
Termyn	Turmenan
Tollenegrosse	Tullynacross
Erreny	Erenagh
Ballycany	Ballycam
Saynct Johne	St John's Point
Ballygylbert or Ballyviger	Ballygilbert
Rectory or Church of St John	
Rectory of Everey in the country of McCarthan & le Duffey	
Rectory of Ballynestrone in Arde	Tener (Reeves:p.25)
Rectory of Kyllerne or Tyllerne in the country of Brian Fertagh	
Rectory of Rincherne or Portnyoce in the country of Brian Fertagh	

Possessions of the Spiritual House [dom' Spiial de Downe]

Milton or Ballenmollye [Grant:1 James I]	Ballymullin
Grange of Ballyntogher	Ballintogher
Tullaghenere or Ballytullaghenere	
Ballylishedryne or Lyssheboy	Lisboy
Ballynegallyncheagh	Killinchy
Rectory of Ballybreene or Ballyntogher	Ballintogher
Rectory of St John in the country of Brian Fertagh	

Possessions of the Canons of St John

Ballynegaryke	Ballynagarrick

Wodanyston or Ballywoddan	Ballywoodan
Carickmallye	
Rectory of Ballyondan	Ballyorgan

Possessions of Monastery of St John the Baptist and St Thomas

Crobyegraunge or Grangeshecany	Grangecam
Ballyalugge	Ballylig
Rynneayse	Ringreagh
Ilynaneaster or Insula Magri (DF)	Horse Island
	[Grant:1 James I] Maister's Island
Ballydogan	Ballydugan
Rectory of Ballygnonyane	Coniamstown
Rectory of Kylbulke	(Reeves:p.29) in Loughinisland
Rectory of Lenlys [Kenlis] in country of McCarthan	Ballykinlar
Rectory of Kylbride	Kilbride
Rectory of Ballyrycherde in Cloneboy in the country of Brian Fertagh	Ballyrichard (Reeves:p.198), near Comber

Possessions of the Abbey of Saul

A church, 2 ruined castles and an [h]ortu[s], (garden)	
Sault and Meryton or Ballysonagh	Ballysugagh
Ballenmott or Ballynnemogh	Ballymote
Hillerteston or Ballyhillerte	Whitehills
Carnarye	Carrowvanny
Ballyntleave	Ballintlieve
Kyllena or Kylleyneyne	Loughkeelan
Casshemoghan	Castlemahon
Snylteston or Ballymylter	Ballyculter
Ballyleynagh	Ballylenagh
Ballyncloute in le Dufferans	Cluntagh
Ballyhillett	Hilletstown (Whitehills)
Rectory of Saul	
Rectory of Ballycalte with the chapel of Kenlys	
Rectory of Castlecryn	Castlescreen
Rectory of Graunge in Arde	(Reeves:p.21) Gransha
Rectory of Cloncaghe in le Dufferans	(Reeves:p.187) Cluntagh

Possessions of Hoare Abbey or Leigh or Iugo Dei in Arde [Grey Abbey]

Sheffelongboge	Sheeplandbeg
Holmegraunge	Tollumgrange
Rectory of Holmegraunge and Sofflottboge	

In addition, the two towns of Balle Edockes are included in the inquisition taken at Downpatrick 13 October 1623
(Patent and Close Rolls, 1627)

Possessions of the Abbey of Bangor in Cloneboy in the country of Brian Fertagh

Baloregan	Ballyorgan
Corbaly	Corbally
Rectory of Ballyurkegan	(Reeves:p.37) in Ballyorgan
Clonnyse in Eveagh	
Ballyagkan and Ballyletyn	
Rectory of Clonnyse in Eveagh	

Possessions of the House of Friars Minor of Down

A church, a dormitory, a brewhouse (*pandoxatoria*), cemetery, gardens and orchard

Ballymaghorlagan	Magheralagan
Ballylegan	Ballylig
Ballentleave called Russells lands	Ballintleave
Crenog in city of Downe	

Possessions of Johes Rawson, Prior of the Hospitallers of St John of Jerusalem in Hibernia

Rectory of Rathmolyn	Rathmullan
Rectory of Ballycrostan in Arde	(Reeves:p.25) Ballytrustan

The Reeves references are to his *Ecclesiastical Antiquities*; some names were further clarified by reference to a grant in the first regnal year of James I

APPENDIX 3

THE 1609 CHARTER

THE PATENT ROLLS OF JAMES I were destroyed in the Public Record Office in Dublin in 1922; fortunately copies, taken earlier, exist of a number of entries. In 1846 J. C. Erck published a volume entitled *A Repertory of the Inrolments on the Patent Rolls of Chancery in Ireland, commencing with the reign of King James I;* there is, in this volume, an abridged copy of a translation of the Charter of 1609. Whilst all the salient details of the charter have been copied, the legalistic terminology, which is extremely repetitive, has been largely omitted.

A further copy translation, handwritten, taken in 1873 by W. M. Hennessy, is among the cathedral archives (as is also a copy of the Latin original). This copy, one can assume, is complete, insofar as the repetitive terminology is included and it is this copy which is transcribed here. Hennessy's judgment on the spelling of place names is much more accurate than Erck's, although it is evident that both translations are taken from the same original.

CHARTER ESTABLISHING THE CATHEDRALS OF DOWN, CONNOR AND DROMORE
PATENT ROLL 7 JAMES 1, PART 2
TRANSLATION BY W.M. HENNESSY, 25 OCTOBER 1873
DOWN CATHEDRAL ARCHIVES

James by the Grace of God of England Scotland France and Ireland King, Defender of the Faith etc., To all to whom these our present shall come,

Greeting

Whereas we desire nothing more earnestly than that true and sincere piety should flourish and strike firm root in the hearts of our subjects, And whereas to this end no more suitable means can be found than by providing for particular churches fit pastors, imbued with doctrine and knowledge of the sacred writings and with gravity of manners, by whose labours and exemplary life the people committed to their charge might learn piety and the true religion of Christ.

Considering moreover that the present Bishop, Most Reverend Father in Christ, John Todd, who now presides over the Bishoprics of Down, Connor and Dromore in our province of Ulster within our Kingdom of Ireland is in want of the solace, assistance and counsel of Deans and Chapters of the said Bishoprics, to the grave danger not alone of the Cathedral Churches of Down, Connor and Dromore aforesaid, but also of piety and religion in the parts subject to the aforesaid Cathedral Churches, Regarding all which the Bishop has humbly entreated us for a remedy.

We therefore of our royal clemency inclining to his pious supplications and greatly desiring the propagation of true piety to the honour of Almighty God and to the progress and augmentation of religion, of our special grace, certain knowledge and mere motion have created and erected, founded and established, and by the presents for us, our heirs and successors do create, found and establish three Cathedral churches in our province of Ulster in the aforesaid Kingdom of Ireland. One of which, now called the Cathedral Church of St Patrick of Down in the County of Down, shall henceforward be and be called The Cathedral Church of the Holy Trinity of Down in our County of Downe – And another which is now called the Cathedral Church of Connor, henceforward shall be and be called the Cathedral Church of St Saviour of Connor in the County Antrim – And the third, which is now called the Cathedral Church of Dromore in the County Down, henceforward shall be and be called the Cathedral Church of Christ the Redeemer of Dromore in the County Down. Every Cathedral Church of which shall be and consist of one Dean and four dignitaries and of certain prebendaries lower down in these presents designated.

viz. of one Dean and four dignitaries in the aforesaid Cathedral Church of the Holy Trinity of Down

And of one Dean and four dignitaries in the aforesaid Cathedral Church of St Saviour of Connor

And of one Dean and four dignitaries in the aforesaid Cathedral Church of Christ the Redeemer of Dromore

And also of three Prebendaries in the aforesaid Cathedral Church of the Holy Trinity of Down

And of four Prebendaries in the aforesaid Cathedral Church of St Saviour of Connor

And of one Prebendary in the aforesaid Cathedral Church of Christ the Redeemer of Dromore

To the honour of Almighty God and to the progress and increase of religion, to continue for ever, we have decreed to be created, erected, founded and established. And the said Cathedral churches and each of them viz.,The said Cathedral Church of the Holy Trinity of Down aforesaid, of one Dean a Presbyter and of four dignitaries Presbyters, with three Prebendaries Presbyters – And the aforesaid Cathedral Church of St Saviour of Connor of one Dean a Presbyter, of four dignitaries Presbyters and of four Prebendaries Presbyters – And the aforesaid Cathedral Church of Christ the Redeemer of Dromore of one Dean a Presbyter and of four dignitaries Presbyters and of one Prebendary a Presbyter, by the tenor of these presents, we do really and fully create, erect, found, establish and to be established and for ever immovably observed, do by the presents command.

We do also will and by the presents ordain that the said Cathedral Church of the Holy Trinity of Down aforesaid may and for ever shall be the Cathedral Church and Episcopal See of the said Reverend Father in Christ John Todd, by Divine Permission Bishop of Down, and of his successors Bishops of Down for ever. And that the said Cathedral Church of St Saviour of Connor aforesaid may and for ever shall be the

Cathedral Church and Episcopal See of the said Reverend Father in Christ John Todd by Divine Permission Bishop of Connor and of his successors Bishops of Connor for ever. And that the said Cathedral Church of Christ the Redeemer of Dromore aforesaid may and for ever shall be the Cathedral Church and Episcopal See of the said Reverend Father in Christ John Todd by Divine Permission Bishop of Dromore and of his successors Bishops of Dromore for ever.

And the said Cathedral Churches and Episcopal Sees and each of them entirely and respectively, with the honors, titles, jurisdictions, eminent privileges, and immunities of Episcopal Sees and Cathedral Churches, by the presents we do fortify and decorate. And the said Episcopal See of the Cathedral Church of the Holy Trinity of Down to the said Reverend Father in Christ John Todd Bishop of Down and to his successors Bishops of the Cathedral Church of the Holy Trinity of Down, we do give and grant, together with all and singular territories, manors, castles, lands, tenements, advowsons, tithes, alterages, woods, underwoods, meadows, pastures & floods, procurations, refections, jurisdictions, privileges, pensions, portions and immunities to the aforesaid Bishoprick of the Cathedral Church of St Patrick of Down heretofore of right and of old belonging. To have & enjoy to the said John Bishop of Down, and to his future successors Bishops of the said Cathedral Church of the Holy Trinity of Down, all & singular to the said late Cathedral Church of St Patrick of Down, and to the said Cathedral Church of the Holy Trinity of Down, or to any one of them in any way belonging or that ought to belong, for ever.

And the said Episcopal See of the Cathedral Church of St Saviour of Connor aforesaid, to the said Reverend Father in Christ John Todd Bishop of Connor and to his successors Bishops of the Cathedral Church of St Saviour of Connor, we do give and grant, together with all and singular territories, manors, castles, lands, tenements, advowsons, tithes, alterages, woods, underwoods, meadows, pastures, rivers, procurations, refections, jurisdictions, privileges, pensions, portions and immunities to the aforesaid Bishoprick of the Cathedral Church of Connor heretofore by right and of old belonging. To have and enjoy to the said John Bishop of Connor and his successors future Bishops of the said Cathedral Church of St Saviour of Connor, all and singular to the said Cathedral Church of St Saviour of Connor, and to the said late Cathedral Church of Connor or to any of them in any way belonging or that ought to belong for ever.

And the said Episcopal See of the Cathedral Church of Christ the Redeemer of Dromore to the said Reverend Father in Christ John Todd Bishop of Dromore and to his successors Bishops of the Cathedral Church of Christ the Redeemer of Dromore, we do give and grant, together with all and singular territories, manors, castles, lands, tenements, advowsons, tithes, alterages, woods, underwoods, meadows, pastures, rivers, procurations, refections, jurisdictions, privileges, pensions, portions and immunities to the aforesaid Bishoprick of the Cathedral Church of Christ the Redeemer of Dromore and to the said late Cathedral Church of Dromore or to either of them, heretofore of right and of old belonging. To have and enjoy to the said John Bishop of the said Cathedral Church of Christ the Redeemer of Dromore and his successors future Bishops of the said Cathedral Church of Christ the Redeemer of

Dromore, all and singular to the said Cathedral Church of Christ the Redeemer of Dromore, and to the said late Cathedral Church of Dromore in any way belonging or ought to belong for ever.

And in order that the aforesaid Cathedral Churches founded by these presents as aforesaid, all and singular, particularly and severally, with fit persons and in their several places, dignities and grades, may be completed & decorated, of our special grace, certain knowledge and mere motion, we have made, appointed, constituted and ordained and by the presents for us, our heirs & successors do make, appoint, constitute and ordain our dearly beloved John Gibbson, Master in Arts & Professor of Sacred Theology, the first, original & modern Dean of the aforesaid Cathedral Church of the Holy Trinity of Down. We have also given and granted and by the presents of our richer special grace and of our certain knowledge and mere motion for us, our heirs and successors do give and grant to the aforesaid John Gibbson, Dean of the Cathedral Church of the Holy Trinity of Down aforesaid and to his successors Deans there for ever, all these our Rectories and Vicarages of Down, Saul, Greencastle, Killmochan, Kilbridache, Bright alias Braten, and the town of Richard White, in our County of Down, with all and singular their rights, members and appurtenances whatsoever.

And likewise we have made, constituted & ordained and by the presents for us, our heirs & successors do make constitute and ordain our well beloved John Blakeborne, Master in Arts and Professor of Sacred Theology, the first and modern Archdeacon of the aforesaid Cathedral Church of the Holy Trinity of Down. We have also given and granted and by the presents of our special grace, certain knowledge and mere motion for us, our heirs and successors, do give and grant to the aforesaid John Blakeborne, Archdeacon of the Cathedral Church of the Holy Trinity of Down, and to his successors, Archdeacons of the Cathedral Church of the Holy Trinity of Down for the time being, all those our Rectories and Vicarages of Killcliff, Killbeg alias Kilbert, Rosglas, Drumbo, Drumbegge and the Chapel of St Malachy in our County of Down with all and singular their rights, members and appurtenances whatsoever.

And likewise we have made, constituted and ordained and by the presents for us, our heirs and successors do make, constitute and ordain our well beloved William Worslye, presbyter, first and present Chancellor of the said Cathedral Church of the Holy Trinity of Down aforesaid. We have also given and granted and by the presents of our special grace, certain knowledge and mere motion for us our heirs and successors, do give and grant to the aforesaid William Worslye, Chancellor of the Cathedral Church of the Holy Trinity of Down aforesaid and to his successors, Chancellors of the Cathedral Church of the Holy Trinity of Down aforesaid for the time being, all those our Rectories and Vicarages of Phillipstown, Trostan, Slane, Rathmullan, Arglas and Ardthuayle, with all and singular their rights, members and appurtenances whatsoever in the County of Down.

We have also made, constituted and ordained and by the presents for us, our heirs and successors do make constitute and ordain our well beloved John Marshall, Master in Arts and Professor in Sacred Theology, first and present Precentor of the said Cathedral Church of the Holy Trinity of Down aforesaid. We have likewise given and granted, and by the presents of our special grace, certain knowledge and mere motion for us, our heirs and successors, do give and grant to the aforesaid John Marshall, Precentor of the Cathedral Church aforesaid and to his successors Precentors of the said Cathedral Church for the time being all those our Rectories and Vicarages of Kinles, Scion, Drumcadd, Racatt, Boriston, Balliraga, Villa bilesa and Ballintympany in the County of Down with all and singular their rights, members and appurtenances whatsoever.

And also we have constituted made and ordained, and by the presents for us, our heirs and successors do constitute, make and ordain the aforesaid Reverend Father John Todd, Professor of Sacred Theology and Bishop of Down, to be the first and present Treasurer of the said Cathedral Church of the Holy Trinity of Down aforesaid. We have likewise given and granted and by the presents of our special grace, certain knowledge and mere motion for us, our heirs and successors do give and grant to the aforesaid John Bishop and Treasurer of Down and to his successors Treasurers of the said Cathedral Church of the Holy Trinity of Down for the time being, all those our Rectories and Vicarages of Kilkaill, Tavlaght, Killingham and Killmedua, with all and singular their rights, members and appurtenances whatsoever in the County of Down.

And we have also constituted, made and ordained, and by the presents for us, our heirs and successors do constitute, make and ordain, our well beloved John Christian, Presbyter and Master in Arts, first Prebendary of the said Cathedral Church of the Holy Trinity of Down; And we will that the said Prebend of the said John Christian be called the Prebend of St Andrew. We have likewise given and granted and by the presents of our special grace, certain knowledge and mere motion, for us our heirs and successors do give and grant to the said John Christian, Prebendary aforesaid, and to his successors Prebendaries of the said Cathedral Church of the Holy Trinity of Down for the Prebend called the Prebend of St Andrew, all & singular our Rectories & Vicarages of St Andrew, Rosse, Killseaclan, Inis, Syth, Carchin & Killinseach, with all their rights, members and appurtenances in our County of Down.

And we have likewise constituted, made and ordained and by the presents for us our heirs and successors, do constitute, make and ordain, our well beloved Patrick Hamilton, Master in Arts, Second Prebendary of the said Cathedral Church of the Holy Trinity of Down aforesaid; And we will that the Prebend of the said Second Prebendary of the said Cathedral Church of the Holy Trinity of Down shall be called the Prebend of Talpestone. We have also given and granted and by the presents for us our heirs and successors of our special grace, certain knowledge and mere motion do give and grant to the aforesaid Patrick Hamilton, Prebendary of Talpestone aforesaid and to his successors Prebendaries of Talpestone aforesaid for the time being, for ever, all those our Rectories and Vicarages of Talpestone, Ruda, Iniscarrge, Drumornan, Clontagh, Leirg & Ballekehulte with all their rights, members and appurtenances in the aforesaid County of Down.

And we have also constituted, made and ordained and by the presents for us, our heirs and successors do constitute make and ordain James Hamilton first and present Third Prebendary of the said Cathedral Church of the Holy Trinity of Down. And we will that the Prebend of the said Third Prebendary of the said Cathedral Church of the Holy Trinity of Down shall be and be called the Prebend of Dunsporte for ever. We have likewise given and granted and by the presents of our richer special grace, and of our certain knowledge and mere motion for us our heirs and successors, we do give and grant to the aforesaid James Hamilton Prebend aforesaid and to his successors Prebendaries of the said Third Prebend for the time being for ever all those our Rectories and Vicarages of Dunsporte, Whitechurch, Donoghdie, Balleristard, Powley, Balleneskeans, Balleoran, Knockcolumkill and Bredagh with all their rights, members and appurtenances in our County of Down.

And we have also made, constituted and ordained and by the presents for us our heirs and successors do make constitute and ordain our well beloved Milo Whale, Presbyter, Master in Arts and Professor of the Divine Word, first and present Dean of the Cathedral Church of St Saviour of Connor. We have given also and granted and by the presents of our special grace, certain knowledge and mere motion for us our heirs and successors do give and grant to the aforesaid Milo Whale, Dean of the Cathedral Church of St Saviour of Connor, and to his successors Deans of the said Cathedral Church of St Saviour of Connor for the time being for ever all and singular those our Rectories and Vicarages of Whitechurch of the Ford, Mablayske, Balleedward, Ralowe, Invermore, Knockfergus and Balloran in our County of Antrim and the Rectories and Vicarages of Blaris and Deriakie in our County of Down with all and singular their rights, members and appurtenances.

We have also made, constituted and ordained and by the presents for us our heirs and successors do make, constitute and ordain, our dearly beloved Nicholas Todd, Presbyter, the first and present Archdeacon of the said Cathedral Church of St Saviour of Connor. We have likewise given and granted and by the presents for us our heirs and successors of our special grace, certain knowledge and mere motion do give and grant to the aforesaid Nicholas Todd, Archdeacon of the said Cathedral Church of St Saviour of Connor and to his successors Archdeacons of the said Cathedral Church of St Saviour of Connor aforesaid for the time being for ever all those our Rectories and Vicarages of Billa, Balleclugg, Armoye, Acheohill, Kilbrid and Dunnager in our County of Antrim with all and singular their rights, members and appurtenances whatsoever.

We have likewise made constituted and ordained and by the presents for us our heirs and successors do make constitute and ordain our well beloved Robert Maxwell, Master in Arts and Professor in Sacred Theology, the first and present Chancellor of the said Cathedral Church of St Saviour of Connor. We have likewise given and granted and by the presents for us our heirs and successors do give and grant to the aforesaid Robert Maxwell, Chancellor of the said Cathedral Church of St Saviour of Connor and to his successors future Chancellors of the Cathedral Church of St Saviour of Connor for the time being for ever all those our Rectories and Vicarages of Miltowne, Culfetryn, Singington, Ramoan, Loughguill, Dundermont, Skyrre and Tacmacremy in our aforesaid County of Antrim with all and singular their rights members and appurtenances whatsoever.

We have also made constituted and ordained and by the presents for us our heirs and successors do make constitute and ordain our well beloved William Todd, Master in Arts and Professor of Sacred Theology first and present Precentor of the Cathedral Church of St Saviour of Connor aforeaaid. We have given and granted likewise and by the presents of our richer special grace and of our certain knowledge and mere motion for us our heirs and successors, we do give and grant to the aforesaid William Todd, Precentor of the said Cathedral Church of St Saviour of Connor and to his successors Precentors of the said Cathedral Church of St Saviour of Connor for the time being for ever all those our Rectories and Vicarages of Portramon, Ballebony, St Cuthberts, Dunluss and Calrad in our aforesaid County of Antrim with all and singular their rights, members and appurtenances whatsoever.

We have likewise made constituted and ordained and by the presents for us our heirs and successors do make constitute and ordain our well beloved Samuel Todd, Presbyter, in Arts a Bachelor, first and present Treasurer of the Cathedral Church of St Saviour of Connor aforesaid. We have also given and granted and by the presents for us our heirs and successors do give and grant to the aforesaid Samuel Todd, Treasurer of the said Cathedral Church of St Saviour of Connor and to his successors Treasurers of the said Cathedral Church of St Saviour of Connor for the time being for ever, all those our Rectories and Vicarages of Culrathan, Agharcon, Arclynnes, Rosrelige and Racavan in our County of Antrim with all and singular their rights members and appurtenances whatsoever.

And we have also made constituted and ordained and by the presents for us our heirs and successors do make constitute and ordain our well beloved John Cotton, Presbyter, first and present Prebendary of the Cathedral Church of St Saviour of Connor aforesaid. And we will that the Prebend of the said John Cotton shall be called the Prebend of Kilroigh. We have also given and granted and by the presents for us our heirs and successors do give and grant to the aforesaid John Cotton, Prebendary of the said Cathedral Church of St Saviour of Connor and to his successors Prebendaries of the said Cathedral Church of St Saviour of Connor of the said Prebend called the Prebend of Kilroigh for the time being for ever, all those our Rectories and Vicarages of Kilroigh, Templecorran, Templeigormagan, Laughnallitten, Ballinure, Insula & Balleprior in our aforesaid County of Antrim with all their rights members and appurtenances

We have also made constituted and ordained and by the presents for us our heirs and successors do make constitute and ordain our well beloved Anthony Hill, Presbyter, Master in Arts and Professor of Sacred Theology, first and present Second Prebendary of the said Cathedral Church of St Saviour of Connor. And we will that the Prebend of the said Anthony Hill shall be called the Prebend of Rasharkan. We have also given and granted and by the presents for us our heirs and successors do give and grant to the aforesaid Anthony Hill, Prebendary aforesaid and to his successors Prebendaries of the said Cathedral Church of St Saviour of Connor and of the said Prebend of Rasharkan for the time being for ever all those our Rectories and Vicarages of Rasharkan, Finvoy, Killoconrola, Kilrates, Kildalage, St Comi, Tullatree and Glinarrm in our aforesaid County of Antrim with all and singular their rights members and appurtenances whatsoever.

We have also made constituted and ordained and by the presents for us our heirs and successors do make constitute and ordain our well beloved Archibald Rowatt, Master in Arts and Professor of Sacred Theology first and present Third Prebendary of the Cathedral Church of St Saviour of Connor aforesaid. And we will that the Prebend of the said Archibald Rowatt shall be called the Prebend of Connor. We have also given and granted and by the presents of our richer special grace, and of our certain knowledge and mere motion for us our heirs and successors do give and grant to the aforesaid Archibald Rowatt, Prebendary aforesaid, and to his successors Prebendaries of the said Cathedral Church of St Saviour of Connor and of the aforesaid Prebend of Connor for the time being for ever, all those our Rectories and Vicarages of Connor, Introia, Kilglia, Solor and Killagan in our aforesaid County of Antrim with all their rights members and appurtenances.

And we have likewise made constituted and ordained and by the presents for us our heirs and successors do make constitute and ordain our well beloved Donald O'Morrey, Presbyter and Professor of Sacred Theology, first and present Fourth Prebendary of the said Cathedral Church of St Saviour of Connor. And we will that the Prebend of the said Donald O'Morrey shall be called the Prebend of Carnecastle. We have also given and granted and by the presents for us our heirs and successors do give and grant to the aforesaid Donald O'Morrey, Prebendary aforesaid and to his successors Prebendaries of the said Cathedral Church of St Saviour of Connor and of the aforesaid Prebend of Carnecastle for the time being for ever all those our Rectories and Vicarages of Carnecastle, Killoutragh, Ballecara, Rathsith and Derikeikan in our aforesaid County of Antrim with all their rights members and appurtenances.

We have likewise made constituted and ordained and by the presents for us our heirs and successors do make constitute and ordain our well beloved William Todd, Presbyter, Master in Arts and Professor of Sacred Theology, first and present Dean of the Cathedral Church of Christ the Redeemer of Dromore aforesaid. We have also given and granted and by the presents for us our heirs and successors do give and grant to the aforesaid William Todd, Dean of the Cathedral Church of Christ the Redeemer of Dromore aforesaid and to his successors Deans of the Cathedral Church of Christ the Redeemer of Dromore for the time being for ever all those our Rectories and Vicarages of Aghederigh, the two Lummars, Magheredroll and Tullaghlisse in our County of Down with all their rights members and appurtenances.

We have also made constituted and ordained and by the presents for us our heirs and successors do make constitute and ordain our well beloved Donald O'Morrey, Presbyter and Professor of Sacred Theology, first and present Archdeacon of the Cathedral Church of Christ the Redeemer of Dromore aforesaid. We have likewise given and granted and by the presents for us our heirs and successors do give and grant to the aforesaid Donald O'Morrey, Archdeacon of the Cathedral Church of Christ the Redeemer of Dromore aforesaid and to his successors Archdeacons of the said Cathedral Church of Christ the Redeemer of Dromore aforesaid for the time being for ever all those our Rectories and Vicarages of Donachglenie with the remainder from of old belonging to the Archdeaconry of Dromore with all their rights members and appurtenances.

We have also made constituted and ordained and by the presents for us our heirs and successors do make constitute and ordain our well beloved William Webbe, Presbyter, Master in Arts and Professor of Sacred Theology, first and present Chancellor of the Cathedral Church of Christ the Redeemer of Dromore. We have also given and granted and by the presents for us our heirs and successors do give and grant to the aforesaid William Webbe, Chancellor of the said Cathedral Church of Christ the Redeemer of Dromore and to his successors Chancellors of the Cathedral Church of Christ the Redeemer of Dromore for the time being for ever all those our Rectory or Prebend and Vicarage of Clondallan in our County of Down with all and singular its right members and appurtenances whatsoever.

We have also made constituted and ordained and by the presents for us our heirs and successors do make constitute and ordain our well beloved James O'Dornan to be the first and present Precentor of the Cathedral Church of Christ the Redeemer of Dromore aforesaid. We have also given and granted and of our special grace, certain knowledge and mere motion for us our heirs and successors do give and grant to the aforesaid James O'Dornan, Precentor of the Cathedral Church of Christ the Redeemer of Dromore and to his successors Precentors of the Cathedral Church of Christ the Redeemer of Dromore for the time being for ever all those our Rectories and Vicarages of Lann and Annecheilth in our aforesaid County of Down together with and singular their rights members and appurtenances whatsoever.

We have also made constituted and ordained and by the presents for us our heirs and successors do make constitute and ordain John McInirny Treasurer of the Cathedral Church of Christ the Redeemer of Dromore aforesaid. We have also given and granted and by the presents of our special grace certain knowledge and mere motion for us our heirs and successors do give and grant to the aforesaid John McInirny Treasurer of the said Cathedral Church of Christ the Redeemer of Dromore aforesaid and to his successors Treasurers of the Cathedral Church of Christ the Redeemer of Dromore for the time being for ever all those our Rectories and Vicarages of Dromore, Drumgath and of Anechloin in our said County of Down with all and singular their rights members and appurtenances whatsoever.

Lastly we have made constituted and ordained and by the presents for us our heirs and successors do make constitute and ordain Nicholas Webbe the first and present Prebendary of the Cathedral Church of Christ the Redeemer of Dromore aforesaid. And we will that the Prebend of the said Nicholas Webbe shall be called the Prebend of Drumarrath. We have also given and granted and by the presents for us our heirs and successors of our special grace certain knowledge and mere motion do give and grant to the aforesaid Nicholas Webbe, Prebendary aforesaid, and to his successors Prebendaries of the said Cathedral Church of Christ the Redeemer of Dromore and of the aforesaid Prebend of Drumarrath for the time being for ever all those our Rectories and Vicarages of Drumarrath, Kilwilke and of Clonduffe in our aforesaid County of Down together with all their rights members and appurtenances whatsoever.

And in order that the aforesaid several Bishops, Deans and Chapters of the Cathedral Churches of Down, Connor and Dromore may severally be honorably endowed to the praise and honor of Almighty God, of our ample special grace and of our certain knowledge and mere motion, we have given and granted and by the presents do give and grant, to the aforesaid John, Bishop of Down and Bishop of Connor and Bishop of Dromore and to his successors respectively in either of the aforesaid Bishopricks, and to the Dean and Chapter of the Cathedral of the Holy Trinity of Down and to the Dean and Chapter of the Cathedral of St Saviour of Connor and to the Dean and Chapter of the Cathedral of Christ the Redeemer of Dromore and to their successors respectively for ever, all and singular the lands commonly called Termon and Irrenough or Errenough lands wheresoever lying and being, situated or found, or which hereafter shall be found or discovered by Inquisition, Office of Record, or by any other title, right or legal manner whatsoever, situate and being within the limits and precincts of our Counties of Down and Antrim aforesaid or of either of them in our Kingdom of Ireland. All and singular which lands above named we will to be shared and divided among the aforesaid Bishops, Deans and Chapters and all and singular their and their successors respectively, by the sound discretion of our Commissioners by us deputed or to be deputed for the plantation of our Province of Ulster in our aforesaid Kingdom of Ireland, within two years next following after the date of these presents. Which partition the aforesaid Bishops, Deans and Chapters and each of them and their and each of their successors respectively shall observe inviolably for ever.

We have also given and granted and by the presents do give and grant to the aforesaid three several Deans and Chapters and their successors for ever all and singular Rectories and impropriate tithes wheresoever situate being, growing, renewing, and which hereafter may exist, grow, renew or may be found and discovered situate and lying within the limits and precincts of our aforesaid Counties of Down and Antrim or of either of them in our Kingdom of Ireland together with all and singular tithes, lands, manors, woods, underwoods, edifices, alterages, obventions, oblations, mortuaries, portions, annual rents, pensions and other profits to the said Rectories or to any one or more of them in any way growing, renewing or issuing, in as ample a manner and form as they of right ought or should have come to our hands or to the hands of any of our Predecessors, Kings and Queens of England and Ireland.

Which Rectories and Impropriate Tithes and other things to the same annexed or appertaining, we will to be partitioned and divided among the aforesaid several Deans and Chapters of the three Cathedral Churches aforesaid by the discretion of the Commissioners by us deputed, or by our heirs or successors hereafter to be deputed, for the plantation of our Province of Ulster in our Kingdom of Ireland within two years next following. To have hold and enjoy all and singular the premises above mentioned to the aforesaid Bishop of Down, Bishop of Connor and Bishop of Dromore and his successors Bishops of Down, Connor and Dromore respectively and to the aforesaid several Deans and Chapters of the aforesaid three Cathedral Churches and of each of them and to their successors respectively for ever. To the sole and proper use and behoof of the said Bishops and their successors respectively and of the aforesaid Deans and Chapters of the aforesaid three Cathedral Churches and their successors respectively for ever.

Always excepting and reserving to the aforesaid Bishop of Down, Bishop of Connor and Bishop of Dromore and to his successors in the several Bishopricks respectively all and singular jurisdictions, procurations, refections, synodals, charities, subsidies, portions and pensions and other things whatsoever of right or from ancient usage or of the privileges of any Bishoprick aforesaid, heretofore paid to or accustomed to be received by the aforesaid Bishop or his Predecessors, in right of the aforesaid three Bishopricks or of any one or more of them.

And excepting also all and singular manors, lands, castles, tenements, houses, edifices, woods, underwoods, meadows, pastures, rivers, mills, annual rents and all other and singular things by whatsoever names called which the said Bishop now enjoys and possesses or in fact and of right ought or should enjoy or possess in right of any of the said two* Bishopricks of Down, Connor and Dromore respectively. All which and singular to the aforesaid Bishop and to his successors respectively we reserve by the presents, together with all and singular thereout growing, renewing and issuing.

We also will and have enacted and ordained and to the said Deans, Dignitaries and Prebendaries, by the presents do grant that the aforesaid Deans of the Cathedral Church of the Holy Trinity of Down and four dignitaries of the said Cathedral Church, viz., the Archdeacon, Chancellor, Precentor and Treasurer aforesaid and three Prebendaries of the said Cathedral, viz., the Prebendary of St Andrew's, the Prebendary of Talpestone and the Prebendary of Dunsport shall henceforth be of themselves in deed, fact and name one body corporate and shall have perpetual succession and shall behave, have and occupy themselves according to and in conformity with the ordinances, rule, statutes. indulgences and privilege granted, ordained or made to the Dean and Chapter of St Patrick's of Dublin in our Kingdom of Ireland.

We also will, enact and ordain by the presents that the aforesaid Dean of the Cathedral Church of St Saviour of Connor aforesaid and the aforesaid four dignitaries of the said Cathedral Church viz., the Archdeacon, Chancellor, Precentor and Treasurer of the Cathedral Church of St Saviour of Connor aforesaid and the aforesaid four Prebendaries of the aforesaid Cathedral Church of St Saviour of Connor, viz., the Prebendary of Kilroigh, the Prebendary of Rasharken, the Prebendary of Connor and the Prebendary of Carnecastle shall henceforth be of themselves in deed, fact and name one body corporate and shall have perpetual succession and exercise, have and occupy themselves after and according to the ordinances, rules, statutes, indulgences and privileges granted ordained and made or hereafter to be granted ordained and made to the Dean and Chapter of St Patrick's of Dublin in our Kingdom of Ireland.

We also will and have enacted and ordained by the presents that the Dean of the Cathedral Church of Christ the Redeemer of Dromore and the four dignitaries of the said Cathedral Church, viz., the Archdeacon, Chancellor, Precentor and Treasurer aforesaid and one Prebendary of the said Cathedral Church of Christ the Redeemer of Dromore, viz., the Prebendary of Drumarrath aforesaid, henceforth shall be of themselves in deed, fact and name one body corporate and shall have perpetual succession and shall bear, exhibit and occupy themselves after and according to the

*Original: Duorum

ordinances, rules, statutes, indulgences and privileges of the Dean and Chapter of St Patrick's of Dublin in our Kingdom of Ireland.

We also grant, enact and ordain that all those several Deans, Dignitaries and Prebendaries and their successors Deans and Chapters of the three Cathedral Churches of Down, Connor and Dromore aforesaid respectively shall be called and named for ever and in the presents be called and named in the following manner, viz., the Dean, Dignitaries and Prebendaries of the said Cathedral Church of the Holy Trinity of Down and their successors shall be called and named for ever the Dean and Chapter of the Cathedral Church of the Holy Trinity of Down.

And the aforesaid Dean, Dignitaries and Prebendaries of the said Cathedral Church of St Saviour of Connor and their successors shall be called and named for ever the Dean and Chapter of the Cathedral Church of St Saviour of Connor.

And that the aforesaid Dean, Dignitaries and Prebendary of the aforesaid Cathedral Church of Christ the Redeemer of Dromore and their successors for ever shall be called and named the Dean and Chapter of the Cathedral Church of Christ the Redeemer of Dromore.

And that the aforesaid Dean and Chapter of the Cathedral Church of the Holy Trinity of Down and their successors may and for ever shall be the Chapter of the Bishop of the Bishoprick of Down and that the said Chapter be annexed, incorporated and united to the aforesaid Bishop of Down and to his successors Bishops of Down for all future time; and those the Dean, Dignitaries and Prebendaries of the Cathedral Church of the Holy Trinity of Down one body corporate in deed, fact and name we do make, create and establish and them for one body we do make, declare, ordain and accept. And that they may and shall have perpetual succession.

And that the aforesaid Dean and Chapter of the Cathedral Church of St Saviour of Connor and their successors be and for ever shall be the Chapter of the Bishop and of the Bishoprick of Connor and that the same Chapter shall be annexed, incorporated and united to the aforesaid John Bishop of Connor and to his successors Bishops of Connor for all future time; and the said Dean, Dignitaries and Prebendaries of the Cathedral Church of St Saviour of Connor one body corporate in deed, fact and name we do make, create and ordain for ever; and them for one body we do make, declare, ordain and accept. And they may and shall have perpetual succession.

And that the aforesaid Dean and Chapter of the Cathedral Church of Christ the Redeemer of Dromore and their successors may and for ever shall be the Chapter of the Bishop and of the Bishoprick of Dromore and the said Chapter be annexed, incorporated and united to the aforesaid John Bishop of Dromore and his successors Bishops of Dromore for all future time; And those the Dean, Dignitaries and Prebendaries of the Cathedral Church of Christ the Redeemer of Dromore one body corporate in deed, fact and name we do make, create and ordain and them for one body we do make, declare, ordain and accept. And they may and shall have perpetual succession.

And that all and singular the aforesaid Deans and Chapters particularly and severally and their successors by the names above given to them of Dean and Chapter of any Cathedral Church aforesaid respectively and each of them respectively shall be able to prosecute, claim and plead and be impleaded, defend and be defended, indict and be indicted in whatsoever courts and places and before whatsoever judges and justiciaries, commissioners and other officers of us our heirs and successors and others whatsoever in our said Kingdom of Ireland and elsewhere wheresoever, in and upon all and singular causes, actions, suits, demands, writs and complaints, real, spiritual, ecclesiastical, personal and mixed, and in all other things and matters whatsoever; and by the same names respectively the manors, lordships, lands, castles, edifices, territories, tenements, possessions, heriditaments, profits and other emoluments whatsoever, as well spiritual or ecclesiastical as temporal, and all other things whatsoever, by us our heirs or successors by the Letters Patent of us our heirs or successors or by any other person or persons whatsoever to them and their successors or otherwise according to the laws of us our heirs or successors to be given or granted. They and each of them may and shall be able to take, receive and perceive, to give, alienate and demise or to do and perform all and singular things respectively, as other Cathedral Churches within our Kingdom, or any of them, are or is able commonly to take, receive, perceive, alienate and demise and to do, observe and perform or confirm in any manner.

And that the singular several Deans and Chapters of any of the three Cathedral Churches aforesaid and their successors forever may and shall have, and every Dean and Chapter respectively may and shall have, a common seal for confirming all manner of causes, evidences and other writings and letters, or of doing other acts in any way touching or concerning themselves respectively, or the Cathedral Churches aforesaid respectively, by which sealing they may and shall be able to bind and oblige themselves and their successors respectively for a time or for ever after and according to the tenor of the writing or writings signed by them.

We also grant and ordain by the presents that the aforesaid Deans of the Cathedral Churches aforesaid and their successors for the time being shall make, constitute, admit and accept from time to time for ever, as the cases or case may require all and singular the inferior officers and ministers of the Cathedral Churches of which they are Deans and may and shall be able, for legitimate cause, not only to correct but also to depose and from the said Cathedral Church and the ministry of the same to amove and expel those persons and each of them so admitted or to be admitted.

Furthermore, we commend and direct the Reverend Father in Christ, John Todd, Bishop of Down, Connor and Dromore aforesaid, that he shall admit all and singular the aforesaid Dean, Dignitaries and Prebendaries and each of them respectively to the Deaneries, Dignities and Prebends aforesaid by us respectively in these presents created and granted; and that he will actually and really assign or cause to be assigned to them all and singular respectively a stall in the choir and a voice in the chapter respectively. And further know ye that we being founders of the said three several Cathedral Churches in our province of Ulster viz., of the aforesaid Cathedral Church of the Holy Trinity of Down in our County of Down and of the aforesaid Cathedral Church of St Saviour of Connor in the aforesaid County of Antrim and of the aforesaid Cathedral Church of Christ the Redeemer of Dromore in the said County of Down, and of the aforesaid several Deans, Dignitaries and Prebendaries in the said several

Cathedral Churches so as aforesaid by us ordained and appointed, and to the said several Deans, Dignitaries and Prebendaries, their successors respectively, having given and granted by our Letters Patent various Manors, Rectories, lands, tenements and heriditaments for their perpetual maintenance in the said Cathedral Churches. And greatly desiring that the said Cathedral Churches and each of them so by us founded to the glory and honor of Almighty God and to the propagation, augmentation and confirmation of religion and Divine Worship in that province shall for ever remain in a good and prosperous state, endowed, enriched and decorated with the issues, rents, profits, manors, lands, tenements and heriditaments necessary and convenient for their perpetual continuance and maintenance.

Considering therefore that the statutes of this our Kingdom of England in that behalf heretofore made and provided were and now are very useful, necessary and conducible to the sustentation of the Cathedral Churches of this Kingdom in a good and happy state, according to the will and intentions of their several founders and towards preserving those churches and all their rents, issues, lands, tenements and heriditaments from spoil, decay and diminution, We, graciously wishing to provide for the good state of the said several Churches so by us founded by the presents in the said Province of Ulster, and to render their state and conservation, as far as in us lies, conformable to similar dignities founded in our Kingdom of England, have willed, ordained and constituted and by the presents for us our heirs and successors do ordain and constitute that neither the aforesaid Dean and Chapter of the said Cathedral Church of the Holy Trinity of Down nor the aforesaid Dean and Chapter of the aforesaid Cathedral Church of St Saviour of Connor, nor the aforesaid Dean and Chapter of the Cathedral Church of Christ the Redeemer of Dromore in the said County of Down nor the aforesaid Dignitaries or Prebendaries nor any of them, nor the successor or successors of any of them, shall have any power by virtue or pretext of these our Letters Patent, of alienating, selling or conveying, or in any manner granting or to farm demising, nor be able to alienate, sell, convey, or in any manner grant or to farm demise, by virtue or colour of these our Letters Patent, or of any clause or concession in these presents contained, any manors, lands, tenements, heriditaments whatsoever to the said Deans, Dignitaries and Prebendaries, or to any of them in these presents mentioned to be given or granted or that may be given or granted, to any person or persons whatsoever, or to any body or bodies corporate or politic whatsoever, of or for any greater estate than for and during a term of 21 years in possession, to be done by indenture, one part of which shall remain in the hands of the aforesaid Deans and Chapters respectively and of their successors, or in the hands of the aforesaid Dignitaries and Prebendaries respectively and with the reservation of all and such annual rents to the said Deans and Chapters respectively and their successors respectively and to the aforesaid Dignitaries and Prebendaries and their successors respectively, in those indentures of such demise or grant to be contained for and in respect of such manors, lands, tenements, heriditaments in or by any such grant or demise or to be granted or demised as according to the discretion of the Deputy of Ireland for the time being and of the Chancellor and Privy Council of the said Kingdom, or of any four or more of them, of whom we will that the aforesaid Deputy and Chancellor shall always be two, after survey and valuation of the premises in due form made and returned into our Exchequer of Ireland, shall appear reasonable and convenient, according to the rate and value of our lands in the same province usually rented and valued.

Which survey and valuation we will and command to be made and returned by such Commissioners as by the Deputy of our said Kingdom of Ireland and by the Chancellor and the rest of the Privy Council of the said Kingdom, or by the greater part of them, shall be appointed and constituted with all celerity and as quickly as it can be commodiously and conveniently be done. We will also that our said Deputy of Ireland and our Chancellor of our said Kingdom of Ireland and the rest of our Privy Council in the said Kingdom, or any four or more of them, of whom we will that the Deputy and Chancellor for the time being shall be two, shall return and describe, in parchment signed by their hands, or with the hands of four or more of them, the said annual rents by them appointed and allowed or reserved as aforesaid. And the said writing so signed by them, or by any four or more of them, they shall deliver into our Exchequer of Ireland, there to be kept together with the Inquisition so as aforesaid to be taken for the declation (sic) of their true annual value for ever.

And likewise we have willed, ordained and constituted, and by the presents for us our heirs and successors do will, ordain and constitute, that neither the aforesaid Dean and Chapter of the said Cathedral Church of the Holy Trinity, nor the aforesaid Dean and Chapter of the Cathedral Church of St Saviour of Connor nor the aforesaid Dean and Chapter of the Cathedral Church of Christ the Redeemer of Dromore, nor the aforesaid Dignitaries and Prebendaries, nor any of them, nor their successors, nor the successors of any of them, shall have any power in any manner of granting or to farm demising their mansion houses or principal seats in which they principally reside or ought to reside or are accustomed to reside nor any manors, lands or tenements usually held or occupied with those seats or mansion houses for maintaining hospitality there.

And also of our richer special grace and of our certain knowledge and mere motion, we have willed, ordained and constituted, and by the presents for us our heirs and successors do will ordain and constitute that the several Deaneries or Dignities of Dean in the aforesaid Cathedral Churches and each of them, in the vacancy of all those Deaneries or of any one or more of them shall belong and appertain to the donation, collation and free disposition of us our heirs and successors. And that we, our heirs and successors, and no other persons, shall be and be reputed patrons of those Deaneries and of each of them and the same when vacant from time shall grant and confer for ever.

And that all and singular the remaining Deaneries and functions aforesaid, the dignity of Deanery alone excepted, and all and singular Prebends of the Cathedral Churches above named, in all vacancies of the same and of each of them respectively, shall belong and appertain to the nomination, collation and disposition of the said Bishops respectively, and of their successors respectively for ever.

And that the aforesaid Bishops respectively and their successors and none other, shall be and be reputed patron or patrons of those Dignities and Prebends and of each of them, and the same when vacant from time to time shall give and confer for ever, anything in the presents to the contrary notwithstanding.

And further we will, and by the presents ordain and grant, that it shall be allowable to the Deputy of our Kingdom of Ireland for the time being, to the Chancellor of the aforesaid Kingdom and the rest of the Privy Council of us our heirs and successors within the said Kingdom, or to any four or more of them of whom we will that the Deputy and Chancellor of the said Kingdom for the time being shall be two, in augmentation and supplement of the aforesaid Deaneries, Dignities and Prebends, to survey all and singular Rectories, Vicarages and other ecclesiastical benefices whatsoever, as well impropriate as not impropriate, and as well with cure of souls as without cure, within the aforesaid three several dioceses and each of them; and after due survey taken thereof and had by such Charters, Letters Patent or other conveyances as by our Counsel, learned in the laws within our said Kingdom of Ireland may be devised according to our directions and mandates in that behalf to be signified by our Treasurer of England, to grant and assign any such Rectories, Vicarages and other benefices impropriate and being within the three aforesaid dioceses of the three several bishopricks aforesaid, according to their sound discretion, to any Deaneries, Dignitaries and Prebendaries aforesaid and to their successors. Provided also that in every such Rectory or church with cure of souls a perpetual vicarage shall be erected and established and endowed for ever with competent tithes, stipends or other profits well and sufficiently assigned to the said Vicars and their successors. Which Vicars shall for ever exercise cure of souls and divine service in the said churches.

We will moreover, that the benefices so as aforesaid respectively to be assigned, in writings and under the seal and handwriting of the persons above nominated for this purpose signed and sealed, all such erections and endowments of Vicarages as aforesaid to be done, to the aforesaid Deaneries, Dignities and Prebends respectively, for all rightful purposes, and inseparably shall be reputed and shall be annexed for ever by the tenor and virtue of the presents.

And we will moreover, and by the presents for us our heirs and successors do ordain that such and suchlike provisions, restrictions and other means shall from time to time be made, had, done and ordained for the restriction as well of the said spiritual Deans and Chapters and their successors, as of the aforesaid Dignitaries and Prebendaries and their successors, from alienating, conveying, granting or demising any manors, Rectories, lands, tenements or heriditaments by virtue or in performance of the intent of these our Letters Patent given and granted or to be given and granted, in any other manner or for any greater estate or term than above by the presents is ordained, and as, for the maintenance and preservation of the aforesaid churches in a good state, by the Deputy, Chancellor and the rest of the Privy Council within the said Kingdom of Ireland, with the advice of our Counsel learned in the law within our said Kingdom shall be better and more firmly devised and advised.

We likewise will and by the presents do grant to the aforesaid Reverend Father in Christ John Todd, now Bishop of the Bishopricks aforesaid that he may and shall have these our Letters Patent made and sealed in due form under our Great Seal of

England, without fine or fee great or small to us in our Hanaper or elsewhere to our use in any way to be rendered, paid or done therefor.

In testimony whereof, we have caused these our Letters to be made Patents. Witness myself at Westminster the 20th day of July in the 7th year of our Reign of England, France and Ireland and of Scotland the 42nd.

By writ of Privy Seal

A correct translation
W.M.HENNESSY
25 OCT. 1873

APPENDIX 4

THE CHAPTER AFTER 1609

DEAN	CHANCELLOR	PRECENTOR
1609 J. Gibson	1609 W. Worsley	1609 J. Marshall
1623 R. Dawson	16 ? P. Ride	1614 D. Fairfull
1627 H. Leslie	1612 M. Hamilton	1668 J. Clewlow
1635 W. Coote	1629 J. Boyle	1700 J. Smyth
1662 T. Bayly	1629 J. Echlin	1703 R. Lambert
1664 D. Witter	1642 R. Echlin	1706 W. Caldwell
1669 W. Sheridan	1661 T. Morgan	1707 J. Laury
1682 B. Phipps	1662 J. Mace	1712 J. Fletcher
1683 J. McNeale	1670 R. Echlin	1720 E. Mathews
1709 R. Lambert	1684 A. MacNeale	1755 B. Ward
1717 B. Pratt	1728 S. Hutchinson	1784 J. Symes
1722 C. Fairfax	1729 A. Rogers	1789 C. Hare
1724 W. Gore	1742 B. Barrington	
1732 R. Daniel	1747 A. Bisset	
1739 T. Fletcher	1757 J. Fortescue	
1744 P. Delany	1781 W. Sturrock	
1769 J. Dickson		
1787 W. Annesley		
1817 E. Knox	1797 R. Mortimer	1791 R. Wolseley
1831 T. Plunket	1800 R. Radcliff	1823 J. Alexander
1839 T. Blakeley	1812 H. Morgan	1828 J. C. Gordon
1856 T. Woodward	1820 E. Montgomery	1841 H. S. Cumming
	1825 C. Davies	1859 T. Drew
	1828 W. St. J. Smyth	
	1843 J. L. M. Scott	
1876 E. B. Moeran	1885 E. Maguire	1870 J. P. Brown
1887 E. Maguire	1888 E. A. Lyle	1899 A. J. Moore
1912 J. P. Brown	1897 H. W. Stewart	1911 G. Smith
1923 W. P. Carmody	1911 A. J. Moore	1911 W. H. Davis
1938 R. C. H. G. Elliott	1919 A. E. Ross	1917 C. W. Harding
1945 F. Hatch	1920 W. L. Twist-Whatham	1922 J. A. Care
1955 W. H. Good	1938 E. H. Blackwood-Price	1925 A. W. Barton
1964 A. W. M. S. Mann	1941 J. Quinn	1927 C. C. Manning
1968 R. W. T. H. Kilpatrick	1956 P. R. Cosgrave	1930 T. B. Brown
1980 J. H. R. Good	1959 H. C. Marshall	1945 F. Matchett
1987 H. Leckey	1964 J. Barry	1949 J. S. Houston
1996 J. F. Dinnen	1974 A. McKelvie	1955 P. R. Cosgrave

	1980 E. S. Barber	1956 A. W. M. S. Mann
	1986 H. Leckey	1964 R. W. T. H. Kilpatrick
	1987 P. J. Synott	1968 J. Hamilton
	1990 A. Maconachie	1979 E. S. Barber
	1991 C. W. M. Cooper	1980 J. H. R. Good
		1981 H. Leckey
		1986 P. J. Synott
		1987 A. Maconachie
		1990 C. W. M. Cooper
		1991 J. A. B. Mayne
TREASURER	PREBENDARIES OF SAINT ANDREW	PREBENDARIES OF DUNSPORT
1609 J. Todd	1609 J. Christian	1609 J. Hamilton
1620 R. Echlin	1616 Andrew Moneypenny	1622 R. Hack
gap until	1620 Arthur Moneypenny	1640 P. Dunkin
	1634 J. Boyle	1661 J. Mace
	1639 John Maxwell*	1661 J. Dale
	1661 T. Morgan	166? R. Echlin
	1662 A. Dunlop	1671 F. Mussenden
	1664 J. Mace	1677 W. Jones
	1664 A. Gordon	1680 H. Leslie
	1670 J. Fineau	
	1675 R. Maxwell	
	1686 G. Lovell	
1693 A. Matthews	1706 E. Benson	1695 S. Foley
1704 C. Ward	1742 P. I. Cornabe	1720 S. Close
1724 J. Matthews	1745 J. Ryder	1721 J. Kenyon
1733 E. Bayly	1759 E. Lodge	1724 S. Hutchinson
1785 L. Waring	1761 E. Trotter	1728 H. Daniel
	1777 A. Traill	1736 V. E. Lonergan
	1782 R. Trail	1755 F. Houston
		1772 F. Hall
		1782 J. Dickson
1823 G. H. McDowal-Johnston		1790 R. Meade
	1842 F. W. Mant	1811 S. L. Montgomery
1864 C. P. Reichel	1845 D. Bell	1812 W. B. Forde
1866 J. H. Freke	1878 A. Creery	1817 L. Creery
1868 E. B. Moeran	1889 G. Smith	1818 J. Alexander
1876 T. Blackwood-Price	1911 J. I. Peacocke	1821 A. Colhoun
1890 J. B. Crozier	1916 W. P. Carmody	1834 T. Thompson
1898 R. A. Kernan	1917 W. L. Twist-Whatham	1836 R. W. Rowan
1914 G. G. Mervyn	1920 F. W. Austin	1839 J. Bradshaw
		1844 J. Free
		1846 F. F. Magrath
		1861 A. Creery
		1864 R. Peacock

		1868 J. Williams
		1883 S. Campbell
		1889 J. B. Crozier
		1890 J. H. Duke
		1905 A. R. Ryder
1916 G. S. Greer	1930 J. C. Rutherford	1920 J. J. Deacon
1921 J. J. Deacon	1931 W. Hannah	1922 C. C. Manning
1921 S. Hemphill	1933 R. C. H. G. Elliott	1927 B. F. White
1923 A. W. Barton	1938 L. W. Crooks	1928 A. Moore
1925 G. Foster	1940 F. Matchett	1938 G. W. Capsey
1935 E. H. Blackwood-Price	1945 G. R. C. Olden	1946 W. H. N. Fisher
	1946 J. S. Houston	1949 J. G. Pooler
1938 A. Moore	1948 P. R. Cosgrove	1953 H. C. Marshall
1946 G. W. Capsey	1955 C. W. A. Huston	1955 C. H. Walsh
1948 J. S. Huston	1959 H. T. Cotter	1966 E. G. Parke
1949 W. H. N. Fisher	1963 A. McKelvie	1970 W. G. L. Walker
1955 H. C. Marshall	1968 G. W. L. Hill	1979 J. H. R. Good
1959 C. W. A. Huston	1974 W. G. Neely	1980 R. J. Chisholm
1966 C. H. Walsh		
1968 A. McKelvie	1976 J. Mehaffey	1981 J. C. Swenarton
1970 E. G. Parke	1980 P. J. Synott	1982 A. Maconachie
1973 T. H. Frizelle	1987 J. C. Bell	1986 C. W. M. Cooper
1980 H. Leckey	1991 S. M. J. Dickson	1990 G. A. McCamley
1981 R. J. Chisholm		1995 T. Keightley
1982 A. J. Douglas		
1986 A. Maconachie		
1987 J. E. Moore		
1990 J. A. B. Mayne		
1991 J. C. Bell		

* PRONI:D 1759/2A/9: Royal Presentations to Benefices 1535-1665
copied by J. S. Reid ex British Museum

PREBENDARIES OF TALPESTONE

1609 P. Hamilton
1691 S. Lightburne (PRONI: T 552,p. 7. Fiants for church preferments)
1692 J. Francis (instituted improperly by Archdeacon Matthews without knowledge of Bishop - Cotton III, p. 241)
1693 Prebend abandoned by Regal Commission
1958 Prebend revived by General Synod bill
1958 J. Hamilton
1968 C. T. Jackson
1974 H. Leckey
1980 A. J. Douglas
1982 J. C. Swenarton
1985 J. E. Moore
1987 J. A. B. Mayne
1990 J. I. H. Stafford
1993 J. F. Dinnen
1997 W. J. R. Laverty

BISHOPS OF DOWN AND CONNOR AFTER 1609

1609 John Todd
1612 James Dundas
1612 Robert Echlin
1635 Henry Leslie
1661 Jeremy Taylor
1667 Roger Boyle
1672 Thomas Hacket
1694 Samuel Foley
1695 Edward Walkington
1699 Edward Smyth
1721 Francis Hutchinson
1739 Charles Reynell
1743 John Ryder
1752 John Whitcombe
1753 Arthut Smyth
1765 James Traill
1783 William Dickson
1804 Nathaniel Alexander
1823 Richard Mant
inc. Dromore after 1842

BISHOPS OF DOWN, CONNOR AND DROMORE

1849 R. B. Knox
1886 W. Reeves
1892 T. J. Welland
1907 J. B. Crozier
1911 C. F. D'Arcy
1919 C. T. P. Grierson
1934 J. F. McNeice
1942 C. K. Irwin

BISHOPS OF DOWN AND DROMORE

1944 W. S. Kerr
1955 F. J. Mitchell
1969 G. A. Quin
1980 R. H. A. Eames
1986 G. McMullan
1997 H. C. Miller

ARCHDEACONS OF DOWN

1606 John Blackburne
1622 John Christian
1628 Robert Maxwell
1640 John Richardson
1647 Henry Maxwell
1654 George Walker
1661 Jeremiah Piddock
1674 Lemuel Matthews
1695 Henry Leslie
1733 Francis Hutchinson
1768 Trevor Benson
1782 Ralph Ward
1784 Edmund Leslie
1790 John Dickson
1814 Robert Alexander
1828 R. M. Mant
1834 W. B. Mant
1869 John Gibbs
1890 T. Blackwood-Price
1899 J. P. Brown
1912 L. A. H. T. Pooler
1923 S. Hemphill
1927 A. W. Barton
1930 C. C. Manning
1945 T. B. Brown
1946 G. R. C. Olden
1950 C. I. Peacocke
1956 G. A. Quin
1970 A. McKelvie
1976 E. S. Barber
1979 G. McMullan
1980 W. A. Macourt
1989 J. E. Moore
1995 G. A. McCamley

APPENDIX 5

THE HERALDIC ACHIEVEMENTS

Lt Col J. R. H. Greeves

HERALDIC ACHIEVEMENTS OF VARIOUS benefactors of the Cathedral are displayed on the walls of the aisles and on some of the piers of the nave. They are cast from plaster, nearly all by Marcus Ward & Co. of Belfast in 1864. The exceptions are Nos. 2 and 16, which were made by Coade of London in 1804, Nos. 5 and 6 on a double plaque with no date and No.14 by Marcus Ward in 1866. They are carefully executed and coloured, although the colouring differs in a number of minor instances from the correct blazon, as quoted in Burke. It is to be presumed that the coats numbered 2, 5, 6, and 16 were erected shortly after the Cathedral was restored and the remainder put up in Dean Woodward's time. The following is a list of the achievements with notes on the families or persons represented. All numbering commences from the East end.

SOUTH AISLE

1.**ARMS:** Azure, 3 boar's heads erased Or,

CREST: Out of a ducal coronet Or, a stag's head and neck affronte erased proper

MOTTO: Animo non astutia

FOR: *Gordon* of Florida Manor and Delamont, Co. Down

David Gordon, J.P., D.L., H.S. Co. Down 1812; b. 1 June 1759, d. 2 March 1837; m. 11 September 1789 Mary, daughter of James Crawford of Crawfordsburn. He was succeeded in turn by his two sons: Robert Gordon, J.P., D.L., H.S. Co. Down 1833; b. 8 September 1791, d.s.p. 1864 and Rev. James Crawford Gordon, B.A. (Cantab) 1821, M.A.1825, M.A. (TCD) 1832, Vicar of Kilmood (Down) 1821-28; Precentor of Down 1828-41; b. 28 April 1796, d.s.p. 12 November 1867

2.**ARMS:** Quarterly, 1st, Sable, on a fess Argent between 3 leopards passant guardant Or, spotted of the field, as many escallops Gules of the 3rd (Hill); 2nd, per bend sinister Ermine and Ermines, a lion rampant Or (Trevor); 3rd, Gules a quatrefoil Or[1] (Rowe of Muswell Hill); 4th, Argent, a chevron Azure between 3 trefoils slipped Vert[2] (Rowe or Roe of Devonshire); in pretence an escutcheon bearing: quarterly, 1st, Or, a fess dancette between 3 cross-crosslets fitche Gules (Sandys); 2nd, Or, on a bend engrailed Azure 3 phaeons Argent[3] (Tipping); 3rd, Argent 3 crescents Gules (Cheeke); 4th, Argent, a lion rampant Gules, on a chief Azure 3 escallops Or[4] (Russell).

CREST: On a Marquis's coronet, a reindeer's head couped Gules, attired and plain-collared Or

SUPPORTERS: Dexter, a leopard Or, spotted Sable, gorged with a Marquis's coronet Or and chained Gules; Sinister, a reindeer Gules, plain collared Or.[5]

MOTTO: Per Deum et ferrum obtinui

FOR: *Arthur Hill*, 2nd Marquis of Downshire, b. 3 March 1753, d. 7 September 1801; m. 29 June 1786, Mary (created Baroness Sandys 19 June 1802, d. 1 August 1836), granddaughter and eventual heir of Samuel Sandys, 1st Baron Sandys, by Letitia, daughter and co-heir of Sir Thomas Tipping, Bt., by Anne, daughter and eventual heir of Thomas Cheeke, of Pirgo, Essex, by Letitia, daughter and eventual sole heir of Edward Russell, 4th son of Francis, 4th Earl of Bedford. The Marquis was grandson of Trevor Hill 1st Viscount Hillsborough (1693-1742) by Mary, elder daughter and co-heir of Anthony Rowe of Muswell Hill, whose mother was Anne, daughter and eventual heir of Sir John Trevor, Master of the Rolls and Speaker of the House of Commons.

3.**ARMS:** [Originally on East pier, nave, north side] Quarterly, 1st and 4th, Or, a bend counter-compony Argent and Azure,[6] between 2 lions rampant Gules (Stewart); 2nd and 3rd, Gules, a saltire Argent.[7]

CREST: None: a Marquis's coronet

SUPPORTERS: Dexter, a Moor (wreathed about the temples Argent and Azure) holding in his exterior hand a shield of the last, garnished Or, charged with the sun in splendour Or; Sinister, a lion Or, collared Argent, on the collar 3 mullets Sable.[8]

MOTTO: Metuenda corolla draconis

FOR: *Stewart*, Marquis of Londonderry

Robert Stewart of Mountstewart, son of Alexander Stewart, M.P. for Londonderry, by Mary, only surviving daughter of Alderman John Cowan of Londonderry, and sister and heir of Sir Robert Cowan, Knt, Governor of Bombay; b. 27 September 1739, m. firstly, 3 June 1766 Sarah Frances (d. 18 July 1770), daughter of Francis, 1st Marquis of Hertford; m. secondly, 7 June 1775, Frances (d. 18 January 1833), daughter of Charles, 1st Earl Camden. He was created Baron Londonderry 20 September 1789, Viscount Castlereagh 1 October 1795, Earl of Londonderry 8 August 1796 and Marquis of Londonderry 13 January 1816; d. 8 April 1821 and was succeeded by his only son by his first marriage, Robert, well known as Lord Castlereagh, b. 18 June 1769, d. 12 August 1822 and was succeeded by his half-brother Charles William 3rd Marquis, b. 18 May 1778, d. 6 March 1854. His son Frederick William Robert, b. 7 July 1805 succeeded and d.s.p. 25 November 1872.

4.**ARMS:** Azure, two flaunches Or, in chief and in base a martlet of the 2nd in fess a rose also Or between two roses on the flaunches Gules.

CREST: A martlet Or

MOTTO: Incorrupta fides nudaque veritas

FOR: *Forde* of Seaforde

Mathew Forde, M.P. for Downpatrick, H.S. Co. Down 1752, b. 1726, d. 6 August 1795; m. 15 August 1750 Elizabeth Knox, sister of 1st Viscount Northland. He was succeeded by his son Mathew Forde, H.S. Co. Down 1803, b.c. 1753, d. 31 March 1812, and was succeeded in turn by his sons Mathew Forde, J.P., D.L., H.S. Co. Down 1820, M.P. Co. Down 1821-6, b. 17 May 1785, d.s.p. 5 August 1837 and Rev. William Brownlow Forde J.P., D.L., b. 1786, d. 11 March 1856; the latter was succeeded by his son W.B. Forde, P.C., J.P., D.L., H.S. Co Down 1853, M.P. Co. Down 1857-74, b. 5 November 1823, d. 8 February 1902.

5.**ARMS:** On a lozenge, the arms of Hill, Marquis of Downshire, as in No. 2 but with a baron's coronet over the escutcheon of pretence

CREST: None: a Marquis's coronet

SUPPORTERS: As in No.2

MOTTO: None

FOR: Mary, Baroness *Sandys* (so created 19 June 1802) granddaughter and eventual heir of Samuel Sandys as widow of Arthur Hill, 2nd Marquis of Downshire (see No.2)

6.**ARMS:** On a lozenge; quarterly, 1st, Or, a fess dancette between 3 cross-crosslets fitche Gules (Sandys) 2nd, Or, on a bend engrailed Azure 3 phaeons Argent (Tipping); 3rd, Argent 3 crescents Gules (Cheeke); 4th, Argent, a lion rampant Gules, on a chief Azure 3 escallops Or (Russell)[9]

CREST: None: a baron's coronet

SUPPORTERS: Two griffins per fess Or and Gules, collared dancette of the last

MOTTO: None

FOR: Mary, Baroness *Sandys* in her own right.
These two achievements, Nos. 5 and 6 are on one plaque.

7.**ARMS:** Quarterly; 1st and 4th, Ermine, 2 bars Gules (Nugent); 2nd and 3rd, Argent, 6 lioncels, 3, 2 and 1 Sable (Savage).

CRESTS:
1. A cockatrice rising Or (Nugent)[10]
2. Out of a ducal coronet Or, a lion's jamb erect (Savage)

MOTTOES:
1. Decrevi (Nugent)
2. Fotis atque fidelis (Savage)

FOR: *Nugent* of Portaferry House

Andrew Savage, of Portaferry, J.P., D.L., H.S. Co. Down 1808; b. 3 June 1770, d. 2 February 1846, m. 13 June 1800 Selina Vesey, youngest daughter of the 1st Viscount de Vesci. He took the name of Nugent on succeeding to the estates of his great-uncle, John Nugent, of Dysart, Co.Westmeath. He was son of Patrick Savage of Portaferry, H.S. Co. Down 1763 (d. 7 March 1797), by Anne, daughter of Roger Hall of Narrowwater and grandson of Andrew Savage by Margaret, daughter and eventual heir of Andrew Nugent of Dysart. He was succeeded by his eldest son, Patrick John Nugent, H.S. Co.Down 1843 b. 1804, m. 29 April 1833 his cousin Catherine Vesey, daughter of the 2nd Viscount de Vesci and d. November 1857 when he was succeeded by his elder son Lt Gen. Andrew Nugent, J.P., D.L., H.S. Co Down 1882

8.**ARMS:** Quarterly; 1st and 4th, Argent, a chevron engrailed between 3 talbot's heads erased Sable (Hall); 2nd and 3rd, Argent, six lioncels, 3, 2 and 1, Sable, (Savage)

CREST: A bear's head couped and muzzled proper

MOTTO: None

FOR: *Hall* of Narrowwater

Savage Hall, of Narrowwater, H.S., Co. Armagh 1795 and Co. Down 1800; son of Roger Hall of Mount Hall, Co. Armagh, by Catherine, only daughter of Rowland Savage of Portaferry; b. 1763, d. ?, m. 3 February 1787 Elizabeth, 4th daughter of John Madden of Hilton, Co. Monaghan (d. 1801). He was succeeded by his eldest son Roger Hall, J.P., D.L., H.S. Co. Down 1816, b. 6 November 1791, d.s.p. 20 September 1864.

9.**ARMS:** Quarterly; 1st and 4th Azure, a cross patonce Or (Ward); 2nd and 3rd, Gules, 3 cinquefoils Ermine on a chief Or a human heart of the first (Hamilton).

CREST: None: a Viscount's coronet

SUPPORTERS: Dexter, a knight in armour proper, on his breast a cross patonce Or, and wearing a flowing robe Gules charged with a maltese cross Argent on the shoulder sinister (his dexter hand resting upon a drawn sword, point downwards proper, hilt and pommel Or); Sinister, a Turkish prince vested Azure and Or, the habit reaching to the ankles, sandals Gules, sash Or and fringe round his waist, wearing a loose brown robe of fur; on his head an antique crown Or enclosing a cap of estate Gules.[11] (The sword is missing)

MOTTO: Sub cruce salus

FOR: *Ward* Viscount Bangor

Nicholas Ward, 2nd Viscount Bangor, b. 1750, d. unmarried 11 September 1827, son of Bernard Ward 1st Viscount Bangor (created 18 January 1781), who d. 20 May 1781, son of Michael Ward of Castle-ward, M.P. Co. Down 1715, Judge of the King's Bench in Ireland 1735, by Anne Catherine, daughter and co-heir of James Hamilton of Bangor, great-nephew of James Hamilton, 1st Viscount Claneboye. He was succeeded by his nephew Edward Southwell, 3rd Viscount, b. March 1790, succeeded in turn by his son Edward, 4th Viscount, b. 23 February 1837, d. unmarried 14 September 1881.

NAVE: SOUTH SIDE
EAST PIER

10.**ARMS:** Gules, a lion rampant Argent within a bordure compony Azure and Argent (Wallace); in pretence an escutcheon bearing Azure a fess Argent between in chief an increscent and decrescent of the second and in base a branch of palm slipped Vert.[12] (Nevin of Shousburgh)

BADGE: (Above the memorial) An ostrich proper holding in its beak a horseshoe Or.

MOTTO: Sperandum est.

FOR: *Wallace*

A memorial to Hugh Wallace,solicitor, Seneschal of Downpatrick d. 4 May 1855, aged 68. He m. Eliza Ann, daughter of William Nevin (d. 1830), son Rev. Thomas Nevin, Presbyterian Minister of Downpatrick 1711-24. They were parents of William Nevin Wallace and grandparents of Col.Robert Hugh Wallace of Myra Castle.[14]

ON 2ND PIER

11.**ARMS:** Quarterly; 1st and 4th, Azure, a fess Or between in chief a crescent Argent between 2 mullets of the second and in base a mascle of the third (Blackwood); 2nd and 3rd, Gules 3 cinquefoils pierced Ermine, on a chief Or a lion passant of the field (Hamilton of Clanbrassil); an escutcheon of Ulster, the shield surrounded by a Collar of the Order of St Patrick, with the badges of St Patrick and the Bath suspended therefrom.

CREST: None: a baron's coronet

SUPPORTERS: Dexter, a lion Gules armed and langued Azure, gorged with a tressure flory-counterflory Or; Sinister, an heraldic tyger ermine gorged with a like tressure Gules. (Armed and langued missing)

MOTTO: None.

FOR: *Blackwood*, Baron Dufferin and Claneboye.

Sir James Blackwood of Ballyleidy (now Clandeboye) Baronet, eldest son of Sir John Blackwood, M.P., by Dorcas, eldest daughter and co-heir of James Stevenson of Killyleagh, son of Hans Stevenson by Anne, daughter and eventual sole heir of James Hamilton of Neilsbrook, Co. Antrim, nephew and eventual heir of James Hamilton, 1st Viscount Claneboye, father of James, 1st Earl of Clanbrassil. Dorcas was created Baroness Dufferin and Claneboye 30 July 1800 and d. 8 February 1808, was succeeded by her eldest son Sir James Blackwood; he was b. 8 July 1755 d. 8 August 1836 and was succeeded by his brother Hans, grandfather of Frederick Temple, 1st Marquis of Dufferin and Ava, sometime Governor General of Canada and Viceroy of India.

ON 3RD PIER:

12.**ARMS:** Argent, 3 bars Gules, over all 3 stag's heads cabossed Or, on a chief of the third a wolf passant of the second between 2 phaeons Sable.

CREST: out of a ducal coronet a greyhound sejant Argent

MOTTO: In te Deus speravi

FOR: *Woodward*

Thomas Woodward, son of Rev. Henry Woodward, Rector of Fethard, Diocese of Cashel, who was 5th son of Rt Rev. Richard Woodward, Bishop of Cloyne, 1781-94. He entered T.C.D. 7 November 1831 aged 17, Scholar 1834, B.A. 1837, M.A. 1849, ordained priest 1841. He was Vicar of Mullingar 1851-6 and installed Dean of Down 15 March 1856. He d. 30 September 1875

NAVE NORTH SIDE
ON 3RD PIER:

13.**ARMS:** Quarterly of eight; 1st, 2nd, 5th and 6th, Stewart as in No.3, impaling, 3rd and 8th, Argent, a cross fleury Gules charged with a plain cross couped of the field, between 4 beech leaves Vert, 4th, on a chief Sable 3 escallops Or and in base Argent a trefoil slipped Vert (Graham); 7th, Gules, on a bend Or 3 martlets Sable (Brabazon).

CREST: a dragon statant Or (The head is missing)

MOTTO: Metuenda corolla draconis

FOR: *Stewart* of Ards and Laurencetown

Alexander John Robert Stewart of Ards, Co. Donegal and Laurencetown House, J.P., D.L. Cos. Down and Donegal, H.S. Co. Donegal 1853, H.S. Co. Down 1861; b. 5 July 1827, m. 17 May 1851 Isabella Rebecca Graham, 7th daughter of Hector John Toler, 2nd Earl of Norbury, (by Elizabeth, only child and heir of William Brabazon of Brabazon Park, Co. Mayo) son of John, 1st Earl of Norbury by Grace, Baroness Norwood, daughter of Hector Graham. Mr Stewart was grandson of Alexander Stewart, brother of Robert, 1st Marquis of Londonderry.[13]

NORTH AISLE

14.**ARMS:** Quarterly; 1st and 4th, Sable a goblet Argent, issuing therefrom a garland between 2 laurel branches Vert, within a bordure of the second charged with 8 boar's heads erased Gules (Laurie) 2nd and 3rd, Ermine a saltire engrailed Gules between in chief a mullet of the second and in base a boar's head erased Azure, the saltire surmounted of a fess Argent charged with 3 crescents Sable (Craig).

CRESTS: 1. An oak branch proper surmounted of a cross patte fitche Argent (Laurie)
2. A knight on horseback proper (Craig).

MOTTOES: (over the crests) 1.Benedictio Dei dicat (Laurie)
2.Vive Deo et vivas (Craig).

FOR: *Craig-Laurie* of Redcastle (Lyon Register 1857)

Rowland Craig-Laurie of Redcastle, Kirkcudbrightshire and Myra Castle, Co. Down, J.P., b. 21 February 1810, d.s.p. 1896, son of John Craig by Jane, daughter of Thomas Anderson, and grandson of Rowland Craig by Margaret Bigham, grandniece of Rev. Walter Laurie of Redcastle. He m. October 1843 his cousin Jane, daughter of Richard Forester Anderson of Walshestown Castle, Co. Down.

15.**ARMS:** Quarterly; 1st and 4th France modern and England; 2nd Scotland; 3rd Ireland; over all a baton sinister Gules charged with 3 roses Argent.

CREST: On a chapeau Gules turned up Ermine, a lion statant guardant Or crowned of the same[14]

MOTTO: Auspicium melioris aevi

FOR: *Beauclerk* of Ardglass Castle

Aubrey William Beauclerk, of Ardglass Castle, eldest son of Charles George Beauclerk, great grandson of the 1st Duke of St Albans, b. 20 February 1801, m. firstly 13 February 1834, Ida, daughter of Sir Charles Foster Goring, 7th baronet who d. 23 April 1838. He m. secondly, 7 December 1840 Rose Matilda daughter of Joshua Robinson and d. 1 February 1854, being succeeded by his son Aubrey de Vere Beauclerk, b. 5 October 1837, d. 9 July 1919, J.P., H.S. Co. Down 1863. George Robert Beauclerk of King's Castle, Ardglass, 3rd son of Charles George Beauclerk (above) b. 28 February 1803, d. 5 December 1871, m. 2 June 1861 Maria Sarah, daughter of Ralph Lonsdale.

16.**ARMS:** Azure, 2 keys in saltire Or, suppressed by a lamb in fess Argent.

CREST: None: a Bishop's mitre

MOTTO: None

FOR: *The See of Down*

These arms have not been registered. They are, however, still used quartered with Argent, 2 keys in saltire Gules, suppressed by an open book proper, between in chief and in base a cross patte fitche Azure (Dromore) for the United Diocese of Down and Dromore

17.**ARMS:** Gules, 3 cinquefoils pierced Ermine on a chief Or a heart of the first.

CREST: A demi-antelope affronte Argent, holding between the forelegs a heart Gules.

MOTTO: Qualis ab incepto.

FOR: *Hamilton* of Killyleagh Castle

Gawen Hamilton, of Killyleagh, H.S. Co.Down 1773, b. 1729, d. 9 April 1805, m. 8 May 1750 Jane, widow of Tichborne Ashton and only child of William Rowan, Barrister-at-Law. He was succeeded by his son Archibald Hamilton Rowan b. 12 May 1752, d. 1 November 1834, m. 6 October 1781 Sarah Anne, daughter of Walter Dawson of Carrickmacross, Co. Monaghan. He was succeeded by his grandson Archibald Rowan Hamilton, J.P., H.S. Co. Down, Captain 5th Dragoon Guards, b. 9 August 1828, whose daughter Hariot Georgina m. 23 October 1862 Frederick, 1st Marquis of Dufferin and Ava.

18.**ARMS:** Argent, a saltire Azure, in base a human heart Gules crowned proper; on a chief of the third 3 cushions Or.

CREST: A winged spur Or

MOTTO: Nun quam non paratus

FOR: *Johnston* of Ballykilbeg

John Brett Johnston of Ballykilbeg, son of William Johnston J.P. of Ballykilbeg by Mary Anne Humphries m. 17 March 1828 Thomasina Anne Brunette, daughter of Thomas Scott and d. 8 March 1853 being succeeded by his eldest son William Johnston M.A., M.P. for Belfast 1868-78 and for South Belfast 1885-1902; b. 22 February 1829, d. 17 July 1902, to whom there is a memorial tablet near the armorial.[15]

19.**ARMS:** Gules, on a chevron Argent 3 mullets of the field

CREST: A Unicorn's head Gules, maned Or

MOTTO: Pro Christo et patria

FOR: *Ker* of Portavo and Montalto

David Ker, of Portavo and Montalto (which latter he bought from the Earl of Moira), b. 1751, d. 1811, m. Maddelena Guardi. He was succeeded by his son David Ker, J.P., D.L. Co. Down, M.P. for Athlone and later for Downpatrick, b. 1779, m. 22 February 1814 Selina Sarah Stewart, daughter of Robert, 1st Marquis of Londonderry and d. 30 December 1844, leaving two sons. The elder, David Stewart Ker of Montalto, J.P., D.L., M.P. for Co. Down, H.S. Co. Down 1852, H.S. Co. Antrim 1857, was b. 1817 and d. 1878. The second son, Richard John Charles Rivers Ker, J.P., D.L., M.P. for Downpatrick, succeeded to Portavo.[15]

20.**ARMS:** Gules, a chevron Or between in chief 3 mullets of the second and in base an anchor Argent

CREST: An anchor erect Azure (part missing)

MOTTO: Fac et spera

GORDON OF FLORIDA MANOR AND DELAMONT

HILL, 2ND MARQUIS OF DOWNSHIRE

STEWART, MARQUIS OF LONDONDERRY

FORDE OF SEAFORDE

LEFT: MARY, BARONESS SANDYS AS WIDOW
OF 2ND MARQUIS OF DOWNSHIRE
RIGHT: MARY, BARONESS SANDYS IN HER OWN RIGHT

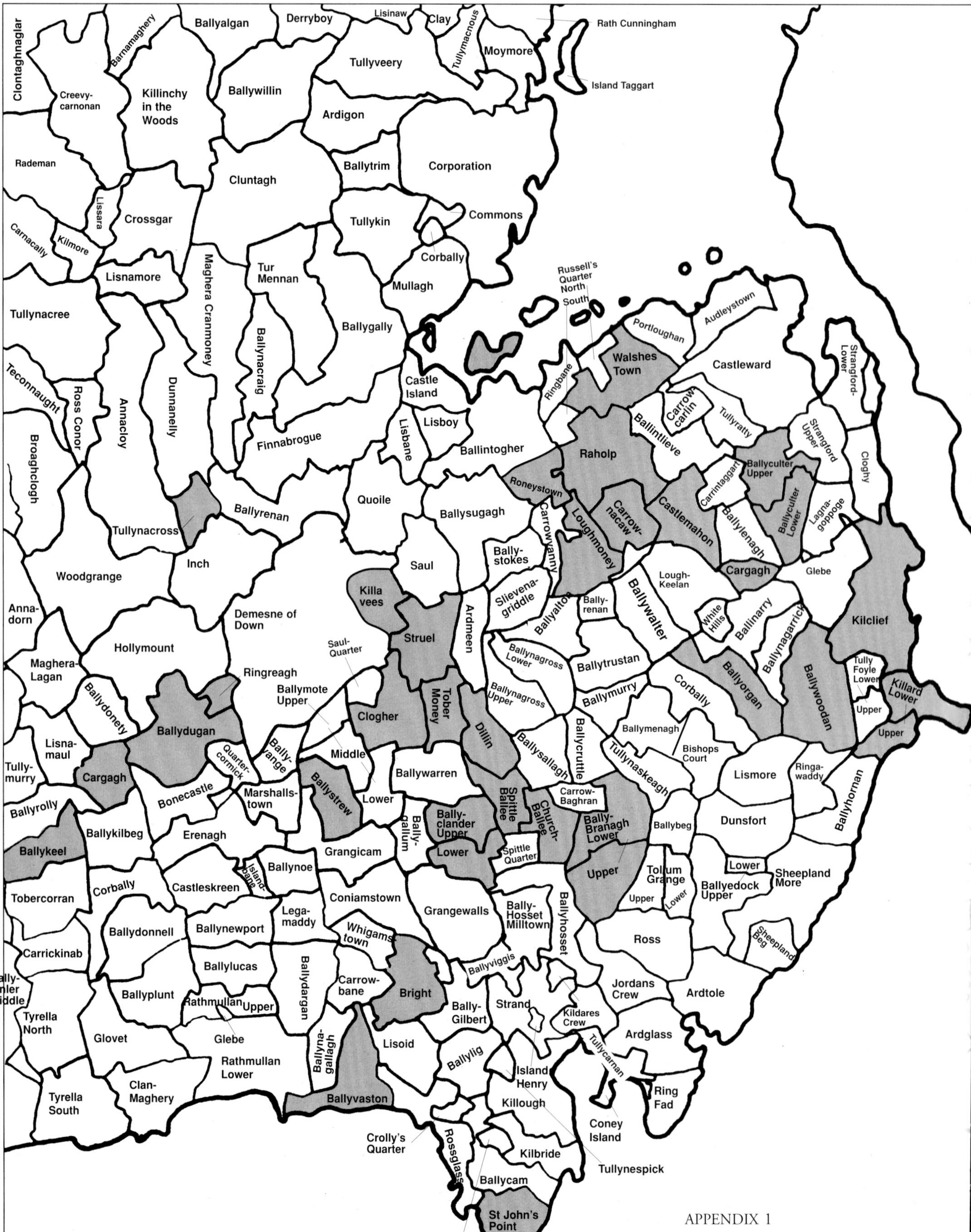

APPENDIX 1

MAP OF LECALE SHOWING LANDS GRANTED BY BISHOP MALACHY III TO THE NEWLY FOUNDED BENEDICTINE MONASTERY, 1183

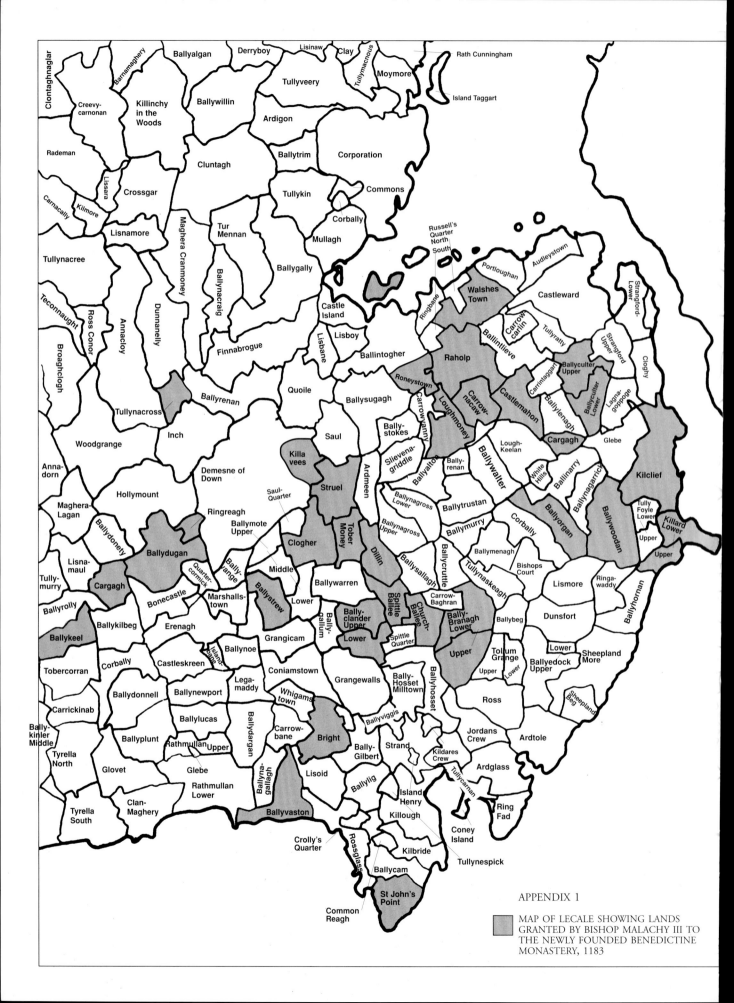

APPENDIX 2

MAP OF LECALE SHOWING LANDS IN THE POSSESSION OF MONASTERIES IN DOWN. 1549 INQUISITION

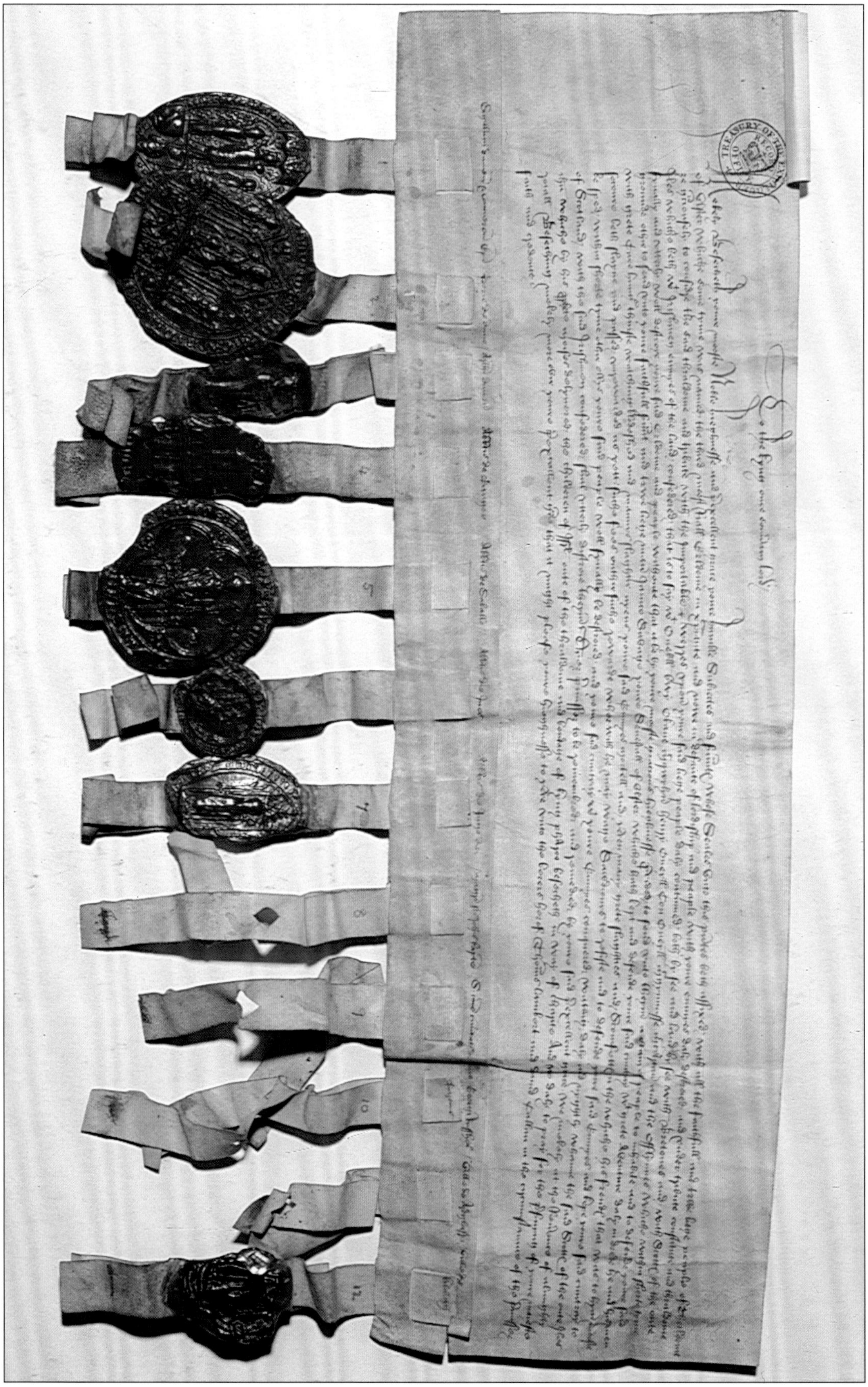

The Down Petition
THE P.R.O., LONDON

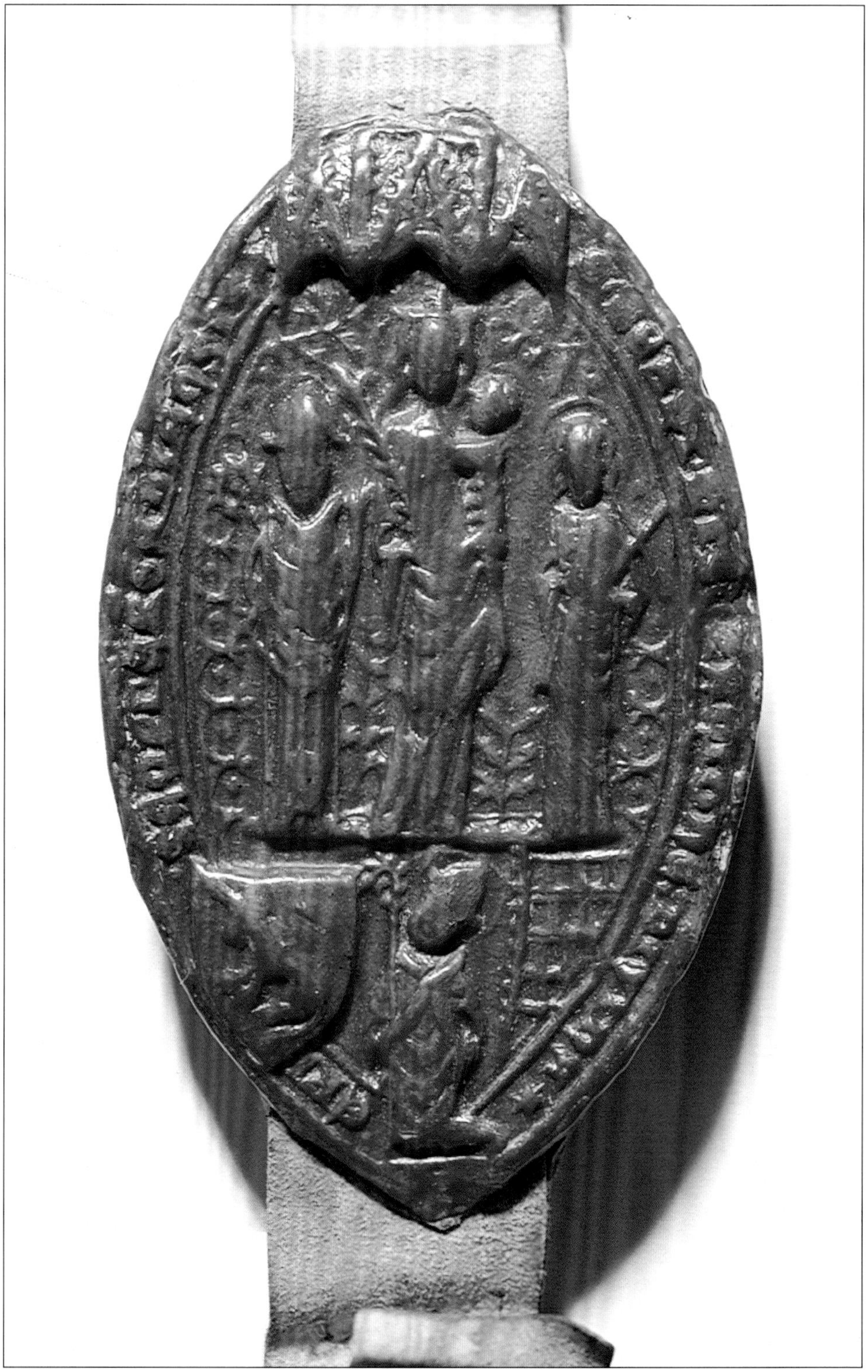

The enlarged seal of the Bishop of Ergal
THE P.R.O., LONDON

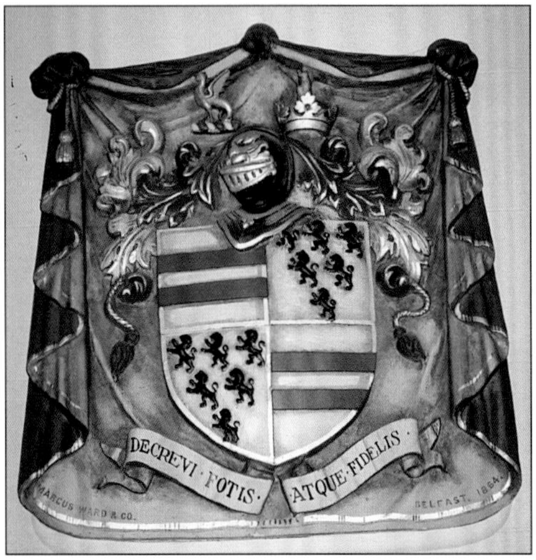

NUGENT OF PORTAFERRY

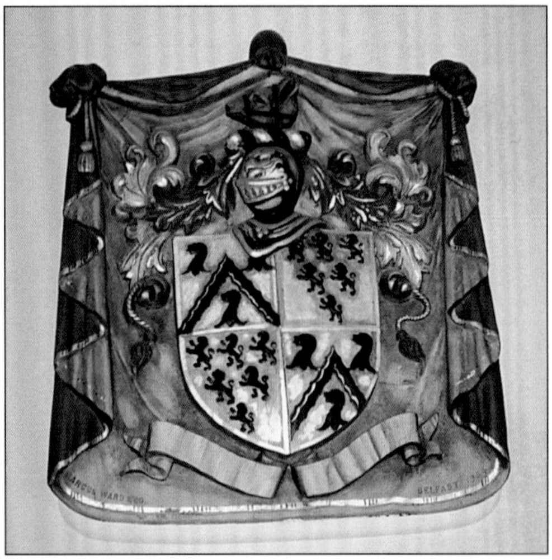

HALL OF NARROWWATER

WARD, VISCOUNT BANGOR

WALLACE
(Below the memorial to Hugh Wallace, Solicitor)

BLACKWOOD, BARON DUFFERIN AND CLANDEBOYE

WOODWARD

STEWART OF ARDS AND LAURENCETOWN

CRAIG-LAURIE OF REDCASTLE

BEAUCLERK OF ARDGLASS

THE SEE OF DOWN

HAMILTON OF KILLYLEAGH

JOHNSTON OF BALLYKILBEG

KER OF PORTAVO AND MONTALTO

DELACHEROIS OF DONAGHADEE

BATESON

ANNESLEY

FOR: *Delacherois* of Donaghadee

Daniel Delacherois of Donaghadee, m. 13 February 1782 Mary, daughter of Alexander Crommelin; his eldest son, Daniel Delacherois, of Donaghadee, J.P., D.L., H.S. Co.Down 1829, b. 1 December 1783, d.s.p. 1850 and was succeeded by his nephew Daniel Delacherois, J.P., D.L., H.S. Co.Down 1863, b. 10 July 1825, d. 1905, son of Samuel Delacherois, J.P., D.L.

21.**ARMS:** Argent, 3 bat's wings erect Sable; on a chief Gules a lion passant Or (Bateson); a canton of Ulster; in pretence an escutcheon bearing quarterly: 1st, per bend sinister Ermine and Ermines a lion rampant Or (Trevor); 2nd, Argent a chevron between 3 ravens Sable (Rice); 3rd, Gules, a lion rampant Or within a bordure engrailed Or (Talbot); 4th, Argent, 2 chevronels Azure between 3 trefoils slipped Vert (de Cardonell)

CREST: A bat's wing erect Sable

MOTTO: Nocte volamus

FOR: *Bateson*

Sir Thomas Bateson, 2nd Baronet, D.L., M.P. for Co. Londonderry 1844-57 and for Devizes 1864-85, b. 4 June 1819, m. 24 February 1849 Caroline Elizabeth Anne (d. 12 August 1887), 2nd daughter and co-heir of George Rice-Trevor, 4th Lord Dynevor, grandson of George Rice, M.P. for Carmarthenshire, by Cecil, Baroness Dynevor, daughter of William Talbot, 1st Earl Talbot and Baron Dynevor, by Mary, daughter and heir of Adam de Cardonell, Secretary at War, temp. Queen Anne. George Rice was son of Edward Rice, M.P. for Carmarthen, by Lucy, daughter and eventual heir of John Morley Trevor, of Glynd, Sussex. Sir Thomas succeeded his father, Sir Robert Bateson, 1st Baronet, 21April 1863 and was created Baron Deramore 18 November 1885 with remainder, in default of issue male, to his brother George. He d.s.p.m. 1 December 1890

22.**ARMS:** Paly of six Argent and Azure overall, a bend Gules

CREST: None: an Earl's coronet

SUPPORTERS: Dexter, A Roman knight in armour Or, short sleeves and apron Azure, face, arms and legs bare, the latter sandalled Or, on his head a helmet (or cap) Or, on the top thereof 3 feathers Argent and Azure, in his exterior hand an antique shield proper; Sinister, A Moorish prince in armour Or, short sleeves and apron Azure, face, neck, arms and legs proper, booted Or; behind him a sheaf of arrows proper fastened by a ribbon Gules; wreathed about the temples Argent and Azure, in his exterior hand a bow proper.

MOTTO: Virtus amore

FOR: *Annesley,* Earl Annesley

Francis Charles, 2nd Viscount Annesley, b. 1740, created Earl Annesley 18 August 1789, with remainder to his brother Richard. He d.s.p. 18 December 1802 and was succeeded by his brother b. 14 April 1745, d. 9 November 1824. His eldest son William Richard succeeded, b. 16 July 1772, d. 25 August 1838, and was followed by his son, also William Richard, 4th Earl, b. 21 February 1830.

NARTHEX:
ON THE SOUTH SIDE OF THE MAIN DOOR, ON ENTERING FROM THE PORCH:

23.**ARMS:** Gules, on a bend Or 3 martlets sable

FOR: *Brabazon*

A brass tablet in memory of Philip Emmanuel Brabazon, who was for a time Surgeon to the Down Infirmary and who d. 26 August 1856

ARMORIAL CARVINGS IN PEWS (1863)

There are nine pews in the aisles which have heraldic achievements carved in wood affixed to the wall behind them. Most of these are duplicates of some already listed, but two additional families are represented, and in the case of Ward, Viscount Bangor, only the arms of Ward are shown, not quartered with Hamilton. These carvings are not coloured, but the correct tinctures are indicated in brackets.

SOUTH AISLE
PEW 36:

ARMS: Quarterly, 1st and 4th, (Argent) a saltire and chief (Sable) with 3 pallets (Argent) on the chief (Maxwell); 2nd and 3rd, (Argent) on a chief indented (Gules) 3 crosses patte (Argent) (Perceval). The shield surrounded by a garter carrying the motto. (These arms are missing)

CRESTS: 1.A stag's head and neck erased (proper) (Maxwell)
2.A thistle slipped and leaved (proper) (Perceval)

MOTTO: Je suis pret – on the garter (missing)

SUPPORTERS: two flying eagles (one missing)[16]

On a scroll – YVERY

FOR: *Perceval-Maxwell*, of Finnebrogue, Co. Down

Robert Perceval-Maxwell, of Finnebrogue and Groomsport House, Co. Down, and of Moore Hill, Co. Waterford, J.P., D.L. Co. Down, J.P. Co. Waterford, H.S. Co. Down 1841 and Co. Waterford 1864, b. 24 June 1813, son of Rev. William Perceval of Kilmore Hill, Co. Waterford by Anne (d. 1861), eldest daughter of John Waring Maxwell of Finnebrogue. He assumed the additional name and arms of Maxwell by Royal Licence 25 July 1839 and d. 9 July 1905, aged 92.

PEW 38:
As Armorial No.1 – *Gordon* of Florida Manor and Delamont (crest missing)

PEW 40:

As Armorial No.11 – *Blackwood*, Baron Dufferin and Claneboye (supporters heads and lion's legs missing)

PEW 42:

As Armorial No.4 – *Forde* of Seaforde

PEW 44:

ARMS: (Azure) a cross patonce (Or)

CREST: None – a Viscount's coronet

SUPPORTERS: Dexter, a knight in armour; Sinister, a Turkish prince, his hands chained (As Armorial No. 9) *Ward Viscount Bangor*

NORTH AISLE

PEW 35: As Armorial No.14 – *Craig-Laurie* of Myra Castle.

PEW 35:

ARMS: (Gules), on a fess between in chief a bow and arrow in full draught to the dexter and in base 3 human legs couped at the thigh (Argent) a lion's head erased (Sable)

CREST: A cubit arm holding an anchor erect (proper)

MOTTO: Arcus artes astra

FOR: *Birnie* or *Birney*

John Birney, J.P., of Glenswinton, Kirkcudbrightshire, and Oakley, Co. Down, d. 1874. He was a cousin of Rowland Craig-Laurie of Redcastle, Kirkcudbrightshire and Myra Castle, Co. Down, (Armorial No.14) and his son, Col John Birney, R.E., who followed him at Oakley, succeeded to Redcastle on the death of Rowland's brother, John Craig-Laurie in 1901.

PEW 39.

As Armorial No. 22 – *Annesley, Earl Annesley*

PEW 41.

As Armorial No. 18 – *Johnston* of Ballykilbeg

CREST: Spur entwined by a serpent

NOTES

1 There appears to be some confusion regarding this charge; Debrett gives 'quatrefoil' while Burke gives 'cinquefoil'.

2 The trefoils should be 'per pale Gules and Vert'; the arms as painted are those of Treadway.

3 The phaeons should be 'of the field'; the bend is sometimes blazoned 'Vert'.

4 This should be 'on a chief Sable 3 escallops Argent'

5 The leopard should be 'ducally gorged'; the reindeer should be 'attired, unguled and plain collared Or'

6 As in Note 2 there is confusion. Debrett gives compony'; Burke gives 'counter-compony'.

7 It is not clear what family is represented by the 2nd and 3rd quarters; this quartering was dropped many years ago. It may have been intended to represent Cowan, but the Cowans bore 'Argent, a saltire and chief Gules, with an escallop Or on the chief', but this coat was not registered (Lyon Reg.) until 1873. The arms quartered here, 'Gules, a saltire Argent' are the very ancient arms of the illustrious family Neville of Raby, and the Stewarts could have no possible descent from this family.

8 Debrett gives '3 lions Sable' instead of 'mullets'.

9 See note 4.

10 The cockatrice should be 'Vert, combed and wattled Gules'.

11 The cross on the breast should be 'a cross moline Gules'; that on the robe 'a cross moline Argent'; the helmet should have 'a plume of feathers Argent'; the sword is missing and may have been broken off; the Turkish prince should have 'white stockings, yellow sandals, and a white turban with black feathers', also 'his hands chained together with a long chain proper'.

12 The palm branch should be 'Or'

13 These arms might also represent John Vandeleur Stewart J.P., D.L., of Rock Hill, Co.Donegal, who was third son of Alexander Stewart, brother of the 1st Marquis of Londonderry. This is unlikely, however, as he had no property in Co.Down.

14 The lion should be 'Or, collared Gules with 3 roses Argent on the collar and crowned with a ducal coronet per pale Argent and Gules.

15 It is doubtful if these arms were ever registered.

16 To which there is, of course, no entitlement. The word YVERY is puzzling. It may be part only of an inscription, as it looks as if there ought to be a second scroll over the other eagle.

APPENDIX 6

THE CATHEDRAL ORGAN

No specification survives of the organ installed by William Hull in 1818, although some of the existing pipes clearly date to that period. The earliest specification extant is that of William Telford's organ of 1854; according to notes left by Mr A.J.H. Coulter, it was a two manual instrument and had the following specification:

GREAT ORGAN

1.	Double open diapason	Tenor C	16 feet
2.	Large open diapason		8 feet
3.	Small open diapason	Tenor C	8 feet
4.	Stop diapason		8 feet
5.	Dulciana	Tenor G	8 feet
6.	Principal		4 feet
7.	Flute	Fiddle G	4 feet
8.	Fifteenth		2 feet
9.	Twelfth		$2^2/_3$ feet
10.	Sesquialtera	3 ranks	
11.	Mixture	2 ranks	
12.	Trumpet		8 feet
13.	Cremona	Tenor F	8 feet

SWELL ORGAN

1.	Double open diapason	Tenor C	16 feet
2.	Open diapason		8 feet
3.	Stop diapason		8 feet
4.	Dulciana		8 feet
5.	Flute		4 feet
6.	Dulciana Flute	Tenor C	4 feet
7.	Principal		4 feet
8.	Piccolo	Tenor C	2 feet
9.	Fifteenth		2 feet
10.	Echo Dulciana Sesquialtera	2 ranks	
11.	Trumpet		8 feet
12.	Hautboy	Tenor C	8 feet
13.	Clarion		4 feet

PEDAL ORGAN

Open diapason	16 feet
Unison diapason	8 feet

Harrison & Harrison enlarged the instrument in 1914 to a three manual organ, although retaining much of the earlier pipework. Again according to Coulter, the case was extended towards the west and the console brought outside the case on the east. The full specification follows:

PEDAL ORGAN 4 STOPS, 3 COUPLERS

1.	Open wood	wood	16 feet 30 pipes
2.	Sub bass (12 from No.9)	wood	16 feet 18 pipes
3.	Octave wood (18 from No.1)	wood	8 feet 12 pipes
4.	Flute (18 from No.2)	wood	8 feet 12 pipes
	I Choir to Pedal		
	II Great to Pedal		
	III Swell to Pedal		

CHOIR ORGAN 4 STOPS, 1 COUPLER

5.	Claribel flute	wood	8 feet 58 pipes
6.	Dulciana	metal	8 feet 58 pipes
7.	Wald flote	wood	4 feet 58 pipes
8.	Clarinet	metal	8 feet 58 pipes
	IV Swell to Choir		

GREAT ORGAN 8 STOPS, 2 COUPLERS

9.	Double open diapason	metal & wood	16 feet 58 pipes
10.	Large open diapason	metal	8 feet 58 pipes
11.	Small open diapason	metal	8 feet 58 pipes
12.	Stopped diapason	metal & wood	8 feet 58 pipes
13.	Octave	metal	4 feet 58 pipes
14.	Super octave	metal	2 feet 58 pipes
15.	Sesquialtera 12, 17, 19	metal	116 pipes
16.	Mixture 22, 26, 29	metal	174 pipes
	V Choir to Great		
	VI Swell to Great		

SWELL ORGAN 8 STOPS, TREMULANT AND 2 COUPLERS

17.	Open diapason	metal & wood	8 feet 58 pipes
18.	Lieblich gedeckt	wood	8 feet 58 pipes
19.	Echo gamba	metal	8 feet 58 pipes
20.	Vox angelica Tenor C	metal	8 feet 46 pipes
21.	Principal	metal	4 feet 58 pipes
22.	Dulciana sesquialtera 12,15,17	metal	174 pipes
23.	Contra oboe	metal	16 feet 58 pipes
24.	Trumpet (harmonic trebles)	metal	8 feet 58 pipes
	VII Tremulant		
	VIII Octave		

IX Octaves alone
(enabling No.23 to be used in 8 ft pitch)

ACCESSORIES

Three combination movements by pedal to the Pedal Organ
Four combination movements by piston to the Great Organ
Four combination movements by piston to the Swell Organ
Reversible pedal to Great to Pedal
Reversible piston to Swell to Great
Reversible pedal to Tremulant
Balanced crescendo pedal to the Swell Organ

WIND PRESSURES

Pedal 3° inches
Choir 3 inches
Great 3 inches
Swell flue-work 3 inches; reeds 5 inches
Action wind 7 inches
The organ was tuned to the new French pitch i.e., 517 vibrations at 60° F

Harrison & Harrison were retained in 1966 to rebuild the instrument; the pulpitum had become structurally unsound which necessitated its rebuilding and the opportunity was taken to carry out both tasks simultaneously. The new specification was as follows:

PEDAL ORGAN

Open diapason (A) Old with new metal pipes from 8' C		16 feet
Sub bass (B)	1914	16 feet
Octave (A) New metal pipes throughout		8 feet
Flute (B) 1914		8 feet
Fifteenth (A) New 12 notes		4 feet
Mixture (from Great) 19,22,26,29 IV Ranks New		
Trumpet New		16 feet

CHOIR ORGAN

Rohr Flute	New	8 feet
Spitz Principal	New	4 feet
Wald flute ex-old Swell Piccolo		4 feet
Block flute	New	2 feet
Quint	New	$1\frac{1}{3}$ feet
Cimbel 29,33,36 III Ranks New		
Cremona 1914 Clarinet revoiced		8 feet

GREAT ORGAN

Double open diapason Old with bottom octave from 1914		
Pedal sub bass		16 feet
Open diapason I	Old	8 feet
Open diapason II	Old	8 feet
Stopped diapason	Old	8 feet

Octave	Old	4 feet
Super octave	Old	2 feet

Sesquialtera 12,17,19 III Ranks Old with Twelfth and 22nd transferred to Sharp Mixture

Full Mixture 12,15,19,22 IV Ranks New

Sharp Mixture 22,26,29 III Ranks Old with 22nd from Sesquialtera

SWELL ORGAN

Open diapason	Old	8 feet
Lieblich Gedeckt ex-stopped diapason	Old	8 feet
Echo Gamba	1914	8 feet
Principal	Old	4 feet

Dulciana Sesquialtera 12,15,17 III Ranks Old with Fifteenth added

Mixture 22,26 II Ranks New with Nineteenth added 1987

Contra oboe	1914	16 feet
Trumpet	1914	8 feet
Tremulant	1914	

COUPLERS

Swell to Pedal, Choir to Pedal, Great to Pedal
Swell to Great, Choir to Great, Swell to Choir
Swell Octaves and Octaves alone

WIND PRESSURES

Pedal flue-work	3° inches
Choir	3 inches
Great	3 inches
Swell flue-work	3 inches
Reeds	5 inches
Action	7 inches

ACTION

Electropneumatic throughout

When the Cathedral was undergoing extensive restoration in 1987, Wells-Kennedy Partnership of Lisburn were retained to overhaul the organ and make a number of minor adjustments. With the exception of a small alteration in the Swell Organ (noted above), no changes were made to the basic specification. The following accessories were added:

Dual level combination capture system
Six pistons to each department and six general pistons
Swell to Great reversible, Great to Pedal reversible
Pedal Trumpet reversible
Great and Pedal combinations coupled
General cancel
Setter

REFERENCES

CHAPTER ONE

1 PRONI, T 808/15018

2 V.B. Proudfoot, *The Downpatrick Gold Find*, Belfast, HMSO, 1955

3 Information from Mr Richard Warner

4 V.B. Proudfoot, 'Excavations at Cathedral Hill, Downpatrick', in *Ulster Journal of Archaeology, Series 3, Vol.17, 1954, pp 97-102: Vol.19, 1956, pp 57-72*

5 N. Brannon, 'Archaeological Excavations at Cathedral Hill, Downpatrick 1987, in *Lecale Miscellany No 6, 1988, pp 3-9*

6 Cecile O'Rahilly, ed., *Táin Bó Cúalnge*, Dublin, 1970, pp 259-260

7 G. Mac Niocaill, *Ireland before the Vikings*, Dublin, 1972 pp 13-14

8 C. Thomas, *Christianity in Roman Britain*, London, 1981

9 D.N. Dumville *et al.*, *Saint Patrick, A.D. 493-1993*, Woodbridge, 1993

10 Ludwig Bieler, ed., *The Patrician Texts in the Book of Armagh*, Dublin, 1979

11 R.P.C. Hanson, *The Life and Writings of the Historical Saint Patrick*, New York, 1983, p.86, Confession 16

12 R.P.C. Hanson, *ibid*, p.88, Confession 19

13 R.P.C. Hanson, *ibid*, p.88, Confession 19

14 R.P.C. Hanson, *ibid*, p.92, Confession 23

15 Ludwig Bieler, *ibid*, p.135

16 Ludwig Bieler, *ibid*, p.79

17 Ludwig Bieler, *ibid*, p.71

18 Ludwig Bieler, *ibid*, p.125

19 R.P.C. Hanson, *ibid*, p.106, Confession 37

20 James F. Kenney, *The Sources for the Early History of Ireland*, 1929, reprint Dublin, 1979, p.324

21 James F. Kenney, *ibid*, p.329

22 D.A. Binchy, 'Patrick and his Biographers, Ancient and Modern', *in Studia Hibernica, No.2, 1962*

23 Ludwig Bieler, *ibid*, p.87

24 Ludwig Bieler, *ibid*, p.121

25 Ann Hamlin, 'The Early Church in County Down to the Twelfth Century', in *L. Proudfoot ed., County Down in History and Society, Dublin, 1996*

26 Richard Sharpe, 'Saint Patrick and the See of Armagh' in *Cambridge Medieval Celtic Studies, No.4, Winter, 1982*

27 Richard Sharpe, *ibid*

CHAPTER TWO

1 Deirdre Flanagan, 'The Names of Downpatrick', in *Dinnseanchas, Vol. IV, No,.4, 1971*

2 N.Brannon, 'Archaeological Excavations at Cathedral Hill, Downpatrick, 1987', in *Lecale Miscellany No. 6, 1988, pp.3-9*

3 F.J. Byrne, *Irish Kings and High-Kings*, London, 1973, p.119

4 Whitley Stokes and John Strachan eds., *Thesaurus Palaeohibernicus Vol II*, Cambridge, 1903, p.285; I am indebted to my daughter Dr Susan Rankin for this reference and to Mr W.C. Kerr for its translation into English

5 Painting in Chapter Room of Down Cathedral

6 National Library of Ireland, 2122 TX (102), redrawn by the Royal Irish Academy for the Historic Atlas of Downpatrick, 1997

7 A. Atkinson, *Ireland exhibited to England, Vol.1*, London, 1823, pp.179-180 & p.293. My thanks to Mr Gordon Wheeler for pointing out this reference.

8 Kathleen Hughes and Ann Hamlin, *The Modern Traveller to the Early Irish Church*, London, 1977, p.33

9 An unsigned note in *Down and Connor Historical Society Journal* Vol. IV, 1931, p.111 suggests that the cross formerly stood over Saint Patrick's grave but was removed and broken into fragments on 19 April 1842

10 P. Harbison, *The High Crosses of Ireland*, Bonn, 1992, pp.67-68 & 231-232

11 P. Harbison, ibid, pp 67-68

12 Unsigned note in *Down and Connor Historical Society Journal* Vol.VI, 1934, p.40

13 F.E. Warren, *The Liturgy and Ritual of the Celtic Church*, Oxford, 1881, reprint 1987, p.113

14 I am indebted to the late Archbishop Dr G.O. Simms for this connection.

15 A.T. Lucas, 'The Plundering and Burning of Churches in Ireland, 7th-16th Centuries', in *North Munster Studies, Limerick, 1967*

16 S. Mac Airt and G. Mac Niocaill eds., *Annals of Ulster to AD 1131*, Dublin, 1983

17 S. Mac Airt and G. Mac Niocaill eds., ibid

18 F.J. Byrne, ibid, pp 119,124

19 H.C. Lawlor, 'The Genesis of the Diocese of Connor including Down and Dromore', in *Proceedings of the Belfast Natural History and Philosophical Society, 1930-31 pp.50-66* H.C. Lawlor, 'Diocesan Anomalies', in *Ulster Journal of Archaeology, Series 3, Vol.2, July 1939, pp.147-157*

20 H.J. Lawlor ed., *Saint Bernard of Clairvaux' Life of Saint Malachy of Armagh*, SPCK, 1920 H.J. Lawlor, 'Notes on Saint Bernard's Life of

Saint Malachy' *in PRIA, 1918-20, Vol.XXXV, Section C, pp.230-264*

21 A. Gwynn and R.N. Hadcock, *Medieval Religious Houses in Ireland,* London, 1970, p.169.

In this Chapter, the 1983 edition of *The Annals of Ulster* edited by Seán Mac Airt and Gearoid Mac Niocaill has been used.

+The 1175 reference is taken from the 1893 3 volume edition of the *Annals of Ulster* edited by W.M. Hennessy and B. MacCarthy

CHAPTER THREE

1 Seámus Ó hInnse ed., *Miscellaneous Irish Annals,* Dublin, 1947, p.65
2 Giraldus Cambrensis, ed. A.B. Scott and F.X. Martin, *Expugnatio Hibernica,* Dublin, 1978, p.175
3 David Bates, *Normandy before 1066,* London, 1982, p.6
4 David Bates, *ibid.*, p.218
5 J. Tait, ed., *The Chartulary or Register of the Abbey of Saint Werburgh,* Chester, Chetham Society, Vol.79, 1920, Part 2, p.471-2
6 J. Tait, ed., *ibid,*p.471-2
7 The Charters have been preserved in an inspeximus of 41 Edward III, PRO, (London) C 66/278. They have been transcribed by Gearoid Mac Niocaill in *Seanchas Ard Mhacha* Vol.5, No.2, 1970, pp. 418-428
8 Mac Niocaill, No.1
9 Liam de Paor, *Saint Patrick's World,* Dublin, 1993, pp.281-294
10 Mac Niocaill, No.4
11 Mac Niocaill, No.5
12 Mac Niocaill, No.8
13 Mac Niocaill, No.7
14 Mac Niocaill, No.3
15 W. Reeves, *Ecclesiastical Antiquities of Down, Connor and Dromore,* Dublin, 1847, pp.163-4
16 A. Gwynn, ed. G. O'Brien, *The Irish Church in the Eleventh and Twelfth Centuries,* Dublin, 1992, p.141
17 R. Stalley, *The Cistercian Monasteries of Ireland* London, 1987, p.246
18 PRO (London) DL 25-219
19 R. Stalley, *ibid*, p.245
20 W. Reeves, *ibid*, p.190-1
21 W. Reeves, *ibid,* p.10-11
22 W. Reeves, *ibid*, p.382
23 A. Gwynn & R.N. Hadcock, *Medieval Religious Houses, Ireland* London, 1970, p.170
24 A. Gwynn and R.N. Hadcock, *ibid,* p.170
25 A. Gwynn and R.N. Hadcock, *ibid,* p.211
26 Mac Niocaill, No.2
27 W. Reeves, *ibid,*p.231
28 Giraldus Cambrensis, *ibid*, pp.179-181
29 Seán Duffy, 'The First Ulster Plantation: John de Courcy and the Men of Cumbria', in *Colony and Frontier in Medieval Ireland, ed. T.B. Barry, Robin Frame & Katherine Simms,* London, 1995
30 G.H. Orpen, *Ireland under the Normans,* Vol.2, Oxford, 1911, p.137
31 G.H. Orpen, *ibid,* p.138
32 H.S. Sweetman ed.,*Calendar of Documents relating to Ireland* [CDI], Vol. 1., No.260, p.40
33 G.H. Orpen, *ibid*, pp.140-1
34 CDI, Vol.1, No.358, p. 54
35 G.H. Orpen, *ibid*, p.143
36 G.H. Orpen, *ibid,* p.143
37 J. Otway-Ruthven, 'Dower Charter of John de Courcy's Wife', *in Ulster Journal of Archaeology, Series 3, Vol.12 1949, pp.77-81*
38 CDI, Vol.1, No.3202, p.476
39 Giraldus Cambrensis, *ibid,* p.235, note.p.353

CHAPTER FOUR

1 R.E. Parkinson, 'The Castle of Down', in *Ulster Journal of Archaeology, Series 3, Vol.3, 1940, pp.55-63*
2 O. Davies and D.B. Quinn, 'Irish Pipe Roll, 14 John, 1211-12' *in Ulster Journal of Archaeology, Series 3, Vol.4, 1941,p.59*
3 J.A. Watt,*The Church and the Two Nations in Medieval Ireland,* Cambridge, 1970, p.72
4 J. O'Laverty, *Historical Account of the Diocese of Down and Connor* Vol.5, Dublin, 1895, p.152
5 H.S. Sweetman, ed., *Calendar of Documents relating to Ireland* [CDI], Vol.1, No.1264, p.191; No. 1360, p.205
6 CDI, Vol.1, No.1377, p.209
7 T.D. Hardy, ed., *Syllabus of Rymer's Foedera,* London, 1869 Vol.1, p.26
8 N. Brannon, 'Recent Discoveries at Down Cathedral', in *Lecale Miscellany, No.5, 1987,* pp.3-9
9 M.P. Sheehy, ed., *Pontificia Hibernica, Medieval Papal Chancery Documents concerning Ireland, 640-1261,* Dublin, 1962, Vol.2, No.259, p.100
10 M.P. Sheehy, ed., *ibid,* Vol.2, No.279, p.122
11 W. Harris, ed., *The Whole Works of Sir James Ware concerning Ireland,* Vol.1, Dublin, 1764, p.197
12 W.H. Bliss and J.A. Tremlow, eds., *Calendar of Papal Letters,* [CPL] Vol.1, April 1265
13 CPL, Vol.1, April 1265
14 CPL, Vol.1, April 1265
15 CDI, Vol.1, No.2551, p.379
16 CDI, Vol.2, No.860, p.139
17 W. Harris, ed., ibid, p.198
18 H. Wood, A.E. Langham and M.C. Griffith eds., *Calendar of Justiciary Rolls, Ireland,* [CJR] Vol.3, 1308, pp.41 & 334
19 CPL, Vol.1, June 1279
20 CJR, Vol.1, 1279, pp.102-3

21 CJR, Vol.1, 1279, p.115
22 *Calendar of Patent Rolls* [CPR] Edward I, Vol.2, 4 March 1289
23 CDI, Vol.5, No.388, p.127
24 J. O'Laverty, *ibid*, p.177
25 CJR, Vol.2,1305, pp.84-5
26 J. O'Laverty, *ibid,* p.180
27 CPR, Edward II, Vol.1, 12 July 1312
28 CPR, Edward II, Vol.2, 24 February and 20 March 1314
29 R. Butler,ed., *Annals of Ireland by J.Grace,* Dublin 1842, p.77
30 W. Harris ed., *ibid*, p.200
31 43rd Report of the Deputy Keeper of the Public Records of Ireland, 2 Edward III, 1912, p.21
32 CPR, Edward III, Vol.1, 1 April 1329
33 CPL, Vol.2, January 1329
34 CPL, Vol.2, January 1329
35 CPR, Edward III, Vol.3, 8 July 1336
36 CPR, Edward III, Vol.3, 8 July 1336
37 CPL, Vol.3, February 1353
38 J. O'Laverty, *ibid,* p.185
39 CPL, Vol.3, December 1353, January 1354
40 H.J. Lawlor, ed., 'Register of Milo Sweteman, Archbishop of Armagh, 1361-1380' in *Proceedings of the Royal Irish Academy, Vol.XXIX, Sect.C, 1911-2, Nos.84-5, p.243*
41 CPR, Edward III, Vol.13, 30 June 1367
42 H.J. Lawlor, ed., *ibid,* Nos.233, 4, 5, p.283
43 W. Harris, ed.,*ibid,* p.201
44 J. O'Laverty, *ibid,* p.196
45 H.J. Lawlor, ed., *ibid,* No.81, p.242
46 W. Harris, ed.,*ibid*, p.201
47 J. O'Laverty, *ibid,* p.190
48 D.A. Chart, ed, *Register of John Swayne, Archbishop of Armagh, 1418-1439,* Belfast 1935, p.11
49 W. Harris, ed.,*ibid,* p.201
50 J. O'Laverty, *ibid*, pp.192-3
51 W. Harris, ed.,*ibid*, p.201
52 Seámus Ó hInnse, ed., *Miscellaneous Irish Annals,* Dublin, 1947, p.173
53 W. Harris, ed.,*ibid*, p.202
54 M. Haren and Y. de Pontfarcy, eds., *The Medieval Pilgrimage to Saint Patrick's Purgatory,* Clogher Historical Society, 1988, p.182
55 CPL, Vol.4, February 1355
56 CPL, Vol.6, August 1413
57 E. Tresham, ed., *Calendar of Patent and Close Rolls of the Irish Chancery,* Vol.1, London, 1828, p.237
58 D.A. Chart, ed., *ibid*, 1430, p.123
59 D.A. Chart, ed., *ibid,* 1427, p.66
60 D.A. Chart, ed., *ibid,* 1434, p.151
61 CPR, Henry VI, Vol.3, 29 July 1438
62 W.G.H. Quigley and E.F.D. Roberts, eds., *Register of John Mey, Archbishop of Armagh, 1443-1456,* Belfast 1972, No.13, p.20
63 W.G.H. Quigley and E.F.D. Roberts, eds., *ibid,* Nos.23, 24, 37 pp.31, 2, 3, 4 and pp.47, 8, 9
64 W. Harris, ed.,*ibid*, p.202
65 W. Harris, ed.,*ibid*, p.203
66 W. Reeves ed., 'Calendar of the Register of John Prene', *Ms 5, Typescript in Diocesan Library, Belfast, Nos.173 and 214*
67 W. Harris, ed.,*ibid*, p.203
68 M.A. Costello and A. Coleman, eds., *De Annatis Hiberniae* Vol.I, Ulster, Maynooth, 1912, p.121
69 M.A. Costello and A. Coleman, eds., *ibid*, p.122
70 W.G.H. Quigley and E.F.D. Roberts, eds., *ibid*, No.135, p.133
71 W.G.H. Quigley and E.F.D. Roberts, eds., *ibid,* No.185, pp.195-6
72 W.G.H. Quigley and E.F.D. Roberts, eds., *ibid,* No.213, pp.211-2
73 W.G.H. Quigley and E.F.D. Roberts, eds., *ibid,* No.190, p.188
74 W.G.H. Quigley and E.F.D. Roberts, eds., *ibid,* No.191, p.189
75 E. Tresham, ed., *ibid,* p.265
76 W.G.H. Quigley and E.F.D. Roberts, eds., *ibid,* No.280, p.286
77 M.A. Costello and A. Coleman, eds., *ibid,* p.122
78 Victoria County History; Staffordshire, Vol.3, Oxford 1970, p.41
79 M.A. Costello and A. Coleman, eds., *ibid,* p.123
80 M.A. Costello and A. Coleman, eds., *ibid,* p.124
81 CPL, Vol.12, July 1463
82 W. Harris, ed., *ibid,* p.203
83 Handbook of British Chronology, Royal Historical Society, 1986, p.326
84 W.A. Pantin, ed., *Documents illustrating the Activities of the General and Provincial Chapters of the English Black Monks, 1215-1540,* Vol.3, Royal Historical Society, 1937, p.107
85 A. Lynch, 'A Calendar of the Reassembled Register of John Bole, Archbishop of Armagh, 1457-1471', in *Seanchas Ardmhacha, Vol.15, No.1, 1992, p.175*
86 M.A. Costello and A. Coleman, eds., *ibid,* pp.125-6
87 CPL, Vol.13, p.651
88 A. Lynch, ed., *ibid,* p.171
89 A. Gwynn, *The Medieval Province of Armagh,* Dundalk, 1946, p.136
90 T.D. Hardy, ed., *ibid,* Vol.2, p.762.
91 L.P. Murray, ed.,'Register of George Dowdall', in *Louth Archaeological Journal, Vol.6, 1926, 7, 8, p.149*
92 A. Gwynn, *ibid*, p.52
93 A. Gwynn, *ibid*, p.138
94 J. Gairdner and R.H. Brodie, eds., *Letters and Papers, Henry VIII,* Vol.14, Part 2, No.621, 1539
95 J. O'Laverty, *ibid,* p.294
96 L.P. Murray ed., *ibid,* Vol.7, No.,114, 1553, p.81

97 W. Harris, ed., *ibid*, p.205

98 Archaeological Survey of County Down, H.M.S.O., Belfast 1966, p.270

99 M.A. Costello and A. Coleman, eds., *ibid*, p.127

100 J. O'Laverty, *ibid*, p.318

101 N. Brannon, 'Archaeological Excavations at Cathedral Hill, Downpatrick, 1987', in *Lecale Miscellany No.6, 1988, pp.3-9*

CHAPTER FIVE

1 W. Reeves, *Ecclesiastical Antiquities of Down, Connor and Dromore,* Dublin, 1847, pp.176-7 M. Archdall, *Monasticon Hibernicum,* London, 1786,pp.115-6

2 M. Archdall, *ibid,* p.115

3 M. Archdall, *ibid*, p.115; CDI, Vol.1, No.3150

4 CPL, Vol.1, July 1266

5 J. Ware, ed. W. Harris, *The Whole Works of Sir James Ware concerning Ireland,* Vol.1, Dublin, 1764, p.198

6 M. Archdall, ibid, p.115

7 H. Wood, A.E. Langham and M.C. Griffiths eds.,*Calendar of Justiciary Rolls, Ireland* [CJR] Vol.3, p.40

8 J. Mills ed., *Calendar of Justiciary Rolls, Ireland.* [CJR] Vol.2, p.84

9 J.Ware, ed.W.Harris, *ibid,* p.200

10 E. Tresham ed., *Calendar of the Patent and Close Rolls of the Irish Chancery,* Vol.1, London, 1828, 11 Edward II, p.22

11 43rd Report of the Deputy Keeper of the Public Records of Ireland, 3 Edward III, 1912, p.33

12 CPR, Edward III, Vol.2, 1336, p.305

13 CPL, Vol.3, December 1353

14 H.J. Lawlor ed., 'Register of Milo Sweteman, Archbishop of Armagh, 1361-1380', *in Proceedings of the Royal Irish Academy, Vol.XXIX, Section C, 1911-12, No.85, pp.213 ff.*, No.93, p.243

15 H.J. Lawlor ed., *ibid,* No.219, p.278

16 CPR, Edward III, Vol.14, 28 April 1369

17 J. Ware, ed.W. Harris, *ibid*, p.201

18 CPL, Vol.4, February 1395

19 CPL, Vol.6, August 1413

20 CPL, Vol.7, November 1419

21 D.A. Chart ed., *Register of John Swayne, Archbishop of Armagh, 1418-1439*, Belfast, 1935, p.151

22 A. Lynch, 'Calendar of the Reassembled Register of John Bole, Archbishop of Armagh, 1457-1471'*, in Seanchas Ardmhacha, Vol.15, No.1, 1992, p.175*

23 W.G.H. Quigley and E.F.D. Roberts eds., *Register of John Mey, Archbishop of Armagh, 1443-1456,* Belfast, 1972, No.166, p.163

24 CPL, Vol.13, 3 June 1474

25 CPL, Vol.13, 7 May 1478

26 CPL, Vol.15, 1484, Appendix, p.962 also W. Reeves ed., *Calendar of the Register of Octavian del Palatio,* Ms 6, Typescript in Diocesan Library, Belfast, No.230

27 CPL, Vol.16, No.335, 7 April 1495

28 CPL, Vol.16, No.645, 1 December 1496

29 CPL, Vol.16, No.666, 24 November 1496

30 CPL, Vol.17, No.391, 29 March 1501

31 L.P. Murray ed., 'Register of Archbishop Cromer', *in Louth Archaeological Journal, Vol.8, 1932-6, No.47, p.46*

32 L.P. Murray ed., *ibid,* p.328

33 L.P. Murray ed., *ibid,* p.328

34 CPL, Vol.3, 1353

35 A. Lynch ed., *ibid*, p.138

36 E. Tresham ed., *ibid,* 5 Henry VI, p.242

37 D. Knowles, *The Monastic Order in England,* Cambridge, 1950, p.541

38 Bodleian Library, Oxford, Rawlinson MS C.892

39 D. Knowles, *ibid,* p.122

40 National Library of Scotland, Adv. MS 18.5.91

41 H.J. Lawlor, *The Rosslyn Missal,* The Henry Bradshaw Society, 1898. There is also a useful discussion on the Missal, along with the Drummond and Corpus Christi Missals in A. Gwynn, ed G. O'Brien, *The Irish Church in the 11th and 12th Centuries,* Dublin, 1992

42 Bodleian Library, Oxford, MS Canon Liturg 215

CHAPTER SIX

1 PRO London, C66/278; The Charters have been transcribed by Gearoid Mac Niocaill in *Seanchas Ard Mhacha*, Vol.5, No.2, 1970, pp.418-428 Mac Niocaill No.9

2 M.D. O'Sullivan, *Italian Merchant Bankers in Ireland in the Thirteenth Century,* Dublin, 1962, pp.28-30

3 CPL, Vol.1, March 1281

4 J.F. Lydon, *The Lordship of Ireland in the Middle Ages,* Dublin, 1972, p.86

5 CPR, Edward I, Vol.2, 4 March 1289

6 A.J. Pollock and D.M. Waterman, 'A Medieval Pottery Kiln at Downpatrick' in *Ulster Journal of Archaeology,* Series 3, Vol.26, 1963, pp.79-81

7 Seámus Ó hInnse ed., *Miscellaneous Irish Annals,* Dublin, 1947, p.103

8 CDI,Vol.2, No.661, p.107

9 R. Butler ed., *Annals of Ireland by J.Grace,* Dublin, 1842, p.77

10 J. O'Donovan, ed., *Annals of the Kingdom of Ireland by the Four Masters*, Dublin, 1856

11 H.G. Richardson and G.O. Sayles, *The Irish Parliament in the Middle Ages,* Oxford, 1952, p.126

12 Proceedings of the Royal Irish Academy, 1851, May 26

13 PRO, London, E/30/1744; For a full discussion of the petition by the author see: Lecale Miscellany No.9, 1991, pp 47-51

14 A.M. Wilson, *Saint Patrick's Town,* Belfast, 1995, p.79

15 H.J. Lawlor, 'The Genesis of the Diocese of Clogher', in *Louth Archaeological Journal, Vol.IV, 1916, p.142*
16 W. Harris, *The Antient and Present State of the County Down,* Dublin, 1744, p.22
17 H.F. Hore, 'The Rental Book of Gerald Fitzgerald, Ninth Earl of Kildare', in *Journal of the Kilkenny Archaeological Society, Vol.2, Part 2, 1859, p.278*
18 *State papers, Henry VIII, Correspondence,* Vol.3, Part 3, No.279, p.156
19 *Letters and Papers, Henry VIII,* Vol.14, Part 1, No.1027, p.471
20 H. Ellis, *Original Letters illustrative of English History,* Series 2, Vol.2, London 1827, p.102
21 *Letters and Papers, Henry VIII,* Vol.13, Part 2, No.1164, p.484
22 R.D. Edwards, *Church and State in Tudor Ireland,* Dublin, 1935, pp.43-44
23 R.D. Edwards, *ibid*, pp.43-44
24 *State Papers, Henry VIII, Correspondence,* Vol.3, Part 3, No.279, p.155
25 *State Papers, Henry VIII, Correspondence,* Vol.3, Part 3, No.295, p.194
26 *State papers, Henry VIII, Correspondence,* Vol.3, Part 3, No.326, pp. 248-263
27 *Letters and Papers, Henry VIII,* Vol.16, No.330, p.153
28 W.M. Hennessy ed., *Annals of Ulster*, Vol.3, 1379-1541
29 Holinshed, *Irish Chronicle, 1577,* Dolmen Edition, 1979, pp.298-9
30 C. Lennon, *The Lords of Dublin in the Age of Reformation*, Dublin, 1989, pp.128-165
31 M.A. Costello and A. Coleman, eds., *de Annatis Hiberniae,* Vol.1, Ulster, Maynooth, 1912, p.121

CHAPTER SEVEN

1 D. Knowles, *The Religious Orders in England, Vol.3,* Cambridge, 1959, p.274
2 *State Papers, Henry VIII, Correspondence,* Vol.2, Part 3, p.371
3 *State Papers, ibid*, p.425
4 *State Papers*, *ibid*, p.433
5 *Letters and Papers, Henry VIII,* Vol.16, No.775, p.372
6 'Calendar of Fiants, Henry VIII, 1543-4, No.409', in *Seventh Report of the Deputy Keeper of the Public Records, Ireland, 1875*
7 J.H. Smith, 'The Shrine of Saint Patrick's Hand', in *Ulster Journal of Archaeology, Series 1, Vol.2, 1854, pp.207-211* C. Bourke, *Patrick, the Archaeology of a Saint*, Belfast 1993, p.51
8 L. Murray, 'Relics of the Penal Days', *in Down and Connor Historical Society Journal, Vol.2, 1929, p.94*
9 E.S. Eames and T. Fanning, *Irish Medieval Tiles*, Royal Irish Academy, 1988, p.78
10 J.S. Brewer and W. Bullen eds., *Calendar of Carew Papers,* [Carew], Vol.1, No.154, p.175
11 Carew, *Vol.1, No.176, p.201*
12 *State Papers*, *ibid*, Vol.3, Part 3, p.337
13 J. Morrin ed., *Calendar of Patent and Close Rolls in Chancery in Ireland*, Vol.1, p.91
14 *Calendar of State Papers, Ireland* [CSPI], Henry VIII-Elizabeth 1, Vol.6, 13 August 1596, p.93
15 W. Reeves ed., 'The Irish Itinerary of Father Edmund McCana', *in Ulster Journal of Archaeology, Series 1, Vol 2, 1854, pp.44-59*
16 W. Harris, *The Antient and Present State of the County Down,* Dublin, 1744, reprint 1977 pp.34-5
17 Carew, *Vol.3, No.270, pp.242, 4, 6*
18 CSPI, *Vol.1, June 1558, p.147*
19 CSPI, *Vol.5, 16 December 1592, p.32*
20 CSPI, *Vol.10, 31 December 1600, p.110*
21 CSPI, *Vol.10, 30 April 1601, p.300*
22 Carew, *Vol.1, No.200, p.242*
23 in Irish Record Commission's Calendar of Inquisitions, PRO (Dublin); see Appendix 2
24 'Calendar of Fiants, Edward VI, 1551, No.837', in *Eighth Report of the Deputy Keeper of the Public Records, Ireland, 1876*
25 CPR, *Edward VI, Vol.4, 25 April 1552, p.327*
26 'Calendar of Fiants, Philip and Mary, 1558, No.232', in *Ninth Report of the Deputy Keeper of the Public Records, Ireland, 1877*
27 'Calendar of Fiants, Elizabeth I, 1570, No.1659', in *Twelfth Report of the Deputy Keeper of the Public Records, Ireland, 1880*

CHAPTER EIGHT

1 CSPI, *James I, Vol.2, 14 January 1607*
2 Translation of Charter from Patent Roll, 7 James I, by W.M. Hennessy, in Cathedral archives; See Appendix 3
3 The Charter clearly states 'Holy Trinity' and does not include the words 'and undivided'
4 W. Reeves, *Ecclesiastical Antiquities*, Dublin, 1847, pp.178-9
5 W.P. Carmody, in *Down Recorder, 9 February 1929*
6 Cathedral Charter
7 H.A. Boyd, personal comment
8 CSPI, *James I, Vol.4, No.362, p.189*
9 CSPI, *Charles I, Vol.2, 24 July 1637, p.164*
10 R. Mant, *History of the Church of Ireland*, London, 1840, Vol.1, p.512
11 Translation of Letters Patent of Charles II to Lisburn Cathedral, 27 October 1662
12 J.S. Reid, *History of the Presbyterian Church in Ireland,* Belfast, 1867, Vol.1, p.102
13 CSPI, *Charles I, Vol.1, 24 July 1626, p.143*
14 CSPI, *Charles I, Vol.2, 4 March 1633, p.3*
15 *Hastings MS*, Historic Manuscripts Commission, Vol.78 HMSO, 1947, p.69
16 J.S. Reid, *ibid,* Vol.2, p.86n

17 J.W. Hanna, *The Deans and Deanery of Down,* 1858; Typescript in the Linen Hall Library; much of the remainder of this chapter is taken from this source without further reference
18 H.J. Lawlor, *The Fasti of Saint Patrick's, Dublin*, Dundalk, 1930, p.121
19 PRONI, Mic 1/38; I am grateful to Canon S.M.J. Dickson, Rector of Down, for permission to quote extensively from this Vestry book
20 J.V. Luce, *The first 400 years, Trinity College,Dublin,* Dublin, 1992, p.40
21 PRONI, T 552, p.121
22 British Library, Southwell MSS, Add.MS 21131. The correspondence is quoted extensively in J. Stevenson, *Two Centuries of Life in Down,* Belfast, 1920, Reprint 1990, pp.218-226
23 W.A. Phillips ed., *History of the Church of Ireland*, Oxford 1934, Vol.3, p.235
24 L.A. Pooler, *Down and its Parish Church*, Downpatrick, 1907, pp.88-9
25 W.A. Philips ed., *ibid*, Vol.3, p.235
26 A. Pilson, in *Downpatrick Recorder, 7 June 1856*
27 J. Magee, 'Some Country Houses in Lecale', in *Lecale Miscellany No.3, 1985, p.6*
28 PRONI, Mic 1/38
29 L.A. Pooler, *ibid*, p.9
A.W. Godfrey Brown, 'Thomas Jackson', in *Bulletin of the Presbyterian Historical Society, No.15, March 1986*
30 W. Harris, *The Antient and Present State of the County Down*, Dublin, 1744, reprint 1977, p.30
31 J. O'Laverty, *Historical Account of the Diocese of Down and Connor*, Dublin, 1878-95, Vol.1, p.312
32 J. O'Laverty, *ibid*, Vol.5, p.547
33 A Pilson, *Downpatrick Recorder*, 30 December 1854; also 26, supra, from a bound volume 'Miscellaneous Essays' in Linen Hall Library
34 CSPI, *Charles I, Vol.1, 21 December 1630, p.593*
35 J. Barry, *Hillsborough, a Parish in the Ulster Plantation*, Belfast, 1962, p.102
36 J.B. Leslie, *Biographical Succession Lists of the Diocese of Down*, Enniskillen, 1936, pp.37-41
37 CSPI, *James I, Vol.4, No.323, p.171; No.419, p.241*
38 1633 Regal Visitation, TCD, Reeves MS 1067, p.27
39 J.B. Leslie, *ibid*, p.70
40 PRONI, T 1075/6 p.7, Fiants for Church preferments
41 BL, Southwell MS, *ibid*

CHAPTER NINE
1 E.R.R. Green and E.M. Jope, 'Patron and Architect', *in Ulster Journal of Archaeology, Series 3, Vol.24-25, 1961-2, p.146*
2 PRONI, T 1254/3
3 Unless otherwise stated, all references are to archive material in the possession of the Cathedral
4 Downshire to Archbishop of Cashel
5 PRONI, D 607/B/338
6 PRONI, D 607/B/339
7 PRONI, D 607/B/343
8 PRONI, D 607/B/340
9 PRONI, D 607/B/341
10 J. Magee, 'Politics and Politicians', *in Lecale, A Study in Local History, Q.U.B., 1970, pp.93 ff*
11 PRONI, D 671/A 18/3A
12 PRONI, D 607/C/183
13 A transcript of Aynsworth Pilson's diaries is in Down County Museum; acknowledgment is made for permission to read and quote from them
14 PRONI, D 671/A/18/2
15 N.Boston and L.Langwill, *Church and Chamber Barrel Organs,* Edinburgh, 1967, p.70
16 PRONI, D 607/I/37
17 PRONI, D 671/A 18/3B
18 H.M.Colvin, *A Biographical Dictionary of British Architects*, London, 1954, pp. 94-96
19 PRONI, D 607/I/159
20 PRONI, D 607/I/158
21 For a history of the firm of Nevin, Sayers & Co., see *Downpatrick Recorder*, 11 November 1876
22 In 1817, Robert McCune was replaced as organist by William McCune, who had, since 1804, been parish clerk at the parish church. It is likely that William and Robert were brothers as an entry in the Down Parish Register records the death in 1828 of Widow McCune, mother of Robert and William. (PRONI, Mic 1/38)
23 private letter, John Holmes to Lord Dunleath
24 G.W.O. Addleshaw and F. Etchells, *The Architectural Setting of Anglican Worship*, London, 1948, p.198; A letter from Dean Mann to the *Down Recorder*, 2 December 1966, refers to a visit to Down Cathedral by The Dean of Chester, The Very Rev G.W.O.Addleshaw in 1948
25 F.L. Harrison, *Music in Medieval Britain*, London, 1958, p.51

CHAPTER TEN
1 J.W. Hanna, *The Deans and Deanery of Down*, 1858, pp.101-2
2 PRONI, D 671/C/181/1
3 PRONI, D 671/C/181/2
4 PRONI, D 671/C/181/3
5 PRONI, D 671/C/181/4
6 PRONI, D 671/C/181/5
7 PRONI, D 671/C/188/6
8 PRONI, D 671/C/188/18a
9 J.W. Hanna, *ibid,*
10 BL:Wellesley Papers, Add MS 37306, pp.414 ff
11 BL:Wellesley Papers, Add MS 37306
12 BL:Wellesley Papers, Add MS 37306

13 PRONI, DIO/1/25A/15A
14 *Downpatrick Recorder*, 1 January 1842
15 *Downpatrick Recorder*, 1 January 1842
16 J.W. Hanna, *ibid,*
17 *Downpatrick Recorder*, 27 April and 11 May 1844
18 J.W. Hanna, *ibid,*
19 J.W. Hanna, *ibid*
20 A recent survey by Wells Kennedy Partnership established that the pipes in the towers are of alloy, while those in the flats were made of zinc.
21 Preachers' Book
22 I am indebted to Mr Aodh O'Tuama, Curator, Cork Public Museum, for making this information available
23 *Downpatrick Recorder*, 15 December 1855
24 *Downpatrick Recorder*, 8 December 1855
25 *Downpatrick Recorder*, 30 August 1856
26 *Downpatrick Recorder*, 4 October 1856
27 *Downpatrick Recorder*, 4 October 1856
28 *Downpatrick Recorder*, 4 October 1856
29 *Downpatrick Recorder*, 4 October 1856
30 *Downpatrick Recorder*, 20 November 1856
31 Letter in Cathedral archive; Armagh and Clogher dioceses were united at this period, thus the reference to two cathedrals.
32 23 & 24 Victoria, Cap.150; An Act to amend certain Acts relating to the Temporalities of the Church in Ireland; 28 August 1860
33 *Downpatrick Recorder*, 12 December 1863
34 *Downpatrick Recorder*, 12 December 1863
35 *Downshire Protestant*, 7 January 1859
36 *Downshire Protestant*, 4 March 1859
37 *Downshire Protestant*, 24 August 1860
38 *Downshire Protestant*, 2 November 1860
39 *Downshire Protestant*, 11 January 1861
40 *Downshire Protestant*, 26 July 1861

CHAPTER ELEVEN

1 *Downpatrick Recorder*, 7 January 1871
2 *Downpatrick Recorder*, 17 October 1868
3 Journal of the General Convention of the Church of Ireland 1870, Dublin, 1871, p.207, No.35
4 *ibid.*, p.207, No.37
5 *Irish Ecclesiastical Gazette*. 21 June 1871
6 N.B. Correct Sarum precedence which has not been followed in practice
7 *Downpatrick Recorder*, 2 October 1875
8 J.B. Leslie, *Biographical Succession Lists of the Diocese of Down,* Enniskillen, 1936, p.68
9 *Down Recorder*, 15 October 1887 (The *Downpatrick Recorder* was renamed *Down Recorder* in 1878)
10 Cathedral archives
11 *Down Recorder*, 26 March 1892
12 F.J. Bigger, 'The Grave of Saint Patrick', in *Ulster Journal of Archaeology, Series 2, Vol VI, No.2, April 1900, pp 61/64*
13 F.J. Bigger, Report to BNFC November 1891, in *Bigger Collection, Belfast Central Library*
14 PRONI, D 1889/5/4
15 *Irish News*, 13 December 1899
16 Bigger Collection, Belfast Central Library, R 241
17 F.J. Bigger, *The Grave of Saint Patrick.*
18 J. Holmes, 'Organs and Organists of Armagh Cathedral', in *Seanchas Ard Mhacha, Vol.13, No.2, 1989, pp.230-285*
19 *Down Recorder*, 9 November 1907
20 *Down Recorder*, 16 November 1907
21 Samuel Green was a noted eighteenth century English organ builder and it had always been assumed that the Down organ had been built by him. The origin of the Green 'legend' is curious; George III, under the influence of the Marquis of Downshire, was reputed to have given an organ, built by Green, from one of the Royal palaces to Down Cathedral on its restoration. This did, in fact, happen in Salisbury Cathedral, but there is no documentary evidence at Down; quite the contrary. How someone of the eminence of Arthur Harrison could have made the mistake remains a mystery.
22 *Down Recorder*, 23 May 1914
23 PRONI, D 1889/5/13
24 *Belfast News Letter*, 24 December 1929 and information from Miss C.M.Wallace
25 RCB Library, MS 529
26 In addition, he published 'Cushendall and its Neighbourhood' anonymously, written when he was curate of Layde, 1892-8. Reprinted 1990, Ballycastle
27 *Belfast News Letter* 8 March 1938
28 *Down Recorder*, 18 May and 22 June 1957
29 *Down Recorder*, 22 June 1957
30 *Down Recorder*, 23 November 1957

CHAPTER TWELVE

1 Useful articles on the Prebend of Talpestone are: W.P.Carmody in *Down Recorder*, 9 February 1929; H.A.Boyd in *Belfast News Letter*, 31 March 1938
2 *Down Recorder*, 25 April and 30 May 1959
3 *Down Recorder*, 2 November 1957
4 *Down Recorder*, 2 December 1966
5 *Down Recorder*, 21 October and 4 November 1966
6 *Down Recorder*, 4 November 1966
7 N.Brannon, *Recent Discoveries at Down Cathedral,* in *Lecale Miscellany*, No.5, 1987, pp.3-9

BIBLIOGRAPHY

MS SOURCES

Bodleian Library, Oxford	Rawlinson C.892
	Canon Liturg 215
National Library of Scotland	Adv. MS 18.5.91
British Library	Southwell Papers: Add MS 21131 Wellesley Papers: Add MS 37306
Public Record Office, London	C 66/278
	E/30/1744
Public Record Office, Northern Ireland	Downshire Papers Wallace Papers Leslie Papers Reeves MSS, ex Diocesan Library of Down, Dromore and Connor
Public Record Office, Dublin	1549 Inquisition in Calendar of Inquisitions
Trinity College, Dublin	Reeves MS 1067 Molyneaux MS 883 1-2
Down Cathedral	Chapter Books; Actuary and Account Books; Preachers' Books; Board Minute Books; Correspondence and Newspaper cuttings.
Down Parish Church	Registers and Vestry Books in PRONI: MIC 1/38 and 1/39
Diocesan Library of Down, Connor and Dromore	Pilson A., *Result of Enquiries as to Religious Houses in Downpatrick* in hand of J.W.Hanna (Reeves MS) (PRONI: DIO/1/24/8/19)
Linen Hall Library	Typescript volumes among Blackwood MSS:
Hanna J.W.	*The Deans and Deanery of Down*, 1858
Pilson A.	*Miscellaneous Essays*, 1854-62
Pilson A.	*Memoirs of notable Inhabitants of Downpatrick*, 1838
Wallace R.H.	*Historical Collections relating to Downpatrick*, nd.
Down County Museum	
Pilson A.	Typescript of diaries, 5 vols., 1799-1863
Boyd H.A.	*The Cathedral System in the Church of Ireland since Disestablishment*, unpublished M.Litt. Thesis, TCD 1950

NEWSPAPERS

Belfast Central Library	Bigger Collection, R.241, various press cuttings

Downpatrick Recorder 1836 until the present day (*Down Recorder* after 1878). Microfilm in SEELB Headquarters, Ballynahinch. The index for the years 1836-1886, compiled by the late Jack McCoy was invaluable

Downshire Protestant: 6 July 1855-20 September 1862
3 Bound Volumes in possession of Down County Museum

ANNALS

Annals of Connacht, ed. A.M. Freeman, Dublin, 1944

Annals of the Kingdom of Ireland by the Four Masters, ed. J.O'Donovan, 7 Vols, Dublin, 1856

Annals of Ulster, 431-1541, ed. W.M. Hennessy and B. MacCarthy 3 Vols, Dublin, 1887-1893

Annals of Ulster to AD 1131, ed. S. Mac Airt and G. Mac Niocaill, Dublin, 1983

Miscellaneous Irish Annals, ed. S.Ó hInnse, Dublin, 1947

Annales Hiberniae, J.Grace, ed. R. Butler, Dublin, 1842

Irish Chronicle, Holinshed, 1577; Dolmen Edition, ed. L. Miller and E. Power, 1979

REGISTERS OF THE ARCHBISHOPS OF ARMAGH

Milo Sweteman, 1361-1380; Calendar ed.H.J. Lawlor in *Proceedings of the Royal Irish Academy*, Vol.XXIX, 1911-12, Section C.

Milo Sweteman, 1361-1380, ed. Brendan Smith, I.M.C., 1996

Nicholas Fleming, 1404-1416; Calendar ed. H.J. Lawlor in *Proceedings of the Royal Irish Academy*, Vol.XXX 1912-1913, Section C.

John Swayne, 1418-1439; Calendar ed. D.A. Chart, Belfast, HMSO,1935; also Typescript of Reeves calendar, MS 5 in *Diocesan Library of Down, Connor and Dromore*

John Prene, 1439-1443; Typescript of Reeves calendar, MS 5 *as above*

John Mey, 1443-1456; Transcript of Register, ed. W.G.H. Quigley and E.F.D. Roberts, Belfast, HMSO, 1972

John Bole 1457-1471; Calendar ed. A. Lynch in *Seanchas ArdMhaca* Vol.14, No.2, 1991 and Vol.15, No.,1, 1992

Octavian del Palacio 1478-1513; Typescript of Reeves calendar, MS 6 in *Diocesan Library*

George Cromer, 1521-1543; Calendar ed. L.P. Murray in *Louth Archaeological Journal, Vol.8, 1932-6* also Typescript of Reeves calendar MS 6 in *Diocesan Library*

George Dowdall, 1543-1558; Calendar ed. L.P. Murray in *Louth Archaeological Journal, Vol.6, 1926-7-8*

CALENDARS

Calendar of Documents relating to Ireland, [CDI] 1171-1307, ed. H.S. Sweetman, 5 Vols., 1875-86

Calendar of Patent Rolls, [CPR] 1216-1509, London, 55 Vols.,1891-1916

Calendar of Papal Letters, [CPL] 1198-1492 ed. W.H. Bliss and J.A. Tremlow, 14 vols., 1894-1961; Vol.15, 1484-92, ed. M.J. Haren, IMC, 1978; Vol.16, 1492-98, ed. Anne

Fuller, IMC, 1986; Vol.17, 1495-1503, ed.Anne Fuller, IMC, 1994; Vol.18, 1503-13, ed. M.J. Haren, IMC, 1989

Calendar of Patent and Close Rolls of the Irish Chancery, Henry II–Henry VII, ed. E. Tresham, 1828

Calendar of Justiciary Rolls, Ireland, 1295-1307 ed. J. Mills, London, 2 Vols., Vol.3, 1308-14, ed. H. Wood et al., Dublin

Calendar of Patent Rolls, [CPR] 1547-78, London, 17 Vols.,1924-82

Letters and Papers, Henry VIII, Vols. 12-16, 1537-41, London, 1890-98

State Papers, Henry VIII, Correspondence relating to Ireland, London, 1835 Vols.2-3

Calendar of Patent and Close Rolls of Chancery in Ireland, Henry VIII, Edward VI, Mary and Elizabeth I and 1-8 Charles I, ed. J. Morrin, 3 Vols., 1861-64

Calendar of Carew Papers at Lambeth, 1515-1624, ed. J.S.Brewer and W.Bullen, 6 Vols., 1867-73

Calendar of State Papers, Ireland [CSP], 1509-1603, 11 Vols., 1860-1912

Calendar of State Papers, Ireland [CSP], 1603-70, 13 Vols., 1872-1910

Inquisitionum in Officio Rotulorum Cancellariae Repertorium, Vol.2, Ulster, 1829

Liber Munerum, 1152-1827, ed. R.Lascelles, 1852

Calendars of Fiants, Henry VIII-Elizabeth I, in *Reports of the Deputy Keeper of the Public Records, Ireland, Nos. 7-22; 1875-90*

Pipe Rolls, Edward III, in *Report of the Deputy Keeper of the Public Records, Ireland, Nos.43-45*

Syllabus of Rymer's Foedera, 1066-1654, ed.T.D.Hardy, 2 Vols., London 1869

Erck J.C. ed., A Repertory of the Inrolments on the Patent Rolls of Chancery in Ireland, commencing with the reign of King James I Vol 1, Dublin, 1846

Calendar of Harris MSS in National Library of Ireland in *Analecta Hibernica No.6, 1934*

Abstract of Inquisitions, Co.Antrim, 12 July 1605, in *Report of the Deputy Keeper of the Public Records, Ireland, No. 26*

Pontificia Hibernica, Medieval Papal Chancery Documents concerning Ireland, 640-1261, ed. M.P.Sheehy, 2 Vols., Dublin, 1962

Hastings MSS, Historical Manuscripts Commission, Vol. 78, HMSO, 1947

PRINTED SOURCES

Addleshaw G.W.O. and Etchells F., *The Architectural Setting of Anglican Worship,* London, 1948

Archaeological Survey of County Down, HMSO, Belfast, 1966

Archdall, Mervyn, *Monasticon Hibernicum*, London, 1786 2nd edition, ed. P.F. Moran, Dublin, 1873

Armagh, Guide to Saint Patrick's Cathedral, 1905

Armstrong G.F., *The Savages of the Ards,* London 1888

Atkinson A., *Ireland exhibited to England,* Vol.1, London, 1823

Barry J., *Hillsborough, a Parish in the Ulster Plantation,* Belfast, 1962

Bagwell, Richard, *Ireland under the Tudors,* 2 Vols., London 1885

Bates D., *Normandy before 1066,* London, 1982

Bernard, Saint, of Clairvaux, ed.Lawlor H.J., *Life of Saint Malachy of Armagh,* London, 1920

Belfast Naturalists' Field Club, Secretary's Report, November 1891

Bieler L., 'Saint Patrick and the coming of Christianity', in *History of Irish Catholicism, Vol.1,* Dublin, 1967
The Patrician Texts in the Book of Armagh, Dublin 1979

Binchy D.A., 'Patrick and his Biographers, Ancient and Modern,' in *Studia Hibernica, No.2, 1962*

Boston N. and Langwill L., *Church and Chamber Barrel Organs,* Edinburgh, 1967

Bourke C., 'Notes on the Relics of Patrick', in *Lecale Miscellany No.7, 1989*
Patrick, the Archaeology of a Saint, HMSO, Belfast 1993

Bradshaw B., *The Dissolution of the Religious Orders in Ireland under Henry VIII,* Cambridge, 1974

Brannon N., 'Recent Archaeological Excavations at Downpatrick and at Inch' in *Lecale Miscellany, No.1, 1983*
'Excavation on Cathedral Hill, Downpatrick' in *Lecale Miscellany, No.4, 1986*
'Recent Discoveries at Down Cathedral', in *Lecale Miscellany, No.5, 1987*
'Archaeological Excavations at Cathedral Hill, Downpatrick, 1987' in *Lecale Miscellany, No.6, 1988*
'Not just a Load of Old Bones: The human and animal remains from the Cathedral Hill excavations, Downpatrick', in *Lecale Miscellany, No.7, 1989*

Brown, A.W.Godfrey, 'Thomas Jackson, Minister of Downpatrick, 1700-08' Lecture 17 April 1985 and printed by *The Presbyterian Historical Society, 1986*

Bury J.B., *The Life of Saint Patrick,* London, 1905

Byrne F.J., *Irish Kings and High Kings,* London, 1973

Chibnall M., 'Some aspects of the Norman Monastic Plantation in England', in *La Normandie Benedictine,* Lille, 1967

Church of Ireland: *Journal of the General Convention, 1870,* Dublin, 1871
Journal of the General Synod, 1871, Dublin 1872

Cobbett W., *State Trials,* Vol.1, London, 1809

Colvin H.M., *A Biographical Dictionary of English Architects,* London, 1954

Costello M.A. and Coleman A., *de Annatis Hiberniae, Vol.1, Ulster,* Maynooth, 1912

Cotton H., *Fasti Ecclesiae Hiberniae,* Vol.3, Dublin, 1849

Davies O. and Quinn D.B., 'Irish Pipe Roll of 14 John 1211-12' in *Ulster Journal of Archaeology, Series 3, Vol.4, 1941*

De Paor, Liam, *Saint Patrick's World,* Dublin, 1993

Dictionary of National Biography

Dobbs M., 'The Dál Fiatach', in *Ulster Journal of Archaeology,* Series 3, Vol.8, 1945

Dolley M., *Anglo-Norman Ireland,* Dublin, 1972

Down and Connor Historical Society Journal:
unsigned note 'Fragments in Narthex of Cathedral', Vol.VI, 1934
unsigned note 'Saint Patrick's cross', Vol.IV, 1931, p.111

Duffy, Seán, 'The First Ulster Plantation: John de Courcy and the Men of Cumbria', in T.B. Barry, Robin Frame and Katherine Simms eds., *Colony and Frontier in Medieval Ireland,* London, 1995

Dugdale W., *Monasticum Anglicanum*, Vol.6, Part 2, London, 1846

Dumville D.N. et al., *Saint Patrick, 493 - 1993*, Woodbridge, 1993

Eames E.S., *Catalogue of Medieval Lead Glazed Earthenware Tiles in the British Museum,* 1980

Eames E.S. and Fanning T., *Irish Medieval Tiles,* Dublin, 1988

Edwards R.D., *Church and State in Tudor Ireland,* Dublin, 1935

Ellis H., *Original Letters illustrative of English History* Series 2, Vol.2, London, 1827

Evans E.Estyn, *Prehistoric and Early Christian Ireland,* London, 1966

Evans S., *Salisbury Cathedral,* Salisbury, 1985

Farmer D.H., *The Oxford Dictionary of Saints*, Oxford, 1978

Ferguson G., *Signs and Symbols in Christian Art,* Oxford, 1954

Flanagan D., 'The Names of Downpatrick', in *Dinnseanchas, Vol.4, No.4, 1971*

Fryde E.B. et al., *Handbook of British Chronology,* 3rd Edition, London, 1986

Gibbs, E.D., *The Complete Peerage,* London, 1913

Giraldus Cambrensis, ed. A.B.Scott and F.X.Martin, *Expugnatio Hibernica* Dublin, 1978

Green E.R.R. and Jope E.M., 'Patron and Architect', in *Ulster Journal of Archaeology, Series 3, Vol.24-25*

Gwynn A., *The Medieval Province of Armagh,* Dundalk, 1946
Anglo-Irish Church Life in the 14th and 15th Centuries, Dublin, 1968
'Saint Malachy of Armagh', in *Irish Ecclesiastical Record,* November 1948, pp.961-978 and February 1949, pp.134-148

Gwynn A., ed.O'Brien G., *The Irish Church in the 11th and 12th Centuries,* Dublin, 1992

Gwynn A. and Hadcock R.N., *Medieval Religious Houses, Ireland* London, 1970

Hamlin Ann, 'The Early Church in County Down to the Twelfth Century', in Proudfoot L. ed., *County Down in History and Society,* Dublin, 1997

Hand G., *The Church in the English Lordship, 1216-1307,* Dublin, 1968

Hanson R.P.C., *Saint Patrick, his Origins and Career,* Oxford, 1968
The Life and Writings of the Historical Saint Patrick, New York, 1983

Harbison P., 'The Earlier Bronze Age in Ireland', in *Journal of the Royal Society of Antiquaries, Ireland, Vol.103, 1973*
The High Crosses of Ireland, Bonn, 1992

Haren M. and de Pontfarcy Y. eds., *The Medieval Pilgrimage to Saint Patrick's Purgatory,* Enniskillen, 1988

Harris W., *The Antient and Present State of the County Down,* Dublin, 1744, Reprint 1977

Harrison F.Ll., *Music in Medieval Britain,* London, 1958

Hayes-McCoy G.A., 'The Ecclesiastical Revolution' in *A New History of Ireland, Vol.3,* Oxford, 1978

Herity M.and Eogan G., *Ireland in Prehistory*, London, 1977

Hill G., ed., *The Montgomery Manuscripts,* Belfast, 1869

Holmes J., 'Organs and Organists of Armagh Cathedral', in *Seanchas ArdMhacha, Vol.13, No.2, 1989*

Hore H.F., 'The Rental Book of Gerald Fitzgerald, Ninth Earl of Kildare', in *Journal of the Kilkenny Archaeological Society, 1859-62*

Hughes, Kathleen, *The Church in Early Irish Society,* London, 1966
Early Christian Ireland, Introduction to the Sources, London, 1972

Hughes, Kathleen and Hamlin, Ann, *The Modern Traveller to the Early Irish Church,* London, 1977

Jackson R.W., *Archbishop Magrath,* Cork, 1974

Kenney J.F., *Sources for the Early History of Ireland, Vol.1, Ecclesiastical,* 1929, reprint, Dublin, 1979

Knowles D., *The Monastic Order in England,* Cambridge, 1950
The Religious Orders in England, 3 Vols., Cambridge, 1948-59

Knowles D. and Hadcock R.N., *Medieval Religious Houses, England and Wales,* London, 1971

Latham R.A., *Revised Medieval Latin Word List,* London, 1965

Lawlor H.C., 'The Genesis of the Diocese of Connor including Down and Dromore', in *Proceedings of the Belfast Natural History and Philosophical Society, 1930-31*
'Diocesan Anomalies', in *Ulster Journal of Archaeology, Series 3,* Vol.2, Part 2, 1939

Lawlor H.J., *The Rosslyn Missal,* Henry Bradshaw Society, 1898

The Fasti of Saint Patrick's, Dublin, Dundalk, 1930
'The Genesis of the Diocese of Clogher', in *Louth Archaeological Journal, Vol.4, 1916*
'Notes on Saint Bernard's Life of Saint Malachy', in *Proceedings of the Royal Irish Academy, 1918-1920, Vol.XXXV,* Sect.C, pp.230-264

Lawrence C.H., *Medieval Monasticism,* London, 1984

Lennon C., *Richard Stanihurst the Dubliner, 1547-1618,* Dublin, 1981
The Lords of Dublin in the Age of Reformation, Dublin, 1989

Leslie J.B., *Biographical Succession Lists of the Diocese of Down*, Enniskillen, 1936

Lucas A.T., 'The Plundering and Burning of Churches in Ireland, 7th-16th Centuries', in *North Munster Studies,* Limerick, 1967

Luce J.V., *Trinity College, Dublin, the first 400 years,* Dublin, 1992

Lydon J.F., *The Lordship of Ireland in the Middle Ages,* Dublin, 1972
The English in Medieval Ireland, Dublin 1984

Magee J., 'Politics and Politicians 1750-1850', in *Lecale, A Study in Local History,* Q.U.B., Belfast, 1970
'Some Country Houses in Lecale', in *Lecale Miscellany, No.3, 1985*

Mant, Richard, *History of the Church of Ireland,* 2 Vols, London, 1840

Mayo, Janet, *A History of Ecclesiastical Dress,* London, 1984

Murray L., 'Relics of the Penal Days', in *Down and Connor Historical Society Journal*, Vol.2, 1929

McKeown L., 'The Burial Place of Saint Patrick', in *Down and Connor Historical Society Journal, Vol.II, 1929*
'The Monastic Houses of County Down', in *Down and Connor Historical Society Journal, Vol.VII, 1936*
'The Islands of Strangford Lough', in *Down and Connor Historical Society Journal, Vol.V, 1933*

McNeill T.E., *Anglo-Norman Ulster,* Edinburgh, 1980

Mac Niocaill G., 'Cartae Dunenses XII-XIII Centuries', in *Seanchas ArdMhacha, Vol.5, No.2, 1970*
Ireland before the Vikings, Dublin, 1972

O'Corrain D., *Ireland before the Normans,* Dublin, 1972

O'Laverty J., *Historical Account of the Diocese of Down and Connor,* 5 Vols., Dublin, 1878-95

O'Rahilly, Cecile, ed., *Táin Bó Cúalnge*, Dublin, 1957

O'Rahilly T.F., *The Two Patricks,* Dublin, 1957

Orpen G.H., *Ireland under the Normans,* 3 Vols., Oxford, 1911

O'Sullivan M.D., *Italian Merchant Bankers in Ireland in the Thirteenth Century,* Dublin, 1962

Otway-Ruthven J., 'Dower Charter of John de Courcy's Wife' in *Ulster Journal of Archaeology, Series 3, Vol.12, 1949*

Pantin W.A., ed., *Documents illustrating the Activities of the General and Provincial Chapters of the English Black Monks, 1215-1540*, Vol.3, Royal Historical Society, 1937

Parkinson R.E., 'The Castle of Down', in *Ulster Journal of Archaeology,* Series 3, Vol.3, 1940

Petrie G., *The Ecclesiastical Architecture of Ireland anterior to the Anglo-Norman Invasion*, Dublin, 1845

Phillips W.A., ed., *History of the Church of Ireland,* 3 Vols., Oxford, 1934

Pollock A.J. and Waterman D.M., 'A Medieval Pottery Kiln at Downpatrick', in *Ulster Journal of Archaeology,* Series 3, Vol.26*, 1963*

Pooler L.A., *Down and its Parish Church,* Downpatrick, 1907

Proudfoot V.B., 'Excavations at Cathedral Hill, Downpatrick', in *Ulster Journal of Archaeology, Series 3, Vol.17, 1954 and* Vol.19, 1956

The Downpatrick Gold Find, HMSO, Belfast, 1955

Raftery B., 'Irish Hill Forts', in *The Iron Age in the Irish Sea Province,* Council for British Archaeology, Research Report 1972

Reeves W., *Ecclesiastical Antiquities of Down, Connor and Dromore,* Dublin, 1847

'Down Petition' in *Proceedings of the Royal Irish Academy, 1851*

Reeves W.,ed., 'The Irish Itinerary of Father Edmund MacCana' in *Ulster Journal of Archaeology,* Series 1, Vol.2, 1854

Reid J.S., *History of the Presbyterian Church in Ireland* 3 Vols., Belfast, 1867

Richardson H.G., 'Some Norman Monastic Foundations in Ireland', in *Medieval Studies presented to Aubrey Gwynn S.J., ed. J.A.Watt et al.,* Dublin, 1961

Richardson H.G. and Sayles G.O., *The Irish Parliament in the Middle Ages,* Oxford, 1952

Rule of Saint Benedict, trans. David Parry O.S.B., London, 1984

Scott A.B., *Malachy,* Dublin, 1976

Seymour St.J.D., *The Twelfth Century Reformation in Ireland,* Dublin, 1932

Sharpe R., 'Saint Patrick and the See of Armagh', in *Cambridge Medieval Celtic Studies, No.4, 1982*

Stalley R., *The Cistercian Monasteries of Ireland,* Yale, 1987

Stevenson J., *Two Centuries of Life in Down,* Belfast, 1920

Swanzy H.B., *Succession Lists of the Diocese of Dromore,* Belfast, 1933

Tait J., ed., *The Chartulary or Register of the Abbey of Saint Werburgh, Chester,* Chetham Society, Part 1, 1920 and Part 2, 1923

Thomas C., *Christianity in Roman Britain,* London, 1981

Victoria County History, Staffordshire, Vol.3, Oxford, 1970

Ware J., ed. Harris W.,*The Whole Works of Sir James Ware concerning Ireland,* Vol.1, Dublin, 1764

Warner R.B., 'Observations on the Beginnings of Fortification in Later Iron Age Ireland', in *Bulletin of the Ulster Place Name Society* Series 2, Vol.3, 1980-1

Warren F.E., *The Liturgy and Ritual of the Celtic Church,* Oxford, 1881

Watt J.A., *The Church and the Two Nations in Medieval Ireland,* Cambridge, 1970
The Church in Medieval Ireland, Dublin, 1972

Wilson, Anthony M., *Saint Patrick's Town,* Belfast, 1995

Wilson J., ed., *Register of the Priory of Saint Bee's,* Surtees Society, Vol.126, 1915

INDEX